Secure Lives

The Meaning and Importance
of Culture in Secure
Hospital Care

D1610370

Secure Lives
The Meaning and Importance of Culture in Secure Hospital Care

Annie Bartlett

OXFORD
UNIVERSITY PRESS

OXFORD
UNIVERSITY PRESS

Great Clarendon Street, Oxford, OX2 6DP,
United Kingdom

Oxford University Press is a department of the University of Oxford.
It furthers the University's objective of excellence in research, scholarship,
and education by publishing worldwide. Oxford is a registered trade mark of
Oxford University Press in the UK and in certain other countries

Published in the United States of America by Oxford University Press
198 Madison Avenue, New York, NY 10016, United States of America

British Library Cataloguing in Publication Data
Data available

Library of Congress Control Number: 2015906130

ISBN 978-0-19-964092-8

Printed and bound by
CPI Group (UK) Ltd, Croydon, CR0 4YY

Foreword

To me as a psychiatrist who has been deeply concerned about the effects of psychiatric institutionalisation, Annie has indeed shared 'a glimpse into lives less lived than they might have been.' My own career rather dramatically changed direction after many years in general practice, followed by general psychiatric training, child psychiatry and psychotherapy. I rather belatedly discovered institutions and was convinced that the culture of these places was detrimental to the lives of the patients who had been thus set apart. This was in the early eighties when the 'ordinary life' movement was just beginning—it was a heady time. If I had known how long ideas about deinstitutionalisation would take effect in my own field of learning disability, perhaps I would have been less optimistic! This book is therefore of great interest dealing as it does with the nature of psychiatric institutions generally as well linking to current issues in non-institutional care.

Annie is very unusual as a psychiatrist who has also studied anthropology, in being able to frame questions about institutions, and to understand and describe so eloquently what happens inside one in particular, in ways that are of interest to clinicians, but also to social scientists and the general public as well as the people known as 'patients'.

Her writing brings to life people whose lives are unknown unless they are sensationalised in the media. The telling detail in the accounts of patients' lives reminds us of their individuality and builds a sense of their own agency and attempts to make sense of their lives, as well as their own difficulties in engaging fully with the culture of the place that they must now call home.

In using historical material she speaks to contemporary issues and reminds us that there are enduring and repeating themes in health care. We continue to think and at times to worry about how we look after vulnerable people. How we consider these questions and how we try and improve care will vary from generation to generation, but Annie shows how much clinicians and managers can learn from other disciplines such as anthropology and social science. A narrower perspective will further diminish the lives of individuals who are dependent on the culture of a secure hospital for their own survival.

This book does not rush to judgement. Instead it is thought provoking about power and influence in hospital care and how they affect both clinical staff and patients, personally and locally.

That her work centres on a population held in secure hospital and deemed to be dangerous does not alter the fundamental questions about how institutional care is provided and maintained. Annie asks a very simple question that generally is hard to answer, which is to whom do we attribute responsibility—whether to systems or individuals in positions of authority. Anything that sheds light on what drives superficial and/or profound change and helps us identify real improvement is to be welcomed. This simple question will always be relevant to health care delivery as are so many of the issues in this imaginative, compassionate and insightful book.

My own research with Jane Hubert, a social anthropologist, involved an ethnographic study of a ward in a hospital for people with learning disabilities, now long closed. Some of the feelings described by this book's researchers about their fieldwork resonated strongly with me. The ethical issues involved in publishing our findings delayed publication for a while but the work has been widely cited. I wish Professor Bartlett the widest possible audience for her book too, focussing as it does on a different but equally complex population.

Professor Sheila the Baroness Hollins Emeritus
Professor of Psychiatry of Disability,
St George's University of London Past President,
Royal College of Psychiatrists Past President,
British Medical Association

Preface

This book is about two key ideas: culture and institutions. It is also about how those ideas can help us understand something that is important, i.e. how and when it is reasonable to lock up people who have mental disorders. All of this is made more digestible and more real by looking in detail at part of one institution, at one time. The institution is an extreme case, as it is a High Secure Hospital; to some people this may be a contradiction in terms. The fact that it is high secure and what that term means is part of the point of the book. It allows a glimpse into lives less lived than they might have been. It is therefore a book both about the function of a particular institution, or at least part of it, as well as how institutions, particularly other secure hospitals, can and do function. This is not to argue from one, single extreme case to unfortunate generalizations about care and secure care but to use the case of high security, as it was at the time of the study, to raise questions that apply, now, elsewhere as well.

There are three High Secure Hospitals in the UK today and their names are well known: Broadmoor, Ashworth and Rampton. Enthusiasm for their existence has varied over the years. They have survived calls for their closure, as well as being full to bursting in the past. Today they are much smaller than they were ten years ago, or twenty or thirty years ago. They remain high-profile institutions. They have housed a small number of well-known people—Ronnie Kray and Graham Young—and continue to house others—Peter Sutcliffe, the 'Yorkshire Ripper', Ian Brady the 'Moors Murderer', the nurse Beverley Allitt, and Christopher Clunis, whose killing of Jonathan Zito prompted a radical overhaul of psychiatric community care. Apart from this handful of household names, most of the men and women sent there will be noteworthy only to a few people: their families and friends, their victims—if they still live—and their victims' families. People admitted to the High Secure Hospitals are thought, at the time of admission, both to be dangerous and to have serious mental health problems. From this, it follows that they are in need of inpatient psychiatric hospital care but in a secure environment. Previously, they were called Special Hospitals, an interesting term in its own right. They were also meant to offer 'maximum' security until it was found they were really no more secure than a local prison. Yet, the historical term seems to conjure an image of an end point; nothing is higher than maximum. This is true. The High Secure Hospitals are end points, both in the sense that there is no higher level of security in hospital care and that the length of stay is years. It is difficult to leave. Many would argue that that is appropriate.

But it is not only those admitted as patients that have caused the three hospitals to be a focus of continuing interest. The people who work in these hospitals and what has happened in what were 'the Specials' have been as much a subject of interest as the patients themselves.

Few would doubt that there are people in England and Wales who need to be contained in order to safeguard the public. The moral, professional and ethical uncertainties so evident in the care, custody and treatment of the 'mad and bad' begin at that point. High Secure Hospitals are maintained by and for all of us. They take people whom society rejects, whose actions we abhor and who are often disowned by those who should be closest to them. In the name of the public, patients can be either vilified or pitied by the media. To imagine that there is no potential for these extremes of sentiment to be further played out when such individuals are concentrated in institutions is naive. Such individuals generate powerful and conflicting feelings in those around them. Just as many of the patients cannot see themselves or others as having good and bad characteristics, only one or the other, the High Secure Hospitals and their staff and patients have been sheared off from the 'good' parts of society. But, what happens within the walls does ultimately connect with all of us; to pretend otherwise is to reinforce the historical isolation of the High Secure Hospitals. In effect, it is to throw away the key.

This book is driven not simply by intellectual curiosity but also by the belief that what happens inside High Secure Hospitals and other secure institutional settings is important. This book includes a lot of information about part of one High Secure Hospital that we will call Smithtown. It looks at how people lived and worked in the hospital in the early 1990s and tries to report what they said and thought. The wards which took part in the study are now different. Patients and staff have moved on. Ward environments are different. Ward philosophies change. The hospital itself is managed by a different organisation. But the questions the book addresses do not go away so easily.

The deinstitutionalization of mental health services continues, but different secure hospital units have been built in the last decade. As one set of institutions fades away, a new set has emerged. The new institutions are much closer to where most people now live, in cities.

The hospital under discussion has a physical reality; it is a series of buildings but it has a social reality too. This book is also about how the culture of the hospital is understood, who owns or acknowledges any of these understandings, how sure we can be that cultural norms exist and what constitutes culture anyway. Given the way in which so many understandings of culture exist—there is an anthropologist who counted and since then no doubt more meanings have appeared—there is a need to be precise. This is not just another sterile academic enterprise, on a par with angels on pinheads. It does matter what cultures are embodied in secure hospitals. There was a view that the culture of the Special Hospitals was a problem. It was said they were too rigid, too much like prisons and insufficiently therapeutic in their approach to patients. The managerial mandate of the then Special Hospital Service Authority was to change that.

So far, nothing much has been said about psychiatry. Smithtown is a psychiatric hospital.

So, the first part of the book is about the history of High Secure Hospitals, and what psychiatry says they are. This is sensible, as, at one level, they are simply hospitals for people with mental disorders. The truth is, they are also highly politicized. They sit in a political, not just a health context.

Part of understanding this in depth is to ask two questions. First, what is known about psychiatric hospitals? Second, what is known about prisons? Both psychiatric hospitals and prisons have been investigated, researched and much talked about by different kinds of people, including representatives of different academic disciplines. They are not the preserve of, respectively, psychiatry and the prison service. This is not a review of everything ever written on either psychiatric hospitals or prisons. It is selective. What has made it into the book it is, is there because it seemed relevant to the two key concepts: culture and institutions. There are many arguments about how these different kinds of institutions should be properly understood. Broadly, psychiatrists and prison staff are on one side, and social scientists and historians are on the other but the devil is in the detail. Below the level of published debate is the impact on real lives caused by changes in public policy and psychiatric and penal practice.

Some of the disagreements in the literature are because people asked different kinds of questions and had different ways of answering those that they thought were important. So, the next section looks at what was a tension throughout the study on which this book is based. This has also been a personal tension throughout much of my adult life, between how psychiatry looks at the world and how anthropology does. Donald Rumsfeld talked about the 'known unknown'; this is more about unknown knowns. Each discipline can silence the other by ignoring its existence. Both claim to be eclectic, both are new kids on the block—psychiatry new in medicine and anthropology new in social science. This book is in the space between and speaks in two directions. This is both uncomfortable and intriguing.

The legitimacy of an anthropological approach to High Secure Hospitals and a debate about the nature of its questions, as opposed to those asked by psychiatric research, are explicitly considered in the study. Social anthropology's reflexive approach to an understanding of the social world, in particular how it frames the understanding of research during the fieldwork described in the book, became apparent. My professional identity is that of psychiatrist, the study approach was anthropological. This made it crucial to consider how the researchers' intentions were understood, what people in the hospital thought about us and the status of our observations, as well as how findings might be translated into writing. This led to some sound ideas on the nature of social relations in Smithtown and who was in charge of what.

Ethnographic material from the empirical study answers a series of basic questions about daily life in High Security.[1] In this specific context,

---

[1] Generous funding was obtained from the Wellcome Trust. They recognized the difficulty and potential impact of the project topic. The Wellcome Trust had the advantage of being independent of all government agencies and had no expressed position on the future of the Special Hospitals.

not previously studied in this way, the meaning of culture became critical. Anthropology, the investigative tool of the study, is preoccupied with culture, a word that is notoriously difficult to define. The construct of culture in atomized or divided societies is very relevant to discussion of ward life, as previous authors thought that patients living together had no shared culture. This part of the book describes and contrasts beliefs, attitudes and social practices in Smithtown with various understandings of culture and cultural knowledge. The managerial identification of a 'cultural problem' among the clinical staff of the Special Hospitals resulted in this being an obvious area of interest.

The recent Francis Report, following deficiencies in the care of the elderly in North Staffordshire, reminds us that problems of clinical and managerial culture are not confined to the care of the dangerously mad. The recent Winterbourne Report reminds us that the care of vulnerable adults in locked units can go badly wrong when a culture of cruelty goes unsuspected.

The wider NHS has been told repeatedly that it must change, and the reasons for this are less to do with care quality than a need to deal with rising demands for health care. Most recently, the financial constraints imposed on the health service have made change imperative. To many health professionals, calls for change have seemed no more than a rhetorical device common to successive governments, signifying little. To others, they have seemed to be a way to channel the creative energy of clinicians who strive for excellence and improvement on behalf of patients whose care might otherwise be tinged with complacency. Many of us who work in the NHS today accept a paradoxical state of permanent change, with or without the impetus of the recent Francis or Winterbourne reports.

So, the last part of this book takes us back into the wider world to explore the relevance of the ideas on both culture and cultural change, emerging from what is, after all, a single case study. There are several reasons why something so particular and, to be frank, so odd, as a High Secure Hospital matters.

Secure hospitals will carry on locking people up. While the last decade has seen investment in this area outstrip that of the rest of mental health services, these high-cost low-volume services are under scrutiny. It is no longer good enough to say clinicians know best and so another bed must be found. In straightened, economic times, better value for money is demanded. How we want Secure Hospital care to work is both a parochial issue for clinicians and managers, as well as patients and relatives but is also important for society more generally. It has been said that the test of a society is how it runs its prisons. How we run our Secure Hospitals is also a good test. The culture of our secure institutions and their reach tell us about ourselves, as much as describing those who do not fit easily into general society. The ethos they express speaks beyond the walls and mesh fences of now regulation height. How and why we lock people up and what it feels like when we do are practical clinical questions but also moral and political ones. For people who think execution is best, this book is not for them. For people who think long-term detention in the name of care and therapy is never justified, this is probably not for them either. For those who want to know a little of what it really can be like in high-security hospital care, it might be. And, in being written, it is there for all of us to consider.

Anthropological accounts often rely on salient detail to bring them to life. In this case, there are still paramount issues of confidentiality, for staff and patients. The reader may be left wanting to know more about given individuals who feature in the study. Both patients and staff in the Special Hospitals have suffered from prurient curiosity and sensationalist writing. Care was taken at all stages of the study on which this book relies to minimize the likelihood of any individual being identifiable.[2] The reader may be surprised to discover that all the staff and patients in an English Special Hospital are French, and that the wards carry the names of French towns and cities. So be it.

---

[2] Empirical data could not always be cited in its entirety; this is indicated in the text. All field-note material is in italics in the text.

Acknowledgements

My thanks go to the people and organizations that have made this book possible. It has had a long gestation period and I hope they will think it was worth the wait.

Nigel Eastman and Gilbert Lewis helped germinate the idea, one night in South London: both gave very practical support. Nigel Eastman continued to look on kindly from a distance and persuaded Hubert Lacey and Deji Oyebode to give me time to complete the doctorate that informs the book. The Wellcome Trust and notably David Gordon had the imagination to fund me with a Wellcome Trust Health Services Fellowship, at a time when no one in a medical school undertook qualitative inquiry. Esther Goody was always an enthusiastic Doctoral supervisor and, unlike me, did not doubt my capacity to complete the original study. The Department of Social Anthropology at the University of Cambridge taught me whatever I know about social anthropology, and my fellow students offered ideas and encouragement. Marilyn Strathern provided thoughtful and pragmatic advice. Sally Beckwith, Marie Clack, Anne Gatenby, Mary Healey Scully and Joan Stevenson, all of whom have been unfortunate enough to be my secretaries, helped with different stages of what is finally a book. Caroline Dacey kindly helped with proofreading.

Smithtown Hospital allowed me access to their staff and patients who were generous enough to talk to me and to my two research assistants. That the project happened was in itself remarkable. I hope those to whom we spoke will feel that I have listened and looked carefully, although the difficulties of doing justice to the experiences of staff and patients' lives and the complexity of the hospital's purpose, in no small measure, account for the delay in publishing this book. Anne Backhouse and Matthew Fiander were my ears and eyes on two wards in Smithtown. Like me, they found the work exciting but demanding. I owe them an immeasurable debt for their conscientious fieldwork but also for their common sense, sensitivity, humour and integrity. I was very lucky to find them.

In their various ways, Ruth Evans, Gill Mezey, Diana Souhami and my anonymous Smithtown reader all helped. Pat Lawton's sensible medical advice allayed some last-minute anxieties. Henrietta Moore's commanding understanding of her subject meant I received detailed anthropological advice at a critical point. Martin Baum was brave enough to commission a work that probably does not fit neatly into his brief with OUP, and Peter Stevenson and Lauren Dunn have cajoled and guided me to publication.

Sandra and Fred were just there, which, it goes without saying, was and is invaluable.

Contents

List of abbreviations

CMHT	Community Mental Health Team	MDO	mentally disordered offender
CNWL FT	Central and North West London NHS Foundation Trust	MIND	National Association for Mental Health
CTO	Community Treatment Order	MSFT	Mid Staffordshire NHS Foundation Trust
DSPD	Dangerous and Severe Personality Disorder	NAs	nursing auxiliaries
HAS	Health Advisory Service	NCCL	National Council for Civil Liberties
HMIP	Her Majesty's Inspectorate of Prisons	NOMS	National Offender Management System
IBVM	Institute of the Blessed Virgin Mary	POA	Prison Officers' Association
IPP	Indefinite Sentences for Public Protection	RCN	Royal College of Nursing
		RMO	Responsible Medical Officer
MAPP	Multi-Agency Public Protection	SHSA	Special Hospitals Service Authority

Part 1

Some abstract nouns: institutions, culture, crime and madness

Chapter 1

Institutions, culture and the culture of institutions

'There's nothing wrong with him medically.'
'Medically?'
'He's just very unpleasant. And therefore incurable.
I'm sorry.'
(Kane 2002: 6)

To invite you, the reader, into an abstract discussion of institutions, culture and the culture of institutions with only the flimsy argument that these are important concepts, might send you off in the direction of detective fiction. So, this chapter tries to make these key concepts both absurdly simple and also very difficult, the latter by refusing to allow the ideas to be thoroughly pinned down, as if in a butterfly collection. Shared understanding of concepts like these, even if achieved, is fleeting. Abstract nouns move on and change meaning. That is the real history of both 'culture' and 'institution' as words. However, if this chapter works, it will provide a context for the discussion carried on through the book and provide enough of a common framework for consideration beyond the pages here.

What is an institution?

This is the question I should have asked myself a long time ago. It is easy to produce a list of types of institution. Having compiled a list, the easy escape from the difficult task of definition, is to suggest that the members of the list are so different from each other that no definition would be adequate. Thus, banks (financial institutions), the Booker Prize (a literary institution), the University of Cambridge (an academic institution) and the Institute of the Blessed Virgin Mary (IBVM, a religious institution) would look similar to each other while being equally, if not more, different from each other.

The class of institutions is a big class. The pupils are different sizes and shapes. They might prove unruly, preferring their own rules to everybody else's, including the teacher's. These things on the list above are institutions but that does not tell us what an institution is. Using the 'without which not' style of definition beloved of the ancients might suggest that rules are necessary to them. Institutions are not anarchic; in fact, this is precisely the feature they share. More than that, they have rules that apply, at least to some extent, to them and not to other things. Their character is a preference for order, not chaos. They do the same things repeatedly. The institutions in my list, respectively, send out your bank statement each month; award, after due process, a literary prize each year; teach, set examinations and award degrees; or admit novices to a religious order to live in accordance with the rules of the order and, should they and the order wish, become nuns in due course. So each institution in the random list has processes in line with their purpose. Their purpose may vary but there may be similarities in their approach at a crude, broad brush-stroke level.

Many institutions are old, like the bank of Monte Paschi di Siena or the University of Cambridge; some, like the Booker Prize and the IBVM, are newer. If they have survived many centuries in changing circumstances they might be thought to be different from when they started out in life. The University of Cambridge has evolved to admit women but it has not changed its fundamental identity. The bank of Monte Paschi di Siena has digital banking; this was not the case in 1472 when the bank was founded. So, some have a capacity for change without loss of identity or erosion of purpose. UBS, a Swiss bank, spent much of the 1990s taking over a number of other financial institutions. These takeovers included Barings Bank. UBS continues but its name no longer reflects all of its acquisitions. Its name makes no mention of Barings, an institution that has gone to the wall. So institutions have lives; some change and some die. Spotting change in institutions is hard. If it were not hard, we would all have predicted the banking crisis of 2008, as we would have been clear that there was something rotten in the mortgage market in the US. We, the public, did not, nor did more than a tiny handful of economic experts or even bankers themselves. This single series of events, on its own, suggests that the assessment of change within institutions might be difficult. This was true even though the organizations in question were both open to a significant level of routine public scrutiny and run by clever people.

Are institutions a good idea?

The financial crisis of 2008 that afflicted the world economy has also called into question the value of banks. A lot of people neither like nor trust them and despise what they do. Some would argue that it has undermined the idea that banks are a good idea. In truth, it is hard to imagine a world without them, for all their recent character defects. Managing personal finance would be reduced to personal transaction, personal and enterprise credits and loans would be shrunk. Economies would be stifled but the bankers would not get their bonuses. Banks, as institutions, are currently a mixed blessing.

They are only one kind of institution. What about other kinds of institution? Institutions go in and out of fashion. Thomas Cromwell did not much like monasteries and his patron Cardinal Wolsey liked universities more, so took money from one kind of institution to give to another (see Mantel 2009, 2012 for these issues brought to life). Universities are easy to defend. However, the two that Wolsey and his king, Henry VIII, did so much to improve are both now accused of elitism. So what might have seemed an acceptable institution at one time might be viewed differently later.

Why concentration camps differ from Butlins

This is not a question. This is to point out something that Goffman, the guru of thought about institutions, did not make entirely clear. Goffman (1961: 23–72) accepts few, if any, of the distinctions between institutions; psychiatric hospitals are boarding schools are prisons and shockingly, concentration camps.[1] He is more convinced of similarity in

---

[1] Townsend (1962) conducted a major study of Old People's Homes. He shares Goffman's view that different kinds of institutions are similar rather than different.

day-to-day function than he is concerned with difference of purpose. Yet, at one level, this is obscene. To compare educational institutions with fine pedigrees and outstanding pupils and teachers to institutions designed for forced labour and murder is inappropriate. Butlins were holiday camps with rules about what time everyone got out of bed. They were enjoyed by thousands of people in their heyday and commercially successful. Concentration camps are different. Even if some boarding schools are sometimes authoritarian or control bullying badly, they do not set out to kill people. Nor do hospitals. Differences of purpose must, at times, be more important than any similarities.

Do institutions fulfil their purpose?

The example of concentrations camps allows a question, not of the goodness or badness of particular kinds of institution, since the atrocities committed there are not in doubt, but of whether they are run in accordance with their purpose. Some are, sometimes, but maybe not forever. Some never are.

Nazi concentration camps, within their remit, were, in fact, only partially effective. They did succeed in killing people and disposing of bodies. The technology of mass killing was improved as the Second World War progressed. The camps were less good as a reliable source of labour, their original intent. The conditions in which the Nazis kept people created illness and starvation, and, even without gas chambers, resulted in many deaths. The camps and the ideology they embodied thankfully failed in their intention to eradicate Jews from Europe, although the Jewish population decreased throughout Europe, particularly in the East (Hoffman 2010; Mazower 2009).

Thomas Cromwell was able to take advantage of the monasteries' and nunneries' failure to keep to their purpose. Where their administration was corrupt and their priests alcoholic and sexually active, it was easy and reasonable to suggest that they did not deserve their wealth. They were not godly institutions full of god-fearing, pious men and women. Echoes of the same arguments have emerged in discussion of the Catholic Church, as it has struggled with allegations of corrupt banking and a failure to tackle sex abuse by priests (BBC 1982, 2013).

Do institutions always live in buildings?

So far, there has been a physical reality to most of the institutions discussed. The exception is the Booker Prize. It may be decided upon somewhere, when the judges meet. It will be awarded somewhere, a large dining room perhaps, but it does not have a continuous physical presence in which institutional life occurs on a daily basis. So, it does not always live in a building, and it can be called into being when required. It is not characterized by a particular order to the day, the regular rhythms of life. It is held together by an idea and the people who are signed up to it. The idea has modest administrative underpinning that makes sure the judging is done properly, and which guarantees the dinner and a prize winner at the end who will briefly claim the media attention. The idea is literary excellence. Behind that, it is a device to boost the value of literature in the public's mind so it can do battle with the X-Factor, help authors survive and keep publishing houses in business.

Perhaps it is an extreme case. There are also institutions which embody ideas, have buildings and rules but rely less on a building than a prison or a concentration camp. An example is the Royal College of Physicians. It has a building in a prestigious location, Regent's Park. It is for senior physicians and promotes competence in a medical discipline. It spreads knowledge about its area of expertise. However, the College is really its membership, without which it could not afford its building. But its membership is scattered. It would not normally meet en masse. Small groups of members will come together for a variety of professional purposes, maybe in the building, maybe not. Members decide, just as in a golf club, who can join; there are rules about membership but not about daily life. Without passing the relevant examinations, membership is impossible.

How virtual is real?

Then there is the institution, a bank, without offices. No branch buildings but an existence in hyperspace. Egg Bank must have had a big computer and a headquarters somewhere but when it was launched it had a novelty value. It was a virtual institution in a field, banking, characterized at the time by a slower approach.

So, to come back to the original question of definition, institutions are many things. They share, to some extent, routines, rules and order and distinct identities but little else. They have varied purpose, embody different values and do what they are supposed to do well or badly. They may or may not have a physical location in which their way of doing things is evident. They have varied lifespans. This is an unsatisfactory definition but a starting point. The alternative to definition is to hide behind the multiple uses of the word 'institution'. This relies upon the assumption of shared understanding which, as what follows makes clear, is far from the case.

What is culture?

If culture is always a word, and an English word at that, and an idea, although contested, would it matter if it were replaced with another, sausages, perhaps? This is not a flippant question. In fact, it is an import-ant one. It addresses the vagueness, the specificity and the cultural par-ticularity of the English word culture, all in one go.

If culture, the word, had been sausages, its multiple meanings and associations would, with their ambiguity, have been lost. People are clear about what is or is not a sausage. The current society-wide preoccupa-tion with all things cultural, from opera and T S Eliot, old-fashioned elitist, high culture to culture as in multicultural education or culture as cultures, contributes to the reader's understanding of culture in this book. To use sausages instead would be to define more precisely, and certainly more concretely, but would absolve the reader of an oppor-tunity to deal with contested meaning, without losing their sense of direction.

Culture has a home in the academic discipline of social anthropol-ogy; this operates in relation to wider discourse not independent of it. Similarly, the diffuse meaning of culture in wider academe and soci-ety is not independent of the historical efforts of anthropology to elu-cidate a concept that, like the world, was changing as it was described. So the contested meaning within anthropology is a genuine reflection of diversity on micro and macro levels. It is testament to the validity of anthropological method, rather than cause for breast beating by anxious anthropologists worried that in saying anything at all, they have said something someone will dispute.

Culture, like other big words such as 'self' and 'society', are often discussed in what has been termed antithesis (Kuper 1999; Peel 1996), the antithesis being to other key concepts such as 'civilization', 'biology', the 'individual' or 'nature' (Geertz 2000: 48; Ortner 1974). The importance of the term can be read from such juxtapositions. Ingold's comment (1996: 57) on society could as well be applied to culture: 'No term is more pivotal to the identity of social anthropology than that of "society" itself, yet none is more contestable.'

Kuper (1999) notes that in Kroeber and Kluckhohn (1952), 164 definitions of culture were classified into two groups, of which 157, most generated by anthropologists, had appeared between 1920 and 1950. The message was unmistakable. Anthropologists were saying this is our 'stuff', even if they were not sure what the 'stuff' was.[2] Such a lack of agreement might have more to do with the differences between the subjects of anthropology than the anthropologists, of course.

Keesing (1981: 68) notes continuing inconsistencies. He helpfully emphasizes the distinction, often lost, between 'observable' culture, as he puts it 'things and events out there in the world', and 'the organised system of knowledge and belief whereby a people structure their experience and perceptions, formulate acts, and choose between alternatives'. Natural science prides itself on its precision. Its words, its 'ohms', 'electrons' and 'Higgs boson', are necessary to its methods and key to its inaccessibility. Writing the last of these I wondered if it was 'Hick's' and 'bison'. Social scientists who strive, it would appear, at times for a similar immunity to informed criticism by the wilful use of words such as 'alterity' or 'personalistic' are losing sight of their natural advantage, that of describing the world in the everyday terms of those who inhabit it. The disputes raging in anthropology can remain accessible to the informed lay reader. Culture is just one of those disputes. Geertz may be right to

---

[2] Kuper (1999) suggests that the enthusiasm for claiming this territory subsequent to 1952 was prompted by the turf war instigated by Talcott Parsons. He writes engagingly on the politics which led to the clarification of disciplinary interests in the 1950s.

point out that when seen from outside, anthropology might be 'a power-ful regenerative force in social and humane studies' and that this may be 'closer to the mark than the Insider view that the passage from South Sea obscurity to worldly celebrity is simply exposing anthropology's lack of internal coherence, its methodological softness, . . . its political hypoc-risy, . . . its practical irrelevance' (2000: 96).

In this book about one institution and its values and practices, cul-ture is a vehicle. It can carry other ideas, while itself being ideational. This applies whoever you are. Specifically, culture can carry ideas about social relations and what constitutes daily life, in this book, within the walls of a High Secure Hospital.

Is culture a thing?

Culture is only one 'thing'. Academic disciplines are full of them, none more so than psychiatry (depression, schizophrenia). Words can break free of their original moorings and sail off into uncharted waters. Per-haps this characteristic of academic abstractions is both evident in, and a product of, styles of writing, where such abstractions are linked with active verbs, e.g. 'post-modern critique wants to address' (Marcus 1998: 218). Academics have a perverse interest in maintaining such entities as well as in shifting their meaning, since to do so is simultaneously both to reinforce the significance of the specific topic and to highlight their own individual contributions. Discrediting topics as obsolete or to attack their usage within disciplines is but a subtle variation on this practice.

Despite such cynicism, the status of the abstractions of disciplines is of historical and contemporary interest. As long ago as 1981, Keesing wor-ried about culture acquiring a life of its own, being a thing that might 'do' things as if separate from the social conditions in which it is discernible.[3] This concern was also echoed by Strathern (1996: 83), in response to a question on the possible obsolescence of the term culture. She would

---

[3] This criticism, applied to society, comprised much of the 1989 debate: 'The concept of society is theoretically obsolete', see Ingold (1996). One observation on this debate was the difficulty participants had in discussing society without mentioning the word culture, which slipped in largely unremarked and undefined.

see the utility of the term waning once 'we begin to manipulate it as an imaginary entity'. It is all too easy to see that discussions of culture in anthropology might arrive at a dead end.

In fact, culture has been taken up again by other academic disciplines, the media and management consultants to name but a few, who are interested in helping culture avoid an unwarranted early death (Kuper 1999; Weiner 1995). Wright (1994: 2) helpfully indicates how this applies in organizational studies, of which this book is one example. She argues that culture has appeared in four different guises in organizational studies. These are national cultures to which multinationals relate, the multi-ethnic work force of a company, the 'concepts, attitudes and values' of the workforce and the 'company culture' of formal managerial values and practices.

This version of culture has immediate appeal, except for the fact that it has no place for the patients of our High Secure Hospital.

Culture: does everyone have one?

This may be easier to answer if the question is put the other way around. Is it possible to be human and not to share to some extent attitudes, views, behaviours, customs, practices and aspects of the material world with other people? If the answer is no, then arguably everyone has a cultural group whether or not they would see it that way. We are social animals with a remarkable capacity to communicate and to generate material culture from natural material, to communicate linguistically and symbolically and to divide ourselves into tribes.

The reason this is important is that it has been said that patients, in contrast to prisoners, lack culture. What seems to be meant by this is that they lack a set of attitudes in common rather than shared practices. Prisoners define themselves in opposition, more or less fiercely expressed, to the order of the prison institution. Patients, by operating with staff, deny themselves that possibility of coherent opposition. This is therefore a critical issue for High Secure Hospital care where there is a conjunction of high security and a patient population with histories of violence.

Culture: can you see it move?

It is a matter of historical fact that societies change and that both cultural values and cultural practices change. That is not the question. The question is whether it is possible to detect change as it is happening.

The French Revolution of 1789 marked a sea change in social attitudes and behaviour leading to the seemingly permanent loss of the monarchy from France and an espousal and articulation of values that persist to this day. No one doubted something momentous was happening at the time. In North London today, already a multicultural community, like other areas of the capital, there is a small but definite French invasion happening now. This has led to the designation of North London as part of a French election, the establishment of a new French school and a remarkably successful French bread stall at a local market where, on Saturdays, as much French as English can be heard. This last point is only a slight exaggeration. Is this a cultural change in North London society? Are these reasonable markers of change, and is that enough of a change to be significant?

Culture and institutions

Having thought a little about both culture and institutions, we can now think about them in the same sentence. We can turn to what might be known about institutional culture, as embodied in mental health and penal institutions.

The potential literature is large. It could be reviewed by academic discipline, by chronology, by location or by theme. To keep a focus,[4] we look first at what we know about psychiatric hospitals and then what we know about prisons. We are principally concerned with these types of institution as repositories and incarnations of particular ideologies, and

---

[4] The literature cited is drawn from an original hand search in 1992 and a subsequent electronic database search derived from ASSIA, IBSS, Psychlit. PsychINFO, Medline, supplemented by further hand-searching of the Haddon and Institute of Criminology Libraries, Cambridge.

their relationship to the wider social world.[5] This leads on to a section on how crime and madness fit together as concepts. We then consider how secure hospital care, i.e. institutions designed to help people who are both mentally disordered and law breakers, are organized and how that relates to the fit between madness and crime.

What do we know about psychiatric hospitals?

When were they invented?

The nineteenth century saw the development and firm establishment of the psychiatric industry (Jones 1993; Scull 1979, 1989). This had three components. First, was the building of psychiatric institutions, asylums, subsequently renamed hospitals. Second, came the emergence of increasingly specialized workers, initially called alienists, subsequently deemed psychiatrists and other mental health workers. The third was the development of a body of specific psychiatric knowledge, a technology of practice for which training was required. As time has gone on, this body of knowledge has shown considerable loyalty to biomedical models of illness and treatment, despite the scepticism of the other medical specialities, many patients, the general public and academic commentators.

Starting history in the nineteenth century is, it has to be confessed, a little arbitrary. What makes it defensible is the radical overhaul of the care of the mad at this time (Allderidge 1979). How this society has coped with madness has been described as an 'academic minefield' (Jones 1993: 4). What marks out the nineteenth century is a new and explicit focus on the warehousing of the mad, notably of 'pauper lunatics', and the scale of the physical building programme that accompanied it.

As the century wore on, critics noted that treatment was failing most patients; they did not often leave hospital. Whatever the strength of the argument, it went largely unheard. Legislative authority had backed a system of categorization of madness still substantially in use today.

---

[5] By implication the study of the individual as one of an aggregate, whether psychiatrically disordered or not, is neglected in this review. Such material is only cited where it addresses the issue of the social.

Categories of madness had previously existed (Berrios and Porter 1995) but in the nineteenth and early twentieth centuries they saw institutional expression on a massive scale. In this country and in America increasingly large numbers of people were detained within psychiatric institutions. In 1827 in England and Wales there had been nine public asylums. In 1930 there were ninety-eight (see Jones 1993: 116). The patient population peaked in the UK in 1955 and fell by more than half in the next four decades (Raftery 1992).

This was a wholesale change in social policy. It was led by politicians and academics, some of whom were disenchanted psychiatrists and some of whom were social scientists. They argued theoretically and practically for a change in the model of care; institutionalization was followed by deinstitutionalization and care in the community. The sheer volume of writing is testament to the seriousness of the attempt to address the inner workings of that embodiment of psychiatric practice, the psychiatric hospital and the social relations of those who lived and worked there.

How do psychiatric hospitals work?

The heyday of social science accounts of psychiatric institutions and the social relations of staff and patients was in the 1950s and 1960s (e.g. Belknap 1956; Caudill 1958; Goffman 1961; Greenblatt et al. 1955). This work was American and often described very large mental hospitals.[6] Subsequent and less radical contributions came from the UK and elsewhere but the important ideas are rooted in this era. It is no accident that these studies emerged at this point of transition between institutional and community care for those with mental health problems.

These empirical approaches were characterized by a reluctance to engage with macroeconomic or political forces. The projects primarily examined the world inside the institution, this focus also being a crucial component of an analysis which emphasized isolation and separation.

---

[6] Rapaport's (1960) anthropological study of the twelve-bedded Henderson Hospital is an exception. The unit's ethos was and is a therapeutic community and the study offers a stark contrast to the finding of work on a large scale. Permissiveness, reality confrontation, democratization and community characterized life in the Henderson.

It is sensible to divide most work on psychiatric institutions into those that 'buy into' psychiatric ideology and those that 'opt out', i.e. where psychiatric discourse is either reframed or problematized as just one of a number of interpretations of the same social phenomena. The main theme in this work is the nature of social relations between staff and patients and understandings of modalities of power within such institutions.

Opting out

The dominant strand of writing about the psychiatric enterprise documents hierarchically differentiated institutions whose social organization is indifferent to the size of the institution or the psychiatric descriptions of the patients (Goffman 1961; Greenblatt et al. 1955; King et al. 1971). These are custodial institutions. Life within them is heavily regulated (Goffman 1961; Morris 1969;[7] Perucci 1974). Staff rule. Some staff rule more than others (Perucci 1974; Segal 1962). Those high up in the formal hierarchy are unaware of individual requests or complaints (Scheff 1961), or communication is only top-down (Greenblatt et al. 1955). Patients entering such institutions lose autonomy (Goffman 1961). Their status plummets, as they are formally designated a patient, their rights are removed and their individuality becomes irrelevant. Their difficulties are seen as a consequence of the institutional processes to which they are now subject rather than intrinsic to them and/or linked to the rationale for incarceration in the first place. Their only room for manoeuvre is to adopt a social role within the institution which enables survival of a sort. Their role, in a fragmented patient community, is often defined by its relationship to staff, and this may provide a mechanism to exit the institution (Perucci 1974). Such an exit bears no discernible relationship to psychiatric or psychological models of mental health.

---

[7] Morris is writing about mental handicap institutions. This term has fallen out of favour in psychiatric circles. It referred to people with significant intellectual and other impairments present from birth but not usually including mental illness. Institutions in the UK followed the US model after 1924, and were explicitly classificatory in intent and deliberately, as opposed to inadvertently highly regimented. She concluded such institutions had only a tenuous claim to the title hospital, as they should be providing social rather than medical care.

Goffman (1961: 11–22), who is still frequently cited, generated a highly determinist but satisfyingly complete model of the 'total institution'. This arose from participant observation in a large US asylum.[8] In his analysis the individual's sense of self is affected by situational factors that are part and parcel of institutional existence; the patient is seen very largely as a passive victim of the process. The inmate world contains two 'constructed categories of person': staff and patients. His understanding of the staff world is limited but his descriptions of the experience of the inmate world constitute a powerful polemic. He argues that the existence of mortification processes, reorganizing influences and limited lines of response for inmates constitute the 'mental patient career'. The mortifying experiences include the destruction of the individual self-image, the intrusive presence of a hierarchical relationship between staff and patients, and the indignities of communal living. He outlines strategies available for the inmates. These consist of paying lip service to the regime, embodied by staff. He assumes that people never want to enter institutions. As he starts inside the institution, he can disregard grossly abnormal behaviour in the community of a kind likely to be seen and labelled as mad by members of that community. Recently, I saw a man sitting on a bench in my local high street wearing only a striped dressing gown. Chatting to friends who had also seen him, they had come to the same conclusion as me that something was mentally wrong with him. They worried for him and about him. Goffman's bleak account[9] of what was designed to be a therapeutic institution suggests the young man in the dressing gown was lucky to escape it, being 50 years too young.

Buying into

There are less dismissive approaches to the concept of madness in this older literature. This school of thought accepts that the institutionalized

---

8 Even if he was a sociologist.

9 Martin (1984) reviews inquiries into UK psychiatric hospitals conducted between 1969 and 1980. Almost all were critical. Although the inquiries themselves identified isolation, poor funding and administration as key problems, Martin's own conclusions echo the social science critique where the intention to alleviate suffering is less important than the smooth running of the hospital.

individual has previously failed to cope in the community. It follows that there may be value, if only humanitarian value, in describing this as illness (as opposed to witchcraft or evil or wilful inertia) (Alaszewski 1986; Stanton and Schwartz 1954). The advent of contemporary ideas about witchcraft, linked at times to exorcism, including that of children should remind us that to be labelled as other by your community can still be both humiliating and dangerous. Exorcism does not cure schizophrenia.

Hospitalization as a response to the identification of madness is based on a philosophy of care. The therapeutic potential of this philosophy may be undermined by scarce resources, the limited independence of subordinate staff (Belknap 1956), unhelpful shift patterns (King et al. 1971) or constant changes of staff (Alaszewski 1986). Individuals' treatment needs are assessed and treatment is arranged to target those needs. Within this framework, it is then legitimate, as a temporary measure, to remove, from the patients, aspects of their non-institutional self, e.g. the right to vote. The temporary nature of patient identity is not a convenient fiction but a reality; the work of staff is to equip those disabled by an illness to return to and remain in the community (Barratt 1988a, b; Belknap 1956; Caudill 1952). The institutional practices which underpin this are uniquely clinical and therefore different from other kinds of institution. Hospitals are not banks, religious orders or boarding schools. The departure of patients is linked with improvement discernible within an illness model but is also affected by levels of social support offered by family and friends outside the hospital (Spillius 1990).

Stanton and Schwartz (1954) exemplify this less critical approach in the historical literature. They conducted a two-year study of a fifteen-bedded disturbed women's ward in a US private hospital. Their ethnography is concerned with whether or not the institution meets its own goals; to do this they used a psychiatrist as an anthropologist.

They suggest convincingly that the real-life interactions between patients and staff are complex and paradoxical. In a disturbed ward, where custody must have been a central issue, they place emphasis on the staff, encouraging change and active therapy as well as being involved in administration. They fail to identify significant areas of inmate culture and stress the importance of the staff–patient dynamic to the life of the unit. Patient information is negatively distorted by omission and selection when staff describe patient activities. They listen to how patients are talked about; the linguistic representation of the patient is invariably passive. The study as a whole is imbued with the psychiatric values of the day and is a long way from today's Recovery model. This new model has generated a tension between the processes resulting in a positive outcome in its own terms (Leamy et al. 2011), conspicuously: 'connectedness; hope and optimism about the future; identity; meaning in life; and empowerment' and the discourse of chronic illness (Lester and Gask 2006). Service User-led services, e.g. the SUN project at Springfield Hospital and Borderline UK, two initiatives, one in a mainstream mental health trust and one a charity, concretize this radically different discourse on life after mental health problems and how the patient or service user or expert by experience is active in determining their destiny, not a passive service or care recipient. The views of service users are now valued as part of the architecture of care quality and their take on ward climate and satisfaction with services eagerly sought.[10]

The concept of psychiatric hospital culture

Accounts of psychiatric institutional life illustrate the confusion present in academe and elsewhere about the term 'culture'. In most cases but not all (Alaszewski 1986) authors have avoided the term, which is interesting in itself. Society, social interaction, roles, strategies and social structure have all found a place. Given the stability of the psychiatric institutions described, it is perhaps surprising that culture is not more often addressed. This is intriguing when the isolation (be it an artefact of method or a social reality) of such institutions (Goffman 1961; Martin 1984) might predispose them to developing distinctive cultures. But the emphasis on staff–patient interaction acknowledged by Goffman (1961: 106) and echoed by other authors undermines any claim to a full understanding of a psychiatric institution.

---

[10] Most early ethnographies of psychiatric hospitals ignored social change. Menzies' (1960) study of a general hospital provided a rare psychodynamic analysis of resistance to change.

Two factors may be more telling. First, to suggest that there is culture, is, on the whole, a positive remark but the tone of much of this writing is negative. Second, Goffman (1961: 23) refers to a process of 'disculturation' that occurs to the patient on admission. This preadmission identity of the patient—who they were before they were a patient—is largely neglected in the study of the psychiatric patient but features strongly in the equivalent prison literature. Staff in institutions have extra-institutional identities which come to work with them, and, unlike most patients most days, leave with them as well. The net effect of these different kinds of partial presence and identity, and the arbitrary collecting and housing of people called patients, may be to undermine a notion of culture within psychiatric institutions. Culture implies similarity rather than difference, and similarities may be hard to find. At best, the difficulty of adequate description is elucidated.

Who lives in psychiatric institutions?

The answer to this question depends partly on whether or not any credence is given to the idea of madness and its particular refinement in mental health services. It also depends on the historical period in question. Two points remain true across time and place: to enter a psychiatric institution you are thought to be suffering from some version of madness (and in all probability a doctor has said which kind) and you are unlikely to want to go there of your own volition.

What is the matter with you?

Descriptions of madness have changed over time. Psychiatric categorization per se has been taken to task for its very existence (Foucault 1967), for its inappropriateness as a metaphor for deviant behaviour (Scheff 1966), for its lack of a biological basis (Szasz 1961), for its discriminatory application to the poor (Scull 1989), to women (Ripa 1990; Showalter 1987) and specific subcultures (Gamwell and Tomes 1995; King and Bartlett 1999; Littlewood and Lipsedge 1988), for the unreliability of its application (Rosenhan 1973, 1981) and the way it legitimized a stigmatizing social process (Scheff 1981). These critical contributions are united by a focus on both social process and cultural groups.

Remarkably, the classificatory systems of psychiatry which focus on individual psychopathology go from strength to strength (APA 1994, 2013; WHO 1992). Indeed, we await, with eager anticipation, the imminent arrival of ICD-11. DSM-5, the latest American contribution to psychiatric classification, provoked controversy as it was developed. Significant criticism related to its lack of scientific validity (Allen 2013). Equally strong voices pointed out that 68% of the task force members had links to the pharmaceutical industry. This, allied to non-disclosure clauses signed by these individuals, created an impression that DSM-5 was created in unhealthy secrecy (Cosgrove et al. 2009). The number and range of disorders has expanded over time, leading to what has been described as 'diagnostic inflation' (Allen 2009: 221). This has left the profession open to ridicule, exemplified by a hoax that suggested taking 'selfies' was actually a psychiatric disorder endorsed by the American Psychiatric Association (Vincent 2014). Although not true, the fact that it was taken at all seriously, suggested that psychiatric classification might be heading in the wrong direction. More importantly, the net effect of more diagnoses may well be more, perhaps unnecessary, treatment.

Psychiatric categories, however flawed, can be said to have a standalone quality, independent of the social conditions in which they are generated. This positivist approach is the one that would strike the reader of any psychiatric textbook forcibly, and informs much mental health teaching and practice. It is also compatible with certain kinds of social criticism, i.e. there is nothing wrong with the categories but there is something wrong with the way they are applied. In the UK this has spawned a debate on the possible racism of British mental health practitioners (Lewis et al. 1990; Minnis et al. 2001), the value of terms such as race, ethnicity and culture in mental health practice (McKenzie and Crowcroft 1996) and the way in which services may have failed particular elements of the UK population (Cooper et al. 2010; Ramon 1996; Singh et al. 2007).[11]

---

11 There is an unresolved debate about the overrepresentation of Afro-Caribbeans in locked psychiatric beds (McGovern and Cope 1987).

Social processes have conspired together to allow psychiatry both to achieve and maintain, against a barrage of criticism, its eclectic[12] dominance of the discourse on madness (Jones 1993; Miller and Rose 1986; Scull 1979, 1989; Treacher and Baruch 1981). The practice of psychiatry has radically altered, moving from institutions to the community. Much of the literature already cited formed part of the impetus for deinstitutionalization, as did more effective medication for major mental illnesses, increased legal rights for patients in the UK and government anxiety about the state of psychiatric institutions. The supposed automatic linkage between madness and confinement (Foucault 1967) broke; this linkage was crucial to the power of almost all of the critiques mentioned here.

The ethnography of illness, allowing people to describe how they are rather than being diagnosed by psychiatrists offers, potentially, an alternative to the diagnostic manuals of psychiatrists. Psychiatric classification is then just one understanding of distress, not the definitive one. Alternative 'symptom' classifications and interventions (e.g. Fabrega 1982; Gaines 1982; Good et al. 1985; Marsella and White 1982) emerge. Good (1994: 25–64) charts the changing practices of medical anthropology over several decades, suggesting that their intentions are in part political. There is a strong desire in the subfield of 'at home' medical anthropology to 'bring the benefits of public health and medical services . . . to cultural minorities and the poor in our own society' (Good 1994: 27).

This can be mediated by what has been termed person-centred ethnography (Hollan 1997). The emphasis is less on the great abstractions of anthropology and more on the relationship of sociocultural processes to an individual's experience (e.g. Krause 1989). The task is to develop local, sensitive, illness narratives that enable people to make sense of their own distress. In many ways, the newer approaches within mainstream psychiatry have done this. Service user involvement in the ethos,

---

[12] The use of the word eclectic is no accident. Psychiatry is a broad church and although the biomedical model takes precedence, psychosocial, cognitive and psychodynamic contributions are relevant to day-to-day psychiatric care.

creation and staffing of mental health services in contemporary NHS Trusts are, in a way, the institutionalization of this critique. The encouraging aspect of this is that they also tailor interventions to these more personal understandings. This is not to forget that increasing routine recording of episodes of illness is done by the state. The Department of Health collects, for planning and monitoring purposes, levels of contact with mental health services. The categories used are not those developed by service users but almost invariably those decided upon by professionals (Department of Health 2013).

So, the medical model has not been jettisoned. It has transformed itself into a bio-psycho-social model (Shah and Mountain 2007) compatible with not only formal diagnostic systems but also with very personal understandings of the reasons for a person's necessary involvement with mental health services. It has adapted and survived into the twenty-first century (Bartlett 2010). Most importantly, from the point of view of this book, its now re-instated 'taken for granted' quality has eclipsed the need to study the place of mental health practice at all. As we will see, work on the other great places of confinement and control, the prisons, has been subject to an unparalleled level of ethnographic interest in the 'beneath the surface phenomena', even as such work has effectively vanished from the psychiatric enterprise.

Mental health law

The long-term confinement of patients, characteristic of Smithtown, was and is legitimated by the joint application of clinical and legal concepts; these establish that a person who is 'clinically mad' may be considered as also 'legally mad'. Much mental health law relates to the possibility or conduct of periods of hospitalization. These clinical and legal concepts have an overwhelming reality for patients in that they, literally, situate the person in the hospital. An alternative ethnography of illness, i.e. the way in which the person frames his/her own experience, can become much less relevant as soon as the law is involved. The law must always be involved in detaining people in mental hospitals. So, it may be helpful to describe the relationship between important legal and psychiatric categories. It is important to say at this point that law and psychiatry are uneasy bedfellows even within the limited area of law that is mental health law, as opposed to the larger area of the law where criminal or civil law is applied and considers inter alia mental health matters. Eastman (2006) observes that they adhere to two different principles, law to justice and psychiatry to welfare.

Within mental health legislation they have to take account of each other's perspective all the time. Clinicians are empowered to different degrees to operate and interpret the law in line with clinical thinking. The most obvious example of this is to decide what constitutes the legal entity of 'Mental Disorder'. This requires a clinician to say, for example, that a mental illness such as schizophrenia is a legal 'Mental Disorder'. If so, the questions about the need for detention in hospital can follow and will be decided initially by clinicians, not lawyers. The need for continued detention in hospital is not left just to clinicians. The checks and balances of the statute demand that non-legal and legal opinion acts as a commentary on clinical practice—not just the psychiatrists but also other kinds of clinicians who have a legal role. So, it is a joint enterprise but one in practice that still relies on the translation of the clinical categories of professional practice, whatever the sociologists said.

The number of psychiatric inpatient beds has stopped falling (Laing 2013). It remains true that a significant component of the psychiatric enterprise involves the use of this legislation for the incarceration of patients in units described, oddly, as open, as well as locked and secure (to different degrees).

What do we know about prisons?

Prisons may look like very different carceral institutions from psychiatric hospitals and academically, politically and governmentally they are usually separate. It may not seem self-evident that some understanding of prison literature is useful in order to understand a psychiatric institution like Smithtown but Smithtown is a High Secure[13] Hospital. Staff

---

[13] The most recent review of security in the Special Hospitals made recommendations that they should be modernized to meet contemporary Category B prison standards. This is one grade below the top level of security available in the UK prison system, Category A, which is used to accommodate only a small proportion of the prison population.

members have historically often belonged to the Prison Officers Association (POA) rather than nursing unions. Like the prison service and secure hospitals in general, Smithtown tries to prevent absconding and escape. It contains dangerous people, many of whom have previously spent much time in prisons (Jamieson et al. 2000).

Purpose and policy

In the past, prisons were often not the punishment for crime but were a stop-off point for other punishments (Morris and Rothman 1998) such as deportation, banishment, the stocks or worse. In the UK, since the abolition of the death penalty, prison is usually the end point. The exceptions are those deported or facing extradition to other jurisdictions.

The punishment, from the point of view of the state, is deprivation of liberty. The purpose is more complex. Prison may be a deterrent. It certainly takes people out of circulation, though whether it helps them desist from crime in the longer term is fiercely debated. From the perspective of the prison service, the purpose includes looking after them well in custody but also preparing them for release and useful lives thereafter (Prison Service, <https://www.gov.uk/government/organisations/hm-prison-service>, accessed 24.04.14). The arrival of the National Offender Management Scheme (NOMS) takes this further, as it intends that anyone sentenced to imprisonment will be managed from the community by their offender manager. Their sentence will be planned with regard both to public safety and the individual's social welfare from the moment they leave court (NOMS 2012). We have travelled some distance from the Spanish Inquisition or the Tudor torture of heretics in England. To some people, we may have travelled too far in the other direction.

The social life of prisons

The intention of prison does not tell us much about the reality of prison. To help, there is a substantial academic body of work (qualitative and quantitative) on informal social organization in prison,[14] supplemented

---

[14] The prison literature is vast and unwieldy, and much is irrelevant to this book, e.g. prevention of recidivism, prison development and current treatment approaches to sex offenders.

by media insights ranging from Bad Girls to fly-on-the-wall documentaries on Strangeways, Wormwood Scrubs and Holloway prisons. England was for a long time oddly silent about its prisons, relying on a well-developed system of prison inspection which has benchmarked prisons over decades against national standards (including decency and respect). This has changed more recently with ethnographic work in, amongst other settings, Maidstone, Wellingborough and Whitemoor prisons, generating fresh insights into contemporary issues including religious affiliation in prison societies. This recent work has also demonstrated how different individual prisons can be, one from another. This is not surprising to those of us who work in different prisons but may be to those outside to whom one prison may look much like another. It is an important observation, not only in the UK context but also when considering the international literature. Contrast, if you will, the use of local GP surgeries and access to jobs in the community, characteristic of Category D prisons in the UK with the Californian supermax (King et al. 2008). There, prisoners are locked up twenty-three hours a day and denied any access to training, education or treatment. Close-circuit cameras monitor the interior of each sparsely furnished cell and face-to-face contact with officers is kept to a minimum. These are very different institutions.

Most academic studies of prison have dealt with male prisons. As in other areas of criminology, women were historically neglected. Given that internationally men invariably outnumber women, this is perhaps not so surprising. Women comprise between 2% and 9% of international prison populations (Bureau of Justice 1997; Home Office 1999; Putkonen and Taylor 2014), although their rates of imprisonment are rising faster than those of men (Walmsley 2012). There are currently circa 3,941 women in prison in England and Wales compared to 81,572 men (Howard League for Penal Reform 2014).

Less attention has been paid to staff than to the inmates. Effort has gone into elucidating staff–inmate interactions, presumably because of their importance in prison control. The distinction between staff and inmate identity has been taken as self-evident. The ideas of the founding fathers of criminology continue to influence the contemporary literature on both sides of the Atlantic.

Inmate culture: men

Emphasis in the early studies of inmates was placed on the effect of the prison, the physical embodiment of penal policy, in generating a distinctive differentiated social system (Clemmer 1940; Sykes 1958), complete with inmate codes, prisoner roles and a prison lexicon. This was termed 'prisonization'. Although individuals' characteristics were not ignored by the early theorists, the significance of factors 'brought in' by prisoners (such as previous experience in institutions or origins within a criminal background) led to a more complete understanding (Irwin and Cressey 1962; Thomas 1973). This model was termed 'importation'.[15] These two concepts have endured, and provide a robust framework with which to examine varied custodial systems.

Wherever identified, inmate codes and culture were seen as oppositional to institutional authority. But the degree of opposition could vary with the severity of the prison regime (Irwin and Cressey 1962; Thomas and Zingraff 1976), how much of their sentence prisoners had served (Schmid and Jones 1993; Wheeler 1961) and the length of their sentences (Wheeler 1961). Traditional interpretations of inmate codes have been influenced by the emergence of gang-related divisions in inmate groups, often ethnically based (Bronson 2006). Clemmer (1940) had identified racial groupings as relevant to social organization but this insight was neglected until much later. Support for Clemner's early work came from Davidson (1974), who clarified the significance of racial allegiance for the informal social organization of male prisoners, and Cardozo-Freeman (1984) whose more up-to-date lexicon confirmed the importance of drug culture and ethnic allegiances. Despite considerable academic energy devoted to the issue, there remains a lack of clarity about the extent to which a prisoner's emotional state and behaviour relates to experience before or in prison (Dhami et al. 2007). However, it is clear that some aspects of imprisonment, e.g. long-term solitary confinement,

---

[15] Quantitative refinement of the key ideas of earlier writers has led to contradictory results. Much of this work has addressed the balance of internal and external factors in adaptation to the prison environment. De Rosia (1998) refers to the 'integrative model'.

are likely to have adverse consequences for the prisoner's mental health (King et al. 2008) and may generate challenging behaviour.

Subtle variations on the notions of inmate role and code are identified by Cohen and Taylor (1972) and King and Elliott (1977) in studies based in the UK. Cohen and Taylor's (1972) 'lifers' relied on strategies from the outside world in a situation of long-term incarceration. King and Elliott (1977) describe strategies prisoners used to cope with Albany prison; these bear some resemblance to those used by Goffman's psychiatric inpatients. What is less easy to discern is the extent to which a strategy is used, or a code adhered to or a role adopted, in sum the extent to which these sociological concepts affect the whole of the prisoner population or the extent to which individual prisoners stick to them. Inmate codes in particular have been described as 'ideal cultural values [that] are contested, shared, or disregarded' (Galanek 2013: 202).

The emergence of inmate sub-culture has been explained as a response to the various deprivations that are part and parcel of a period of imprisonment (Sykes 1958). Inmate sub-culture may also contribute to continuing delinquency. Multiple authors have seen prisons as schools of crime, i.e. despite their supposed role in reforming the criminal, they encourage further delinquency (Thomas and Foster 1972). Foucault (1979) suggests this is a product of inmate association and conditions both in prison and on parole.

Similarities exist between the prison systems in the US and the UK but there are also important differences (size of the prison system, rates of imprisonment, levels of internal prison violence, patterns of supervision), any or all of which may affect informal social systems inside a prison. In the UK, where the Ministry of Justice controls all research and access to prisons, the official interest in informal social organization was historically minimal. The social commentary provided by social science was substantially separate from the practicalities of prison management (HM Chief Inspector of Prisons 1990, 1992; Home Office 1984, 1991; King and McDermott 1989; Mott 1985). This was curious given the importance of some prison issues. Prison riots (Carrabine 2005; Home Office 1991; Thomas and Pooley 1981), drug use, physical and sexual violence (Ireland 1999, 2000) and the prevalence of HIV-related disease are hard to investigate without understanding inmate culture. In the US, the site of much early ethnographic work, such work is now rare and prison management has come to the fore, not least because of extraordinarily high rates of imprisonment (Galanek 2013).

Until recently, the best and most detailed information, compiled on a prison-by-prison basis, came through the work of Her Majesty's Inspectorate of Prisons (HMIP). This body is independent of government and undertakes both routine and unannounced visits to all prisons in England and Wales, and also does periodic thematic reviews, e.g. HMIP 1997. They are empiricists, and they pay attention to the material culture of prison life, e.g. the physical state of the prison, aspects of prison regime such as access to outside space, workshops and quality of the food and staff–prisoner relations but have less to say about prisoners per se except when there is bullying or theft between prisoners or harshness from staff. This is a reflection both of their need to report against a template of predetermined issues as well as the brevity of their visits, which last only a week. Having said that, their work is better than almost anything else, being comprehensive, evidence based and conducted by experienced inspectors. It will not tell what it is like to be there but it does clearly indicate how different prisons can be from each other.

Recent academic work in the UK has been ethnographic. De Viggiani (2012), drawing on fieldwork in a Category C prison, comments on the relationship addressed by multiple authors on the prisoners' presentation of self as, in some way, either stereotypically masculine or hypermasculine in order to deal with perceived risk within a difficult social arena. His work specifically links such display and the absence of intimacy it engenders with a threat to well-being. Crewe (2007, 2012) provides fieldwork material of considerable depth, focusing on power and its softening in contemporary UK prisons. In the less overtly controlling environment of modern-day HMP Wellingborough, the inmate code is revised for the times. In line with de Viggiani, Crewe notes public compliance with the prison regime and suggests that below the surface is greater defiance, evidenced by, e.g., drug taking and brewing of alcohol, which, if found out, would provoke punishment. Developing older typologies of prisoner adaptation, he delineates multiple degrees of compliance with the new technology of measurement and documentation, all differentiated from open resistance to the regime. Simultaneously, he identifies a weakening of local staff power; power is both more hierarchical and more distant than in earlier times, being located beyond the wing, not on the wing, and also in other disciplines, e.g. psychology, making it hard for prisoners to influence or even locate.

Crewe and Bennett (2012) comment on both new UK ethnography and also the absence of the prisoner voice itself, often only mediated through the analysis of the researcher. In a compilation of accounts of and from different types of prisoner, a range of first-hand experiences do emerge.

In the US, the previously substantial interest in undertaking studies of informal social organization has dwindled (Wacquant 2002) in favour of analyses of incarceration rates and prison management in an era of highly restrictive prisons (Galanek 2013).

Inmate culture: women

Although there is an almost universal finding among male prisoners of inmate codes, the results from women prisoners have been inconsistent (Giallombardo 1966, 1974; Jensen and Jones 1976; Mandaraka-Shepherd 1986; Mawby 1982; Ward 1982). Recent support for the importance of an oppositional code, governed in this case by prisoner 'queens', comes from a closed Swedish prison (Lindberg 2005). In contrast, Einat and Chen (2012) report on the prevalence of gossip in an Israeli prison, noting the frequency of inmates reporting and inventing information about fellow inmates to staff, clearly breaching the inmate code and undermining inmate solidarity.

The patterns of social networking in women's prisons are characterized by affective and sexual ties; much of this writing emphasizes the centrality of lesbian or other close relationships in prison (Rowe A. 2012; Giallombardo 1966). Goldingay (2007) describes affective bonds mirroring to some extent mother–daughter relationships in New Zealand prisons, where the importation of a relationship of respect, embedded in Maori culture, may have affected the social world of the prison.

More generally, a recognition of gendered social networking and women's distinctive pre-prison experience, notably high levels of physical and sexual abuse (Covington 1998; Genders and Player 1986; Giallombardo 1966, 1974; Halleck and Hersko 1962; Peugh and Belenko 1999; Ward and Kassebaum 1966) has emerged. In the UK, Carlen (1998) has argued that biological, social and cultural differences between male and female prisoners give rise to qualitatively different experiences. The situation of women prisoners who are mothers has been emphasized (Casale 1989; HM Chief Inspector of Prisons 1997; Kesteven 2002; McCellan, Farabee and Crouch 1997; Ministry of Justice 2012) and Einat and Chen (2012) review the literature on the pains of imprisonment for women, which brings out the importance of missing their children. The literature suggests that women import gender into prison, while failing to see that men do this too.

However, any attempt to explain gender differences in inmate social organization needs to incorporate the relative atypicality of any women's prisons as well as the typicality or otherwise of women prisoners, as women. The extent to which women prisoners are 'typical women' in experience or expectation must be in doubt. The type and frequency of their offending, as well as their duration of imprisonment, are very different from that of male prisoners (Ministry of Justice 2012). Women prisoners were and probably still are seen as socially and psychiatrically deviant (Heidensohn 1985).

Staff culture

Prison staff received far less attention. Staff–inmate interactions feature but staff internal social relations are neglected. This rather lopsided picture of prison life fails to differentiate between the intended prison regime and what might be termed staff culture. No coherent view emerges from the academic literature and there is conflicting data on the degree of similarity and difference in demographic profile and belief systems between prison officers and inmates (Davidson 1974; Jones and Cornes 1977; Liebling and Price 2001; Marsh et al. 1985).[16] Kauffman's

---

[16] Robben Island's prisons were staffed by Afrikaaners, who lived in a small isolated community on the island. There were two prisons, one a maximum secure prison for political prisoners belonging to the ANC and one medium secure for serious offenders. The warders had little or nothing in common with their political prisoners whom they viewed through the prism of apartheid. Personal Communication from a former Robben Island prison doctor.

work is a rare example of a study looking exclusively at prison officers. She found officers in four US men's prisons united by a code, where 'officer subculture is basically defined by its opposition to inmates' (1988: 111).

In contrast, Liebling and Price (2001) provide information of the staff group in a high-security prison in the UK. They identify largely positive relationships between staff and prisoners. They comment favourably on qualities of the staff group including the 'common sense' of officers, something that represents a considerable skill, sifting of information and complex judgement. Liebling (2007) (cited in Johnsen et al. 2011) has also argued that the staff–prisoner relationship is most critical to the experience of prisoners as they serve their time. In a recent Norwegian study, Johnsen et al. (2011) examine how this is nuanced within prisons of different sizes. Their empirical work suggests that in a country known to have a humane prison system, smaller prisons allow for more positive relationships between staff and prisoners. The enduring relationships they describe may be similar to those of a long-stay hospital ward with consistent staff and patients residing there for months or years and very different from large, high turnover prisons.

More recent work also in Whitemoor paints a different picture (Liebling and Arnold 2012) from the earlier study. Staff remain committed to rehabilitation but the prison has altered. The prison population in the UK has changed, with more young men on long sentences and with a change in the religious affiliation of the prisoner group so that in 2009/10 35% of the population was Muslim. The staff group had become less confident partly because of this single issue. Adherence to Islam was a vehicle for dissent in prison as well as religious observance and an expression of group identity. Conversions to Islam were common among prisoners but misinformation about the religion and its practices circulated in the prison as a whole. The local staff group had been ill equipped to deal with this complex social change. The consequence was a discernible difference in the atmosphere of the prison. This is a comprehensive and sensitive study and is a rare example of its kind in the British prison estate. It speaks to the issue of change and how previously competent staff can be severely challenged by it.

In the UK over the last ten years additional work has emerged (see Bennett et al. 2012) on prison staff. In this volume, Crewe et al. (2012) observe that this has led to an understanding of the heterogeneity of UK prisons, where staff attitudes and behaviour vary in part but not solely because of the function of the prison. In addition, male and female staff have discernibly different approaches to prison craft. This book also carefully documents the contrast to what may be the public's view of prisons; in fact, prison staff are also heterogeneous, no longer just officers but also health, education and welfare staff who contribute to the ethos of a given prison.

Who is in prison?

In England and Wales the really important answer is many more people than there used to be. Ministry of Justice figures show an increase of 66%, 32,500 people in the prison population of England and Wales between 1995 and 2009. This was a far greater rate of increase than between 1945 and 1995. It was caused by a change in legislation leading to both longer sentences and more recalls to prison as well as by an increase in serious offending, especially violence against the person (Ministry of Justice 2013).

The total prison population in the UK in September 2012 was 86,457 (OMS 2013). Men constitute the overwhelming majority of both the remand and sentenced prison population. There were 69,860 sentenced men and only 11,054 remanded men. There were 3,409 sentenced women and only 695 remanded women. Three in seven sentenced men and three in nine women were imprisoned for either violent or sexual offences. Women are rarely convicted of sexual offences, and there were only eighty such women against 10,466 men.

There is telling information about both the social origins and the health and social care needs of prisoners. They are much more likely than the general community to have experienced adversity in childhood. A large number come from families that already have experience of imprisonment. Many have been in local authority care, been excluded or truanted from school and have poor literacy and numeracy. Their work history is poor. They have unstable housing and significant debt (Ministry of Justice 2012; Williamson 2006).

Repeated surveys of the English prison population have indicated that many prisoners suffer from mental health and substance misuse problems (Coid 1984, 1988a, b; Maden et al. 1994, 1995; Singleton et al. 1998) and that suicide rates are high (Dooley 1990; Fazel and Benning 2009).[17] This situation is not unique to the UK. Fazel and Seewald (2012) found high rates of mental disorder in prisoners worldwide and over four decades. The last major review of psychiatric morbidity in the prison population in the UK is now over a decade old but routine data collected by the National Confidential inquiry team continue to suggest high levels of suicide and self-harm in the prison population (NCI 2011). The criminological and demographic characteristics of the population have changed (Ginn 2012) and new comprehensive mental health data for the UK would be helpful.

Prison policy on mental health has been set since 1990. Both government guidance (Circ 66/90) and a review of services to mentally disordered offenders (Department of Health/Home Office 1992) were clear that offenders with mental health problems should be the responsibility of the NHS. At that time, this meant that they should be looked after outside of prison (i.e. moved). In 2005 commissioning of health care in prison became the responsibility of the DH, devolved down to local Primary Care Trusts (Department of Health/HMPS 2001). This meant that prison health, including mental health, was provided in a different way. The NHS provides services inside prisons in a more coherent way than was ever possible under the Prison Medical Service. Many prisoners with major mental health difficulties have multi-disciplinary teams inside prison, although transfers out are still needed and still often slow (Bartlett et al. 2012; Forrester et al. 2009).

---

[17] This is matched by similar findings in the US where epidemiological work is usually of greater rigour (see Bartlett 2002). There is also substantial psychological literature, e.g. Toch (1977).

More recently, the Corston (Home Office 2007) and Bradley (2009) reports have emphasized alternatives to custody both for women (as their offending is usually minor) and for mentally disordered offenders (who might be diverted to mainstream NHS services before remand or from prison). Most recently, in contrast to this general principle, there has been enthusiasm for locating services for offenders who have personality disorder who are thought dangerous (or high harm in the language of the NOMS) either in prison or within NOMS agencies in the community (Department of Health 2011).

The current picture seems mixed and the sorting processes for prisoners imperfect. It is clear that there are individuals with diagnosable mental disorders in prison, and that there always have been and still are conflicting policy directions in terms of who should help them and where they should be to receive that help.

Chapter 2

Crime and madness

How do crime and madness fit together?

The point about current sorting processes for individuals with mental disorders could have been made at any time over the last two centuries and perhaps before that, too. The relationship between crime and madness is of enduring interest. English common law connected violence and madness many centuries ago. There has been little doubt that at times the connection is real but the frequency and mechanism of connection can be less clear (see Burke 2010). It remains an important topic and from it should follow a better understanding of who is and who should be in prison.

We have already considered in outline how common mental disorders are in the contemporary prison population. Other ways of getting at the relationship of crime and madness include both looking at the frequency of mental disorders and criminal behaviour in hospital and community samples and examining the nature of the connections between criminality or violence, and particular types of disorder. The issue is not so much that there may or may not be a connection but rather how significant it is in accounting for overall crime rates, which themselves change over time and vary by jurisdiction and corresponding definitions of crime.

Some simple observations emerge from existing research. First, being young and male and addicted to or using drugs and alcohol are risk factors for criminality and violence (Joliffe 2010). Second, certain kinds of mental illness create specific links to certain criminal acts. Schizophrenia is characterized by symptoms such as delusional beliefs, instructional voices and intense paranoia. The experience of these symptoms is common but in a small proportion of cases they do lead to violent acts. Third, people who might anyway commit criminal acts can also have mental disorders that are unrelated to their criminality. So, there are direct, indirect and coincidental connections between a loose idea of madness and crime.

Different mental disorders warrant different kinds of intervention, i.e. currently, few people with addictions, a kind of mental disorder, are in hospital; many are in prison. A small proportion of people with major mental illness will ever be in prison, and when they are, some will be sent out to hospital. Personality disorders of different kinds are common amongst prisoners and mental health patients and not uncommon in community populations (Coid et al. 2006; Singleton et al. 1998). Their treatment is debated (NICE 2009, 2009a), and current government policy is eclectic in the sense that it recommends treatment in different settings but prefers that risky individuals, where there is a clear connection between the disorder and the violence, be managed by the NOMS, not the NHS.

From the outside, decisions about who ends up where could seem arbitrary, despite clear rules in both criminal courts and mental health law about how these issues can be decided.

Who decides what to do?

Just as law and psychiatry work together to decide on admission to psychiatric hospitals in general, both law and psychiatry are also key to decisions about the fate of individuals with some combination of madness and criminality. The balance in the operation of the law is different, as criminality rather than madness will lead. That is to say, a person will enter the criminal justice system and be considered in relation to an alleged crime. The job of mental health services is to decide whether or not it needs to offer the criminal justice system information that would allow it to decide if the person should be diverted in some way towards the health service. This can happen anywhere along the pathway of criminal justice processing, e.g. the police station, courts or prison, and at any legal stage of criminal prosecution.

The secure hospital system, of which Smithtown is one component, comes into play where the alleged or proven criminal act is serious, usually amounting to a violent crime such as grievous bodily harm or worse. It is true to say though that both prisons and secure hospitals look after individuals who are a risk to others and have mental disorders.

How does secure hospital care work?

What is it for?

Secure hospital care embodies the relationship between madness and crime in a way that prisons do not. Their explicit remit is to provide treatment to those legally detained within a secure building with high walls.

The High Secure Hospital population was c. 1,800 at the time of the study (Butwell et al. 2000). These institutions are the oldest part but only one part of the complex social system dealing with mentally disordered offenders. They were originally criminal lunatic asylums, then Special Hospitals, and now High Secure Hospitals.

The term mentally disordered offender (MDO) is both immediately comprehensible, implying both a mental health problem and unwanted antisocial behaviour, and in need of qualification. The term is the latest in a long line of terms seeking to encapsulate similar meanings, e.g. criminal lunatic, criminal insanity, moral insanity and psychopathy. It has its origins in the 1980s review of services for MDOs (Department of Health and Home Office 1992), which recognized that the gravity of offending by people with mental health problems varied, and that they required different approaches from the criminal justice and health care systems. The High Secure Hospitals deal with MDOs who are considered most dangerous, and are intended to assess and treat them and manage their risks so that they can leave to a less secure environment. The same is true of the other components of the secure hospital system, which has grown larger as the high secure population has decreased.

The numbers of people detained as patients under the parts of the Mental Health Act that relate to criminal offences have not changed radically in the last fifteen years (Department of Health 2000; CQC 2013). In 2012/13 there were 1,788 such hospital detentions; a quarter were under Section 37/41, an order that usually results in hospitalization over a period of years.

The organizational philosophy is that most patients will move through the system en route to community rehabilitation. The end point is intended to be similar to that of the prison system: people go home.

This is to explain the operation of the secure hospital system in its own terms; not everyone accepts this account (Gostin 1986). There are good reasons to see secure hospital care as part of a wider system of surveillance and control, and to dispute the value of the clinical and legal frameworks on which its operations depend.

Forensic psychiatry as social control

To place the development of psychiatric institutions in a wider socio-historical context is valuable (Foucault 1967; Jones 1993; Scull 1979, 1989) and a necessary counterpoint to focusing only on the inside of potentially isolated institutions (Etzioni 1960), exemplified by the early hospital ethnographies. But there is a tension between writers whose preference is for historical precision, such as Scull and Jones, and those whose strength is grand theory, such as Foucault. Both strands of thought are relevant to reframing the psychiatric enterprise historically and providing a way of understanding contemporary psychiatric practice. As so much historical service provision was locked, and patients were confined against their will, this is particularly pertinent to the study of secure care.

The emphasis on power, and its legitimation through particular bodies of knowledge, fit well with the position of forensic psychiatry. Miller (1986) argued that the practices of social control evident in institutional psychiatry outlined here could be laid at the feet of the capitalist state. The category 'state' was and is far from being unproblematic. Even a cursory examination of two major branches of government, the Department of Health and the Ministry of Justice, demonstrates inconsistency in their attitudes to those with mental health problems, for example in relation to those who are both homeless and mad. The relationship of psychiatry and the state has implications for the practice of forensic psychiatry, whose practitioners staff secure hospitals. Forensic psychiatry's sphere of operations includes not only hospitals but also prisons and courts. The authority of forensic psychiatry stems directly from government, which has legitimized the decisions of forensic psychiatrists using both the criminal justice and civil sections of the Mental Health Act 1983. Furthermore, forensic psychiatrists have specific working relations with the Ministry of Justice. They, more than those in any other branch of psychiatry, practise overtly custodial psychiatry, sanctioned by the state, using the argument of public safety.

However, forensic psychiatry is morally complex. The difficulty for any global, as opposed to detailed, analysis is beautifully illustrated by four phenomena, which occurred simultaneously. First is that Jack Straw, a Labour Home Secretary, argued for an extension of medico-legal power to allow the hospitalization of those untreated and unconvicted dangerous individuals (Hansard 1999), even if they are untreatable. Second, he was opposed by a wide range of organizations, including the Royal College of Psychiatrists and Liberty. Third, these same forensic psychiatrists then expanded institutional provision for the dangerously mad. The climate of blame that rendered this a necessity (in defiance of actuarial risk to the public (Taylor and Gunn 1999)) was the same as that propelling the Home Secretary's policy. Fourth, the Home Secretary required the cooperation of psychiatrists to implement his policy shift (Eastman 1999) as it was finally represented in the amended Mental Health Act 1983, finally revised in 2007. This much might have made Foucault smile.

This political detail should also be seen against the symbolic and physical practices of surveillance, inside and outside locked institutions. Interest in Bentham's panopticon was rekindled (Boyne 2000; Foucault 1979). Originally, it was intended to allow inspection from the centre of activities of the periphery, and to be used as a template for prisons, hospitals and educational facilities. Wandsworth prison, amongst others, relies on a central space from which radiate wings. Staff standing in that space can see the landings and who goes in and out of a cell, though not inside the men's cells. It is efficient, as not many staff are needed. Alternative prison designs require more staff. Foucault (1979: 195 and 212) argued that regimented practices of surveillance, such as those in use in a prison with this kind of architecture, acknowledged and perpetuated power relations. He considered a desire for surveillance that both originated in the wider community and spread outside the buildings in which disciplinary practices were perfected. Thus they both do and do not require the physical paraphernalia of the panopticon. Boyne (2000:

302) refers to the panopticon as an 'ideal type', necessary to generate thought about more contemporary surveillance techniques (Jones 2000) using modern technology. These can represent surveillance not by the Foucaultian state but by the local community anxious to reduce street robbery.

This attempt to link ideology, physical structure and social practice was not an obvious feature of early studies of institutions. Social relations and their relationship to psychiatry were discussed but with only occasional mention of the symbolic dimensions of literal space (Perucci 1974: 25). This is striking given that the designers of early asylums certainly thought about segregation, isolation and internal and external space, with particular reference to gender (Alaszewski 1986: 7–13; Bartlett 1994). It is likely that they also thought about air and light. Cramped and airless institutional and private spaces increased the likelihood of disease transmission. This is evident from the way in which Nightingale wards were designed and also maintained, as well as from the ceiling heights, long corridors and spaciousness of many still extant nineteenth-century psychiatric hospitals which could, at least at the beginning, be seen as a serious attempt to create more healing environments. The absence of engagement with the aesthetics and practicalities of building design and a neglect of the symbolism of institutional buildings is important, compromising a day-to-day grasp of patients' quality of life, and how active movement and passive processing in the space of a hospital is informed and constrained by design. It is now a more obvious weakness in empirical studies of hospital life given the substantial interdisciplinary investigation of space as an analytic coat hanger in recent years, which has permitted multiple and local formulations of the connections between physical structures, ideology and personal meaning.

It is the link to the community that brings this discussion up to date. Jack Straw's intervention in 1999 followed increasing concern about dangerous madmen running amok in the streets of Britain (BBC 1998). The sensationalist language in the previous sentence is deliberate; it is exactly the way in which the small numbers of killings of strangers by individuals, usually with badly controlled mental illness, was rehearsed by the tabloid press. The consequence for forensic psychiatry (and to some extent other branches of mental health services) was the introduc-tion of risk management with a vengeance (Bartlett and Kesteven 2010). There were three arms to this: statute law to increase surveillance of the mentally ill in the community; clinical practice measures to standardize recording of risk formulations; and greater use of mathematically based risk instruments designed to predict violence with greater accuracy. Much of this was intended to extend the surveillance possible within the institution to the home and the street.

There was a parallel shift in community-based criminal justice ser-vices. Homicide by individuals under the active supervision of the Pro-bation service helped push the Probation service away from a welfare agenda towards the prevention of reoffending. The latest initiative in Transforming Rehabilitation (Ministry of Justice 2013) is firmly focused on reducing reoffending and requires increased supervision of those emerging from short sentences of imprisonment. It is possible to see this as benign in the sense that it may enhance support for offenders at obvious high risk of reoffending. However, it may not feel like that if, in practice, it requires an ongoing demand for compliance with supervi-sion and prescribed activity in the community. Foucault would not be smiling now.

How is secure hospital care organized?

Contemporary secure hospital care is one component of this multi-agency approach to the care and management of individuals with men-tal health needs who come into contact with the criminal justice system. The secure psychiatric hospital system nationally comprises three tiers of security: high, medium and low. Staff in these units, who include forensic psychiatrists, have additional specialization in criminal and mental health law and the management of violence. Secure hospital care fits into a wider system (see Fig. 2.1).

The complex web of interconnections between MDOs and organizations

Different parts of government have ultimate responsibility for these individuals. Depending on where someone is in the system, they will be

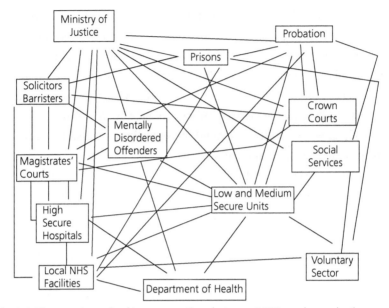

Fig. 2.1 The complex web of interconnections between MDOs and organizations.
Reproduced from Bartlett and McGauley, *Forensic Mental Health: Concepts, Systems, and Practice*, Copyright (2009), with permission from Oxford University Press.

the primary responsibility of either the health care system or the criminal justice system. People in prison or in the community post sentence, for instance, are usually the responsibility of an offender manager based in a local probation office. People who have gone through the secure hospital system out into the community will be the responsibility of the health care system. However, at different times in their lives an individual person could find themselves known to probation, on a short prison sentence, or in a secure hospital bed (Hales et al. 2015). The principles underlying care and management are that there is a plan leading to independence with safety, i.e. that the risk posed by someone is managed as well as their welfare, and in the case of those needing treatment that they get this even if they move around the system.

High secure services such as Smithtown are only one part of this complex system. Their size and relevance was greater at the time of the study than is true today. High secure services take individuals deemed the most dangerous of the Mentally Disordered Offender population. For many years the threshold was that they posed a 'grave and immediate danger' to life but this has been altered recently to requiring 'treatment under conditions of high security on account of their dangerous, violent or criminal propensities. (NHS Commissioning Board 2013)

Why were High Secure Hospitals built?

The High Secure Hospitals have a long and convoluted history. Their origins can be traced back at least to the mental health issues and legislation of the nineteenth century which resulted in widespread institutional care for the mad. The first half of the nineteenth century was marked by ad hoc provision for the 'criminal lunatics', and it was not until the early 1860s that specific provision in purpose-built accommodation was created (Parker 1985).

In 1863 Broadmoor was built, followed in 1912 by Rampton, and by 1933 Moss Side was also operating. These three institutions subsequently became 'Special Hospitals' following the Mental Health Act 1959. Their histories, management and patient population show significant differences (Bartlett 1993), both over time and between themselves. A further Special Hospital, Park Lane, was built in 1974; Ashworth was created in 1989 by the merger of Park Lane and Moss Side.

The organization of the Special Hospitals was quite different in the early years of their existence (Department of Health 1994; Hamilton 1985). Broadmoor was run by the Home Office until 1948, when it was taken over by the Ministry of Health. Managerially many functions had been transferred but admissions and discharges remained the responsibility of the Home Office. Moss Side and Rampton were run by the Board of Control (established under the Mental Deficiency Act 1913) during the years they functioned as institutions for violent and dangerous 'mental defectives'. They also became part of the NHS in 1948. Between 1948 and 1959 the Board of Control managed all three Special Hospitals on behalf of the Ministry of Health. Both the Home Office and the NHS continued to be important to their activity but the role of the Home Office became highly circumscribed and has now moved to the Ministry of Justice.

The involvement of two government departments in this way, and the historical alteration in the level of their involvement, is a reflection of the ways in which the individuals contained in such institutions are socially constructed. This debate about 'madness' and 'badness' is well rehearsed in forensic arenas. The definitions change from time to time because there neither has been nor is consensus about who is mad and bad (Foucault 1967; Grounds 1987; Home Office 1990; Lewis 1974; Porter 1987). The significance of this in terms of all secure hospitals is that clinicians designate the patient population to be mad and in need of treatment, rather than bad and in need of punishment. The tabloid press often refers to prisoners and inmates rather than to patients (<http://www.wlmht.nhs.uk/bm/broadmoor-hospital/>).

Who was in the High Secure Hospitals?

In secure hospitals generally and in High Secure Hospitals in particular, most people have schizophrenia, a major mental illness and/or clinical personality disorders, and they are admitted for assessment and treatment. Schizophrenia is a powerful social construct; there is a debate about its value (e.g. Barrett 1998; Clare 1980; Ingleby 1981) but less doubt about its impact on someone's ability to live an ordinary life. Personality disorder also affects many High Secure Hospital patients. This is the group of people who are most often the focus of the discussion 'mad or bad'. The presence of large numbers of individuals with personality disorder in the prison *and* secure hospital systems highlights the rather arbitrary application of madness or badness explanations for antisocial behaviour.

The ratio of men to women in high secure services was, for many years, *c*. 5:1. The length of stay of patients has varied; some individuals are more likely to stay longer, e.g. men convicted of sexual offences who are not mentally ill. Current length of stay is in the region of five to six years (<http://www.wlmht.nhs.uk/bm/broadmoor-hospital/>) but used to be ten years (Butwell et al. 2000). Men and women detained in the then Special Hospitals, now High Secure Hospitals, have had different profiles (Bartlett 1993; Hassell and Bartlett 2001).

Men were likely to have committed serious offences, to have been convicted by the courts and to have been sent to hospital under Part III (Criminal) of the 1983 Mental Health Act. Most entered hospital because they were mentally ill, with the most common psychiatric diagnosis being schizophrenia. They were less likely than women to be held in terms of the 1983 Mental Health Act under the legal category of Psychopathic Disorder, and were more likely to be held under Mental Illness.[1]

One-third of the men had committed a homicide and were very likely to have had a history of previous criminal convictions. Women were less likely to have committed serious offences, although a number had killed and they were more likely than men to have committed arson. Women were more likely than men to have had previous experience of mental health care. They were less likely than men to have gone before the criminal courts and more likely to be detained under Part II (Civil) of the Mental Health Act 1983. They were more likely than male patients to be held under the legal category of Psychopathic Disorder (Coid et al. 2000; Jamieson et al. 2000).

The secure hospital population is very different from the general psychiatric hospital population. The number of beds available for psychiatric care is c. 35,000 today, a number that has altered little in the last twenty years (Laing 2013); this period of stability has followed the steep, post-war reductions in bed numbers during which time community care became usual. Most inpatients in non-secure psychiatric beds are suffering from mental illness. Roughly similar numbers of men and women are detained (Care Quality Commission 2013). Historically these people have been detained under the legal category of Mental Illness, very few under Psychopathic Disorder (Department of Health 2000).

What has changed recently in secure hospital care?

The system of secure hospital care has never been static, and recent changes in the size and distribution of beds and patients are worth

---

[1] The Mental Health Act 1983 had four categories of mental disorder, and suffering from one of these is a prerequisite of being subject to the Mental Health Act. These four categories are mental illness, psychopathic disorder, mental impairment, and severe mental impairment. These do not correspond easily to clinical categories, and in clinical practice the relationship was clarified on an individual basis (Jones 1996).

rehearsing. In 1991 there were 1,740 men and women in high secure services: women constituted 20% of the population (Special Hospitals Service Authority (SHSA) 1991). There were 551 men and women in NHS regional medium secure services at the same time (Murray 1996). There has been a downsizing of the High Secure Hospital estate notably since the Tilt report (Tilt et al. 2000) and increases in the number of medium and other secure services. Laing (2013) reported a current total of 8,115 high, medium and low secure beds in the NHS and Independent Sector, an increase from 5,522 in 2006. The Independent Sector has become a major provider of secure hospital treatment (Harty et al. 2012). By 2013 bed capacity in high security had been reduced to *c.* 828. There are 240 beds at Broadmoor (<http://www.wlmht.nhs.uk/bm/broadmoor-hospital/>), 228 beds at Ashworth (<http://www.mersey-care.nhs.uk/Eligibility_and_selection_Criteria.aspx>) and *c.* 360 beds at Rampton (<http://www.nottinghamshirehealthcare.nhs.uk/information/annual-reports-2012–13/>). Only fifty beds at Rampton are available for women. The NHS Commissioning Board (see Laing 2013: 31) thought 680 individuals were actually detained in these high secure beds at the end of 2012.

Comprehensive, detailed data are hard to obtain but it is clear from the overall financial spend (Mental Health Strategies 2010), the interest shown in this market by the Independent Sector (Laing 2013) and the number of beds available that secure hospital care has developed in size and complexity over the last twenty years (Bartlett et al. 2014). The same comment could have been made about the period 1973–93.

Common to all secure hospitals is a considerable level of physical security (locks, cameras, internal building design, fences and walls), and relational and procedural security designed to minimize risks of escape or of harm to other people. This enhanced level of surveillance and monitoring is part of routine clinical work as well as part of the architecture and practice in units. The impact of the Tilt report and the introduction of security standards for medium secure care (Department of Health 2007) was to bring in national definitions of physical security and allied practice.

It is likely that the change in the climate of risk following well-publicized killings by psychiatric patients in the 1990s contributed to what, overall, seems to be an increase in secure care. So, too, did the introduction of new mental health law explicitly aim at risk reduction, and this may have had a direct effect on clinical practice in clinicians becoming risk averse.

There is now concern that these medium secure services have grown large and stagnant (Wilson et al. 2011). It is difficult to obtain timely admissions to some units despite increasing numbers of beds. Length of stay for some patients is longer than that thought suitable for this tier of security (Bartlett et al. 2007). They are expensive, high-cost, low-volume services whose cost to the health service has outstripped by some distance the rate of growth seen elsewhere in mental health services (Mental Health Strategies 2010). The Department of Health is now taking steps to provide financial incentives for patients, not to occupy secure beds but to be treated, improved and moved on to less expensive facilities. The Health and Social Care Bill 2012 contains new measures to revamp commissioning arrangements for secure hospital beds, which seems likely to ensure more coherent pathways of care linked to financial arrangements; these were introduced in April 2013.

Cultural problems in high secure hospital care

To date, the hugely expanded low and medium secure hospital estate has largely escaped the kind of criticism aimed at the then Special Hospitals in 1988, 1992 and 1999. The worst that has been said of them has been that mini-Special Hospitals are being built in cities, that they have a tendency to let people escape and that they are slow to admit because they are slow to discharge. The CQC inspections have replaced those of the Mental Health Act Commission. It is interesting that at a time when institutional care is once again under the spotlight (Department of Health 2012; Francis 2013) that some secure hospital care has been criticised but with relatively little publicity (<http://www.cqc.org.uk/directory/1–129,389,340>).

All three Special Hospitals (Ashworth, Broadmoor and Rampton) were subject to individual, critical scrutiny (Department of Health 1989,

1992; Department of Health and Social Security 1980; Fallon et al. 1999; Health Advisory Service 1988; Hospital Advisory Service 1975; Prins et al. 1993) and lumped together in policy terms. If one Special Hospital is criticized, they can all be criticized. The decrease in the size of the high secure population and the corresponding development of smaller, local units (Department of Health 1994; SHSA 1995) make those that detain dangerous patients less conspicuous than the well-known high secure units. Given the recurrent political embarrassment generated by discussion of high secure care, this may be politically adroit. Given what we know about scandal in small and scattered children's homes, it does not make any kind of secure care intrinsically immune to the kind of criticism aimed at the then Special Hospitals.

The inquiry literature argued that the Special Hospitals were geographically and professionally isolated from the rest of the health service. These observations matched much of the earlier and subsequent inquiry literature into a range of different kinds of institutions (BMJ 1978; Department of Health 2012; DHSS 1980; Martin 1984). In addition, they were criticized for rigid and impersonal regimes, with little awareness of contemporary treatment approaches. It is a moot point as to how many other institutions might have had the same comments made but did not. In the mid-1980s, as a junior doctor working just outside London, I went to a ward I did not usually visit within a large hospital complex. It was known as the Polish ward. It had polished lino and was very clean but it was a barren physical environment. Entering the nursing office, I saw the nurse in charge hide a bottle of alcohol in the drawer in front of him. He called the patient I had been asked to review into the nursing office. The man stood to attention. He did not speak English and there was no interpreter. The ward was full of men who were, ultimately, casualties of war, existing in a time warp of long-stay care without rehabilitation. They had become ill either during the war or soon after; their country, Poland, had become part of the Soviet Union and they could not return home. They had minimal ties in the UK and so could not be discharged but this was not seen as a problem.

The then Special Hospitals had two additional interrelated concerns: first was the relationship and distribution of power and authority between central government and the local management structures; second was the local balance of power between the main Special Hospital union, the POA and the management in each hospital.

Power was concentrated in the Department of Health. This is evident in the failed attempt to produce an effective outward-looking local management system in Broadmoor. After some years of wrangling and the final creation of the Broadmoor Hospital Board, an attempt at the devolution of power, the critical Health Advisory Service report on Broadmoor said: 'Board members, members of the HMT and hospital staff are uncertain about management roles and responsibilities' (1988: 22).

Paradoxically, it was also argued that central government was insignificant in terms of its ability to influence life on the ground. This was because of the power wielded locally by the POA, the main trade union in the Special Hospitals. The POA owed its pre-eminence to historical management structures in the Special Hospitals (Kaye and Franey 1998a: 39–50).

The publication of the 1988 Health Advisory Service report on Broadmoor signalled a turning point (Anderson 1988; Evans 1988; Smith 1988). It brought wholesale managerial change to the Special Hospital world, and heralded the arrival of a new management body, the SHSA, in 1989. The report linked organizational issues with an overreliance by staff on historical practices. It found fault with the emphasis on custodial procedures and the corresponding neglect of therapy (Burrow 1991a, b). It was not the first time that these criticisms had been made but the Department of Health believed the rest of psychiatry had moved on, and was obliged to conclude that the Special Hospitals had been left behind (Millar 1991).

The industrial relations disputes in the Special Hospitals were well covered in the media of the time. Even after the introduction of the SHSA and local, larger hospital management teams led by general managers, the POA could, in the early 1990s, bring the system to a halt. Patients would remain locked up for long periods of the day in their rooms or dormitories. Senior hospital staff and the small number of nursing staff who were members of the Royal College of Nursing would man the wards (Carvel 1990a, b, c; Department of Health 1992; Naish 1991).

The creation of the SHSA in 1989 had demonstrable consequences for the three hospitals managed by the authority. The SHSA review indicated how the authority understood its role:

> improved commitment, visibility and understanding of the role of special hospitals within society and in the national health framework ... We are starting to get over to people the message that we are hospitals ... slowly but surely the old image of the hospitals as prisons is being whittled away (1991a: 3).

Yet more explicit is the following passage from the five-year development plan:

> [W]e register our intention to introduce ward management in all our hospitals. This will devolve management further down the organisation, . . . and be a key factor in changing the existing culture (SHSA 1991b: 6).

The SHSA saw itself as having a 'culture' problem but believed it was actively addressing it and thought it could be changed. The worry was that their institutions might still be seen as prisons for the bad, not hospitals for the mad. But there was and still is an undeniable overlap of intended, rather than inadvertent function between prisons and psychiatric hospitals (Dolan and Coid 1993: 157–70; Genders and Player 1995). Built into mental health legislation since its inception are powers to detain. All psychiatric hospitals contain some patients held against their will, whose own view is often that they are imprisoned, whatever the medical rationale. The High Secure Hospitals lock up dangerous patients; they are high secure institutions. Prison populations include people with established mental illness; many will remain in prison and receive psychiatric treatment there.

For the SHSA there was no positive value attached to the way things have been done in the past; positive value derived from doing things differently. As Kaye and Franey (1998: 52) later put it, their task was 'to make change happen'. The solution outlined in 1991 was to introduce more managers in a lower-down-the-line management system, so that they impacted on the clinical coalface, the ward. They wanted to win the 'hearts and minds' of the staff.

The SHSA spoke as managers, fluent in management discourse. This carries its own assumptions and norms but:

> Critics have focused on the emptiness or hollowness of its language—usually when confronted by visions, mission statements or strategic plans . . . seen as testimony

to the fact that managerialism is just an ideological con trick or smokescreen being used to conceal 'real changes' (Newman and Clarke 1994: 28–9).

Newman and Clarke argued that what the 'smokescreen' hides, or is usually thought to hide, is a profit motivation based on increased efficiency. They suggest that the empty spaces of management talk can be the battleground for various interests, e.g. political, professional, who can act on the language in accordance with their own aims. This seems curiously relevant, as, after a period of sustained real increases in NHS funding, the NHS now faces flat-line funding and increasing demand. The level of efficiency savings currently required within solvent parts of the NHS is in the order of 7% per year; this will be achieved by managers.

In this (brave new) world, 'downsizing' the workforce sanitizes compulsory redundancy. Linguistic exclusion, that is, an inability to speak in management jargon, limits communication with those in charge of the budget. The promise of this kind of managerialism is not only that it is a good in itself but that it delivers; wherever it is, it not only brings its language and its meetings but also improvement. The assessment of managerialism's achievements is made more difficult by the flexibility of the language itself. We may have a bad case of the emperor's new clothes but if the vocabulary of evaluation is also 'hollow', this may be hard to establish.

Certainly the style of management preferred by the SHSA had something in common with that outlined by Clarke et al. (1994). The documents of the SHSA suggested that managers, rather than clinicians, knew what was good for patients.

The Chief Executive of the SHSA (SHSA 1991b: 5) said, 'We start with the patient'. His 'personal view' emphasized his personal contact with the patients in the hospital; he knew their cases, something that might normally be confined to the individual and his/her clinical team. Amongst the strategies of the SHSA was the wish to introduce a 'fair and effective complaints procedure' for patients, and parts of the labour force of the Special Hospitals were contracted out. In a bid to improve management efficacy, 'systems' were to be introduced 'to control and develop resources, including hospital sites and buildings, personnel and finance' (SHSA 1991a: 13).

The then Chief Executive described the challenge for the SHSA as 'Changing the Spots: Tackling the Culture' (Kaye and Franey 1998: 51). The new management, which had been introduced well before this study was undertaken, was explicitly charged with bringing about cultural change. It was widely thought that this would be opposed by those already working in the Special Hospitals (Bynoe 1992), so, although cultural change was demanded, it was less clear whether it had happened or would happen, or what it really constituted.

This study in Smithtown was conducted at a key political moment in the hospital's history, and culture was a key word for the hospital at that time. There was a need both to see beyond visible formal activities and publicly voiced opinion, and to understand social relations as they were embodied in the daily life of an institution committed to long-term care. Part of the remit was to look at power between and within social groups. Given the concerns about stagnation and resistance to change in the work force, this was also a focus for the fieldwork; this was new research terrain.

So, the empirical study of Smithtown wards allows for a wider discussion of concepts of culture than was evident in early psychiatric ethnography, but it starts from and relies upon daily life. The strategy of the SHSA (1991a, b) identified a problem of culture and the need for cultural change. The issue of culture, raised so clearly in management rhetoric, perhaps paradoxically, placed it in the real world. The concept of culture was not sterile; it had political weight and had become an idea embedded in people's lives.

Culture is of course a key anthropological concept, an abstraction which shapes inquiry and the production of accounts of social phenomena within the external world. This study is located in an institution where at first glance, psychological rather than social constructs like culture appear to dominate. The institution is both in and separate from a society where personal and media discourse is badly infected by the virus of 'psychologizing'. All of this makes it possible to explore these different ideas and to examine which, if any, are useful.

Part 2

Methods and their meaning

Part 2

Methods and their
meaning

Chapter 3

What we actually did and why

This part of the book describes what techniques of inquiry we used to document daily life in Smithtown. It is the part that many readers skip, though a few will dwell. In this case it sticks to essentials. Without a section on method, it would be hard to know if our reporting was in any sense fair. In many write-ups of research, the readership is familiar with how research in their field is usually done and how it is judged. This may be less true here.

So, with that last point in mind, the first issue discussed is the way in which doing a certain style of research, in this case social anthropology, was understood in an institution, a psychiatric hospital, that thought about research in a very different way. The second issue is to describe in simple terms how the research team went about gathering information and sorting it out. Some of the 'nuts and bolts' detail is put in Appendix A at the back of the book. The third issue is to discuss the status and identity of the research team. Thinking reflexively, not just about what is out there to be investigated but also about how you can make a difference to what is happening in front of you, as well as how you respond to doing this kind of research, is a particular anthropological contribution to understanding. Common sense suggests that doing research in a High Secure Hospital is not for everyone. Curiosity alone might lead someone to ask about the team who actually did it. Anthropological reflexive thinking and understanding has a counterpart in psychiatric practice and this comparison, undertaken here, adds another layer to a discussion of cultural knowledge and practice. The lenses of social anthropology and psychiatry, how they look at the world and people in it, are distinctive. But this part of the book demonstrates that what they highlight can be only subtly different. This is a way of framing what comes after, the meat of the book, which is how people lived and worked in part of this particular High Secure Hospital.

Are social anthropology and psychiatry old bedfellows?

The short answer is yes, but they are uncomfortable bedfellows. The relationship between anthropology and psychiatry is old but continues to preoccupy contemporary writers. The dimensions of this relationship have changed over time but there is a focus, as before, on the problem of categories (e.g. Barratt 1988a, b; Carstairs and Kapur 1976; Kleinman 1977, 1980, 1987; Littlewood 1990, 1991; Marsella and White 1982; Yap 1965). Psychiatrists take people's distress and experiences and sort them into illness categories, in a way that is designed to be useful to the people concerned, the patients, but which also allows psychiatrists to be clear with each other. This 'medical model' is much the same as is found in other areas of medical practice (Bartlett 2010).

In Britain, there has been an important debate between British psychiatrists and medical anthropologists (Krause 1989; Littlewood and Lipsedge 1985, 1988) because it has been thought that mental health services have been at best insensitive to and at worst discriminatory towards certain Black and Minority Ethnic Groups. Anthropological critiques of categorization of illness behaviour have been very challenging to psychiatry and have probably helped change mental health services. Psychiatrists have been compelled, within an increasingly multicultural society, to engage with issues of disadvantage and discrimination (Lewis et al. 1990; McKenzie and Crowcroft 1996; Minnis et al. 2001; Singh 1997) and to an extent be anthropologically informed about the cultural values of their patients, not just their psychiatric symptoms. Cultural competence, an ability to work knowledgeably and sensitively with patients from a range of cultural backgrounds (and a range of equality issues), is now a routine requirement of clinicians working in mental health services. Such competence makes it less likely that cultural differences are seen as evidence of mental disorder. For mental health practitioners within custodial settings, an additional dimension is a grasp of an individual's previous experience of state systems of authority (Kapoor et al. 2013).

Psychiatry and social anthropology also fell out about styles of inquiry, i.e. how they found things out. In the field of what was called transcultural psychiatry, psychiatrists looked at how psychiatric illnesses appeared in different parts of the world and specifically, whether they were as common and whether they looked the same. The conflict centred on the status of epidemiological and anthropological insights (Bartlett 2002; Kleinman 1987; Leff 1988; Sartorius et al. 1986). There are important and obvious differences that are worth outlining, crudely, as this became an issue in the research at Smithtown.

Social anthropology is concerned with the social world and cultural understandings. Psychiatry is concerned with the individual's mental processes, in so far as they deviate from the normal. To produce their own, distinct bodies of knowledge, they generate material in different ways. Anthropology builds on existing ideas and has aims of inquiry which alter in the light of data gathered. This is circular hypothesis testing involving both refinement of inquiry in the field and rereading of written research data in the light of conceptual advance. The knowledge base is asserted to have high validity being based on indigenous societal modes of thinking and being. The linear hypothesis testing of much psychiatric research, based on pre-existing psychiatric categories, leaves little room for the unexpected in research. Data is often subject to statistical analysis. Social anthropology is best at producing in-depth small-scale studies, psychiatry best at large-scale studies, where whatever the validity of the instruments used, they are reliable. Psychiatry likes to be scientific, by which it means numerically based, and social anthropology likes to be learned.

Both are concerned with disciplinary boundaries and the status of their knowledge but for different reasons. Social anthropology continues to reel from the assaults of the post-modernists who dismantled its claims to be able to describe social phenomena objectively. Psychiatry worries about the scepticism of medical and scientific colleagues, to whom it is neither medical nor scientific.

These ideas, and assertions, should not just be taken at face value. They will be tested out in the pages that follow.

What might it mean to 'do' anthropology in a High Secure Hospital?

The High Secure Hospitals were the cornerstone and are an important element of the forensic mental health system; as such, they are responsive to and participate in the implementation of social policy and criminal law on the dangerously mad. Many of their decisions are guided by the principles of mental health law. It is easy to see from this that they, and their staff and patients, are involved in and sometimes buffeted by competing ideas on how the hospitals should work and what they actually are.

Anthropology enters this world like an agnostic; the belief systems enshrined in psychiatric textbooks and practice, the assumptions of the legal system and practical issues of social policy are subjected to the anthropological gaze. In marked contrast to these three perspectives, psychiatry, law and social policy, anthropology observes, understands and assesses this world, and the people in it, without *having to* make decisions for, or about, the people concerned. In this, the anthropologist as individual may be separate from the anthropologist as professional researcher. The primary object of anthropology must be to identify and describe the 'insider' view as illuminated by consideration of a suitable combination of beliefs, behaviour and institutions. Anthropology as consultancy, or as explicit contribution to policy formation does exist but individual responsibility and power are not of the same order as in medicine, law and social work. Good (2006: 91–113) notes the 'disdain' (p. 95) with which academic anthropologists viewed practical overseas development work. Put at its most basic, psychiatry and the law decide where anthropology informs. This fundamental difference affects interdisciplinary work and understanding in a High Secure Hospital setting.

There is an expression in forensic psychiatry of writing 'past the court';[1] this means that in writing psychiatric reports for court it is

---

[1] Forensic psychiatrists assess and treat individuals with a coincidence of offending behaviour and mental health problems. In this capacity they are frequently required both to produce written reports and give oral evidence to courts in the course of criminal proceedings.

useful to bear in mind that the report will inform the clinical approach to the person concerned. It needs to read in a way the court understands and speak to its medico-legal agenda but also be helpful to future clinicians. This project was similar. The empirical basis of this book is a piece of anthropological research but the point of it is also to speak to policy and practice in forensic mental health. Publication means it is likely to be read by those working within different traditions. This book and the research data in it could be judged by standards intrinsic to those disciplines rather than to anthropology (see Good 2008: 91–113). Equally, it seems a long way away from the theoretical preoccupations of many contemporary anthropologists, so it might get a rather cool reception from them too. In an ideal world it might go beyond academic pretensions of whatever kind and be accessible and useful to those living and working in forensic mental health settings. Though this is something of a tall order, it is true that interdisciplinary work, where anthropology reaches out, often into health arenas, can be seen as inherently useful (Unnithan-Kumar 2006: 129–48), even as it loosens its original moorings in 'deep' ethnography (Gooberman-Hill 2006: 117–28).

What were we trying to find out?

The point of the research was to document daily life at the level of three wards in the hospital. Our intention was that the description and analysis would do justice to the experience of people who lived and worked there. That meant primarily observing and, to some extent, participating in networks of social interaction as well as observing how decisions were made. This would form the basis of an analysis of the social functioning of those units of the hospital. This seemed the best approach, as it was a sensitive time in the hospital's history. Social anthropology, precisely because it is agnostic, lends itself to a non-judgemental approach.

More specifically, the aims (see Appendix A for full list) included a question about possible resistance to change in the staff group. More generally, the intention was to find out about currencies of power. This meant considering what evidence was available on how power was manifest informally and formally on the wards, by looking at the particular sets of social interaction between members of staff, between patients and between staff and patients to see who controlled and who decided what. These aspects of the study are reported in the following sections of the book.

Getting into the hospital

Researchers cannot just walk into hospitals and begin doing research. The process of getting permission is, nowadays, fairly standard. This was less true at the time of the research. The Smithtown process was very lengthy and, with the benefit of what I now know, unusually complex and political. The advantages of the way we were approaching the study was explained in the following way.

Why anthropology would be useful

The research proposal argued that in the light of recent criticism of the Special Hospitals and the absence of detailed knowledge about the daily life of patients in such settings, there would be an advantage to the unit concerned if it commissioned independent research in this area. The proposal acknowledged the external hostility to Smithtown and the tone of much published information on High Secure Hospitals. It pointed out the methodological advantages both in the duration and the open-endedness of participant observation. First, it was assumed that there would be a level of suspicion and distrust from both staff and patients, both of whom were to be clearly designated subjects of the study. Daily contact with researchers and the slow process of getting to know them would be vital to eliciting valid material from ward staff and patients. There would be little in the way of presumptive questioning early in the project.

This was contrasted with the limitations of the artificial methods of cold questionnaires and structured interviewing which we thought would generate information biased severely in the direction of what staff and patients thought the research team should hear. The research team would be hampered unless there was observational material with which to assess the quality of informants.

The status of anthropological research

It appeared that no qualitative project had previously been passed by the Smithtown Research Committee. Scepticism was evident about the lack of a 'scientific' basis for the research but an external review was favourable.

Consultations were then necessary with representatives of all the unions, professional representatives for all the clinical disciplines and negotiations at ground level with patients and staff from the wards that were to be the focus of the study. The advice we received was that the study could be stopped at any stage if there was opposition from any group. It was thought by senior figures in the hospital hierarchy that opposition was likely to come from the POA, which represented most of the nursing staff.

Issues that were raised in the course of these negotiations, and who raised them, provide insights into the way Smithtown worked and how power was manifest in the hospital hierarchy. This is an interesting counterpoint to what happens at ward level.

Further consultation involved the then management body for the hospital itself, which also raised questions about research method. Ethical approval was received from the hospital Ethics Committee, as was normal at that time. The Hospital Management Team allowed us to proceed. The Chair of the POA and the Secretary of the Royal College of Nursing (RCN) were thought to be 'quite favourable' to the project. The politics of the institution were clearer. Senior managers recalled that a different attempt to get to grips with life inside the institution had foundered and hoped this one would succeed.

Meanwhile, more thought went into the detail of the project and its theoretical context. Revisions were made to the protocol which did not change its broad intention but flagged up issues inevitably present within Special Hospital life, e.g. understandings of violence and the construction of dangerousness, as well as internal discussion of the Special Hospitals' public profile. As a matter of courtesy, this was forwarded to Smithtown to keep them abreast of the project's development. Those initially in receipt of it agreed with our view that the alterations represented a refinement of the proposal and went on to express confidence in the researchers and the approach we were taking. Additional comments included the view that 'Smithtown is a complex institution with an important public purpose and the operation of its functions can only be understood not only by virtue of its internal culture but also as part of the wider community to which it belongs.'

The next meeting was with the Hospital Management Team. We were told the project was viewed with suspicion; this derived in part from its association with the higher tiers of management. Individual researchers might, they surmised, be 'management spies' in the minds of other staff. Paradoxical strategies were discussed, including attaching researchers to what were termed 'resistant' nurses. The best way in, we were informed, was to build on what was a key aspect of the staff identity, pride in the hospital. It was suggested that at some time, if not now, the largest of the nurses' unions had the power of veto over management decisions.

However, despite encouragement, the revised proposal had hit a serious problem. Perhaps, despite what we had thought was a clear statement of the intended method and its intrinsic open-ended quality, this had not been understood. There is a clear commitment in anthropological method to analyse and refine data, including unexpected data, as it arises within a piece of work. The level of opposition to the revised proposal was such that the only sensible thing to do was to work from the originally approved proposal. The risk in doing anything else was to have to start all over again.

Whatever people's genuine understanding of the project's aims, it remains my view that the project had hit a degree of institutional opposition disguised by procedure. One explanation was that within the higher echelons of Smithtown there were long-standing members of staff who did not share the Hospital Management Team's enthusiasm.

Coincidental attendance by me at a meeting of the Medical Advisory Committee (in connection with a less contentious project) indicated in contrast how quickly less controversial projects could be approved.

Two intriguing juxtapositions to the journey of this project are the place of ethnography in other tightly controlled environments where the ethnographer has been seen as a risk (see Galanek 2013) and the fact that documentary film makers have been allowed essentially free access to film, as well as independent editorial control over their material, in HMP/YOI Holloway, HMP Wormwood Scrubs and HMP Strangeways in the last few years.

Talking to a ward

The single most important task at this point was to gain access to a ward. Although one had been identified, acceptance was not a foregone conclusion. An information sheet was prepared and approved. Its purpose was to outline the project and its likely impact on the ward, and to discuss the ethical issues of participation and anonymity to staff and patients. I was told that if this ward did not accept me, then nowhere in Smithtown would do so. The meeting with staff on the ward was revealing in that it suggested what I came later to see as true, that the staff of the ward are nurses. At this meeting no other disciplines were represented, e.g. social work, psychology. The consultant was present but acceptance hinged on the nursing staff. The issues discussed were much more practical at this point in the negotiations.

The concern was for my safety. It was agreed that I could have access to informal and formal ward settings and that it would be possible to be present during all three shifts, i.e. to obtain data over a twenty-four-hour timeframe. However, I was told to get the project running during the day and then approach the night staff, who were culturally distinct. Lastly, I should have keys. Otherwise, I would have to have an escort every time I came and went from the ward. Interpretation of these instructions became clearer as the project progressed.

One month later, I attended the patients' meeting on the ward. Staff, once again exclusively nurses, attended. The project took up most of the meeting. No one had indicated that patients as well as staff could block the project, so the 'sales pitch' took this into account. It also stressed the fact that I was not a member of the hospital staff, medical or otherwise, and that the project had an unusual degree of independence. Patients' concerns at this juncture were different but revealing. What was anthropology? one man inquired. Would I be asking awkward questions? Another quizzed me as to what sort of doctor I was, and smiled wryly at the news that I was a psychiatrist. Would the research lead to changes? What would I do if the Hospital Management Team objected to what I wrote? I understood later that this meeting had attracted a large number of the patients on the ward and some from adjacent wards as well. There was a question about whether the project would cover the whole twenty-four-hour period. There was a supportive remark from the staff to the effect that they were 'in' the project too.

Not quite there yet

Soon after this, and for unrelated reasons, the POA met with the Hospital Management Team. The senior staff had done some initial talking to the Chair of the POA. The comments gave clues to the state of affairs in the institution. It seemed that, from the point of view of the union, a project focused, at least in part, on the work of the nurses might to them appear advantageous. They might want to use it politically. But there was also evidence of the kind of distrust that had characterized the POA's response to the Committee of Inquiry into Complaints about Ashworth Hospital (Department of Health 1992). We were told that staff would feel spied on, and material would be taken out of context. Also, the project would take up staff time because the other researchers and I would need to be tied to staff. The alternative, which was presented as equally alarming, was that we would simply be wandering around. Luckily it was possible to say that liaison at ward level had been fruitful and that there was a ward ready to host the project.

At that point it was no longer a question of whether the project should happen but how. Representation from the ward was helpful. Training to safeguard the researchers in a secure hospital setting was offered. Safety was a nursing issue.

The last Committee before starting was the first where the POA had joined the other unions in discussion with management. The symbolism of this should not be underestimated; it meant that instead of being 'the union', it was in fact 'a union'. Perhaps this accounted for the relative lack of questioning about the project. At the end of the meeting it was possible to state a meaningful start date.

The final project was hosted on three wards. Access to the second and third wards was uneventful by comparison. Ward-level explanations were undertaken for both staff and patients. Staff wondered what we would do if we knew of possible acts of violence or self-harm. A staff worry was whether the study would be the 'truth'. Patients commented on the possibility that everyone would be on their best behaviour but welcomed the way the study would look at round-the-clock ward life.

It seemed to the researchers from the way the project was introduced to staff and patients, that neither the second or third ward would have a power of veto about the project. The contrast with the first ward was striking.

Reflections on the access story

The access story is important both because it illustrated the 'Realpolitik' of Smithtown and because it underlined the tensions of interdisciplinary work.

Although painfully slow, the access negotiations gave invaluable information on the relationship of management, unions and the wards. In the process, the status of anthropology was called into question by both Smithtown and on one occasion by the funders' body.[2] Both displayed not outright rejection but ambivalence. In both cases a lack of knowledge of anthropology played some part. As a medically qualified person doing anthropology, I was the embodiment, on the one hand, of the possibility of interdisciplinary work, and on the other hand, of this ambivalence. It seemed to me, in this process, that for Smithtown, and perhaps for the Wellcome Trust, that I was the acceptable face of anthropology because I was a doctor.

How did we go about getting information?

Study design and implementation

Three researchers spent time on three wards, one ward each. In total we spent twenty months collecting information through participating in what happened, observing life as it unfolded and talking to staff and patients (either chatting informally or checking and expanding systematically on ideas that were emerging). We did not visit the wards every day. This was in keeping with the behaviour of staff but at odds with the life of patients who had no choice but to be there. We would go for the duration of a nursing shift, in total covering 214 shifts including some

---

[2] Even in higher education, anthropology may not be fully recognized. Shore and Wright (2000: 76) mention the QAA review of university activity, which refused to acknowledge anthropology as a separate discipline and put it in sociology.

weekends and night shifts. Most things happened during the day, so relatively little time was spent on the night shift: all patients were locked in from 9 p.m. until 7 a.m.

All three of us, two women and a man, took notes as we went along and then transcribed them. We approached the day-to-day conduct of research in the same way and met regularly to review practicalities, discuss ideas and for mutual support in an unusual and potentially testing research setting.

We spent most of our time in the hospital on our allocated wards. The three wards were Toulouse, a men's ward where I was based, Lille, a women's ward where the other female researcher was based, and Paris, a men's ward where the male researcher was based. Toulouse and Lille were in the older parts of the hospital site and Paris was in a new part.

Senior staff at Smithtown had firmly suggested that the original title of the study, 'An Anthropological Study of Smithtown Special Hospital', was grandiose beyond belief. Different parts of the hospital were said to have their own character. Choosing three wards gave us the opportunity to compare and contrast two male wards, whose institutionally determined functions were distinct, as well as to compare and contrast male and female wards. There are probably no wards which are representative of Smithtown but the concept of 'a ward' is an interesting one, dating from Florence Nightingale and Scutari, and the project allowed us to think about what wards meant in Smithtown.

A few words on the theory of research

The mechanics of research

It is a truism of qualitative research that data collection, recording and analysis and writing are integrated activities.[3] But some points are more pertinent to the earlier 'conduct of fieldwork' phase of a project

---

[3] This subsection may appear redundant to those who believe Shweder (1997: 153), who says, 'In anthropology . . . most PhD training programs are big on long term ethnographic fieldwork but do not require courses in methodology at all . . . They think that if you are really serious and want to get to know a place well, the most important thing to do is to muck around a lot, somewhat like a good journalist and follow your nose. This is participant observation.'

and some to the later 'post fieldwork' stage. This is about that earlier phase. The approach to data collection and analysis throughout the project was informed by ideas put forward by Glaser and Strauss in a number of publications on grounded theory. Grounded theory 'is a detailed grounding by systematically' and intensively 'analysing data, often sentence by sentence, or phrase by phrase of the field note, interview, or other document: by "constant comparison", data are extensively collected and coded . . . thus producing a well constructed theory' (Strauss 1987: 22). The appeal of the approach is its iterative nature and that the process of data analysis in qualitative investigation is more systematic. It does not solve the problem identified by Miles and Huberman (1984: 16), that 'we have few agreed on canons for qualitative data analysis, in the sense of shared ground rules for drawing conclusions and verifying their sturdiness'.

The use of grounded theory does not, and perhaps cannot, guarantee transparency. But it does give the researcher some rules of conduct, albeit without the guarantee that they will adhere to them. This begins to address the problematic issue of what they term 'speculative' theory with little obvious relation to data.

It is reassuring to the novice ethnographer that Hammersley and Atkinson (1995) acknowledge the ideal world status of grounded theory in relation to the reality of ethnographic inquiry. The regular and orderly processes of data collection, review, memo writing, sampling and coding are hard to sustain in practice. They also point out that grounded theory was driven by a desire to produce theory but the skills are transferable to descriptive accounts of which this study is one. Strauss (1987) suggests the techniques are atheoretical but the relationship to naturalism is complex. Naturalism, were it possible, would seem the most sensible approach to the study of such a closed and secret place as Smithtown.

This project was naturalistic in that the fieldwork allowed for the unfolding of events over protracted periods of months, fifteen months in total. But it adopted a more proactive approach to certain topics through interviewing and was systematic in the way it gained access to individuals whose voices might have been drowned out in the noise of ward life.

Hammersley and Atkinson (1995: 12) suggest that the critique of Kuhn is fatally undermining of naturalism.[4] This critique suggests, in their words, that 'all knowledge of the world is mediated by paradigmatic presupposition'. Naturalism collapses as soon as a question is asked. To do so is to alter how things really are and to bring in an observer effect in at least two ways. First, questions are likely to be influenced by the observer's immediate experience but also by ideas (background reading, political perspective, personal issues) present in the observer when they entered the field. In order to take this point seriously, considerable attention is devoted to reflexivity in a later section. Second, questions require answers, so field data loses the quality of spontaneity essential to the naturalistic ideal. This is to suggest that the naturalist ideal could never be achieved. Certainly in this purist sense it seemed an inappropriate ideal in Smithtown; uncertainties require clarification, and refutation of early, perhaps misleading, ideas must be a possibility in the implementation of method.

So, the final position taken in this project is of a broadly naturalistic approach, tempered by systematic inquiry and underpinned by a reflexive attitude.

Practical issues: time and place

The focus of participant observation, on each ward, was to document daily life, examining a range of planned and unplanned activities and the social interaction that constituted and accompanied them. Attention was paid to the use of space, and events were recorded in relation to the layout of each ward and to mealtimes, in more detail.[5]

Researchers noted the regular and irregular activities undertaken by the staff and patients, and followed the unfolding both of ward events and hospital-wide events through the recording of spontaneous conversation. Because of the focus on informal and formal systems of power

---

[4] They also believe that this undermines positivism, but this never constituted the philosophical underpinning of this project.

[5] Maps of the ward were constructed by all three researchers, but for reasons of confidentiality these cannot be reproduced.

in the study (see aims), particular attention was paid to the content of different social interactions, i.e. staff: staff, staff: patient and patient: patient. These were clearly differentiated in what we wrote in the field notes.

Different parts of the wards were the scenes of different activities. This was not immediately obvious to us but wards are just another place where people live and work. So what might at first have seemed an undifferentiated space was subdivided and characterized by activity as we understood it better. In a recent visit to a similar institution in Scotland, I was struck by not understanding the layout or who people were as I entered a ward. This was a brief return to the state of not knowing that we experienced at the start of our data collection. We recorded social interactions systematically and noted what happened where. Key areas were nursing offices, the nurses' mess, day areas and rooms used for formal meetings, e.g. ward rounds, case conferences (both characterized by relatively in-depth clinical discussion of individual patients) and community meetings. Relatively less time was spent in areas considered to be private by researchers and potentially unsafe and private by staff, i.e. bedrooms, dormitories and washrooms. Aspects of the built environment and other elements of the material world were also documented. Gradually, it appeared that particular spaces were associated with the different social groups, and care was taken to include adequate information on whether staff or patients or both groups occupied spaces and what rules determined occupancy.

The relative neutrality of researcher identity (discussed in full later) and the mobility of staff and patients within the ward environment made this easier than for other researchers. Some ethnographers in secure settings have been more restricted. Davidson's (1974) work on San Quentin is almost exclusively concerned with prisoners, partly due to the mechanisms of control and segregation in the US prison system. Also in the US, Schmid and Jones (1993) reported on fieldwork in a maximum secure prison where Jones' real identity provided limited access to staff arenas. Cardoza-Freeman (1984), reporting on language in prisons, was reliant on key informants; her focus may have resulted from access difficulties as a woman in a US male prison.

The researchers visited other parts of Smithtown systematically but relatively infrequently. Areas covered included work areas (e.g. print shop, carpentry area, bricklayers' yards and sewing room), social activities which happened in the Central Hall, the canteen, the Chapel, the education centre, the sports ground, the area of Smithtown designated for Control and Restraint courses, the Staff Club and the medical centre.

The technique of participant observation can seem easy to grasp, until you actually do it. At that point, its nature seems more fluid and exactly what it is has been debated (Agar 1980; Ellen 1984; Hammersley and Atkinson 1995). Certainly the balance between participating and observing can vary. The researchers actively participated in specific activities, e.g. sitting watching television, having meals with staff, clearing up after patient meals, playing snooker. Equally, there were other activities in which researchers participated passively, i.e. they had opted to be there specifically but took no active part in the usual activity, e.g. ward rounds, handovers, workshop tasks. Finally, there was simply being part of events as they unfolded. Observation formed an integral part of being there but necessarily varied with the degree of interaction. This itself could vary between episodes of the same activity and according to the nature of the activity.

Observation could feel covert, despite the intentions of the project being openly aired and discussed. This stemmed from an inability in practice to explain, in detail, to everyone encountered, e.g. on the sports field, what we were doing. This is recognized as a long-standing ethical dilemma in anthropology and one on which there is little agreement. Our intention was to inform individuals encountered as clearly as possible without thoroughly distorting the field with intrusive and potentially unnecessary explanation. In practice, we answered all questions throughout the project and often gave more information than had been required of us by the Smithtown ethics committee. Nonetheless, some people we encountered would not have known who we were or even crudely what we were doing. This approach is within the norms of social research where, as in our project 'even when operating in an overt manner, ethnographers rarely tell *all* the people they are studying *everything* about the research' (Hammersley and Atkinson 1995: 265).

As the fieldwork progressed, all three researchers felt increasingly bored. As Hammersley and Atkinson (1995: 116) point out, this may represent a significant degree of data saturation. The less appealing interpretation was that the researchers were lazy and not thinking enough about the work. As boredom was a regular complaint from both staff and patients, it must at least have represented some empathy with their situation. As it was rather different from our state of mind at the start, it is more likely that we were increasingly re-experiencing what we had already witnessed.

Practical issues: persons

Although all three researchers were obviously strangers to their wards, our remit, as indicated earlier, was to blend in as much as possible. If not, I had been warned, the project would be halted by the hospital authorities. The consequence of this was, at first, to enhance the naturalistic style of the project; it seemed unwise to ask too many questions. The project could not have happened in another village, another hospital, another town. It only had permission to take place in Smithtown.

Not asking questions ensured that people told us what they wanted us to hear. Also, certain people wanted to tell us much more than others and would talk individually for long periods of time. It was hard initially to check out the origins of individuals' verbosity or reticence. It transpired later that the reasons were rich and varied. Our key informants no doubt had their own reasons for talking. Whatever these reasons were, they were very helpful and told us much that was valuable about themselves and their lives in Smithtown. But they said little about other people. This is a valuable insight into the way Smithtown worked. The dilemma was that if the project relied on willing talkers, although this was naturalistic, it effectively excluded the views of the relatively quiet and self-effacing. This was important to clarify given that the project was concerned with the nature of power and relationships.

All three researchers had unprecedented freedom in this unique setting but without behaving very strangely there were places we could not go. No doubt the Staff Club would have been revealing but becoming a regular there was unrealistic for any of the researchers. Similarly, information from patients was unavailable because it was what was discussed in private places or just out of earshot. This made us sometimes reliant on reported, rather than witnessed, information.

Practical issues: adding focus and detail

To add detail to what was emerging as an appropriate focus of the study and to increase the likelihood of hearing from as many potential informants as possible, longer interviews were conducted with both staff and patients. But, for both staff and patients perhaps rendered silent in the ward, it was an opportunity for them to describe their experiences in a way that did not invite public comment, not that privacy guarantees honesty.

Forty-five members of staff (a mixture of nursing staff, doctors and other clinicians) and forty-four male patients agreed to discuss the various topics. No member of staff refused to be interviewed. It is reassuring that on both Toulouse and Paris a few men refused, eight in total. Reasons included concern that the project would not change anything and a view that not talking represented an area of autonomy they valued. Reasons were not always forthcoming but in some cases came from men who had previously avoided contact with researchers. Informants could and did talk for as long as they wanted. A conversational style was possible because the informants were very well known to the researcher, and the schedule allowed topics to be addressed in different orders. Most interviews took place on the ward; they were not overheard, and offered people an escape from overcrowded ward life and more privacy.

Participation should not be read as unbridled enthusiasm for the project. It can be seen as a consequence of months of participant observation and relationships on the ward. The researchers did feel that one or two staff interviews were almost useless as a guide to what interviewees really felt. The opinions uttered were at odds with other information about how people were perceived or so guarded as to be self-evidently limited. Equally, previously reticent members of staff took advantage of the relative privacy of the interview space to speak their minds, and at times to bare their souls. The emotional pitch of the staff interviews was unexpected. It indicated that we had tapped into issues which were inherently important. Researchers often felt privileged being told information by patients.

Hammersley and Atkinson (1995: 131) note the advantages of combining participant observation with more systematic interviewing in this way. Schmid and Jones (1993) contemporaneously adopted the same strategy in a maximum secure prison. This combination of techniques is a triangulation of data sources. Interviews can lack spontaneity and fail to match the informant's world view (concepts, language, format) but they add detail and allow for the eliciting of specific information otherwise hard to obtain.

Interviews were based on topics that had come up in the field notes and were informed by overall aims. The main topics covered were individuals' personal experience of life or work in Smithtown, their relationships with members of other social groups, their understanding of change in Smithtown and their views on the progress either of themselves or the patient group through Smithtown. We also asked a question about the impact of the researcher on the life of the ward.

Practical issues: writing things down

We wrote field notes as soon as was practicable without being rude. The idea was that they should be as contemporaneous as possible. In a mental hospital setting, taking notes is not a neutral activity; it has specific connotations. Notes are written both in the presence of the patient, characteristically by doctors, and in the absence of patients, characteristically by nurses. The content of the notes is personal. Often what is recorded is negative, sometimes banal and seldom shared with the person concerned.[6] For patients to take notes is rare; in Smithtown (and in my experience elsewhere) it was viewed as opposition to the staff. Rosenhan (1973) reports that writing notes was seen as pathological in psychiatric patients.

The levels of interaction, opportunity and the sensitivity of the material all affected researchers' note taking. Note taking in the course of

---

[6] Access to notes by patients has undergone legislative change in recent years. The current process involves a request to the hospital administrators and the agreement of the senior doctor. In certain circumstances agreement can be withheld e.g. third party risk.

chatting to staff and patients was usually not possible, the exception being where they had agreed to discuss specific topics. Ward rounds, where other notes were written and the researcher was a silent presence, also allowed for exactly contemporaneous notes. In practice, mealtimes and the lavatory offered good opportunities for writing. We dictated our handwritten notes partly to encode the identities of all staff and patients, to protect all informants. Dictation also offered a valuable opportunity for reflection. Analytic notes and memos were dictated at the same time. The three of us met regularly to discuss the practicalities of fieldwork, to ensure sampling was adequate and to discuss emerging analytic issues and how to code notes in order to make more sense of them. Many researchers record conversations and interviews on tape and nowadays digitally. This would have been at odds with the informality we achieved in the fieldwork and also was not permitted in this setting. Where we could, we recorded verbatim accounts.

What issues emerge in sorting out the information?

Data processing: coding, concepts, computers and memos

As the field notes were transcribed, we talked about what they might mean. There was a lot of data and the initial plan was to chunk it, technically, to allocate descriptive codes in an effort to get an overview of the material. Similarly, at the end of fieldwork the entire database, i.e. all field notes and interviews, was read twice through, with analytic notes and revisions to preliminary codes being made contemporaneously. The purpose of this was to see what ideas came out of the data. More detailed analysis was done by hand and checked by frequent returns to the raw text. This resulted in analytic ideas cutting across basic descriptive codes and there was significant recoding. Throughout this process of analysis, analytic memos were written, which proved a valuable source of ideas. Analytic concepts were both observer identified, as, for instance, in the overarching idea of institutional change, and indigenous, as in the extensive Smithtown lexicon. Going back to the raw material is crucial and this was done in order to compare and contrast material particularly between researchers, to note negative case material and where there was an absence of information.

Writing matters: problems of ethnographic authority

The interdisciplinary concerns voiced at the start of this section come into play when thinking about how the project has been written up. Doing anthropology was just that. Sitting in an office writing brought into focus not just post-fieldwork anxieties but also two additional issues: first, what has been called the crisis of representation in anthropology, and second, the specifics of audience for this piece of work. What had become apparent was that in the process of writing about what we had found out—the culture of the field—it was just as necessary to think about the culture or cultures in which the whole project sat.

Writing anthropology

Early social anthropologists were curious, lived abroad, thought seriously about what they had seen and experienced and, perhaps in line with the colonial perspective of the day, wrote with considerable certainty about their discoveries. These early assertions of authority were blown away in the wind of methodological doubt. The position of the 'objective' and 'scientific' anthropologist became increasingly untenable. This 'crisis of representation' (Marcus and Fischer 1986: 8) has generated a large amount of literature in its own right. More attention has been devoted to writing and the finished products of anthropological fieldwork than to the philosophy and technicalities of inquiry. Although it is unfair to characterize a whole discipline, it is arguable that having acknowledged the limitations of the art, not a lot has changed.

Anthropologists are still happy to write books about, sit on committees about, advise the United Nations about and talk about other cultures. The 'other' may have blurred at the edges, become shadowy, indistinct, at times a mere figment of the anthropological imagination but as such it is still there. It is possible to suggest that whatever the change in theoretical outlook, little may have happened in practice.

Even where the anthropologist is at home, s\he continues to create another culture, most commonly on paper, not always an indigenous medium. How this is done and what weight it carries is interesting. Whatever the methodological qualifiers put in to avoid criticism by fellow professionals, cultures are harvested after time is spent in the field.

The social identity of the anthropologist and the site of anthropology

The 'crisis of representation' literature has several discernible strands. They explain why it is rare for social anthropology to stray into areas of medical dominance.

Key to these strands is an anxiety on the part of a Western academic discipline about its capacity to represent the 'other', where the other is believed to be significantly different from the Western academic (Said 1989). Geertz (1983: 56) asked, 'how is anthropological knowledge of the way natives think, feel and perceive possible?' The responses to this question have over the subsequent nineteen years become more convoluted. Although Geertz (1983: 57) himself appears to believe, like the founding fathers of anthropology, that 'you don't have to be one to know one', not everyone has agreed with him.

Early feminist critique (Ardener 1975: 19–27) had already noted the difficulty for male anthropologists of accessing the woman's perspective in certain societies. This marked the beginning of a sophisticated debate about woman ethnographers and their capacity to document women's lives and also men's lives, and concerns about the dominant concepts used to articulate gender distinctions (MacCormack and Strathern 1980; Moore 1988: 4–11; Rosaldo and Lamphere 1974; Strathern 1981). Alongside was a concern about the separate and overlapping issue of ethnocentricity. A Western discipline in a post-colonial age still purported to describe non-Western cultures. It also forgot that not all anthropologists were white and not all came from Western Europe, and that much that was written about anthropological concerns came from those they disregarded, the non-anthropologists, who simply knew the history of their non-Western society well (Moore 1996a). Appadurai (1992: 34–47) comments that Western thought has three approaches to the other: it 'essentialize's the other, it 'exoticise's the other and it 'totalise's the other. All approaches emphasize difference; none is satisfactory. The net effect of these arguments has been a perceived need to reflect on the social identity of the anthropologist. They inform the now characteristically anthropological reflexivity,[7] where for want of a better definition, '[t]he self reflexive ethnographic approach is understood as one that questions its authenticity but does not abandon interpretation' (Josephides 1997: 17).

The language of anthropology

Another dimension to the crisis of representation is language; by this I mean both languages learnt and the specific vocabulary of anthropological expression.

Clifford's (1988: 92–113) erudite commentary on Malinowski, a founding father of anthropology, and Conrad notes the need for anthropologists to learn languages. Both Malinowski and Conrad had to, and did, move between languages, literally languages, not modes of expression. My own observation is that it is rare for anthropologists to discuss as linguists might, the possibility of linguistic incompetence. Yet it must affect the realities of fieldwork and give rise at times to fundamental misunderstanding. Equally, as Clifford more positively points out, by virtue of their polyphony and the personal and cultural references of the languages, Conrad's and Malinowski's writing took particular courses. This generated partial accounts informed by 'a consciousness deeply aware of the arbitrariness of conventions' (Clifford 1988: 96), a remark to which I relate from my own awareness of psychiatric and anthropological styles of writing.

The awareness of convention within a discipline is linked to a recognition of the possible artificiality of the subject matter of anthropology. The theoretical touchstones of anthropology, the ways in which you know what you are reading is anthropology, may limit its audience. Marcus (1998: 203) argues that in the 1990s, anthropology had to consider 'the nature of representation, description, subjectivity, objectivity, even of the notions of "society" and "culture" themselves'.

But the potential inaccessibility of anthropological topics can be defended. Strathern is reluctant to relinquish the anthropologist's traditional preference for ethnography addressing discipline-specific

---

[7] Reflexivity is explored at length in a later section.

theoretical questions. She makes no apology for being an 'academic': 'there is always a discontinuity between indigenous understandings and the analytic concepts which frame the ethnography itself' (1987: 18).

She is scathing about experimental ethnography that purports to include the authentic voice of the subject other. Implied multiple authorship, where text is talk and where such conversation is a substitute for analysis, does not impress her. Her point is that one is left guessing as to the circumstance and choice of contributors. It is uncertain who they are in their world, and why they might want to appear in another. A legitimate role of the anthropologist is to generate theory.

The construction of ethnographic authority

So, to take stock, ethnographic authority has been undermined, though not to the extent that anthropology has died out. None of the criticisms has much to say to the novice ethnographer struggling with early ideas and dubious interpretation. Becoming an author, as Geertz has noted, is not resolved by dealing with the relationship of 'observer and observed', as he continues: 'the oddity of constructing texts ostensibly scientific out of experiences broadly biographical . . . is thoroughly obscured' (1988: 10).

Hammersley (1992) offers more practical advice, which begins to address the likely views of an audience outside anthropology. There are, he suggests, three lines of argument. First, that the criteria by which ethnography should be judged are the same as for quantitative research. Second, that ethnography is a distinctive approach, and as such requires its own criteria. He suggests that this is a more heterogeneous view than it seems at first glance, including not only Clifford but also those who see qualitative work of this kind as closer to the physical sciences than is quantitative social research. Third, there are those who argue that there are no criteria by which ethnography can be sensibly assessed, as to do so would rely on a belief in a social world separable from our description of it.

My point here is more to flag up the problem of judging ethnographic work than to adopt a particular position. While the relation of the social world to phenomena in it remains, as it must, disputed, there will be no resolution of the debate. Hammersley himself proposes criteria of validity and relevance (1992: 68). In painting pictures of the social world we edit, we do not 'reproduce reality' as Google Glasses purport to do (The Economist 2013). In fact, we swop modes of representation, highlight, underline, summarize, emphasize, reduce and ignore, as well as provide a conceptual, analytic order to the totality of material. There is no doubt he is correct to say that the exact relation, of kind or of degree, to the original cannot be known. But, he would like to judge the 'adequacy' of the claims in support of the analysis. Weighting evidence will depend on its validity and its relevance. Validity itself would be based on 'plausibility and credibility', the extent to which the important arguments are evidentially solid and the 'type of claim' in relation to the evidence produced. Relevance would be based on the intrinsic importance of the work and 'contribution to the literature'.

Despite this, agreement on criteria by which to assess value seems a still distant goal. Conflicting views about the value of work will occur. The existence of criteria is no guarantee that they will be used, or if used, used scrupulously. The fact that they are not, does not, per se, invalidate the expressed opinion. The lack of explication of the process of opinion formation either in the work or in the assessment of the work does not render either automatically invalid, and agreement can be fool's gold. The reputation of academics, like that of biographers and novelists, can easily change over time.

Hammersley is reluctant to deal with writing. This is not to say that literary criticism is all. We will not all believe Goffman's (1961) rhetoric but we know who he is, and what he says. These two things may be as important as being believed. *They* are a tribute to his choice of words rather than his explication of method, because as Clifford (1986: 1–26) said, ethnography is fiction and arguably characterized by rather male rhetorical strategies of control (Moore 1994b: 124). Fiction is capable of profound reflections on the human condition. But as Clifford allows, texts of whatever kind are 'partial', that is, the reader gets the edited highlights, or lowlights, of the world of the other. It is therefore always incomplete but 'it is always writing' (1988: 26). Whether or not the writing is deemed good or bad will vary. Anthropology has no agreed criteria and, such as they are, they are changing.

Consequently, the distance and relationship to the original cultural experience may be hard for the reader to delineate. This difficulty is pronounced where little attention has been paid to spelling out the details of data collection and analysis. To the person in the other culture, the published version of their existence may be unrecognizable. It remains an open question whether or not this matters, or when.

Writing with authority about high secure hospitals

The local audience

The luxury of anthropology is that on many occasions this crisis of representation is simply an internal matter. The anthropologist has both in their style of writing, and literally, simply retreated to another country. Debates about their work will be conducted, if at all, in the rarefied atmosphere of higher education establishments, where, relatively speaking, their work is supported and their careers advanced.[8]

Writing about High Secure Hospitals in the UK contributes to an existing public debate on secure hospital provision. Anthropology can address a potentially more critical audience, outside its comfort zone, with a distinct and real capacity for 'creative' readings. Being out there and visible to professionals and to the media would seem as valuable as hiding in a redbrick or ivory tower but it could be much less enjoyable. Very few pieces of social anthropology ever do this. Two examples that spring to mind are Moore's (2013) recent contribution on Female Circumcision, and La Fontaine (1998) on satanic abuse. In both cases the material seemed so exotic that it would be hard to challenge. Given the extensive policy development and NHS vested interests in forensic mental health, the rules of engagement around this project were always going to be different.

It remains to be seen whether or not in this specific instance the distinctive ethnographic approach and the clear blue water between it and the research approaches favoured within psychiatric research institutions,

---

[8] Bell (1993: 40) makes the interesting point that in working with Aborigines, the anthropologist cannot produce one set of 'outputs' for local consumption and one set for home consumption. This parallels the situation of this fieldwork, but is rare.

of which Smithtown is one, truly matter. Randomized control trials, the gold standard of proof in much medical research, are a long way away.

Time has also passed since the basic research was undertaken. While the data sheds light on persistent issues about quality of life and ways of working in secure health settings, it may be less likely than it was at the outset to be caught up in debates about investigative techniques and their intrinsic value.

This study sat and this book sits 'between the lines'. For this reason it seems more than usually important to consider aspects of reflexivity before looking at the 'out there' findings. Reflexivity can qualify and contextualize research findings. In this study, there are particular aspects of reflexivity that demand attention. Without them it is impossible to assess the status of other findings. The following discussion of the nature and process of reflexive anthropology raises questions as to the constitution and consciousness of the inquiring self.

Chapter 4

Reflexivity: who am I to ask questions?

Reflexivity is one way in which social anthropology has made a distinctive contribution to the development of research methods. Its importance, as a technique, lies in the depth it can add to a research study. Anthropologists reflecting on their experience, as fieldworkers gathering information, can in turn create insights into the cultural norms and practices of the group being studied. In the context of Smithtown, a psychiatric hospital, it becomes interesting to compare and contrast the way in which the practitioners of psychiatry and anthropology can think about themselves. So, this part of the book both provides a context for what we found out as well as being some of what we discovered.

What is reflexivity?

> If I am not necessarily the person that others see, and if I am not necessarily the person who I *imagine* that others see, and if I am not merely the persona whom I present to others (for whatever reason), who am I, and how might I discover the answer? (Cohen 1992: 229)

Cohen is worried about the status of findings in anthropological studies. He warns us too that it is rash to assume that adequate description of others is easy, particularly if we describe them only as examples of 'kinds' of people. In so doing, he provides a justification for a serious interest in reflexive anthropology. This worry derives from scrupulousness about how 'the self' and therefore 'the other' can be identified, and to what extent categories do justice to individual variation.

Malinowski kept diaries. So, if he is any guide, anthropologists have always thought reflexively, at least in private. His diaries were published posthumously (Malinowski 1967); they might have landed their author in trouble had they emerged sooner. Such reticence has been frowned upon more recently. Reflexive musings are now considered to add to the totality and vitality of the account, to put anthropologists into their own research frames and to ward off criticism of unacknowledged subjectivities. Not everyone approves. This essentially methodological concern can be confused with self-absorption (see Okely 1992: 2), when the narcissistic inclusion of autobiographical material tells you only about the anthropologist's personal life. De Neve (2006: 67–89) suggests this is because anthropologists are uncertain both about what reflexivity is and how self-reflection can be used in fieldwork and writing to enhance accounts. There are some implicit limits to the level of self-disclosure. Core aspects of a 'social' self, such as educational background, country of origin and gender, can be publicly displayed (e.g. Calloway 1992; Cohen 1992; Hastrup 1987), although other components of the self, such as sexual practice in the field, usually remain private (Kulick and Wilson 1995).

Where did reflexive practice come from?

Reflexive anthropology has several origins. First, concern about the colonial encounter (i.e. that Western anthropologists studied non-Western societies), when those societies were in the grip of colonial political systems, spawned a critique of the apparent but largely implicit, value systems of these researchers. These value systems were assumed on the basis of a particular interpretation of the anthropologists' social positions and origins, as well as from the anthropological account. Second, there was an assault on the rhetorical strategy of scientific objectivity in early writing which arguably made anthropologists ponder on the nature of their own subjective take on what they observed. Third, feminist writing pointed out the absence both of women in the field and women informants, and that 'the' account of a culture was a largely 'male' account (Ardener 1975;

Moore 1988). Recent work has focused on anthropology done 'at home', where subtleties of social similarity and difference between anthropologist and other are highlighted (Bodenhorn 2006; Jackson 1987; Okely 1996).

As a result, both the social identity of the anthropologist and the values and interests associated with their social position have become part of anthropological inquiry. This is the complete opposite of other styles of inquiry, where the imperative is to squeeze out 'researcher bias', not to understand it. Such reflections on the self of the anthropologist have necessarily included not only the response of the informants, their perception of the researcher and thus the effect of social identity on the research process and outcome but also the response of the anthropologist to the field encounter. All this material can be analysed, polished and honed for publication; it can and often does add depth and complexity to the account.

From my own position in these uncharted waters between contemporary psychiatric practice and research anthropology, three issues stand out. First, there are remarkable parallels between reflexive anthropology and the work of psychotherapy—most obviously the articulation of the components of transference and countertransference, in both individual and group psychotherapy.[1] From within anthropology, Okely (1996: 39) has argued the same point. She introduces the term 'cultural countertransference' but what she intends by this term is incomplete. In indicating that it includes only cultural and social history she leaves out the personal, which she sees as the proper consideration only of psychotherapy. Second, there can be deceptive rhetoric in the apparent self-disclosure by the anthropologist, which deserves attention. Third, writing in this seam of anthropology, although it appears close to psychiatry at first glance, is really only close to psychotherapy. It is, perhaps

---

[1] Transference is the term used to describe the emotions and thoughts that the psychotherapy patient has about the therapist which stem from ways of relating to real figures from their past life. Countertransference is a term used to encompass the therapist's thoughts and feelings about the patient both in relation to isolated events in the therapy and more generally (Rycroft 1972).

paradoxically,[2] as far away as it is possible to be from that which psychiatry characterizes as research.

Psychological and social selves

The parallels between psychotherapy and reflexive anthropology prompt questions more generally about the relative value of 'psychological' and 'social' models of people and process. The distinction of psychological and social is mine but not uniquely so. It is problematic, as are other words in this area, e.g. self, person, individual. Though such terms can be distinguished, and need to be, sometimes the distinctions are little more than artefacts of academic disciplines. They are models, academic constructs, that sometimes escape into the outside world. What people say and do may not be so conveniently classifiable. Even within the world of academe there are difficulties in disentangling the psychological and the social, how they relate and how both are conceptualized in terms of the self, or the person. Anthropology has dipped its toes into this discussion (Delvecchio Good et al. 2008: 1–40). The unitary person has been dismantled and can be considered to demonstrate multiple and interacting social subjectivities, e.g. of gender and ethnicity (Moore 2007). This can be considered as anxiety about the constitution of the self and the idea of a person as an autonomous social actor, an individual who says and does things.

Some anthropologists have tackled psychoanalytic theory head on (Moore 1994a: 28–48, 2007: 43–62). The self-evident cultural relativism of developmental models based on a particularly Judeo-Christian view of family and sexuality is easy to spot, and the related concept of an individualized and separated adult person is necessarily to some degree

---

[2] The distinction between psychiatry and psychotherapy is important. Psychiatry is a medical speciality which includes some exposure to psychotherapy. Psychotherapy has its own training schemes and many practitioners with no medical background. The term is sometimes used synonymously with psychoanalysis but this is inaccurate. The situation is further confused by the fact that doctors with psychoanalytic training will often be employed within the National Health Service as psychotherapists. Research into the efficacy of psychotherapy is difficult. Many practitioners have been uninspired by the medical models of inquiry favoured by more biologically orientated colleagues.

culturally specific. Freud's contribution, as a nineteenth-century Viennese man, is much more remarkable for the way in which he transcends his own history and values to address the universal issues of the human condition, than it is handicapped by simplistic attacks.

However, psychological models, including those of psychotherapy, do attach less importance to social and cultural norms and their variation, and more to aspects of the local individual. They highlight traits or personality characteristics, latent or visible tendencies wherein lie the essence of an adult person and which influence their emotional or behavioural responses to environmental cues, and perhaps how people react to them. Even group analytic psychotherapy, which is much more alert to social norms, remains primarily interested in their final common pathway, the individual's psyche.

Delvecchio Good et al. (2008: 1–40) despair of the separation between psychological and social models. They recommend the integration of several streams of academic writing ('post-structuralist writing on agency', 'clinically influenced writing on trauma and other forms of psychopathology' and 'the ethnography of "social suffering"') (p. 14), at least in looking internationally at colonialism, civil conflict and their legacies. In essence, they are still talking about the 'out there' bit of anthropology, the study of the other, not the context or person of the anthropologist, both arguably influencing what is then found out.

Who is the anthropologist?

Reflexive anthropology demands an appreciation of an 'I', the anthropologist, in whom certain social characteristics meet. The identification and description of this 'I' is problematic. The initial response to the field is in terms of a person's perception, feelings and thoughts. Through these individual processes appear field notes, photographs, tape recordings and memories. A recurring problem is how at a given point, or more generally, you decide whether the fieldwork material is a consequence of an irritable, tired anthropologist impatient with informants that morning—a psychological sequence, or because you are a woman with a small baby not sleeping well and these social facts are important and known to your informants. It would seem self-evident that within long periods of fieldwork different aspects of the 'social' self and the 'psychological' self of the anthropologist will matter on different occasions. It may depend on the congruity of indigenous models of behaviour and the social and psychological frameworks the anthropologist brings to the field. But anthropologists who are, in my terms, shy, exuberant, personable or habitually irritable may end up very differently informed—even while they share crucial social identities. The process by which it is possible to move from the individual to the social, where N = 1, is less than clear, the robustness of the conclusion debatable. It is a matter of great import that '[w]hile . . . the fieldworker writes extensive and personal notes in the field about others, we simply do not know how to explore the specificity of the fieldworker in those relationships (Okely 1996: 13). Bell (1993: 29) sees this as a further assault on 'scientific' anthropology, which excludes psychological responses to the field, and does not include the 'self . . . interacting, or as an element in a relational field'.

Equally, there must be concern about the resolution of the possible discrepancy between the perceived anthropological 'I', the one visible to informants, and the active perceiving 'I', who is physically and intellectually there. Cohen (1994) makes the point that even where there is no consciously mediated attempt to disguise or conceal aspects of the person, this can happen anyway.[3]

How reflexivity illuminates cultural norms

In sum, it is worth considering how, using a reflexive approach, the final product, the self of the anthropologist, is generated and the extent to which this self is owned by the anthropologist, as opposed to signalling the cultural values of the researched. The next two sections do exactly that for Smithtown. The analysis is of the social relations established between researchers and people in Smithtown, using an understanding

---

[3] The language and practice of psychotherapy encourage exploration of such discrepancy. The analysis of the fantasy in the transference as a central aspect of psychotherapeutic work and the therapist is deliberately opaque.

of who we were thought to be in the field and who we thought we were. All three fieldworkers manipulated aspects of their social identity in order to conceal certain parts of themselves from informants. Both the ethics and rationale for this discretion are considered. The discrepancies between and within the personae of the fieldworkers are described, as are the cultural values in Smithtown that they illuminate. In this project there was no single opaque 'anthropologist'.

Who we were as far as other people were concerned

Researchers are quite common in secure hospitals but none had spent such a long time just being there, watching television and playing snooker. The only people who spend prolonged periods of time on wards are patients or nursing staff but in our own minds, we were not either of those kinds of people. The long period of fieldwork gave rise to much material from which to reflect on the nature of the researcher's identity.

Not being like anyone else

Patients did not sit in the staff mess (with honourable exceptions) and nursing staff did not have notebooks, wear their own clothes or participate in yoga classes. Neither our behaviour nor what we said about ourselves fitted neatly with an available institutional identity. In this we were different from previous researchers—Goffman, the games teacher, Alasewski, the nursing assistant or Stanton and Schwartz, the psychiatrists—but the ways we did and did not overlap with obvious types of people told us much about who those people were.

We came and went from Smithtown according to our own timetable and on our own. Both the possibility of determining the working day and its contents, as well as passing in and out of the hospital, are defining characteristics of different social groups. No one else in Smithtown had this kind of freedom to determine their own working day. Staff of various disciplines were constrained by fixed points on their timetables or their duty rotas. These were times when they had to be there. Entering and leaving on our own was required of us by the ward staff. Escorting of individual researchers on a regular basis would have been an unreasonable demand. Patients were in no cases free to move around the whole hospital site and none was allowed to enter and leave the hospital grounds at will. When they did go out of the hospital it was invariably with at least one escorting member of staff. When they moved around the hospital site it would be in accordance with the rules governing parole or, more commonly, in escorted parties en route to 'work' or 'social functions'.

Our relative flexibility and mobility as researchers were determined by our keys; these keys made us neither patients nor visitors (professional nor personal). We came in through the staff entrance, and as we did so we exchanged an outside identification tag for internal keys attached to a lead and belt; there are several keys on the ring. Women staff (and all the researchers) had pouches[4] for the keys when not in use, while men use their trouser pockets. This system is almost identical to that in use in many English prisons.

That we were allowed to do this, in the same way as all members of staff, seemed curious. We had moved rapidly from a position of relative distrust where the project had required prolonged negotiation, to one where free access to the hospital was given unconditionally. This suggested that you were either trusted as one of the Smithtown staff group or significantly distrusted.

Being no one in particular

Despite keys being very obvious—large and noisy—not everyone remembered that the researchers had them. This continued throughout the project. It was not always possible to understand how certain staff and certain patients could continue not to notice. For others, this distinguishing feature could be and was used ironically or practically. For example, one patient would ask me to open doors on the ward that he needed opening; he asked me because I was nearby. To refuse seemed churlish but to accede to his request was to move from a position of neutrality to one of staff behaviour. To act 'as staff' might have long-term consequences in my research relationship with him and other people.

---

[4] Pouches are made in Smithtown work areas by patients.

Later in the project patients would tease me about possession of the keys *and* how they were often hidden under my clothing; for them to be very visible seemed a kind of flaunting of the paraphernalia of power that did not fit with the project's intention. I was told that a preoccupation with keys, verging on enjoyment of them, was associated with a staff attitude to patients which included revelling in the power differential. My keys were deliberately downplayed.

Once on the ward the issues of access and its meaning took on different dimensions, not necessarily dependent on keys. Access to or exclusion from physical spaces, at particular times, implied access to or exclusion from congruent social arenas. What kinds of people were allowed into such arenas became clearer as the fieldwork progressed and as we broke the rules for particular categories. Though the experiences of the three researchers were often the same, there were also important distinctions.

Being a woman

For me there were special considerations which did not apply to the other two researchers. As a woman working on a male ward, where many of the patients had committed serious sexual offences against adult women, and where no woman, staff or patient, had ever spent long periods of time, there were concerns about my safety. It was suggested that I wore no jewellery. On a tour of the ward, it was indicated to me that some places were likely to be safer than others, safety being determined by nearness to the nursing staff. It was agreed that the nursing staff should know where I was at all times. This restriction on movement did not apply to either of the other two researchers who were on wards where they were the same gender as the patients and the bulk of the staff. However, unlike Rawlings (2005), who found attention to security unnerving, these measures were both perfectly manageable and seemed reasonable. However, the precautions of staff did add to my initial oddness.

I was initially chaperoned by staff as I wandered around the ward. This was obvious to patients and they commented on it. When male patients are chaperoned, or 'specialled', by staff in psychiatric hospitals this is because of concern that they might harm themselves or others, not that *they* might be attacked. Staff took this seriously. When I failed to tell anyone I had gone to the lavatory, it appeared I was missing. One of the patients then told staff where I was but they were about to sound the alarm and were in the process of searching the ward. Some hours after this incident, it was brought up by the ward manager and I was publicly chastised. Routinely, I was escorted up a flight of stairs to the ward, and escorted down again. This was to stop me, and to stop other women, being attacked on the stairs. Other women familiar to the hospital had thought it absurd. When I returned for the last part of the fieldwork, the practice had reduced and staff were inconsistent in their approach. Sometimes they escorted me, sometimes they did not. This seemed to follow the addition of a female nurse to the otherwise entirely male staff group on an adjacent ward.

Being included or not

There were peculiarities about access to information that indicated the researchers were in a unique position. Attendance at the various clinical meetings illustrates this. It had been agreed by nursing staff and consultants that researchers would have access as observers to meetings and discussions which focused on patients' clinical care. This meant we were not patients. Patients would not sit in on staff discussions about other patients (but they might eavesdrop on staff conversations about someone). Patients viewed this in several ways. A few argued that if researchers were allowed into 'case conferences' about a given patient, the patient him/herself had a right to be present throughout. Patients did not have this right and it was certainly not a normal expectation as it would be in contemporary practice. It was feared that we would tell staff what we had learnt about patients as part of the general discussion, as we were not patients. The fact that one of the researchers was a psychiatrist created additional dilemmas. The consultant on that ward was frustrated about being unable to access clinical information from the researcher who was obliged to stonewall periodic requests as to how certain patients appeared. Patients would occasionally request clinical information they thought they could obtain more easily from me than from their own doctors. If this information were available to the 'intelligent layperson' I would give it to them but if not, then I would stonewall them too. In particular, if the questions related to their own care, I declined; the potential for complicating the clinical supervision of a patient seemed all too obvious to me, even if not to them.

With time, it became clear that information was not being fed back to staff. Equally, it became apparent that we did not tell the patients what we had learnt about them from staff. We responded to such requests with clear statements about our position, which tended to provoke disappointment and, on occasion, an accusation from the patient concerned that we were not on their side. Sides were real. Our decision to behave in this way can be criticised. For example, information about patients might have been ultimately helpful to them if the staff had been told. Equally, entering staff social areas would preclude our getting certain kinds of information from patients.

Access to certain areas helped us understand what was important, as did exclusion. Such exclusions were sometimes attributable to the social conventions of the ward, sometimes to the sensitivities of the researcher, and sometimes to the active intention on the part of staff to exclude. No researcher regularly entered patients' rooms and we did not use the patients' wash areas. Entering patients' rooms was rare for anyone other than the patient concerned. Staff lavatories were demarcated and locked; we were told where they were. Researchers spontaneously withdrew from sensitive meetings, e.g. where staff suspensions were being discussed. We offered all patients the option of excluding us from their 'case conferences', the one occasion in the year when their history was discussed in great detail. One of the researchers also withdrew from a set of therapy groups which required patients to divulge personal material. Staff occasionally made it clear that the researcher was unwelcome, e.g. by not including them in mealtimes or explaining they needed to have a private meeting the content of which was usually subsequently divulged. Significantly, we were never excluded from staff discussion of patients, even though this might have involved very intimate material. In this regard, I am not sure that High Secure Hospitals are unique. Patients' encounters were less formal, and there were opportunities for patients to have private conversations, as there were for staff. Occasionally we overheard conversations intended to be private, e.g. patients obtaining pornography, or witnessed private moments, e.g. male patients kissing.

In maintaining the same levels of confidentiality to staff and to patients, and treating both groups as subjects of equal importance for the study, we differed from other researchers in polarized societies. In Smithtown, as has been well documented in other work on hospitals and prisons, the distinction between 'them' and 'us' is so obvious that you ignore it at your peril. Most researchers opt, implicitly or explicitly, to study and/or favour either 'them' or 'us'. Davidson (1974) conducted research in San Quentin prison, the layout and social organization of which meant there was a separate prisoner social world in which he chose to immerse himself. As a consequence, his ethnography contains little material about prison staff. In contrast, Barratt (1988a), a psychiatrist, investigating discourse *about* patients in an acute (i.e. short-stay) psychiatric unit learnt this from staff. These restricted views were not open to us. The point was to study the patterns of social relations, not just to observe them from one single vantage point. The fact that 'confidentiality' of information was an issue that had to be considered as such was itself a reflection of the broader context of this research and our social flexibility. The social flexibility of the outsider was brought home to me in a trip to the Lebanon. In conversation with a wine maker in the Christian area north of Beirut, I said I was going to go to Baalbek in the Bekaa Valley, the base for Hezbullah. His grapes came from the Bekaa Valley each year to make his world-renowned wine. All except two vintages had been made during the Civil War. Yet, he said he could not go where I was going due to the ongoing religious divide in Lebanese society. As a stranger, I was more socially flexible than he was.

Perception and attribution of identity

From the discussion in the previous section, it is clear that we had complex identities which were created and adjusted in the course of the project. This is a well-known phenomenon; e.g. Halstead (2008, 48–66) describes how, in her fieldwork, she could be seen as an academic but also as an East Indian. Depending on the East Indian individuals' sense of themselves as modern or not, her inquiry was or was not welcomed.

Similarly, our identities could be seen to overlap partially with those of the most obvious social groups. Yet, we could be made into certain kinds of people, even by those who knew us to be researchers. Though infrequent, its importance lies both in the fact that this was spontaneous behaviour and that it made us into kinds of people which did not fit with our sense of self, all variants of the category of patient. The incidents described next are variants on covert research; individuals were unaware of the project and its methods, and provided data that might otherwise have been inaccessible.

Three examples of this illustrate the following kinds of perceptions: being seen as a patient by other patients; being taken for a patient by staff; being seen as a patient by visitors.

Being a patient to other patients is illustrated as follows. The new arrival of a woman was something to be remarked upon, because the men outnumbered the women in Smithtown by 5:1. One of the female researchers recalled the day when she, for no particular reason, wore a short skirt to work. During the day she went to the sports field. Both male and female patients went to events on the sports field. In contrast to her experience on the female ward, she felt uncomfortable. She became an object of sexual attention in the way a woman newly arriving as a patient might, particularly when they moved out of a sexually segregated ward.

This makes an interesting comparison with an excerpt from the poetry of a woman prisoner venturing out of the women's prison into a mixed county jail.

> . . . here are the inmates of the county jail. The inmates display mean and lustful stares at me. The eyes of the men undress me. The men say derogatory things to me and they make me feel like a piece of meat. (Latisha M., in Brooks and Johnson 2010: 155)

The discomfort was caused by being able to guess the likely reasons why many of the male patients were in Smithtown, in many cases after committing crimes of sexual violence.

The second scenario, being a patient to staff, was evident when one of the researchers was working at night. At the suggestion of the night staff, the researcher agreed to pretend to be a patient but pointed out that the other night staff would not be convinced if they saw the researcher's keys. It was suggested that the researcher remove them and leave them behind the curtain, which was done. The night man said that to make it convincing, the researcher should move away from the table and sit elsewhere when instructed by him. When the visiting night staff arrived they were surprised to see a 'patient' drinking tea at the table with staff. The field notes read as follows:

> Antoine said that he had seen me somewhere before. Bertrand said that of course he had seen me before as I had been in Paris for the last two and a half years. Bertrand said I had been a bit upset so they had got me up and given me a cup of tea. He said, "What with this 24-hour care business they thought they would make a start with some of the 'good patients.'" Bertrand asked me to change places so I moved. . . . Antoine looked uncertain. Bertrand asked Antoine if he wanted any milk. Antoine nodded towards me and Bertrand said, "Oh, he's O.K." Antoine still looked uncertain but took a pint from the fridge and left. Once he had gone Bertrand handed me my key pouch and he and Claude and I laughed . . . later Antoine came back and I introduced my real self and he laughed. He collected some vinegar . . . and left.

The anxiety in the visiting night staff is about taking the 'patient's' milk. He will only be anxious about this in front of a patient who knows the rules and might object. The second time he visits he is reassured by the evident shared joke between the researcher and night staff, in which rules about the key pouch, based on obvious security implications, are breached, and does not hesitate in sharing the joke and taking the 'patient's' vinegar. The researcher, who was briefly a patient, obeying staff by moving places at the table, is now a member of staff, sharing potentially embarrassing knowledge.

This is a rich vignette, as it also had great significance for the researcher. He reflected, having read this account, that this incident had stood out for him as the single most frightening moment of the fieldwork. For a period of time, brief but measurable, he had been without keys. He became intensely aware of the flimsiness of his non-patient identity. Keys were the only thing he had on him that made him not a patient and therefore able to leave. He had wondered what would happen if he did not get his keys back; he would be like Rosenhan's (1973) patients, thought of as mad because he took notes. De Neve (2006: 67–89) writes of how the reflexivity of the research assistant is a neglected component of fieldwork. As M. and I discussed this incident he reminded me that he had said years ago, in supervision, that it had been alarming. In effect, I had not noticed this in my earlier analysis. It had only now resurfaced and contributed to the depth of understanding of the interaction. So, to create a thicker (in the Geetzian sense) description, it is belatedly added to the account.

The third case of mistaken identity, being a patient to visitors, was illustrated at a social event at which outside visitors were present. The event was a quiz, and the researcher sat with the patients. The field notes read:

> There were several late middle-aged women (Women's Institute types) who came and spoke to Didier and I in a very patronising manner. They asked if we had managed to answer any of the questions. (My key pouch was out of sight and she must have thought that I was a patient). I said that we had answered the questions but had not written the answers down. The first WI woman said that we should try even if we could only get one or two. (She completely ignored the fact that I had said we had answered the questions but that we had not written the answers down). She obviously assumed that we were stupid.

These mistaken identities follow from the behaviour of the researchers. We were perceived in accordance with a set of other people's preconceptions about what people *do*. This exemplifies how attributed identity can only be informed, not determined, by the subject concerned. The acquisition and maintenance of identity is a social process subject to related processes, including restatement and revision. The balance between these two processes in turn informs the extent to which an evident identity is reinforced or amended.

Being who we said we were

Throughout the project all three researchers were persuading people legitimately that we were who we said we were. This is a common research task. In a society based on 'them' and 'us', it has to be important. If we were not 'them', then we must be 'us'. During my fieldwork I was for staff a *'management spy'* just as predicted in the negotiations, as well as a *'fly on the wall'*, *'part of the furniture'* and *'one of the men'*. For patients I was *'special'*, i.e. what I said I was, as well as *'not a lady . . . a screw'*, and *'an undercover doctor'*. For staff I was rarely a patient but I might be management; for patients I might be staff. Exactly who 'them' and 'us' are depend on who you are. None of these identities was incompatible with being a researcher; they were in fact subtleties that told me both how the project was understood and which were the overriding important identities in the minds of the people concerned.

The other two researchers had their own experiences. Neither was a doctor and neither was perceived in this way. The other woman researcher was like me, and thought by staff to be a *'spycat'*, and questioned as to whether or not she was from the *News of the World* and in a moment of humour *Catherine Cookson*. From the patients, no single attribution stood out but she was told several times that she looked like a patient that had left. Patients seemed to value the researcher, occasionally confiding in her. The third researcher was referred to by some of the staff as *'that fucking spy'* or the *'mole'*. The concern about what might be written was maintained until the end. To the first researcher it was expressed as an anxiety about the staff losing their jobs but to the third researcher it was expressed as a threat. Staff wanted to know where he lived in order that *'we can beat the fuck out of you'* if the report was not to their liking.

If everyone had made the attribution of 'spy', the project would have ground to a halt as far as the staff were concerned but it was not. We received practical help, information, opinion and invitations from the staff group, who went out of their way to be helpful. We gathered key informants and their information was, where possible, systematically cross-checked. Whatever else, spies find things out, especially secrets. It is also axiomatic in the world of espionage that it is never completely certain whose side you are on.

Also critical to the success of the project was the extent to which the ward settled down after an initial period of fieldwork. This was done in two ways: periodic checking from key informants as the project progressed, and retrospective evaluation from all interviewees. The key informants explained that I was both sought out and avoided, depending on the individual. Both staff and patient groups contained seekers-out, avoiders and those seemingly indifferent to my presence. Amongst the staff there was no correlation between length of service in Smithtown and patterns of seeking-out or avoiding. I made little difference to what happened, except people swore less. This matched my own observations of being increasingly unremarkable the longer I spent on the ward. This was also true for the other researchers, who were initially less peculiar than I had been in that they were the same gender as all the patients and most of the staff on their ward. This may well be why they were less of a magnet for certain individuals.

While we were sure of our roles and their boundaries, we could still 'be' other people, but this did not so much hamper the research process, as constitute a crucial part of it. To have encountered bland answers about the way things were done, without evasion, distortion, hostility, enthusiasm, humour or attempts at monopolizing, would have been less interesting and less true to Smithtown. We would have known a lot but not necessarily what mattered. We may have felt uncomfortable about the process but without the prompting of discomfort we would have learnt rather less than we did.

What we thought about what we did

The researchers did not have to travel too far. This was not geographically exotic anthropology. This looks at first glance like anthropology 'at home'. Being 'at home' is not just about place but also about fitting in socially. This is an interesting idea in a community of apparently dangerous people. So, the next section explores both the idea of being 'at home' and the extent to which we were 'at home'. Part of my identity is to be a psychiatrist, another is being gay. These identities are to some extent separable. So this is an opportunity to discuss how researchers' identities may need to be dealt with differently depending on the society in question.

Linked with this is an articulation of how we responded to doing the fieldwork. This creates an opportunity for cross-referencing with how we were viewed by others. This was difficult research and negative responses to fieldwork are relatively neglected in anthropological writing; there is a need for the anthropologist to return as a conquering hero. Common sense would suggest that anyone who works in a High Secure Hospital should think about personal safety, and it was very much part of our induction. All three researchers had concerns about this at different times and for different reasons. The issue of safety informed the conduct and ultimate content of the fieldwork.

Anthropology at home

Strathern (1987: 17) has asked 'how one knows when one is at home' as an anthropologist.[5] This is an important check on the appealing but too simple idea that similarity of one social variable, e.g. researcher and subjects sharing a country of origin, is enough to constitute 'at homeness'. Her argument is that

> [t]he personal credentials of the anthropologist do not tell us whether he/she is at home . . . what he/she in the end writes, does: whether there is cultural continuity between the products of his/her labours and what people in the society being studied produce by way of accounts of themselves. (1987: 17)

She avoids discussing what the anthropologist's personal credentials do tell us. In obstetric practice there has been a long-standing debate about the position of the male obstetrician and the extent to which he understands childbirth. If he does not understand, goes the argument, he should step aside and let women deliver babies. The parallel argument in anthropology is that shared social background between researchers and informants increases the likelihood of an illuminating ethnography. The opposite argument is that coming into the field from afar brings out the otherwise 'taken for granted' quality of the field. Strathern points out that the force of one or other of these arguments may well depend not on a universal truth but on the specifics of the society under scrutiny. It is relevant, she argues, to consider a given society's approach to someone 'near' and someone 'further away', as well as that society's grasp of the other elements and consequences of the anthropological process. As an illustration of this last point, Bell talks of the social policy influence of insiders and outsiders in relation to her work with Aboriginal women, where although she had

> a deeper appreciation of the political process than an outsider . . . as an insider one's views were never taken as seriously as the 'expert' from abroad. But critiques heard from overseas experts can be contained: dismissed as insensitive to 'local conditions' (1993: 31).

---

[5] Jackson (1987) uses this term mainly about European anthropologists researching in Europe.

In the Smithtown project there were obvious but crude indicators of this being anthropology 'at home'. There were none of the issues that beset many going into the field; there was for instance a common language and a shared experience of living in Britain for many years. Although I did my fieldwork on a male ward, the other two researchers were on gender-congruent wards. More than that, there were subtleties of personal history that resonated with obvious elements of Smithtown. One of the researchers had been in the police force; whatever else the police do, they certainly lock people up and restrain them, both activities that were features of Smithtown life. The other researcher had worked in hospital units in Britain and abroad, and had experienced previously being in new hospital environments. For me, the experiences and previous contact with Smithtown and other institutions that shared the goal of caring for forensic patients were probably more crucial to my sense of self. That one is a forensic psychiatrist is no easier to forget than that one is a teacher, an anthropologist or a fishmonger. Occupational identities fill our days and carry with them social roles and expectations.

The presentation of self in everyday fieldwork

That being a doctor was important to others was obvious in negotiations for access and funding. That it was an issue for *me* really only became apparent at the start of contact with my chosen ward. I began to wonder how who I was, influenced what I noticed. This obsession with the detail of method becomes more interesting if it is borne in mind that we could, in theory, have been anyone (in reality, for anyone to access Smithtown is very hard). Our responses to the field might be very different or very similar to Joanna Bloggs, who finds herself transported from the local bus stop to the inside of a High Secure Hospital. Anthropologists, when they are not anthropologists, are anyone but also someone.

Psychiatry both sharpens and dulls the senses. When visiting wards late at night as a junior doctor, there were rows of demented elderly women in beds and sometimes in cots. I recall the constant stench of urine and the wailing and the mutterings. Someone's mother, someone's sister in every bed, even if they no longer knew that themselves—time often so altered that they would believe themselves to be children again. A colleague of mine told a story about a prison visit; the man he saw had smeared the walls of his cell in faeces and poked faeces through the wicket of the door. Inside the cell he had no clothes on and would let no one approach without attacking them. This is an example of what psychiatry would call old-fashioned, untreated madness. It is seldom seen in Britain except in prison. Now, working in a women's prison, I too have seen this level of distress and degradation, though infrequently. It is deeply affecting, and as a psychiatrist there is an obligation to *do* something. There is often the possibility of helping, and always the need to try. This distinguishes the doctor from the journalist or the anthropologist. They *may* help but they do not have to do so. Simply to watch or be with someone was therefore a new role for me.

Thinking about how you look at the world and how you therefore see it is hard. That this is important is evident from Mary Douglas's comments on ethnography. The risk is that we imbue other people with unacknowledged aspects of ourselves in a way that may not be true to their identity. It begins to matter if Mary Douglas was right to suggest that unluckily for societies studied by anthropologists,

> they inevitably end up resembling the anthropologists who study them. Thus, the Nuer—studied by the British—turned out to be phlegmatic politicians, while the Dogon—studied by the French—are aesthetes with an interest in language and systems of signification (Moore 1994c: 130).

The implication in Smithtown is that as a psychiatrist, I would use the psychiatric gaze and be complacent about 'patient' experience. Many social scientists, lawyers and 'patients' see the practice of psychiatry as coercive and insensitive to real needs. This was a more pertinent concern in the days of electroconvulsive therapy for everything, insulin coma therapy for schizophrenia and aversion therapy for gay men (Mackay 1948). Nonetheless, it remains relevant at times. The category of psychiatric or mental health patients is one of negative difference. Doctors present themselves as caring professionals who deal with illness; this has enabled them to disregard, both individually and collectively (Clare 1980), pertinent criticism of practice (Hare 1983; Scull 1989). Patients, they might say, do not know what is good for them because they are mad. The question for this project was the extent to which the data and analytic focus would reflect this outlook. The danger was failing in this way to do justice to lived experience by sanitizing the account. Well-intentioned others had silenced patients with a reluctance or an inability to hear their comments.

Stanton and Schwartz (1954), in their study of a locked ward in the US at the time of *One Flew Over The Cuckoo's Nest*, write cheerfully about treatment and its usefulness. They never problematize the psychiatric discourse. Categories of madness were self-evidently true to them. This, it should be remembered was during the heyday of surgical management of schizophrenia, with widespread use of the now discredited lobotomy. They do not assess the impact of having a psychiatrist in their research team.

Equally worrying was the possibility of ignoring disability, such that all madness was rendered inconsequential. Patient testimony could not just be taken at face value but sensitive material could be the most difficult to triangulate.

These are similar but different dangers to those which Moore (1994c: 130) notes later in the same passage:

> The anthropological gaze risks turning subjects into objects; othering them in a permanent relation to an anthropological self which by virtue of disciplinary training and philosophical orientation, if by nothing else, is frequently a kind of quasi North American or European self.

In my case no convenient anthropological self could be reasonably and safely separated from other subjectivities, i.e. psychiatrist, woman, lesbian, which were relevant to the fieldwork.

The evidence for the presence of a given element of the self is fragmentary. To notice it in field notes requires reflection on the self and its documentation. One *is* some kind of person all the time but this is not a necessary component of much conscious thought. Much of this kind of material remains *potential* material in the mind of the anthropologist. It may be retrieved. It may not have been recorded. It may not be recoverable by the prompting of bare field notes. But these elements of a complex self and the nature of their relationship to the field can be partially explored.

The psychiatric intruder

The field notes given here indicate how these subjectivities can relate. Alphonse had a case conference, which he allowed me to attend.

> The three of us displace Alphonse from his place in the Games Room and information comes from Bertrand who says it is very much as the previous case conference . . . Alphonse has never been in Intensive Care, he has never been secluded. His parents are now elderly and they visit him. They now live in Solihull. He attacked his mother; he was thought to be psychotic and always hallucinated. He reads 'Ciao'. . . . Bertrand was rather vague about his education but mentioned some kind of assessment for which he did not know the outcome. His consultant raised the issue of his continuing dangerousness to his mother, wondering why it might be construed as any different, and also the possibility of absconding. Bertrand says this is not a problem. Claude comments that he would look after 30 Alphonses. Apparently, Alphonse as a young man used to get into very frequent fights. There is a work area staff member who has joined us and he says that he works very well and that he is actually less hallucinated.

> Alphonse comes in and sits next to the consultant who asks most of the questions. He was in Rome aged 15 and this has sparked his interest in Italian. His Italian is obviously better than his consultant's. He is mad at times and keeps mentioning hostages. He, when asked who I was, said, 'I do operations on the female side.' He says he does not want to leave Smithtown. He said that . . . television told him to attack his mother. He thinks his mother is safe whilst he is here and I wondered myself about the implications of that statement. There is a long conversation in which this is all discussed, some of which is in Italian and some in English. He says the staff are not too bad but mentions being beaten up by them. It is quite interesting, as this case conference contains no social work and no psychology input and I note how humorous he is really, despite his level of obvious thought disorder.

This is not a straightforward passage. As I listened to Alphonse talking in Italian, I listened for 'thought disorder'. I listened as a psychiatrist. At the end, I made a spontaneous comment on it and everyone laughed because I had dropped out of the anthropologist role for a moment. Thought disorder is a technical term which describes an abnormality evidenced in speech, whereby despite grammatically correct use of language, the sentences do not make sense. Classically this is found in individuals with schizophrenic illnesses. It is of minor psychiatric interest to see if thought disorder is apparent in a second language. There are other clues in the passage to double vision, and the casual and non-problematized use of 'hallucinated', 'psychotic' and the suggestion of a risk assessment in the phrase 'I wondered myself about the implications of that state-ment'. Risk assessment is the raison d'être of forensic psychiatrists. Other terms are attributable to a version of going native—'secluded' and 'inten-sive care'. But as a record of the social event of the case conference it looks very unlike the minutes taken at a case conference for one of my own patients. There is note taken of the venue and the order of inter-actions but not of a 'management plan', because I could not take notes contemporaneously without distorting the field.

These notes are a mishmash of choice, chance and preoccupation. The impossibility of recording everything is well known. The absurdity of a rigid adherence to schedules with the inherent danger of missing the subtle and important points is the rallying cry of anthropology. In their mix of the systematic and idiosyncratic, they are perhaps typical anthropology, but they are also a clear example of how the subject self can inform the specific appearance of the object self.

The secret self

Being a psychiatrist was an obvious available self. It could be talked about, asked questions about, and only its internal workings were covert. Being a lesbian was deliberately hidden. High Secure Hospitals had developed a reputation for homophobia. Discussion in the public domain had been about the difficulties confronting gay and lesbian patients (Department of Health 1992), and little had been said on the topic of gay and lesbian staff; it was as if they did not exist. In deciding on self-presentation, it had seemed prudent not to discuss much of me either with staff or patients. In fact, all three researchers edited our present and past lives to make us as acceptable as possible to Smithtown. Who we were to informants was different in important ways from who we thought we were.

The consequence of my decision to disguise, by rendering opaque, my sexuality was that material emerged that might not have done if my lesbian self had been known. The absence of an overt heterosexual self allowed speculation which was partly determined by the field—baggy androgynous clothing, which I would not normally wear, and no jewellery—such that no one knew if I wore a wedding ring. The clothing was to discourage staff or patients chatting me up.

Ex-Smithtown patients have recounted to me, both before and since the fieldwork, how their sexual orientation was played out when they were there. It lacked the ordinariness of contemporary, metropolitan gay and lesbian life, and had more in common with historical methods of negotiation, fear of disclosure and the need to explain. During fieldwork, and in the absence of systematic inquiry, similar anecdotal material emerged. Gay sex was invariably negatively construed. 'Homosexual', a word with medical and psychoanalytic overtones of pathology (King and Bartlett 1999), was used as part of critical descriptions of both staff and patients, by both staff and patients. Staff recounted how 'queer' was an insult used to other staff; at the same time, *male staff would play games and sit on each other's laps to psyche each other out by suggesting that there was a gay fraternity.* An incident of professional misconduct arose when a male member of staff appears to have formed too close a relationship with a male patient and was sacked. Other stories were told of a staff–patient lesbian relationship that was formed in hospital and continued outside it. Reports were made of the threat of, or the fact of, non-consensual sex between male patients. The patients concerned would often not mention it or fail to identify the perpetrators for fear of retribution. One staff member told me he would need a shotgun to sleep in the male dormitory. The situation on the women's ward was slightly different, where it appeared that there was less hostility to women patients' sexual liaisons with each other and some women staff were openly lesbian.

But there was little evidence of positive role models for patients which incorporated gay or lesbian identity. Gay patients were cautious both about self-disclosure and also their behaviour, which could be construed as breaking institutional codes of behaviour.[6] The position of gay and lesbian staff and patients was no doubt made more problematic by

---

6 A colleague of mine, who had been attached to a High Secure Hospital as a trainee, reported an incident where two male patients were found having sex in a shower. One was put in seclusion. My colleague asked if anyone had inquired of these patients whether or not they were enjoying themselves and, if no one had, why not? Staff greeted this question with baffled gazes.

the deliberate use of same-sex sexual behaviours by certain patients profoundly opposed to the institution. If their intention was to demonstrate dissent, they might well have been gratified by the staff response. These patients may or may not have self identified as being gay.

Transgression has a long and honourable history among gays and lesbians, with many different purposes (Garber 1993). Recent writing has addressed the idea of heterosexual city and public space where the recognition of the presence of gays and lesbians challenges a heterosexual norm, and its implicit or explicit homophobia (Graham 1998; Probyn 1995), and creates queer space. Conscious transgression along the lines of queer politics had literally no place in Smithtown. On the rare occasions where same-sex behaviour was used deliberately, it would be better read as the invocation of a despised identity to challenge institutional competence.

A further complication was the homicide of a patient by another patient in one of the then Special Hospitals (Department of Health 1992: 151). Staff in Smithtown thought it had occurred in the context of a 'homosexual' liaison. The Rowe report into this death illustrates the institutional confusion about gay sex in the Special Hospitals:

> ... homosexual conduct took place in bedrooms on Forster ward, ... senior social workers accepted that it took place and said that the nursing staff obviously turned a blind eye to its activity: such activity took place either as predatory chance encounters, or in pursuance of a committed sexual association.

Smithtown is not unique in psychiatry in the difficulties it has in relation to things gay and lesbian (King and Bartlett 1999). The belated recognition by mental health authorities of gay and lesbian identity as part of the normal expression of human sexuality, resulting in the removal of the 'homosexualities' from the diagnostic canon, followed a protracted period in which many gay and lesbian patients fared badly (Bartlett et al. 2001; Smith et al. 2004). There is no real equivalent understanding of the expression of sexuality within closed psychiatric institutions to that found in rich, extensive and illuminating prison ethnographies (e.g. Hensley et al. 2003; Sykes 1958).

Having a visible acceptable identity, psychiatrist, and disguising a less acceptable identity, lesbian, was both about maximizing access and about self-protection. Staff greeted slippage from neutrality into psychiatrist with friendliness. It is hard to imagine that revelation of lesbian sexuality would have been greeted similarly. Being a psychiatrist in this case was doing anthropology at home but carried with it the danger that it would leave me ill equipped to consider Smithtown critically. Being a lesbian in Smithtown left me feeling uncomfortable in a way most people do not associate with being 'at home'. Yet the sense that part of me was negatively different, a secret area of unacceptability, was to make me more imaginative about patients to whom disapprobation is familiar. This would look different now. Since the fieldwork was carried out, social attitudes and legislation have changed rapidly. The public sector has had to respond and many hospital trusts have LBGT networks for staff, if not for patients.

Going on to write about this in an anthropological text, i.e. writing anthropology as a lesbian ethnographer, is of course very unusual (Graham 1998: 113). Writing as a psychiatrist ethnographer is much more common, if often underplayed and not problematized. Writing as a woman ethnographer is now utterly unremarkable.

The difference between fact and fiction

Like other anthropologists approaching the field, all three researchers had expectations. We had all anticipated discomfort: smoke-filled dayrooms, early morning starts to get to the hospital for the morning shift. In the evenings, I had warned my fellow researchers that they would have to stay until nine-thirty at night—not a job for the uncommitted.

Fiction

In Patricia Duncker's (1996: 94–6) novel *Hallucinating Foucault*, the hero walks, accompanied by one of the doctors, into a secure hospital. It reads as follows:

> She unlocked the door carefully and looked around as we entered. Then she relocked the door. It was a large open space, sparsely furnished; a television muttered, high up on the wall. The windows were barred and blocked out with thick, opaque squares of reinforced glass. There was dirt on the floor, crumpled paper flung behind chairs, the smell was unmistakable, urine and excrement. Two men with horribly distorted purple faces and vacant stares, shuffled endlessly in the

space. They were white, thin, gaunt; one of them had an arm, twisted and stiff, held against his chest. They smelt unwashed, fusty and old.

Dr Vaury greeted both of them by name and shook hands with them as if they were rational, living beings. . . . Two more doors, unlocked and relocked. And then we were in a corridor with separate bedrooms. The smell was unbearable, a sharp acrid gust of recent human piss. I glanced through one of the open doors; the room was in chaos, with clothes flung on the floor, against the radiator, a broken plastic pot still spinning on the floor, the walls were smeared with fresh excrement.

The hero has come to see one of the patients. Waiting for Paul Michel, he leans against the wall, 'shaking'. They meet; the patient stands very close, breaking the code between strangers that you maintain a particular interpersonal distance. They converse, alone and unsupervised, over a cigarette. Paul Michel, the patient, says,

'Ah-uh. I can't risk the lighter. They won't let me smoke unsupervised.'

'Why not?'

I was horribly afraid of this thin unshaven ghost. He laughed slightly.

'I set fire to the ward.'

Fact

The gap here between fiction at £8.99 and fact at £35 (Department of Health 1992) is narrower than it might appear. Duncker's powerful many-layered fable appeared after we did the research. In its detailing of the ward environment it is similar to some of the descriptions found in the Inquiry into Ashworth Special Hospital (Department of Health 1992: 146):

We observed on our visits to Ashworth that the physical environment at Ashworth North, the old Park Lane site, is potentially very good. All patients have their own rooms and separate sanitation facilities. Some wards had indeed encouraged patients to decorate and 'personalise' their rooms and use the garden area constructively. Overall, however, the layout of the communal rooms, the domination of the day area by the ubiquitous snooker table and the style of furnishings remain institutional. For a relatively new hospital the fabric shows signs of wear and tear in excess of its age. The 'garden area' . . . is bare and barrack like . . .

Ashworth South wards were unacceptably bare and unwelcoming and were pervaded by an atmosphere of hopeless inactivity. Two of us . . . witnessed a young male patient on Beeches ward, encased in a restraint garment preventing movement of the arms and legs, rolling repetitively back and forth on a bare patch of courtyard floor, observed in a desultory fashion by a member of staff sitting on a chair in the corner of the yard. Other patients stood or sat around in the dayroom, there being little communication between patients. The women's wards showed no signs of attempts to create a homely environment.

Both fact and fiction convey succinctly what we could all have been worried about before we began. They are part of the public, as opposed to the professional, discourse about the dangerously mad. They are outside images of the inside of a world which few ever see first hand. Both this and other kinds of information contribute to the expectations of anyone entering a secure Hospital. They also both demand a reaction from the reader. Such writing is not neutral; it invites different kinds of responses: gut reaction, views on civil liberties and fundamental rights and human dignity, on punishment, suffering and one's own ability to cope—whatever coping would be in such circumstances. Fiction, rather than inquiry literature, allows in particular for the unsayable—that perhaps the mad are not quite human. The most consistent feature of hospital inquiry literature is its tone of outrage at various affronts to human dignity. Duncker, being a novelist, is allowed to raise the issue of disgust. In some ways this is liberating for researchers who personally and professionally would not like to be seen as lacking in basic humanity. Writing like Duncker's creates a space for possible responses in a way the authoritative and depersonalized tones of inquiry literature do not.

Showalter (1987) recalls that at one time the public paid to go and look at the mad in Bedlam. In the nineteenth century the public were still entitled, not to say frankly encouraged, to go to look at the mad. There was pride in the new asylums and those running them wanted to show them off; one can only speculate why visitors came, sometimes in large numbers. Even the academic interest in the mad at the turn of the century veered towards an unseemly voyeurism, with the demonstrations by Charcot in Paris of 'cases' of hysteria, mostly, inevitably, women.[7] Charcot held public lectures at Salpetriere in Paris attended by students

---

[7] The diagnosis of hysteria is and was most commonly made in women. This gender imbalance was particularly marked in nineteenth-century psychiatry and is indicated in the origins of the term hysteria, wandering womb, itself.

and members of the public, including Freud. In England and France, the mad were photographed and their images scrutinized. Today there is a waiting list for the guided tour round Broadmoor for professionals. Medical students prefer this trip even to going to prisons. The tabloid press rush into print the latest news of Peter Sutcliffe, the 'Yorkshire Ripper', and Ian Brady, one of the 'Moors Murderers'. The High Secure Hospitals have engendered fascination, revulsion and fear.

We as researchers shared in these kinds of expectations but our responses were also informed by different personal histories and different readings of the background to the project. Unlike Dunker's hero, our reading of background material raised issues about staff and patients.

Being scared of the patients

In my working life I have been assaulted three times by patients; someone tried to kill me with broken glass. I have grown used to being the object of unwelcome sexual fantasy, the detail of which is often unnerving. On a more mundane level, intrusion into personal space or intrusive questioning by potentially dangerous patients is a regular occurrence. But the professional role of psychiatry and the social conventions that follow in terms of the behaviours and expectations of both patients and staff within psychiatric settings confer both a sense of safety and, in reality, a variety of protective measures. Psychiatrists may worry about being killed but this is highly unlikely. Where mental health workers have been killed by patients, it is often because they have failed to notice the possibility (Blom-Cooper et al. 1995).

A difference for me in fieldwork was the sense of being potentially psychologically and physically 'unaccompanied'. In the Duncker passage cited earlier, the hero feels afraid, not when walking with the doctor but when alone with the patient. It is in the patient that the fantasy and possibility of danger primarily reside.

Used chronologically, fieldwork notes shed more light on these experiences. In the first few days of fieldwork I noticed how close together the chairs were in the patients' dayroom. What, I wondered, was I doing sitting and chatting to a bunch of men, a good proportion of whom had raped and killed? I did not know who had done what. Paradoxically the effect of being told by a number of them why they were there was curiously reassuring. For some weeks nothing happened that could be construed as alarming. One or two men stood too close and many, staff and patients, asked personal questions but it was manageable. Strasser and Kronsteiner (1993) worked in rural Turkey. They, as two unaccompanied women in the field, were constantly asked if they were alone. I became familiar with the many possible variations on this question.

My sense of safety relied on the absence of physical contact; this was crucial. Given the nature of the men's offences, their own experiences of abuse and uncertainties about their own physical boundaries, psychotic and otherwise, I relied on their anxiety and the possibility of institutional sanction to maintain distance. The yoga class threw all of this into sharp relief. The class was run by an external yoga teacher. I participated, as did a handful of patients, each week. On the occasion when the teacher suggested partner work, I would have liked to drop out but this did not seem possible, as it would so clearly have indicated a lack of trust. For men who barely converse with women and whose intimate contact with them has often been violent, holding one gingerly around the ankle or waist assumes an unusual importance—however closely supervised. But for the most part this was not an issue, and I felt safe most of the time.

One incident unnerved me. Standing chatting in the corridor of the ward with one of the friendliest of the staff, one of the patients came up to him and hugged him; then the same patient hugged me. Perhaps inadvertently—one will never know—the patient squeezed my left breast. This was not apparent to the member of staff concerned. To me this constituted violation. That it did so, and that it preoccupied me, was to do with where this happened. It signalled my vulnerability to other patients. Like other sexually vulnerable individuals in locked settings (Gilligan 2000; Kauffman 1988: 23–46; Lockwood 1980), I was tied to the ward and to this group of patients. Unlike them, my period in Smithtown was clearly time limited. The sense of vulnerability was increased because it went unremarked by friendly staff—although they did, at my request, talk to the patient in question later in the week. It was the symbolism of this incident, rather than its reality, that was perturbing. In a way I had become an honorary man, whereby it was possible for physical contact to happen between some staff and some patients and for it to be construed as appropriate. But I was a woman.

In another incident I, as the anthropologist, was invited to watch a film about Grendon Underwood, the therapeutic prison for serious sexual and violent offenders. That I am a woman lent another, private, dimension to the experience. Sitting on the ward with a group of men, chosen primarily for their sex-related problems and history of sexual violence, I watched a film about the female victim of a rape and a man who had raped someone else. The film established a dialogue between the two via the presenters. It was impossible in that room not to be aware of my gender and that it made me a potential victim. It was a powerful film that reduced one of the staff to tears and made my snooker partners attentive. The staff aggression (probably unconsciously to do with my having invaded their ward) in inviting me to do this was probably only clear to me. On the one hand, it was an opportunity for a novel piece of participant observation—I did not usually sit in on treatment groups. On the other hand, the staff behaviour mirrored that of the patients in their indifference to women's experiences. The feeling of accompanying passivity was enhanced by being asked to leave at the end of the film so that they could discuss their responses privately. Such a request was not a real request, it was an instruction in keeping with good psychiatric nursing practice—the patients took the decision—but it resonated with the gender-based dynamics and power differential of sexual violence.

My reaction to these incidents was quite at odds with the possibility of psychotic, non-specific violence where the choice of you as victim is arbitrary. The staff were concerned enough to warn me of the possibility of this kind of incident. At the time I responded with complete indifference.

The last supper

This marked the end of my initial period of fieldwork. A group of patients and I were invited to supper cooked by one of the most informative patients. A serious effort was made, involving at least one member of staff going strawberry picking for pudding. The patients' exquisite sensitivity to the reason for inviting me was evident in their comments that Didier too had been invited and could not come because of his shift pattern. To invite me alone was to risk institutional disapproval. In the ward history an invitation to someone had provoked opprobrium—for the woman concerned and for the patients. Tea was too intimate; it created anxiety about the therapist's role—perhaps she was invited as a woman who was liked because of her gender. There was concern that her response was not in keeping with her professional role. She was not the patients' friend. We, with approval, ate fish and chips and peas with plastic cutlery and drank a lot of alcohol-free wine. The formality of this meal, and the contrast with the usual rush of patients' meals, lent the event a strange 'let's pretend' quality.

Thinking about it later

It was only after I left the field and reflected on it that I felt the full impact of being asked to dinner by a group of men who had histories of such serious violence. It was both deeply personal, in that it was me there, and also impersonal, in the sense that anyone else who had been doing my work would have been so asked.

The timing of these reactions had some significance; as Josephides (1997: 25) noted, 'with fieldwork, time and return are crucial factors'. The emotional impact of this indicated something about the nature of participant experience. There is a temporary suspension of real self that allows you into the field. McKnight (1986: 138–9), working in an Aboriginal supercamp where physical fights were common, wrote:

> I was often in the thick of the brawls—not fighting but recording. . . . recently acquired Aboriginal friends and relatives would vehemently threaten that if anyone hit me they would be killed. . . . I now realise that they helped to ensure my safe stay in the field.

He reports a sense of invulnerability in the face of real danger; he needed it to conduct his fieldwork but only later did it occur to him that this was the case. Away from the field, experience percolates through the mind and is distilled out. In my own case it also re-established a sense of difference—and social distance—between a heavily stigmatized group and myself. This meant that I came to a different appreciation of my snooker partners, and one in which the details of their past violence took precedence over their kindness in cooking me dinner. Also, the details of their past serious violence took precedence over the violence of the man who had assaulted me, which seemed of less consequence in the end. The mad are always second-class citizens; the dangerously mad are yet more so. Proximity is contaminating. It may be that in addition to the ordinary process of anthropological analysis, this provided an imperative to distancing.

Being scared of the staff

Despite this focus on fear, and the possibility of violence, most of the time life on the ward was mundane and boring. This is a reflection of the routine nature of institutional life, the lack of new stimuli for staff and patients and the habituation to the social and physical world of the field. They were also the experiences of staff and patients for much of the time.

It had been stated that some staff in the then Special Hospitals had intimidated individuals perceived as antagonistic to certain staff interests and we thought this might be an issue for us. In Ashworth it was stated that there was

> a developed pattern of intimidatory behaviour against those who have been brave enough to speak up about the 'culture' at Ashworth. We have both direct and hearsay evidence of intimidating telephone calls, threats to family, damage to cars and property; even physical assaults (Department of Health 1992: 247).

Given the project's remit and how it had been initially received, this was worrying. We did not know what we were going to find, nor how the attempt at research would be received by any member of staff. It occurred to us that we might not be able to rely on support. Although staff might come to the aid of colleagues in tricky situations, they might be less keen to come to the help of a researcher.

Several stories gave us pause for thought; they were hard to evaluate but could not be ignored. One informant said he had been accosted by patients who had been tipped off by a member of staff. He had feared for his safety in this encounter, which had occurred in a quiet corner of the ward, involving patients who had previously been career criminals and had reputations to match. We were told that a new member of staff had been escorted off his designated ward because he had divulged the fact that staff were eating patients' food, and that a manager had had fake explosives placed under his car. It was therefore comforting to be told by patients that if anything did occur, then other patients would come to my rescue.

The experience of one of the other researchers was revealing. Although taken out for a drink at the end of the fieldwork and presented with a case history of themselves in good spirit, they were also slightly unnerved. One member of staff asked where the researcher lived, leaving the impression that retribution could be inflicted if the 'report' was not to the staff's liking. The researcher was concerned but grateful that the real address had been kept secret. Other staff also saw the fieldwork as sufficiently worrying to provoke jokes about finding another job.

Concern for our safety was an element of the fieldwork experience. It had an impact on, and was part of, the participant observation. The relevance of these considerations to our conduct should be acknowledged. As the coordinator of the research team, I could not put anyone in a position of unacceptable risk from any of our informants.

The fearless anthropologist

There is relatively little anthropological writing on safety and related conduct in the field. This may be because anxiety and fear are individual emotions and thus of only secondary interest to a discipline focused on sociocultural phenomena. However, the field of forensic psychiatry is not exactly full of contributions on how the patients can be frightening. Possibly the common issue is that acknowledgement of fear is seen as a personal weakness and a professional failing. In contrast, both disciplines have much to say on the subject of violence. This has an 'out there' quality, not an 'in here' quality. This spatial imagery is deliberate, with its resonances with bodily boundaries. The impact of fear may be about maintaining the illusion of an objective version of what has happened, which physiological states of high arousal (of which fear is one) undoubtedly compromise. Discomfort is inevitable and unremarkable but fear is too much. Lutz shares my surprise at its conspicuous absence:

> The anthropological denial of danger and hence fear is common and powerful, however, and this is so despite the fact that it might be expected that fieldwork

provides more opportunities than does the home context for the construction of a sense of threat (1988: 191).

We were not the only ones to experience fear in Smithtown but getting it into any kind of perspective seemed important. It was not in any way self-evident that what frightened us would shed light on the experiences of our informants. Fear is socially constructed and different societies do that differently.

Lutz draws attention to what she got wrong. Thus, during her fieldwork in Micronesia she wanted to sleep on her own. To the Ifaluk with whom she was staying, this seemed very dangerous. To her, a man coming into her home at night symbolized possible sexual violence; when this happened, her adoptive Ifaluk family thought it very funny, as the man's wish was for consensual sex. She emphasizes the relative quality of fear, and also the way fear relies on learnt symbols. To anyone who watches late-night movies, the clichéd music and camera work can be both effective and familiar. Reading Patricia Cornwell's crime novels late at night makes you at least temporarily want to check all your window locks are firmly fastened. The feared object and just how frightened you are, are context-dependent.

However, there may be good reasons why anthropology has not dared to tackle fear—other than the difficulty mentioned earlier of incorporating individual responses into participant experience to contribute to what is overtly cultural analysis. The first reason is a preference for the anthropologist to be 'conquering hero'; the second, which relates to women researchers, is of having to be just as heroic, if not more so, as the aptly named Napoleon Chagnon.

Okely argues that Chagnon (1983) avoids self-disclosure while pretending to explain his involvement in his fieldwork with the Yanomamo. She observes that

> on every page the exotic or bizarre as would be understood by the North American or European general reader. The chapters make exciting and sensational reading. We are rarely presented with the range of Chagnon's inner feelings, instead his escapades and heroism in the pursuit of science (Okely 1996: 30).

Given the real threat he encountered among this inhospitable group it would seem understandable if he resorted to manic indifference as a coping strategy but a shame that he stooped to satisfying the reader's base appetites. In Smithtown it might well be tempting to succumb to telling tales of Gothic horror in an effort to transform ethnography into a 'good read' or even 'a gripping yarn'. The patients' stories, either in terms of what happened to them as children or what some have done as adults, would be more than enough to satisfy the most prurient of imaginations.

An alternative response to Smithtown would be to adopt in writing a kind of fearlessness, to downplay issues of personal safety, not with bravado but with indifference. This approach is evident in Codere, writing about a society characterized from outside by recent brutality. With a distinctly stiff upper lip, she says of her work in Rwanda at a time of revolution when physical danger was a distinct possibility and when it would have been odd not to have thought it:

> There were several occasions when the possibility of physical harm was an actuality—all in crowd situations—but their most frightening aspect was my discovery that I was quite fatalistic, an attitude I never held and still do not hold in ordinary circumstances (1986: 162).

She discusses her association with Gahenda, a research assistant in Rwanda, who was said to have killed a Hutu child with a spear. In terse understatement, Codere adds:

> Then there were later stories . . . of how Gahenda . . . had been making various charges against me to the effect that I had not paid him. In any event I had no confrontation with Gahenda, and no more reason to worry about him than about other impersonal reports (1986: 163).

Her concern is that she 'over responded'—her term. Perhaps at the time of the fieldwork—the early 1960s—this was as much to do with the expectations of women and women anthropologists as with the reality of her situation.

In Smithtown it was important for the three researchers to be able to talk about fear and dangerousness, at least amongst themselves. To neglect this would seem negligent if the site of anthropological study is a place you go to when you are in 'grave and immediate danger' if you remain at liberty. Phillips and Earle (2010) comment on the need for prison ethnography to consider reflexivity, hitherto almost entirely ignored. In a compelling account of issues raised in the course of ethnographic work, they discuss the impact of race and gender but never mention what might be seen as inevitable within a similar but different secure setting, i.e. consideration of personal risk.

Being good enough for the job

Our response to the field was sensibly informed by what we knew before we got there. It included a degree of caution about all informants. Once there, we acted on what we already knew to present ourselves. To some extent the wisdom of doing this was borne out by the response to us, which, overall, was more positive than we had been led to believe it might be. To a considerable extent both staff and patients saw us as separate from the institution and took on our research at face value, though they could have doubted its ultimate utility and worried about its impact. There was also evidence that our identities as researchers, as far as our informants were concerned, were flexible and this offered otherwise unavailable insights. Equally, we altered certain aspects of ourselves to elicit certain information. Key features of our identities were central to people's response to us, and these were not mutable. As far as we could tell, our incorporation into ward existence provoked little in the way of permanent alteration, and it was possible both to elicit and evaluate these subtle changes.

Although by the standards of anthropological adventure there were clear components of anthropology 'at home', the passages quoted outline the extent to which that was meaningfully true, how it can affect information gathering, and the extent to which appearances can be deceptive. There are unresolved issues as to the construction of the anthropological self but I have attempted to fill the potential space around the perceived and perceiving self, and indicate the necessity, at least in this fieldwork, for articulating the impact of the social relationships intrinsic to the project. Inevitably, in this case, this has included discussion of our fears and concerns in a setting where safety is a real issue.

This seemed essential. To report on information we established without putting it into a reflexive context would be a serious misrepresentation. Now it is possible to move on to describe the three wards of Smithtown as we found them.

Part 3

Power and praxis: who is in charge of the ward?

Chapter 5

Daily life

These days, anthropologists get remarkably nervous when they discuss culture—which is surprising on the face of it, since the anthropology of culture is something of a success story . . . although everyone is now talking about culture, they do not look to the anthropologists for guidance.
(Kuper 1999: 226–8)

First impressions

When you enter Smithtown there is little to signify that it is any different from many public buildings. Staff sit behind a glass screen, furniture is modern but impersonal and there are the usual, random pot plants. Like visits to prisons, the route you take into the building tells you what kind of person you are. But you may not know this until sometime afterwards. There is a classification process on entry. There are 'staff' entrances and 'other' entrances.

If you are staff, you enter through the staff entrance, are recognized by the reception staff and retrieve your keys. If you are a professional visitor, e.g. lawyer or doctor, you will have your visit pre-booked; on arrival, the unit you are visiting will be informed. You will then wait. After some time a relevant member of staff will appear. You will be let in through the 'other' entrance controlled by the staff keys. You will not pass the racks of keys. You will be escorted until you reach a ward. If you are a friend or relative of a patient you will arrive with others like you, more often than not. You too will wait. You may pass an electronic screen of the kind used before boarding aeroplanes. The purpose of this is to make sure you are not bringing in anything undesirable, e.g. knives or metal saws. You will be let in through the 'other' entrance by staff with keys. You will form a herd and be shepherded, by escorting staff, to the communal meeting place. Again, you do not pass the keys.

If you are a patient, you will not arrive alone; you will come with guards or escorts—in a van. Where other people leave their cars in a car park, the van with you inside will pass into the 'airlock' between two large electronically controlled gates. You will have escorts from where you came and from Smithtown. You may well be driven to the ward.

As Parker-Pearson and Richards (1994: 3) have said, 'architectural discourse can be psychologically persuasive, or experienced inattentively'. Entering Smithtown is both. There is a high wall. There is no mistaking its significance; it symbolizes protection and privacy, and in so doing is ambiguous. It keeps people both in and out. Low boundaries are about friendliness and openness; a high brick wall is not. They do not build such walls, yet, around children's nurseries. As Foucault (1979: 116) notes, the high wall of medieval cities was about protection, as any casual visitor to Italy and France will observe. While his argument is persuasive, it is also true that the Tower of London is old, high walled and protective but it has also proven useful over centuries for the incarceration of politically troublesome rivals. Fairy-tale representations of damsels in distress often feature incarceration within castle walls. The meaning of the high wall in the past has depended on your relation to it. The more contemporary association is more straightforward and is with the state prison and the power to punish (Foucault 1979: 101). This is true whether it is the familiar turreted entrance of HMP Wormwood Scrubs, vaguely reminiscent of a castle, or the small entrance set in a modern, unremarkable brick wall at HMP/YOI Holloway.

In contrast, the divisions of social identity allocated by the route of entry may be less clear to the occasional visitor. For staff and patients they will be echoed and reinforced and challenged in the course of prolonged, daily usage of the physical environment of the wards and the rest of Smithtown. That is the strength of ethnography. It starts with daily life, sees it, thinks about it and analyses it. Based on the three wards, the ethnographic material creates a general outline of ward life, who are the key players and how the key players relate to each other. This involves thinking both about life as it is timetabled and also what else happens. This lends itself to a meaningful analysis of power—who is in charge and in what domains and how, at the level of the ward, is power exerted. An interesting juxtaposition is to think just how many times and in what ways our own lives are affected by institutionalized micro-power: parking fines, stopping at a barrier to produce a railway ticket on demand, not driving as fast as you might like, waiting in a lunch queue in a café. This is a dimension of understanding that is seldom articulated in either prison or psychiatric literature. Freedom is not absolute. Non-institutional life has rules too and most of us are compliant, most of the time.

Against a canvas of institutional norms, it is also possible to see how individuals achieve a degree of individual expression. This is not necessarily defiance of the rules. Traditionally, in prison writing, this is thought of as prisoners being antagonistic to a defining regime. Often termed resistance, it may be a group phenomenon and thus a cultural phenomenon. Sometimes, it is an assertion of individual identity and difference. Smithtown is not a prison and so it is more sensible to ask what individual expression can mean, rather than assuming we understand either its intent or impact.

The three wards discussed in detail are Toulouse, Paris and Lille. They had institutionally distinct purposes, different timetables and staff specifically allocated to each one to look after the particular population living there. Unlike prisons, where the turnover of inmates can be very rapid, these wards had fairly static populations.

What is a ward?

Wards constitute the central focus of the study. Ward is an old word whose archaic meaning in Middle English and Norman French was to guard or to protect. To guard someone is to protect them from harm but also to keep them in. There is an ambiguity in the word that has been handed down through the centuries and which has now found a home in general and psychiatric hospitals. Closely related etymologically are the words warder and warden; the first relates to prisons, the second to another kind of institution, as in Oxford University colleges.

Smithtown wards have an inescapable physical and organizational reality. Everyone knew their ward, staff and patients. Staff had responsibility for the running of particular wards. Wards have operational policies and ward meetings of various kinds. Patients in their own newspaper were referred to by their ward, never their name. In institutional correspondence, the ward of the patient was usually given.

Patients were admitted to, transferred between and discharged from particular wards; the passive verb was deliberate. As far as staff were concerned patients do not come to, move between or leave wards or Smithtown itself. Patients are physical objects to whom things are done, linguistic objects about whom words are said, as Stanton and Schwartz (1954) observed earlier. In non-secure hospitals, psychiatric and general, patients are admitted and discharged, interviewed and examined. There is a linguistic reinforcement in medical discourse of the passivity of all patients; yet many *people*, rather than *patients*, go and see doctors, go to hospital, decide to have treatment. So too, now do service users. This is the politically preferred term for patients in mental health services. The term's active tense is deliberate and currently linked with the 'Recovery Agenda', which emphasizes choice, self-determination and engaging on your own terms with mental health services, with a view to not needing much, if anything at all (Leamy et al. 2011). In Smithtown, patients said of themselves that they moved wards and left hospital. They were ahead of their time. Wards have parties, get post and have reputations.

Patients were absent from the ward for much of the day. Many were checked out of the ward early in the day and returned at the end of the day. They went to work and came home after work. Patient existence on these study wards had a stability strikingly absent from that of the acute psychiatric patient or the acute medical patient. Bed occupancy levels in metropolitan psychiatric hospitals are high. The person who returns from weekend leave on Monday morning can find their possessions in a plastic bag and a different duvet cover on the bed. The acute medical patient is likely to find him/herself daily moved further away from the nursing station as their condition improved. The pace of life was slower in Smithtown. Most patients did not venture outside the hospital from one year to the next; they might well visit the outside world only in their imagination.

By comparison, staff occupied many more physical and social arenas. They went home at the end of their working day and had lives which existed spatially and temporally beyond the perimeter wall. Nursing staff were allocated to particular wards. They would spend most of the nursing shift on the ward, only leaving it for short periods, commonly to escort people to and from the entrance or to work areas. In contrast, medical, social work, education and psychology staff would usually only come onto the ward for specified meetings or interviews and only rarely spent more than half a day there. They worked on more than one ward. Nursing staff sometimes opted to do overtime on wards other than their own but this did not change their formal attachment to a single ward. The experience of overtime on another ward was often very different from work on their own ward; it brought with it a lack of familiarity with routines and with patients; the main incentive was financial. Clinical work on wards was based around a 'multidisciplinary team', which over-lapped, but not entirely, with the ward. All nursing staff on the ward were part of the multidisciplinary team but some members of that team were members of other teams too. The term multidisciplinary team is com-mon in contemporary psychiatric practice. It was introduced to indicate and probably encourage team working, combating both the isolation and individualism of the past. The elements of a team would routinely include junior and senior psychiatrists, junior and senior nurses, a social worker, a psychologist and an occupational therapist. Such teams are led with differing styles and degrees of autocracy by a consultant psych-iatrist. This is periodically disputed and debated but the system remains the same, not least because the combination of medico-legal authority, weight of numbers and access to administrators continue to favour doc-tors. Decision-making will play out the tensions in teams; input and presence at key venues such as ward rounds will indicate the state of the game to interested observers.

The ward was central to an analysis of Smithtown life but lines of com-munication stretched out from it. There was an administrative hierarchy, a disciplinary hierarchy for the different professions and a political hier-archy in the form of unions. For patients there were friendships, rela-tionships, work and recreational activities that both emotionally and literally crossed the boundaries of the ward. The physical boundary of the ward was socially permeable but it was still a place of confinement.

Wards had an individual 'operational policy'. They said something about what was supposed to be happening, why and to whom. They were also useful here because they suggested that the patients' groups on the three study wards differed according to institutional, though not strictly psychiatric, criteria. Operational policies gave a flavour of the wards from a semi-official perspective. From this arbitrary starting point, a picture can develop of the ways in which the wards were different from, and similar to, each other on a daily basis (see Box 5.1).

Box 5.1 Differences between the three wards: Toulouse, Paris and Lille

Toulouse

- a male ward
- 'low dependency'
- emphasizes the relaxed atmosphere of the ward
- range of group therapies
- physical environment not recently improved
- patients should be able to use group therapy
- complete multidisciplinary team
- day shift: five nurses on duty, all male

Paris

- a male ward
- 'medium- and high-dependency' patients
- small number of 'low-dependency' patients
- high security for the protection of patients and staff
- no outside exercise space
- variable lengths of stay

Box 5.1 Differences between the three wards: Toulouse, Paris and Lille *(continued)*

- ◆ complete multidisciplinary team
- ◆ day shift: six nurses on duty, all male

Lille

- ◆ a female ward
- ◆ heterogeneous group of patients
- ◆ ward environment not refurbished
- ◆ incomplete multidisciplinary team
- ◆ day shift: nine nurses on duty, mostly female

What are people supposed to do all day?

Daily routines were evident to the researchers on arrival. They proved to be of enduring significance. Visible routines were tributes to the power of temporal and spatial rhythms imposed by this institution, just as had been true elsewhere over time.

> The time table is an old inheritance. The strict model was no doubt suggested by the monastic communities. It soon spread. Its three great methods—establish rhythms, impose particular occupations, regulate the cycles of repetition—were soon to be found in schools, workshops and hospitals (Foucault 1979: 149).

A thin version of daily life on the wards was mapped out on noticeboards on all three wards. One noticeboard consisted of the 'work' allocations for patients for the day; another indicated ward activities for the week. Information about patients referred to administratively critical features of their identities: their names, admission dates, section status (i.e. classification under the Mental Health Act) and dates of birth. This information was compiled by staff and kept within ward offices into which patients would infrequently venture. In contrast, the staff duty rota, an equivalent piece of paper, was kept more privately in the staff mess on Toulouse ward. Ward life was, however, lived beyond the administrative summaries, in the repetition and individuality of the day, the week and the year(s).

Daytime: being up and about

All wards in Smithtown had the same shift system for nursing staff. Day staff worked either an 'a.m.' or a 'p.m.' shift on any given day, sometimes doing overtime by working 'long days'. Night staff only worked nights. Although the other clinical staff, and the more senior nursing staff, worked hours which crossed over the shift times, the formal boundaries of the patients' days and nights corresponded with the shift systems in operation at that time.

The consequence of this was that much of the day was officially night, in the sense that patients were confined to their rooms and dormitories for longer than they needed to sleep. During fieldwork, patients were locked into their rooms or dormitories from nine o'clock in the evening to seven in the morning. Night staff arrived just before locking up and left just after opening up. They had very little contact with patients.

On all three wards, patients rose, washed and dressed. For men, shaving was supervised by staff before breakfast; razors were counted. Patients dressed at their own pace and in their own clothes. It is recorded that in previous years in Special Hospitals, patients would collect clothes each morning from the ward stores, dress either in a main corridor or in the billiard room, and hand back night clothes to the store-man (Department of Health and Social Security 1980).

Within a 9-to-5 day, there were formal meetings held on each ward. They varied in frequency and intent but most had a clinical objective (see Appendix A). Their official quality was evident from the fact that they tended to make it onto a staff noticeboard. Their impact on ward life was a function both of this and the geography of the ward; where groups or meetings happened, this required the attendance of staff and patients in variable numbers and proportions. When this occurred, one of the large rooms on the ward would inevitably be occupied, potentially displacing other would-be inhabitants.

On all three wards smoking was relevant to the pattern of subsequent activity; smoking areas on all three wards were restricted.[1]

---

[1] In line with hospital policy nationwide. This was in some contrast to prisons.

Cancellation of meetings was not unknown. Clinical team meetings, management rounds and case conferences only happened if the RMO (Responsible Medical Officer, always the consultant psychiatrist for the ward) was available. The community meeting on Paris was also dependent on the presence of the RMO or the ward manager. The groups on Toulouse varied. The groups run singly by the social worker and the psychologist were most vulnerable. Those run under the supervision of the psychotherapist were more resilient and were assisted by the interchangeability of the nursing staff. The groups run by specific nursing staff required a high degree of commitment from staff, who, though no doubt paid extra, were expected to come in on days off and did so. The emphasis on group work was something of which the staff on Toulouse were proud. It was part of their image of themselves as having a specialist function, one which originated in the energy and enthusiasm specifically of the nursing staff. By contrast, Paris nursing staff attached importance not only to the hospital being the end of the line in terms of dangerous patients but also that they managed particularly problematic patients. No such clear pattern of their task was discernible on the women's ward. Comparisons of nursing style were made by those on the ward, suggesting that some were 'office wallahs' and others more ready to engage with patients.

What else was there to do?

The formal, largely clinical meetings did not fill much time. How much time people spent on the ward depended first, on whether they were staff or patients, and second, if they were patients, whether or not they had a range of off-ward activities.

Ward-based nursing staff were just that. During a shift, the opportunities to be off the ward were few and far between (occasional escorting of patients on trips to external hospitals or family, occasional cover on other wards). Other professionals flitted in and out for meetings or to see specific patients.

Some patients were truly ward-based; others had a range of activities they went to during the day and in the early evening. These off-ward activities, work and recreation included a variety of mixed social functions (films, music and parties), educational activities (classroom teaching on basic subjects and independent study) and a range of work (including sewing, brick laying, print work, gardening), and playing different sports or attending sports functions. It may come as a surprise that patients were able to participate in quite such a large range of activities. The organizational skills required to build a doll's house or play in a football team conflict with stereotypes of madness. Certainly it is true that some people did not and could not undertake a complex range of activities but many did. Equally, others exerted active choices about how they wanted to fill their day, which might include choosing *not* to do things.

So far, everything has been written in terms of staff and patients. These are key categories but they need to be fleshed out, as neither category is self-explanatory. Most obviously different from the analyses of power within prisons is that the staff group was more heterogeneous. One consequence of this was that their spheres of influence correspondingly varied. Within the microcosm of a ward, it is possible to see how staff behaved generically and how they could bring individuality to their particular roles. So too could, and did, the patients. The combination of talk and observation makes it possible to add depth to an understanding of the social identities of both types of staff and types of patient.

What is it that staff do?

Never before or since have I had so much understanding of what staff actually do at work, as opposed to who is in the team. As training for clinical management, ethnography is hard to beat.

Each ward had a staff team that followed the same basic structure: ward manager, team leaders, staff nurses, enrolled nurses and nursing auxiliaries (NAs). The exact proportions of these varied. In addition, there was, in principle, a social worker, a psychologist and a consultant psychiatrist for the ward (RMO for the ward's patients) and a staff-grade doctor (non-training grade). Non-nursing staff were considered as part of their own discipline's department, e.g. psychology department or social work department. Doctors did not have a department as such. Only one of the wards studied had input from training psychiatrists.[2] Senior medical staff complained that the absence of training grades was unsatisfactory, as it meant highly trained staff did the work normally done by juniors, and they considered that this made it impossible for them to carry out their jobs as they would wish.

In addition to the basic complement of staff outlined, the wards had other inputs, e.g. psychotherapists, a yoga teacher, an art therapist and staff from the Rehabilitation Therapy Services (occupations) department and education department, who appeared on the ward sporadically.

However, in many ways the wards were the preserve of the nursing staff. They spent most of their day there and were on duty for at least four days out of six. This was so true that the term 'staff' tended to mean only nurses, rather than including other professions. Nursing staff, unlike other staff, worked on wards of their own gender. The only exception to this was that a small number of male nurses worked on the women's side. The social workers, doctors and psychologist would spend limited periods of time on the ward. Historically, this pattern of doctors' work is well documented (Scheff 1961). How they used this time was very different. Doctors spent most of the time either in meetings, which were a mixture of administration and clinical activity, or talking alone to patients. Doctors spent short periods of time in informal conversation with anyone; the same was true of social workers and psychologists. How nursing staff spent their time depended in part on their grade, this being most noticeable in the different activities undertaken by trained and untrained nursing staff.

It was quite possible for doctors not to speak to nursing assistants, as they would not occupy the same physical space. The status distinctions of the hospital's formal hierarchy informed patterns of interaction between staff.

Routine and security were critical to trained nursing staff. Characteristic of conversation was not patient-centred information but rather the repetitive elements of ward life, i.e. unlocking and locking patients' rooms, checking diaries, serving meals, supervising razors for shaving,

---

[2] Elsewhere in psychiatric hospitals around the UK there were Senior House Officers and, often, Specialist Registrars. These are training grades and lead to consultant appointments.

dealing with visitors and escorting. This is apparent in the account of an experienced staff nurse:

> Etienne felt the shifts are different but that if he works in the morning he will check out if anything of significance has occurred during the night, whether anyone is in seclusion. When the rooms and dormitories are opened he will check the patients are 'alive'. The patients will wash and shave and some will require prompting for self-care. The patients' breakfast is for him a full security check. Then follows medication and getting patients off to 'work', education or the multi-gym. The visit of the doctor and telephoning around the hospital may then happen, and also running groups. He sees the patients filtering back for lunch, more medication and having a relaxation period before they go back to 'OT'. In the second half of the day he notices that the 'multidisciplinary team wanes away' after 4 p.m. and he will do primary nursing in the second shift. He remarked that this can be 'difficult with patients who go to a lot of social functions'.

Etienne's observations suggested that limited overtime meant he was not on the ward as often as others. As a non-smoker, he frequented the smoking areas of the ward mainly to play snooker. He would attend case conferences, go on occasional trips out with his own patients and attend handovers. He was not infrequently seen doing the crossword in the privacy of the mess or the nursing office.

A regular activity, and one unique to qualified staff, was giving out medication; this happened three times a day. Giving infrequent but regular injections of medication was also their job. Other medical tasks included monitoring or reporting patients' physical health problems, e.g. testing of diabetics' blood sugars. These were presented in interview, since they were observed by the researchers as activities that precluded in-depth conversation of any kind—personal or otherwise. Senior ward-based nurses found their time taken up with administration, usually paperwork, but in the case of ward managers, also meetings. Half volunteered, as an aspect of a typical day, activity where the patient himself was the primary focus, e.g. seeing patients for whom staff were primary nurses or shared recreational activity (snooker, dominoes), which allowed for prolonged conversation or observation.

> Eric preferred to describe his work in terms of a long day, saying this reflected the amount of overtime he undertook. He said, 'You work as per things crop up . . . and at the same time you keep in mind your patients.' By this he meant the patients to whom he was primary nurse; if the primary nurse was not present he would

take on the task of sorting problems out. He took part in groups, and liaised with doctors. He would deal with telephone queries to the ward, serve meals, arrange external trips to see transferred patients in less secure units around the country. He will help patients sort things out. "You make a lot of phone calls for the patients because they have got nothing; they rely on you to ring.' He added, "He can't ring, he can't walk there, and you start putting yourself in his place . . . who is going to do it if not the nurses?' Other tasks he undertook included taking requisitions to the canteen, 'portering jobs', escorting to 'the gate or reception'. He added, ironically, that this is what staff nurses do. Later, he said, 'You sit down, you play your dominoes . . . you make the best of it.'

Observation of his activities showed that he went to case conferences when he was primary nurse for a patient, dispensed medication, served meals, attended handovers, played dominoes with the patients and dealt with ward paperwork, interspersed with talking to patients, often in a bantering tone which they enjoyed, sometimes swapping gambling tips.

These trained staff nurses were either Registered Mental nurses or enrolled nurses, who were called[3] 'Qualified Staff'. Their grading system for pay meant not all staff nurses were paid the same. The grading system extends high into the nursing hierarchy, past team leaders and ward managers into the truly managerial nursing posts. Because of changes in the nursing structure (the introduction of the ward manager post with two team leaders rather than three charge nurses), anomalies existed. Among the staff nurse group were nurses who had been charge nurses and continued to be paid at that level.

NAs are unqualified staff. In the past, in Smithtown, as elsewhere, their job was often a stepping stone to nurse training. The numbers in the hospital were small. NAs are cheaper than qualified nurses. None of those encountered either nurtured ambitions to train as nurses, nor did they view it as expected. Several staff commented on the increase in the numbers throughout the hospital and their use on difficult wards with high levels of interpersonal violence. Many patients on Toulouse commented on their appreciation of nursing assistants. Without nurse training, their union affiliation was necessarily non-nursing. They had very varied

---

[3] Systematic interview material on what staff did on an individual basis is only available for male wards. Scrutiny of fieldwork material for the women's ward shows similarities in nursing and other roles.

backgrounds and some had worked in the hospital in other capacities. The fact that they have not been professionally induced in the nursing or medical role can lead to views that contrast with professional ideas of illness. The development and utilization of common-sense categories by such staff has been known to be a feature of work in psychiatric hospitals for many years (Bucher and Schatzman 1962).

> Francois comes to work 'to do a little bit more than necessary'. He sees his work as things that are not nursing, and says he steers clear of anything that smacks of 'mental health'. His day requires him to undertake a variety of different tasks, which might include the following: encouraging the patients to get up, supervising razors, booking the patients out to work, helping with the laundry, 'condemning' clothes and acquiring replacements, supervising the cutlery for meals and empty- ing the rubbish bags. He perceives half jokingly a 'labyrinthine bureaucracy' as a challenge to the achievement even of basic tasks, such that the faint-hearted will give in all too gracefully.

He was most often to be seen working; he was infrequently seen in the mess reading the papers and drinking tea, or even eating meals there. In addition to the jobs outlined, he would often supervise the patients' use of the telephone in the evening. He never attended clinical meetings and was only occasionally present in nursing handovers.

In terms of typical tasks, there was considerable overlap with trained staff but a greater emphasis on unskilled activities. Nursing assistants, like trained staff, unlocked and locked patients' rooms, served meals, checked cutlery and escorted patients and visitors. They were more likely to hand out work chits for off-ward activity and escort people around, and uniquely dealt with laundry and rubbish bins and undertook the role of 'radio man'.[4] They played a different role in relation to other rou- tine activities, e.g. not serving medication but washing medicine pots.

> Gerard describes the components of his working day as follows: on a laundry day the dirty linen comes in. He supervises one of the patients bagging it up. He sorts out escorts for the morning to take patients for their various activities. Halfway through the morning he checks rooms, both for forgotten laundry and items not allowed in rooms such as plastic bags. He also serves meals and washes up medi- cation pots after medication rounds. He may escort patients himself to external

---

[4] See glossary of terms, Appendix E.

activities like the sports field, though this is rare on his ward, or to evening functions. He comments, 'In the evening there is not that much to do; you usually play snooker, table tennis or watch TV.' At nine o'clock he locks up the patients and goes off-duty twenty minutes later.

Observation of his work showed that he was often radio man for the ward, in charge of arranging and monitoring patients' and visitors' movements in and out of the ward. He escorted patients himself and spent time on the ward chatting in the nursing mess and watching TV. The notes do not record him in spontaneous conversation with a patient.

Ward differences are apparent in terms of NA work. The patient group on Toulouse had ward work, which overlapped with the NA role, e.g. putting out the rubbish and washing medicine pots.

Despite the differences between wards and between grades of staff in terms of activities, there was surprising uniformity of opinion among the day nurses in terms of what kept them coming to work. Crucial to a sense of fulfilment for these staff was working in a team characterized by team spirit and good working relationships and helping patients, both in a day-to-day sense (either explicitly therapeutically or by having a good rapport with them) and in helping them move on, perhaps even to leave Smithtown. It was also true that among the Paris staff there were men who declared there was nothing satisfying about their job; this was not true of Toulouse.

Problems with their work were more varied, although it was easy to identify managerial action either as the explicit cause of perceived difficulties or as being behind them. A second group of concerns voiced by male and female nurses were to do with dealing with patients when they were aggressive or antagonistic, particularly where this led to the use of physical restraint. Staff could get hurt, and even if they were not physically injured, such incidents were demanding:

> The consultant challenged Xavier (patient) about it (drug taking) and this made him angry. The patient was sitting in a chair when the nurses went to take him to seclusion. Yves went up to him first and, as he approached, the patient sprang to his feet and punched him twice in the face very quickly. During the incident five members of staff were hit with chairs. Yves said he was hit twice with a chair and eventually managed to get in close. He was then punched repeatedly . . .

Staff were aware that incidents like this might lead to patient complaints and were pleased if other staff members, especially consultants, were witnesses.

Persistent verbal abuse was very wearing and not uncommon on Paris. On rare occasions, it was witnessed that staff lost their capacity to deal with this:

> Through the glass partition I can see Jean-Jacques (staff) at the far end of the games room. He is being shouted at by Guillaume. I hear Guillaume (patient) shout, 'You fuck off, you fucking bastard.' Jean-Jacques then shouted, 'You are the worst fucker I have ever come across, you fucking wanker.' As Guillaume shouted this, Gerard (staff) was next to him, along with Etienne (staff). They both stared in my direction. Jean-Jacques then looked in my direction. Guillaume continued shouting abuse but Jean-Jacques was then quietly spoken and I could not hear what he was saying.

Dealing with stresses of this kind was a necessary part of Smithtown nursing life but it seldom directly affected other disciplines. It is well recognized that being a secure hospital nurse was likely to be more stressful than working elsewhere, partly because of the likelihood and gravity of major incidents (Jones 1987). The climate of the work environment could also affect enthusiasm for using physical restraint (Griffin 1999). It is also recognized that the role of management is to provide sensible support structures for injured or traumatized staff, which go some way to reducing the likelihood of burnout in the staff group (Kidd and Stark 1995).

Day staff had significant levels of patient contact; however, they chose to inhabit their role. This was not true for night staff. Descriptions and observation of night-shift work emphasized that it was fundamentally about maintaining security both on and off the ward. The imperative was to prevent escapes and suicides, which, as in other psychiatric institutions, were not unknown. When not actually checking these things, staff watched videos. If they slept, which would be understandable in view of the tedium of the job, they did so when the researchers were absent.

Dormitories were checked by walking into them and shining torches around. Individual rooms were checked by flashing lights through the locked door. Going into dormitories had been decided upon following a well-publicized escape. Night staff wore slippers in order that their regular perambulations did not wake everyone up. However, observation material showed that the presence of five or six men in the middle of your dormitory did not make for an uninterrupted night's sleep for everyone.

Night staff were few in number. All had previously worked on days. Their comments were distinctive in tone and content. Imposing security was their main source of satisfaction. One man said he got most satisfaction out of

> [l]ocking the fuckers up! You are not in touch with the patients on nights because they are locked up . . . Some patients have a nice side to them and you can build up a rapport with them and some even respect you. Some are fucking horrible assholes . . .

Segal (1962) and Perucci (1974) both highlight major differences between day and night hospital staff, which relate to the small number of staff on night shift. They have little contact with high-status staff and have few colleagues to reinforce their attitudes, and are thus dependent on strict interpretation of overtly custodial rule. Reliable night shifts, or day shifts make planning for individual members of staff easier. There are still health services that have separate staff groups. Health staff in HMP/YOI Holloway maintained this system, even after health provision passed to the NHS, and are only now moving to integrated rotas.

The repetitive practical tasks that characterized nurses' roles were less evident in the accounts of other clinical disciplines. Social workers and consultant psychiatrists spent much of their time off the wards and outside the hospital. Although the content of their day differed considerably, *all* the non-nursing staff included working with patients as an element of their typical work. Seeing patients was a deliberate activity and aspects of patient care were the most rewarding part of their job, e.g. seeing patients leave. This contrasted with the more incidental contact, observed by all three researchers to be the main component of nursing staff interactions with patients. Discontent was generated by bureaucracy, meetings and memos, as well as concerns about having to deal individually with too many patients.

What is it that patients do all day?

Although Smithtown was cut off from the world in the sense of very few patients in a given year going outside the hospital walls, inside there was considerable movement. The detail patients provided about their days revealed the absence of variety and new challenges, down to small elements of their tasks; their existence remained essentially the same day in, day out.[5]

Patients' accounts express a vision both of the group movements—the troop formations necessary to travel round the hospital escorted by nursing staff, the meals en masse—and of their own private rituals, e.g. tea in the morning. Much is mundane. Within their accounts there is an almost total absence of either acknowledgement of therapy (which was observed happening) or of activity that might make them stand out from the crowd.

> Boris on a typical day will get up and shower. He has breakfast and then goes to work. He comes back for dinner and then has a pot of tea. He is out at work in the afternoon, returning at four o'clock to do some ward work. He will have tea, relax and then go out in the evening to see his partner. The social evening ends at 8 pm. He will watch some television, go to bed and watch more television. Getting off the ward is a high priority for him, as he says, 'Time in other areas is well spent.' Boris is not conspicuous on the ward. This is in part because he attends as many social activities as possible. He is likely to check whether social functions are happening and if not, to want to have this communicated to his partner.

The absence of a preoccupation with therapy is a feature of staff accounts. Absence can be interpreted in several ways, e.g. it is so pervasive that it is unnecessary to say it, or it is truly absent. In the case of these male patients it is likely to be complicated in many cases by a disagreement with psychiatry as to whether or not they needed to be in hospital or have treatment. Patients did mention medication. Only rarely did patients identify 'groups' therapy in which almost all of the patients on one ward were involved. Examples of activity that might make them stand out from the crowd were learning foreign languages or writing creatively; these were non-prescribed activities and thus were different from going to particular work areas or to education. The following patient excerpts are chosen to illustrate these general points:

---

[5] As in the previous section information for the male wards is more robust than for the female ward, and uses all field notes and interviews except where stated.

Up at 7.30. Get dressed. Plug in my tape so I have music when I'm getting up. I have a cigarette. I have selected breakfast, a mug of drink. Have medication, have a cigarette and a cup of coffee if you can and then get ready to go to education (i.e. put your jacket on), e.g. Monday to education where I am writing a science fiction story. I would have a drink in the school and then go back to the ward. I'd have a mug of coffee, have a chat and a smoke and have lunch.

Get up. Shave and wash. Collect lighter. Cup of coffee in the quiet room. Breakfast— open boxes, put everything in place. Make teas for breakfast. Put milk out and 9 small teapots. Clear up the scullery. Goes to the kitchen gardens. Comes back. At dinner mop floor, clean up . . . 6–6.15 checks the scullery for cleanliness and p.m. gets a couple of hot water bottles ready for Christophe and Dominic. Finishes by asking everyone if they want hot water. Last chance coffee and tea announcement. 8.10 that's when my day ends.

Toulouse and Paris were very different in terms of the number of patients who remained on the ward during the day. Among the Paris patients were some who were physically confined to the ward, sometimes also lacking access to their rooms for much of the day. These were the patients the researcher was most likely to encounter, as they had to be in the day areas of the ward. Exactly what this meant is illustrated here:

After breakfast I do the washing up and then have my own breakfast (on my own). I have another cigarette and go to my room and stay for a while. I just lie on the bed. I come out now and again for a cigarette and go back to my room. I do writing in my room. I wrote a play. I try to learn German. . . . I come out again at lunchtime. I make the tea and put out some water for them to drink and after lunch I do the washing up again. I might play a game of snooker or table-tennis and then it might be tea time. I put out the plates, make the tea and then wait until Etienne has finished clearing up and then wash up again. I go to my room for some of the afternoon. After tea I smoke and watch TV. After that I might read the papers and play snooker or table-tennis. Then I will wait for meds and go to bed.

On Toulouse there were one or two patients whose reluctance to go to any kind of activity marked them out. Their days were limited to what was at times an almost empty ward in which they sat one could say watching television but it might be more accurate to say with the television on in the same room. This is very different from the levels of physical confinement found in segregation units in prison or the levels of supervision and confinement found in intensive care psychiatric settings but might involve a similar level of social isolation.

It is significant that whether or not these men gave detailed accounts of their day, none of them suggested that life was so varied that it was difficult to describe. This is in contrast to almost all the non-nursing staff and a few of the nursing staff. The days of the male patients were constrained by the institutional timetable. This is also true in broad terms for the women's ward, even though the same individualized accounts were not obtained. The following field note excerpt from Lille, from a typical morning, also illustrates this balance of individual desire and institutional rule:

> The conversation moved on to the patient day. Laure was saying that during the week a lot of patients were getting up late because they do not have to go to breakfast. They get up at 8.45, get dressed and go straight to work and some of them were beginning to smell but there is nothing the staff can do about it. . . . She said that the patients used to queue for breakfast but not any more. The only ones who do so are those who are so institutionalized they do not know any different. . . . The dayroom was a real mess. There were brimming ashtrays all over the place, tables with coffee spilt over them, magazines scattered around on the chairs and on the floor and a horrendous stale smell of cigarette smoke hanging around. There were not many patients around and mainly they were in their dressing gowns. . . . All of them were waiting for medication to be finished so they could have a cigarette. Francoise was complaining, as it had taken 25 minutes. She said it never used to take that long before they started this business with the lighter. Isabelle said it did. It took longer but patients did not notice, as they were allowed to smoke. Everyone was waiting for Suzanne, who would not get out of bed to get her medication. . . . In the end it took 45 minutes before the lighter was switched back on. Ongline told me to write that down. Ongline had been getting up and down to see how medication had been getting on. She came back in and said medication was finished and offered her lighter around. Patients immediately lit up. Isobelle, who had been in the office, came rapidly back into the dayroom and said sarcastically, "I assume medication is finished ladies," and unlocked the lighter. This caused cheeky smiles from Ongline, Nathalie and Renate, who had snuffed out the lit cigarettes.

The tedium of daily life is not unique to High Secure Hospitals but the level of interest created by new faces in the community indicates the poverty of the social world. Weekends, when work activities ceased, were particularly uneventful for patients without visitors:

> Helene repeated that she wanted to be free because she is a free person. She does not like to be shut in like this. She said Smithtown is very boring and the same things happen every day. Each day is exactly the same. She could not think of

anything that would improve this; nothing could be exciting in here. The one good thing she said was that she went to school, because at least she could use her mind there. Irene also said that she just wanted to get out . . . She agreed with Helene that it was very boring at Smithtown. . . . Helene said she put on two stone in a year. She said it was the medication and the inactivity.

A break in the tedium of daily life could be generated by emotional crisis. At these times, patients discernibly needed privacy and this could be hard to achieve because of the need to be seen out of your room. Staff were praised by patients for their concern at these difficult times but the nearness of other patients and the need to negotiate alterations in routine was visibly taxing. Such events were hard to manage, though other patients were often tactfully avoidant as news of serious events seeped out into the ward.

What they thought of one another: categories, cohesion and divisions

It is already obvious that staff and patients are key categories in Smithtown life with practical impact. Now we explore them conceptually from different perspectives.[6] Symbolic meaning may be separable from day-to-day experiences but if the category of meaning has resilience, there will be a relationship between what happens on the ground, in social action, and what resides in the individual or collective mind.

What kinds of staff are there really?

The heterogeneity of the staff group is underlined by the way in which they themselves created multiple others (by gender, by ward location, by race, by being of Smithtown, by being nurses). The multidisciplinary team may function as such in clinical decision-making but it does not describe the reality of social allegiance for staff. In contrast, a point of consensus was an antipathy to management; all clinical staff recognized 'management' as other, providing an otherwise divided staff group with a focus for cohesion.

---

[6] This relies on fieldwork material from all researchers.

There were also tensions within the nursing group. The fault lines varied. Some staff felt outside the Smithtown network, with its emphasis on looking out for each other. It was hard to ascertain the importance of a network among nursing staff operating outside formal organizational lines. If you were part of it you did not talk about it, and if you were outside, you had an incomplete picture. Certainly there were families in Smithtown, both horizontal and vertical. A third of nursing staff had either partners who worked in Smithtown or came from a family in which more than one person had been employed by Smithtown.[7] In addition, there were nursing staff who lived, worked and socialized adjacent to the hospital. This was much less true of the non-nursing staff, and when it occurred might be thought odd.

It was alleged that these kinds of connections gave people an investment in Smithtown and its history that went far beyond the ordinary. The information and support it offered could be thought both to exclude relative outsiders from job opportunities and cover up for people. As one person commented, 'the job he had applied for on Lyon had already been taken before it was advertised. It had already been decided who was going to get the job. He said it is just jobs for the boys.'

Almost all nursing staff in Smithtown at the time of the study were white, and only one of the study wards had black staff. This simple mathematical fact made the position of the handful of black staff very interesting. That the Special Hospitals have had to discuss their approaches to the relatively high proportion of black, predominantly Afro-Caribbean, patients makes this yet more interesting (Prins et al. 1993). During the study racism was not openly discussed except where white staff irritably refuted it to three white researchers. Despite such refutation, individual white staff were noted to express frankly racist views on occasion. One member of staff was called a 'black dickhead' and there was irritation expressed about 'coloured people, Mauritian, West Indian and Nigerian staff' obtaining overtime and taking long holidays. The tiny numbers of

---

7 These are almost certainly underestimates, as this was sensitive information that could only be documented when it occurred spontaneously.

black staff were aware of the range of attitudes in their fellow staff members and wider society.[8]

Gender was more frequently an issue. There were no female nursing staff on the male wards but women were well represented among senior positions in other disciplines. There were male staff on the female ward. Field notes suggest that men discussed women, in ways that, at times, could only be construed as sexist:

> Henri asks Antoinette if she enjoyed dancing in the club . . . She said she did. He said he had heard that she was doing cartwheels in the car park. She said it was handstands and it was a pretty poor state of affairs if a girl cannot go out and enjoy herself without everyone checking up on her. Ivan said that he would write an article about this. He asked if she was wearing a skirt for the handstands. She replied, 'Trousers.' He said it would have been more interesting if it was a skirt. He said he would do a cartoon of her.

There were also discussions of the sexual practices of women senior staff by men, out of earshot, which were not only sexist but also insulting. Women caught up in these open discussions were sometimes having their sense of humour tested. This was sometimes a form of initiation ritual for new women on the ward. Women had little choice but to go along with this, since they risked unpopularity if they could not laugh at the joke. This is in keeping with patterns of behaviour in custodial settings where the introduction of women into male staff groups is viewed as an intrusion (see Rader 2005). However, women nursing staff, and at times other women staff, would discuss men and male staff and make bawdy jokes. Unlike men talking about women, this was a regular feature of life on the women's ward. Jokes first told by staff would spread rapidly to the patient group, where they were retold with *elan*. Male staff were teased, and that teasing had a sexual dimension; one woman said that in order to get the overtime she wanted she would cheerfully flash her suspenders! Senior women would not make bawdy jokes. At times they would alter their self-presentation, and occasionally swear, when

---

[8] The more general construction of ethnic identity and issues of racism in Smithtown has been discussed more fully by the author elsewhere. See Bartlett (2000) *Racism and the Expression of Identity.*

'talking to the troops'; this temporary disruption of the usual codes of gender- and status-appropriate behaviour was related to crisis and went down well.

When asked about men's and women's wards, respondents had difficulty pinpointing the source of what they perceived to be significant differences between them. Many staff had no experience of the other side of the hospital, despite members of their families and close friends working there. The characterization of the women's wards was uniformly more negative than the men's side. Women patients were thought to go to extraordinary lengths to self-harm and were more frequently violent. Both of these observations are well founded, as studies have echoed these impressions in a variety of clinical and non-clinical secure settings, with the consequence that a more gender-specific approach has since been adopted (Department of Health 2002). One man said that it was '*bloody terrible*' on the women's side. His kindly expressed concern was that women patients' incidents were unpredictable and that he might end up being assaulted because the women were '*very ill*'.

One member of staff who had the advantage of working on both male and female wards at the same time said:

> Female wards have become more defensive. They have been under scrutiny a lot and they get fewer resources. They have more problems . . . It is a general feeling. The women staff are not prepared to take risks like the men would. The women crack down a little earlier than the men would. . . . Also on male wards things are more relaxed, as men patients are encouraged to do things off the ward. On the female side, the patients are rarely pushed to do things. There is more anxiety about patients sitting around all day.

Women staff were aware that their ward had difficulty reconciling disparate staff groups used to working only with specific groups of patients, and knew that certain staff were struggling with this and were stressed.

> Discussion moved to Marthe and Giselle in particular and the various dirty jokes that seemed to be the mainstay of Lille humour. Jean said he reckoned the raucous humour had something to do with stress and that if I thought it was quite bawdy on this ward, it was much worse on —, where it was really raunchy and very loud and quite over the top. . . . He said it was difficult to estimate the levels of sick leave among the staff . . . He said the attitude of the male staff to working on the female side was that it was much harder . . . He said there was a myth that women patients were far more difficult than the male patients and that the staff were much more

bitchy. He said it was not true and that the male staff were just as bitchy but it came out in different ways.

Doctors were not always dealt with kindly by other staff. They would be criticized for seeing patients alone, not communicating with nursing staff and particularly for not taking the advice of nursing staff and for not backing them up in times of crisis.

> Pierre said Thierry, he was the sort of doctor you would want as your GP. He would chat for hours. Quentin said that when Phillippe came on to the ward he was not on medication and Claude tried to get Thierry to put Phillippe on medication. In the end, Phillippe smashed up a room. Thierry said he had better go in and see him. Claude and Frederic went with him. Phillippe was standing there and Claude pushed Thierry in first. . . . When he came out, he (Phillippe) was on medication (laughing).

Doctors were more likely to be praised for not believing patients than for the more classic skill of being able to discuss difficult problems sympathetically.

These multiple categories of often negative difference were not as important in terms of the ward ethos as the wholesale negative characterization of managers. Managers were described as incompetent in day-to-day administration, guilty of a misplaced enthusiasm for management initiatives and viewed with disdain for their lack of familiarity with clinical reality. Comments included personal invective, including accusations of personal insensitivity and cowardice. The following illustrative extracts relate to a visit by managers to the ward—in practice, a rarely observed event:

> Genevieve said she had a real go at Didier and Henriette (managers) that afternoon saying that the staffing levels were inadequate for the levels of dangerousness of the patients and that there were insufficient staff to cope and what happened if there was a major incident when there were so few staff available and that all this contributed to considerable staff stress. She was very annoyed that Didier's response to this was to make sarcastic comments about the dangerousness of staff stress. He went into the dayroom during activities time and commented on the three patients there who I can imagine would be elderly, that they looked really 'dangerous'. He also said that the two staff in the dayroom with them did not look very stressed to him, as they were both reading newspapers at the time. Genevieve went into overdrive, talking about the fact that Didier had no idea because this was at activity time when very few patients are around . . . She went on to say that

Didier has no idea about the situation on the ward, he does not listen and he will not meet the staff halfway about anything at all and you cannot trust him.

In the end, Robert (manager) didn't come to open the ----. He cancelled at the last minute and sent Valery instead. Jacques was obviously disappointed. Staff were absolutely delighted that Robert hadn't come. After the barbecue, in the staff mess, staff were having tea. Sylvie was talking with Claudette about how she would like to shit in Robert's shoes and pee on his clothes. Bernadette was talking about how Valery used to be a porter apparently, and now he was director of something or other. Apparently, he left to go to another Special Hospital and then came back. Bernadette said he left one of us and came back one of them.

The scatological nature of these comments makes more sense given that staff agreed that having full '*potties*' thrown at them, which could happen in intensive care wards, was very hard to bear.

Even where staff agreed with a managerial initiative they might have reservations about how it was being implemented. The effect of such discussions about managers was to create a sense of solidarity, which enabled staff of all grades and disciplines to gloss over more subtle differences, albeit perhaps only briefly.

What do staff think about patients?

There is a striking 'them and us' quality for staff thinking about patients and patients thinking about staff. This is not always negative but there is a distinction that is unquestioned, regardless of whether or not it is tinged with empathy or sympathy.

The three wards in the study had different formal designations, and they were intended to be dealing with patients with different needs. This should be borne in mind in this section, as the challenges the staff felt they faced were different on the three wards.

The field notes for Toulouse ward show the patients being discussed individually either in case conferences, ward round or handovers or in casual conversation. They tend not to be referred to as a group or type. This is in contrast to the global statements made about management. Dominant themes are that patients make progress and that they should move on, perhaps outside the hospital. Discussion of patients in interview material is characterized by an enjoyment of contact with patients and a concern for the vulnerability of the mentally ill. Only two nurses on Toulouse suggested that patients had too much by way of rights or material goods. One man mentioned explicitly his view of psychopaths being manipulative and clever.

Both these themes pervade the material from the other wards. On Lille the women patients as a group were generally and specifically repeatedly referred to as undeserving of clothing, leisure activities and payment for work, as the following field note extract illustrates:

> There was a lot said about the social budget and there was irritation at how much money was spent on leisure activities for the patients. Francoise said how many patients do you know who can go out seven nights a week if they want to? Similarly with the hairdressers, they were totally unrealistic prices. £4 for a perm is about £30 outside. She said they would soon change their habits, meaning the patients, if they had to pay full whack. Ghislaine said the patients here run up an overdraft of £1,000 and then they just leave here and it is just written off. They can just walk away from it. There was more discussion about clothes and the availability of clothing issue for the patients. This is quite a hot topic at the moment, as patients seem to be going to and from the stores quite regularly. There have been many comments that some of the staff would not mind having the opportunity to go to the stores themselves.

This in part relates to the distinction between the mentally ill and those with personality disorders. It was thought that women with personality disorders would play staff off against each other and that some staff would be unaware of this. Such skills could also be employed to get other patients to do their work for them and their word was not to be believed. That patient testimony was at times at odds with what was observed was noted by the researcher. In contrast, older women with mental illness were construed as vulnerable, unthreatening and more deserving by comparison:

> Helene said that she loved working with the patients and that she loved them all. She said she liked to think that if ever she was mentally ill she would be looked after like this. She told me that she had wanted to take Isabelle home with her for a visit but Smithtown would not let her. She and Jeanne had wanted to take some of the oldies out, Isabelle, Karine and Laure but again they were not allowed to. Helaine said the reason for them wanting to do it was that by taking them out they may spark something in them if they saw what it was like outside, and so they would not be quite so frightened of the outside world and might be less resistant to any change.

This recognition of patients, and indeed themselves, as very institution-alized was fairly common, but the characterization of patients as children meant the incentive to allow women more independence and decision-making was tempered by a belief that they would not be up to it. Women patients needed to be taught the difference between right and wrong and could only manage children's Trivial Pursuit, as many were illiterate.

Paris was designed to be, and was, a very different ward from Toulouse. Interview material from Paris staff gives an impression of a staff group under siege from patients perceived as constantly trying to catch them out:

> The manipulative patients can be really stressful. Some days they never leave you alone. They think they are the only patients on the ward and you are the only staff man. They think it's your fault when things are not going right for them. When you talk to them you have your hands tied because there are so many things you cannot say.

Largely patients were seen as undeserving of their rights and privileges (the latter reducing the possibility of incentives), and, when thwarted, very ready to complain. The same small group of patients were named by staff as manipulative, and disproportionately affected the staff per-ception of the patient group as a whole. As on Lille, their demanding behaviour was seen to penalize the mentally ill.

However, the Paris patients were thought to be more alarming than those on either Lille or Toulouse. This assessment of the patient group was informed not only by the particular past offending of the Paris group but also by their activities inside Smithtown. Patients were discussed as generally dangerous to staff, whereas on Toulouse the only mentions of dangerousness applied to concerns for the researcher. One man strug-gling with a desire to be caring said, 'Knowing what crimes the patients have done . . . I don't know how you can feel nice things about people who have raped and killed.' Women patients were also described at times as dangerous, though this might be more about throwing pots of urine at staff and their self-harming potential than serious violence towards oth-ers. Male staff working on other wards viewed women patients as poten-tially dangerous to them by virtue of their capacity to make allegations of sexual impropriety. Consistent across the three wards, however, was mention of possible hostage taking by both male and female patients.

What do patients think about staff?

On all three wards a handful of socially dominant patients tried to monopolize the researchers. Their views on staff were largely negative, and often referred to a sense of personal persecution by staff. There was an opportunity to set reported remarks against observed behaviour. Unremitting complaints, voiced loudly, affected the atmosphere on the ward but could tell us more about the patient than what routinely happened. The following excerpts are characteristic of frequent complainers:[9]

> Bernadette, a patient, had borrowed an item from Cecile (staff) and was asked to return it. As she was in the middle of a game she said she would get it later. Cecile's response was to scream over the Tannoy at her to fetch it. She went to get it and then said that Cecile was winding her up and speaking to her very rudely. She said that in the dayroom Cecile took the opportunity to elbow her very hard as she was going past. Bernadette's comment was, 'Who was Cecile? Just someone coming here to boss people around.' She said she should go to the prison service where she would be better off.

> Jean said that the nurses were thieves. . . . He said . . . it is not paranoid to believe that the known thief is responsible. He referred to them as 'thieving bastards' . . . He said that the psychiatrists are mad. Stark raving mad.

These interactions told us a lot about the dynamics of the ward, particularly as these patients were often in the Smithtown technical sense privileged (in terms of rooms and finances) but did not give the full range of patients' perspectives. Having said that, the general pattern of spontaneous comments was clear. Common threads in this material showed that staff were understood to be those largely based on the ward, in most immediate contact with them. Staff that were thought to patronize patients, who did little to assist, had a disrespectful personal manner towards patients, which might include shouting or being dismissive, and/or who withheld information from patients or lied to them, were viewed unfavourably. Field note extracts illustrate how these ideas might be expressed:

> Luc said that he thought that 'everyone was a screw'. He commented favourably on Marc, saying when he tells you off he never raises his voice, which others do. Indeed, one of the more senior staff, who I think was—since his role was designated—Noel, is known for picking on the vulnerable.

---

[9] Based on all field note material and interviews.

> Someone was telling me about reading the BNF. Apparently, Olaf gave the patients a copy to read about side effects, and Pierre got very cross and went to Quentin, who then 'carpeted' Pierre about it.

> She said they talk to them, meaning the patients, as if 'they', the staff, are superior human beings. She said they should not talk to them like that. Delphine said they do not know how to treat people . . . Delphine repeated her remarks about patients not being treated as human beings and asked for Edith's agreement on this that they do not treat them properly, and Edith agreed.

The elements of praise came from consideration shown about major events in patients' lives and respect shown to them. This is very much in keeping with the literature on respect in prisons, where courtesy demonstrated by officers is highly valued and where being treated not just as a member of a group but as an individual is key (Hulley et al. 2012). As Butler and Drake (2007) argue, respectful relationships are complicated in secure environments where those detained have failed to be independent, have offended society and have done much to jeopardize their status as individuals worthy of esteem. Consideration, they suggest, is less likely to be affected by the actions of the detained individual and is a more achievable goal than esteem, with the added advantage that it assists the maintenance of order in the institution. The gap between the 'caring officer' articulated by Tait (2012) and the popular and well-respected nurse looks small, and disciplinary training looks less important than discernible humanity.

Patients were also observant of tensions between staff groups on all wards and noted this with amusement. As more information was obtained from patients who were quieter, it transpired that 'staff' is a far from homogeneous category in many patients' minds, whilst it is for others.

Male patients had relatively little experience of women staff, and a range of attitudes was expressed. Women staff were sometimes described in insulting and sexualized terms and viewed as more strict, while the presence of women in a male staff group was also seen as helpful. Many male patients had a significant history of violence towards women, both psychotic and non-psychotic, so this is perhaps unsurprising. Women patients similarly had little experience of male staff, and depending on their role, as for male patients, this might be quite remote. Supportive relationships were observed between male nursing staff and women patients, together with well-received joking incidents which relied on gender difference.

It would be easy to attribute these views and behaviours to Smithtown and to neglect the potential significance of patients' earlier experiences. A small proportion of patients had either been in other secure hospitals or had left this one and had to come back. Many more had spent time in other institutions either as children or as adults, or both. Many male patients had been in prison and many women in other psychiatric hospitals. These detentions, admissions and placements must have resonated with and differed from Smithtown even though they shared two crucial characteristics: a negative difference from mainstream society and an experience of relative powerlessness. It would be a mistake to assume that the ethos of Smithtown was operating on a blank canvas.

Chapter 6

What are the mechanisms of power?

It is already apparent from the description of ward life so far that power was contested in the sense that what might be seen as legitimate, reasonable, understandable or unfair depended on who you were. The accounts of life on the ward, built out of daily interactions, give a flavour of the mechanisms of power. Here, these mechanisms are considered in more detail. Critical to the analysis is whether or not staff based on the ward had defining control or were themselves subject to external authority.

Mechanisms of power: asking for items and getting stuff done

Patients' spontaneous interactions with ward staff shed more light on the relationship with nursing staff; this is the critical dynamic of ward life. Their approaches to staff were largely instrumental, that is, they wanted the staff to *do* things for them. This is a reflection of what they could not do for themselves because of the control the hospital exerted over certain items; there were restrictions attached to a range of materials that could be construed as a potential weapon. Many such materials were items regularly found in daily life, not explosives or guns. They included aftershave, spray deodorants and razor blades; these were locked away, creating a need for patients to ask and a need for staff to respond. This practical issue of power and authority also encompassed requests for doors to be opened, to get a dentist appointment, to get cutlery or towels, to put in requisition slips for the canteen, toothbrushes, phone calls and plugs for the bath. This reflects both the degree of confinement and enforced dependency. A small number of patients said they might go to a nurse with a problem, but absent from their thinking was the idea that staff, of any discipline, represented a therapeutic resource.

> When Rolf is on the ward he is visible—his work makes him so, but by his own admission he will seldom chat with staff, saying, "I hardly have much to say to staff. Here they leave you to get on with it."

In keeping with this was how the staff were construed. Kindness and friendliness were valued, and patients often sorted staff by these categories and their opposites; being security minded, custodial or like a prison officer was unlikely to endear you to patients.

> Best blokes in here are the NAs because they treat you like people. Can have a laugh and a joke with most staff. Staff on ward are like prison officers and that's why we call them screws. Some you like, some you don't.

Black patients operating in a predominantly white environment were clear that they would have welcomed more black staff on the wards, and thought that their placement within Smithtown was affected by being black, though this was impossible for researchers to evaluate. A small number of individual patients said aloud that staff were racist, though to the researchers such accusations could seem misdirected. One reason for this was that overt racist comments, which were rare, were more likely to be made out of earshot of all patients and black staff.

In general terms, staff who exerted power by regularly being too busy to attend to patient requests, or saying they were going to do things and then not doing them, were unpopular: 'Bloody idle—won't get stuff out of the cupboard.'

Mental health nurses have been thought, in other settings, both to have considerable power because of their proximity to patients compared to other staff groups (Barrett 1998) and to have to be preoccupied with the minutiae and practicalities of patient life since otherwise, the hospital could not function (Deacon 2004).

If tasks were not undertaken by staff, the patients had limited options. They could approach someone else or they could wait, but they could not sort them out independently and for these types of activity were very much at the mercy of staff. About half of the patients were therefore strategic in whom they approached; they had worked out for themselves who were useful and for what purpose. Others were at a disadvantage. Thus, the intrinsic passivity of the patient position could be tempered by active and strategic consideration about how to achieve goals.

In prison studies, the responsiveness of staff has been termed 'organizational respect' (Hulley et al, 2012) as opposed to the interpersonal courtesy described earlier. This aspect of relationship seems to be independent of the purpose of the organization, and emerges and acquires analytic power where non-negotiable disparities of power between social groups apply.

These practical displays of power were overt. Covert decision-making was also hard for patients to understand and/or challenge, and some thought of staff as secretive in the sense of never explaining how decisions were made. One man cited his confusion about how rooms were allocated and taken away, and could see little consistency in the decision-making. Another said that information about the patients' use of the telephone had been kept from them.

Some staff got routinely bad press. One of the wards had experienced a scandal, after which staff were brought into the ward to sort it out and to reintroduce standards of incorruptibility. An ethos of being hard but fair had been thought necessary. The following field note indicates their approach:

> Rolf came out to get his razor. He went to the wet shaver box on the trolley next to Sylvan. Rolf hesitated and then reached out for his razor. Sylvan snapped the box shut, saying, 'You are too fucking late, pal.' Rolf turned away and looked upset and uncertain. As Sylvan wheeled the trolley away, he added, 'You will have to have an electric shave.' Rolf went to the electric razor trolley. He does not have an electric razor. He looked at the razors on the electric razor trolley but did not take one (as they are all other people's). He walked away looking dejected. Thierry and Vivien heard and saw all this. Thierry seemed embarrassed and muttered something about there being a spare electric razor which was not working at the moment because it needed cleaning, and if Rolf could not be bothered to clean it, then he cannot have a shave. But even this second-rate option was not presented to Rolf.

This personal approach was unpopular with the patients.

Staff who demonstrably responded quickly, cheerfully and kindly to patients' requests were praised by patients. Such staff, with one exception, were all nursing assistants. Very little mention was made of

non-nursing staff, and they received mixed comments. However, the contrast between staff on the wards and in work areas was pronounced. Most patients felt that at work they were treated with greater friendliness and less as patients. They valued a greater sense of equality apparent to them when not on the ward.

Mechanisms of power: beyond the immediate availability of a toothbrush

Patient accounts also provided insights into other aspects of their lives over which they had little control. These were matters that involved considerable depth of feeling, but which ward-based nursing staff had little, if any, power to influence.

The overarching context in this section is that almost all patients disliked being in the hospital; sometimes, they also thought it was wrong or unjust that they were there. Complex views were expressed:

> [I've] always hated Smithtown, but it's the best thing that ever happened to me. He also spends a little time off the ward, attending both education and the main shops more than once a week. He sees himself as institutionalized, his term. But he says of himself, 'To me I'm not part of Smithtown . . . I don't want to take part.' He adds, 'I just want to forget I was ever here.'

A tiny number of patients actually welcome the security it provides, e.g. one man described feeling 'lonely' and 'unsafe' outside and saw his return to Smithtown as coming to a place of 'refuge'. Even for such men whose circumstances were unusual, the experience of living there year after year was not without its drawbacks.

Sykes' (1958) contribution to the prison literature provides an interesting comparison to that found in Smithtown. Both institutions are maximum secure in intention, though one is a prison and one a hospital. Sykes outlines the 'pains of imprisonment' as follows: association with other prisoners who were mutually considered dangerous, loss of liberty, reduction in autonomy, absence of heterosexual contact and paucity of goods and services. This is both similar to but also different from the situation in Smithtown. The following sections deal with the 'pains of hospitalization' not already discussed in relation to ward staff control. These relate both to fellow patients and to the wider institution. For male patients these are sensibly considered as uncertainty about likely discharge, aspects of relationships with fellow patients, heterosexual relationships and infringements of privacy.

Being there forever

Patients stayed in Smithtown for years, rather than weeks and days. However, even when it was decided they should move on, there was a complex system with frequent delays. Many staff were also frustrated by this. The very slow rate at which patients were discharged following recommendation by the clinical team had been repeatedly demonstrated, but still affected the patients to whom we spoke (Bartlett et al. 1996; Dell 1980).

Making matters worse was the uncertainty attached to detention in hospital. This is one of the major differences between most people in jail and everyone in a secure hospital. There is no fixed duration of hospital stay. In addition, there is no recommended term of detention or tariff as applies to life-sentence prisoners or those held on Indefinite Sentences for Public Protection (IPP).[1] This aspect of confinement is unique to the mental health system and is often expressed by patients as the experience of an indefinite sentence, i.e. they made an explicit comparison to criminal justice sanctions. There is evidence that it is this single facet of life in Smithtown that is hardest to bear for almost all patients.

At that time, a further obstacle to the transfer of patients out of Smithtown was the Aarvold process (Aarvold Committee 1973), which added unpredictability and postponed discharge at best. A patient who was clinically ready for discharge could be referred to an Aarvold Committee,

---

[1] All patients in Smithtown are detained in hospital under the Mental Health Act (except a tiny number held under the Crime and Insanity Act). This has two main parts: a Civil part (Part II) and a Criminal part (Part III). Individuals may be admitted under either part, and there are significant differences with each in terms of renewal procedures and the power of the clinical team and the Home Office. What all of these detentions have in common is that there is no point at which the detention will definitely end. In this way they differ from finite-term prison sentences and even from life sentences, where there is a recommendation from the judge as to the minimum sentence.

which would then reconsider the decision. This trumped all other decisions, and took a long time, adding automatic further delay to an already cumbersome mechanism. It was designed as a further safeguard for society with regard to the release of dangerous patients. It came into being following the outcry surrounding further homicides by Graham Young, a former Special Hospital patient, in the early 1970s (Hansard 1972: 74).

The day-to-day restrictions on movement and access are of much less import for patients than the issue of not knowing when they might actually leave:

> I am uncertain about when I will go. It would be so wonderful to know that I'd be going on a certain date. The length of the sentence is indefinite and this concerns most people.

This is despite the fact that only a few patients linked confinement with deprivation in the sense that they had interrupted relationships with friends, family and children (Flanagan 1980). For people in the secure hospital system, such ties, if they continue to exist, can be problematic. Often, they always have been. Relationships can atrophy over the years and parents may die. Entry to the secure hospital system by virtue of serious crime can mean the sudden dissolution of friendships and partnerships even when the offence is not against someone intimate. Leaving implied not so much the resumption of old ties, but freedom per se.

> Marcel got a bit annoyed and said Christmas should be cancelled. He said he has had many Christmases in Smithtown and they have all been unenjoyable. He said everyday he has been in Smithtown has been unenjoyable. He said, 'I hate it. You ask me what I think. Do I need to be here?' Luc said, 'I don't know.' Marcel said, 'Well, some bloke at the gate just has to press a button and I will be out. Christmas is just another day'. . . Marcel was clearly upset and this is the first time I have seen him like that.

There was a certain mystery about getting out. Patients could hazard guesses at what constituted progress, but were very uncertain. This may be more understandable in light of the fact that it is men with sexual offences and no mental illness who stay the longest (Dell et al. 1987). Also, patients were not well informed about the pre-Smithtown crimes of their fellow patients.

> She was looking to get parole, which she thought would be good because it would show that she was improving and help to get her out. She said that getting out took

a long time. Marie-Glycine agreed and said that an additional problem was that you did not know what was happening and did not seem to be able to do anything about it. She had recently been told that she was not going to be recommended to be moved before her next Tribunal and said that she cannot do anything to change it. She said all these decisions were taken by someone else and the patients feel helpless. Ghislaine agreed and said she just has to wait.

This lack of agency and real understanding of the process resonates with Crewe's analysis of prisoners grappling with uncertainty about concepts of progress and the possibility of early release on time-limited sentences. The bureaucracy of assessment, he argues, based on mathematical prediction and reports to prison authorities, is opaque. Conclusions can seem inconsistent (Crewe 2011).

Though less important, there were also physical aspects of confinement within Smithtown which reinforced the fact that patients cannot leave of their own volition, e.g. 'all you can see is a wall outside. The closer you are, the bigger it seems . . . ' or sardonically, one man liked 'the view'. The security apparatus bothered someone else. However, by comparison with prison experience, the day-to-day restrictions were far fewer. Those with prison experience were unanimous that Smithtown was greatly preferable to being locked in a cell all day.

The Groucho Marx problem: club membership

Groucho Marx wondered why he would want to be the member of any club that would admit him to the membership; he should not join anything so suspect. For Smithtown patients there is a similar issue. The pertinent question is whether or not you want to be part of a society which will have you. Patients expressed concerns linked to the idea of confinement with the mentally unwell and, separately, they could be fearful of their fellow patients.

Many people were alarmed by the idea of coming to Smithtown, some, though not all, of which was due to their expectations of their fellow patients. These fears are encapsulated here: '. . . thought it was a loony bin . . . all nutters running about. I knew G---- was here . . . I knew it was long term'. Even if they were not fearful, patients differentiated themselves from others.

Sometimes, patients used ideas of mental illness to establish negative difference in others. Field note extracts illustrate how, left with the practical problem of living together, everyday observations of mental illness in others occurred and how patients managed the impact of this as part of a peaceful life on the ward.

> While Jean-Paul went on and on, Ludovic was sitting nearby and listening to the conversation. While Jean-Paul was speaking his most nonsensical statements . . . Ludovic smiled at me conspiratorially.

> After the game I sat next to Michel. Michel leant over and said quietly to me, 'If he looks at you don't look back at him. Just ignore Patrice. He is mad.' . . . Michel involved Roger by calling him. 'Roger, at lunch he had a go at me and I did nothing. I was just eating some crisps.' Roger laughed almost uncontrollably and Michel joined in. I could see the humour of the situation and laughed too. This caused Roger to laugh more heavily so that he could barely sit in his chair. When Michel stopped laughing he said to me never to look at Patrice. He said I should just wait to see if he wants to speak. He added, 'He is mad.'

Although there were examples on both the men's and women's wards of patients showing kindness to others who were obviously distressed or unable to manage, it is true that a third of the male patients expressed fear of their fellow patients, independent of their previous expectations. This was more of an issue for patients on Paris than Toulouse. Not all hostility or violence between patients was picked up by staff, and some men felt vulnerable. Even where staff suspected intimidation, they were unable to intervene unless they had proof; one experienced nurse said of his ward, 'Richard, Victor, Christian, and Jean-Paul are fearful of Claude and they pay him off to leave them alone. I can't prove it yet, but I will.' The possible truth of this idea was perhaps borne out by Claude persecuting Victor; he was both personally insulting and teased him cruelly. Intimidation and bullying were also known to occur on the women's ward. Part of the anxiety on the men's side stemmed from what had been done in the past, when a number of patients colluded in very serious violence.

Even if someone was in a volatile mood, there was a limit to what could be done about the situation. If not sufficiently disturbed to warrant seclusion, s/he would wander the ward. Staff and patients could respond kindly if the patient was popular but temporarily disturbed. I was warned by both staff and patients when one patient on the ward was particularly irritable, and their tone of voice expressed a degree of concern not only for me but also for the man in question. On the other hand, the levels of tension on the ward can rise when the person is very intimidating. This is not unique to Smithtown. Victimization of patients by patients is not uncommon in non-forensic hospital settings (Thomas et al. 1995) and patients will respond by retreating (Van Dongen 1997).

Both staff and patients occasionally mentioned the possibility of coercive sexual relations between men in dormitories; such coercion is common in prisons (Gilligan 2000; Struckman-Johnson et al. 1996) and unwanted sexualized behaviour is a common feature of in-patient psychiatric settings (Bowers et al. 2014). Steps were taken to minimize this possibility. The number of incidents of physical violence appeared quite small—perhaps small enough to confound people's expectations of a secure hospital. The majority were between patients. The question of appearances is important. Psychiatric hospitals are unsafe in practice and many incidents never come to the attention of staff or go unmentioned in records (Mezey et al. 2005; Thomas et al. 1995); this profoundly conflicts with the psychiatric practitioners' idea of asylum as a place of safety for those with chronic illness (see Chow and Priebe 2013).

This study did not seek out material on safety, but what emerged is not inconsistent with what is known about other not dissimilar environments. Also, how people behave will depend as much on what they believe as on what actually happens. There is no necessary correlation between what people fear and what happens to them. In Smithtown, paranoia is rife and likely to be a feature of many people's experience of their immediate world. But it is well known that although the general public's view of crime is at odds with the real risk of being a crime victim, it is their perceptions that will govern their behaviour.

Fear of others is important as a measure of the climate of the ward, though not given much importance in quantitative measures of ward atmosphere or institutional quality of life (Kirby 1997; Swinton et al. 1999). This was an area of concern for many patients. On Paris, vulnerable patients were often given little choice but to go along with aggressive joking from fellow patients, which could include racist and homophobic elements:

> He asked why Marc had touched 'that researcher bloke's leg'. Marc laughed. He asked Marc if he was 'gay'. Marc said, 'No, he's my mate,' and indicated me. Patrice told Marc that he had some special soap to get him white like Michael Jackson. Marc did not laugh at this.

Some people felt permanently unsafe

There is, however, an important qualification to the previous point. For sex offenders, Smithtown was much safer than prison.[2] Some of the patients in the study had spent time in prison for offences against children. 'Nonces', to use the prison term, were likely to be beaten up if their crimes were discovered while they were in prison. 'Rule 43' exists to allow prisoners who are vulnerable for a variety of reasons to be in a segregated part of the prison; sex offenders often choose this option. In Smithtown, the proportion of sex offenders in the hospital population is high, but they are not segregated. The feeling of safety was something of a welcome novelty for potential victims, and could demonstrate a change in perpetrators' behaviour.

> Jean-Claude thought he was coming to 'a terrible place'. For him his first ward confirmed his fears; it was 'a bit tight'. In addition, he was frightened about being beaten up because of the nature of his offences, as he had been in prison. He was concerned about what would happen to him if he got into arguments; he thought he might be moved to a ward from which it might take years to move. He was told about privileges on other 'blocks'. He began to have hope from the information he obtained from other patients he met on the sports field.

> Frederic commented on the issue of sharing space with sex offenders. He explained he was convicted of serious violence. In prison he would have joined in beating them up, whereas being here had made him more 'tolerant'. He said he thought he had gone 'soft' and that this would be the case if he were to return to prison.

The company of women

Psychiatric hospitals have taken different approaches over time to the levels of contact between men and women detained in hospital. Historically,

---

[2] Genders and Player (1995) make the same distinction. The therapeutic environment of Grendon Prison, with a high proportion of sex offenders, made it unlike the rest of the prison system.

asylums created sexually segregated wards. With the advent of medium secure hospital care in the 1970s came a period when mixed psychiatric wards were thought best, medium secure hospital patients could share ward spaces and it was not automatic that their bathrooms or bedrooms were significantly private from each other. High secure care had not moved on so quickly, and twenty years ago, when all three High Secure Hospitals had male and female patients, there was much discussion about how contact should be managed. This was an area of institutional power, where staff surveillance was delicate and potentially intrusive.

Consensual sex between a male and female patient as far as Smithtown was concerned was a bad idea, and staff surveillance was necessary to prevent it; a baby would have been a tabloid disaster. Sexual practices between psychiatric in-patients are usually unwelcome (Commons et al. 1992), but there are several reasons why sex is such a delicate and important issue in Smithtown. Staff have responsibility for the patients. Many of the women have histories of systematic and permanently damaging sexual abuse (Bland et al. 1999; Heads and Taylor 1997), whilst many of the men have committed sexual offences against adult women. This throws into sharp relief the desirability of friendships and relationships, as well as actual sexual contact between these people. Legally there is no bar to patients marrying, though this would be a civil wedding and there is no way married patients can live together inside Smithtown. The wisdom of such marriages is hotly disputed.

Be that all as it may, the reality for many men, the majority of whom have not offended against women and may have successful or unsuccessful relationships behind and ahead of them, is that they miss the company of women. For some this is about missing particular women who may visit them, but, as in prison, they sit at tables being scrutinized by staff. For others it is the oddity of living for the most part in an all-male environment. For others, notably those with relationships inside Smithtown, they were unhappy with the restrictions on current intimacy, tempered by the recognition that the situation was a little easier than before.

> Marcel thinks that the attitude of Smithtown towards couples has altered, describing this as Smithtown being a 'lot more lenient on couples'. Though he has no visits

himself, he is able to have joint visits with his partner when her family visit. This accommodation of couples is one of the changes he has seen since his arrival.

But for most men, the issue was an irrelevance, whilst for some it was a relief not to have to deal with women in any sense.

Given that the gender ratio was five men for each woman, there are specific institutional dimensions to cross-gender relationships of any kind. First, meetings can only take place off the ward, and second, such meetings are always supervised by staff. This brings an additional element of artificiality to an already highly charged situation, usually a social function.

The experience of women was varied. There are no comparable interviews from the women's ward. However, certain women from Lille clearly went to functions to meet specific men, and only rarely did they go without a known partner. Equally, there were examples of women avoiding social functions because of the level of unwanted male interest. One woman explained that as a consequence of a number of men writing to her, she had been sent eight bars of soap as presents. Despite her request, one of her admirers continued to write. She had not replied to any of them and felt disconcerted when one man referred to her in his letters as his wife and wrote about their children. Finally, this correspondence ceased and she was grateful. Another woman was careful not to go to functions without her boyfriend, as she knew from experience that she was likely to be approached by all and sundry, something she did not want. This also happened to one of the researchers. As one woman put it:

> . . . when she arrived . . . she received a lot of letters from male patients. She reckoned there was some sort of Tom-Tom system operating whereby when a new female patient arrives, the male patients become aware of it quite rapidly. She was concerned if she went down to the sports field or to any function that the men might approach her, as some had been quite persistent in writing to her and even though she had not replied, she felt they could well come up to her when she did not wish to be bothered.

Other women were known to take advantage of the gender imbalance and play the field. It was possible for them to gain materially from such relations and for men to see themselves as exploited. Older women at

Smithtown had social contact with men outside of the usual social functions, where there was better scope for entertainment.

> Celine said she liked going to the ------. I asked her what she does there and she said, 'Sweet fuck all.' I asked her about the functions and whether or not she goes and she pulled a face. She says she sees enough of men at the ------. Celine told me that the men kiss her when she arrives at the ------, just a peck on the cheek. She demonstrated herself regally accepting pecks and it was clear this was not unwelcome. She told me depending on how many men are there she gets a different number of kisses, and it ranges from two on an ordinary day to four on a Wednesday.

This complex issue is one part of a broader discussion about personal privacy.

Personal privacy

It is easy to understand why in a life that was recorded in detail in court transcripts and clinical notes, and scrutinized by clinical staff in daily observations, privacy might be a core value. But privacy from each other was a key patient issue.

In Smithtown, if a clear patient-value system existed it could be summed up as follows: 'Patients don't ask, patients don't say'. Inmate codes in prison that involve neither inquiring into other prisoners' lives nor telling tales to staff are well known, but may be more talked about than lived (Copes et al. 2013). In contrast, this seemed to be more lived than talked about. Patients did not ask each other why they were there, although sometimes it would be apparent from the media. They might tell a few people, though they might be deliberately misleading. At no time did the researchers hear public discussion of such things, though they were confided in at times. There was also a telling example of what could happen if this simple rule of patient behaviour was broken:

> There is some knowledge, but people cannot know it is the truth. Generally people don't tell each other. It's a strictly unwritten law that no one is allowed to mention what other people are in here for. That's why Eugene smacked Joseph in the head a couple of weeks ago and I stood to make sure no fucker pressed the bell. Joseph went flying across the room and over his bed. It's because he said, 'You are a rapist,' and that is very wrong to say. Joseph deserved it. If Eugene had been half Joseph's size I'd have held Joseph down. Joseph had been annoying him and this was where Joseph stepped over the line.

The imposition of this sanction was also made possible by the powerful position of these patients in the running of the ward.

The exception to this rule of privacy was group work, which was offence focused. The vulnerability was shared, and patients had a mutual interest in maintaining the confidentiality of the group. This is similar to the conscious decision of patients not to discuss therapy with each other, noted long ago (Caudill et al. 1952).

The other element of patients 'not saying' is 'not grassing'. The point about grassing was that it did happen, but it was recognized as such and not done without thought. The system of life on wards allowed for infringements of the institutional rules which remained unknown to staff. Surveillance was not so tight that acts motivated by personal social relations or individual preference could not happen. Pornography or drugs might be exchanged, displays of physical affection between patients of any sex did occur and these are examples of secrets shared between patients. They might be discovered later by staff, patients might tell staff or contraband could be discovered during a room search (occasionally, minor infringements were tolerated because they did not cause a problem; in this case they provided incentives for cooperation, as did other privileges).

Grassing could be instrumental, as the total number of valued goods was small. It could be indirectly beneficial to the grass, for instance in terms of getting a room. Similarly, it could be motivated by dislike of the activity per se. We observed one man complaining about dormitory sex. Malice seemed to account for the case of this man, who teasingly pointed out the absence of a couple who had disappeared from sight.

Personal privacy may be required due to anxiety and/or shame about the reasons for admission. This is an individual matter and several high-profile patients who wished to leave were painfully aware that further publicity would remind people of their actions and be unhelpful. At a more mundane and generic level, some echo of the prisoner code was evident in the behaviour of patients. Individual infractions of what were known to be the rules became part of shared private patient knowledge, hidden from the institutional gaze.

Indigenous categories

Smithtown had an indigenous lexicon that was tiny compared to the large prison lexicons described in early prison ethnography, e.g. Sykes (1958) and Cardoza-Freeman (1984). There were several terms in regular use about staff and patients, which, even if not used by an individual, were likely to be understood.

Staff lexicon

They do not cover all members of the staff group, nor do they encompass all aspects of any individual. They are included because they had some local currency.

Dinosaur

Any member of staff could be a dinosaur, and suggested that they had been in Smithtown for a long time. They revered the past and the ways in which things were done years ago. They may or may not still work on the wards. Their main source of frustration was with the introduction of changes, notably of new-style ward management packages. They may at this point or soon after have moved to other posts, e.g. supervising visits. Dinosaurs are at best honourable individuals who were genuinely concerned about an institution, to which they were proud to belong, going to the dogs.

Screw

This is a term used by patients about staff. It is never used to indicate approval, but it may be relatively neutral in the sense that all staff are screws or it may be used to differentiate those whose manner and behaviour is least appealing. The following field note indicates this:

> Xavier says there are nurses and there are screws and the proportions vary on different wards. Down here he said there were in fact three screws, another phrase for them being key men. Individuals who like telling you that they are going off for a pint. He said it was much worse on Agen and Calais. He asks Yves if Alain is a screw and Yves says yes, and Xavier says for Yves that everyone is a screw.

This is understandable in the context of Smithtown, both because so many members of staff were members of the Prison Officers Association and because it is an institution which detains people, many of whom have been in prison. Perhaps the second point is pertinent, as it was very infrequently heard on the female ward where a much smaller proportion of the patients had experience of the prison system. It was used discreetly by patients so that the screws would not hear it. Nurses who were not screws heard it as a general term, rarely deliberately applied to specific individuals. Only the most cavalier of patients would use it indiscriminately. Although it has its origins in prison argot, it was used both by patients who had spent time in prison and those who had not. It meant staff whose preference was for a custodial role and who did not turn a blind eye to minor misdemeanours such as having food in bedrooms. It did not imply unfair treatment but suggested the absence of friendliness in staff–patient relations and, if humour was present, it was at the expense of the patient. It said little about the length of time someone had worked in Smithtown. It probably indicated that they preferred to keep a staff uniform—though there were many staff who would who were not screws. It was likely that they supported automatic deference to staff. They used the word respect where they meant immediate and unquestioning obedience.

Nurse

This rather obvious word had meaning in a vocabulary where it was regularly juxtaposed with screw. It implied either wholehearted or grudging approval of the person in question. This depended on the patients' view of their own circumstances, in particular whether or not they agreed they needed psychiatric help. It suggested diligence in the role. It was often used for someone who would seek out patients for conversation of varying degrees of formality and someone who could be trusted to do what was requested as opposed to promising but not delivering. It carried with it an idea of formality in interaction; the professional nurse was unlikely to think water fights with patients were a good idea or to take part in one. They were signed up to the idea of professional boundaries and details of their private life would be unknown to patients, giving the interaction both distance and an unequal quality. This was someone who was likely to believe that treatment was a good thing and, whatever its form, was something to be delivered by staff as their primary task.

Patient lexicon

As with terms applied to staff, what follows are words that were used in Smithtown. They did not encompass all patients, but do tell us something important about the relevance of mental illness to patient and, more generally, ward life. Equally, they tell us something about how status differentials within the patient group can be represented in language rather than action.

Chronics

This was a term used by older staff about older patients; the latter would not use it about themselves. Its meaning is close to the psychiatric term 'chronic schizophrenic', in that it turns an adjective into a noun with the same absorption of self into disability. It did not include everyone with mental illness or everyone who had chronic schizophrenia but it meant someone was obviously mad, even after many years in hospital. In the world of Smithtown it signified their inability to compete in the social world; these were a group of men and women who would not win in the political games of the ward, and who might lose their rooms through chance misfortune rather than deliberately subversive activity. They could not compete at social functions because they gave themselves away with the side effects of medication (being overweight, odd physical movements) or ongoing strange speech and obvious bizarre preoccupations. They could not go to the gym because they were slowed up by sedating medication.

> One patient said nowadays half the bowls team are psychotic and in the past significantly less were and that medication or their illness affect them. He says you can tell from their shakes and from their body posture and their facial movements. He said one mentally ill man won something requiring physical activity; I forget what he said exactly. Clearly Emile viewed this as very much against the odds.

Chronics were likely to be older rather than younger. They would talk of going to work, but for the men this was likely to be the easiest of ward tasks or the least demanding of the work areas. They were vulnerable to exploitation, teasing and physical intimidation; in some patients and some staff they evoked protective feelings. These were a group of people who were left out of the high-status activities of Smithtown. In the kingdom of the mad, the very obviously and irredeemably mad are second-class citizens.

Psychopaths

Within psychiatry this is a highly problematic term. Here we are concerned not with the specifics of medico-legal psychiatry, but rather with the related social meaning of the term in Smithtown. Psychopaths had a number of attributes in Smithtown, and it depended on who was speaking as to what was said. This was a term predominantly but not exclusively used about young men. Patients used it to express apprehension or reluctant admiration. Thus, these were men intrinsically dangerous and/or successful, e.g. with desirable women, as well as daring, e.g. planning escapes. The term carries a resonance of opposition to the system, a wish to be bloodied but unbowed by the experience of patienthood. These were women likely to exploit others where possible and to complain without foundation. For staff, too many intelligent psychopaths in one place at one time was a problem, as they were considered likely to behave as 'collusive psychopaths' and test the system. Although its close cousin, the formal term 'Psychopathic Disorder' was proportionately more likely to be applied to women than men, the social term was predominantly reserved for men. If you were not so far beyond the pale on your ward, you were likely to get well-paid jobs where it was possible to reward yourself and your friends on the ward. You might organize patient social events or order food. There was scope for entrepreneurial flair, though if caught out you would plummet from your privileged position. This position was testament to your competence and allowed because it kept you out of further mischief. You would dress well, with little evidence of the clothing time warp produced by long-term hospitalization. You might keep yourself fit and play in sports teams; even if untalented, you might discover the delights of participating enthusiastically in the hospital show. You would be someone to watch.

Girls

Girls were women patients in the eyes of staff. Some staff recognized it as at best an odd term for adult women, whilst others thought the drive to eradicate it a laughable example of political correctness. It was not derogatory as such, in contrast to the terms commonly used on the male wards, but its use betrayed an implicitly patronizing attitude in which patients had a childlike quality rather than being truly adult. At the same time it carried a hint of affection, again not found in terms used on the male wards.

Power and social structure: how would you know who is in charge?

This preliminary analysis of power is based on a fundamental truth about High Secure Hospital life, which is that there were staff and there were patients. These were formal institutional designations, neither unusual nor as terms particularly contested at that time. They were manifest in mental health law and guidance, and official communications, and had a quality of legitimacy. In fact, at the level of a ward, these identities relied on action and its representation in talk. The mutual perspective, i.e. the way in which each group thought about itself and the way it saw what, at ward level, was the critical other, created a complex sense of identity in both cases, belying the simplicity of the words. This begins to tell us something about modalities of power and influence, both in terms of legitimacy and role congruent power, and in other ways relating to the embodiment of social roles. Precisely because this is not a study of a prison, the analysis does not need to be so weighted down with earlier ethnographies, helpful though these are. Equally, early ethnographies of hospitals, useful because they do deal with detained patients, as does Smithtown, are of limited use because of the failure to theorize power beyond social structure and role, both being curiously static and failing to do justice to individual agency. Instead, in line with what we found, we explore the relationship between what Rapport (2009) has termed 'individual energy' and structural power.

Staff and patient identity is filled out by that which individuals bring to their roles. To this is added a layer of periodically ascribed identity, based on a shared lexicon of social meaning: the indigenous typology. Further, the social relations of staff and patients are informed both by the specific characters of the three wards and a more distant idea of institutionalized power, precisely that which dictates the fundamental social hierarchy from beyond the ward.

The analysis in the previous chapter, which generated an understanding of the complex and fluctuating selves of the researchers within the process of fieldwork, resonates with this picture of ward-based daily life. The researchers maintained a sense of themselves as researchers, but were ascribed other identities. Similarly, staff and patients were always that, but the kind of staff member or patient they were varied.

Staff and patients were the two dominant social categories in that they were the stuff of everyday speech, and belonging to one or another group determined both possible and actual kinds of behaviour on the ward. Giddens (see Rapport 2009) argued that key social concepts (in his argument politicized categories such as culture and society) have meaning and are used instrumentally. Then, having entered a social arena they are contested and revised. Correspondingly, the understanding of the terms 'staff' and 'patient' is informed by how individuals embody their roles and, in turn, as this new information is processed in the collective memory of the ward, must inform their contemporary meaning.

Structural power and real people

Staff recognized their formal subdivisions of role as meaningful. Doctors were not nurses and staff nurses were not nursing assistants. Among nursing staff these subdivisions included significant degrees of overlap in the staff nurse and nursing assistant roles, but nursing assistants had less paperwork, less ward responsibility and more unskilled tasks. Night nurses of whatever grade seemed a different breed, their work involved virtually no patient contact. All nurses were strongly allied to their wards, whereas other clinical staff were both less physically present and had diffuse allegiances. Other clinical staff were likely to comment on purposeful activity with patients. Nurses were action focused, and the patient contact was only implicit in the description of their activity.

Ward staff embodied, from the point of view of the institution, legitimate roles, and though praxis, the power relations of the wider institution and at some level, the intentions of law and the state. This could be tacitly understood, although not articulated in speech. They did not necessarily see that external forces reached in to inform and to impose a wider set of rules and regulations and status differentials. Legitimate behaviour (attendance at CPA meetings, doing group therapy or locking away knives) was seen as role-specific action, and involved ways of working and living. The categories of person might be substantially determined outside the ward but were lived within it. These external forces could be seen, regardless of their expressed intent, as by Goffman and Foucault for instance, as determining, controlling and largely malign. The wider principles of the NHS and its wish for patients to receive appropriate good care and treatment may mean that the social structuring of a hospital is viewed more kindly by the reader.

We live now in the aftermath of the Francis (2013) report. It is the latest in a long line of hospital inquiries, and stands out because of the gravity of the findings, the elegance of the writing and the common sense infusing the report. It is an indictment of many errors and misjudgements at different levels of Mid Staffordshire NHS Foundation Trust (MSFT), creating a culture not of care but of indifference. What stands out is that the way in which clinical staff related to patients was not characterized by qualities compatible with caring professions. Individuals at work were unkind and incompetent, tarnishing the meaning of the words nurse and doctor. Central and North West London NHS Foundation Trust (CNWL FT), like many health organizations, has a 'hidden gem' award, an award for precisely opposite behaviours, where individuals bring, often to lowly roles, personal qualities as rated by colleagues and patients, which make them stand out as beacons of excellence. CNWL FT and MSFT shared Foundation Trusts status. The 'individual energy' Rapport (2009) identifies as contributing to the structural power of an institution need not be a function of the institutional ethos and indeed may be at odds with it.

Smithtown was and is a hospital, but spontaneous mention by nursing staff or patients of work that could meaningfully be described as therapeutic was uncommon, yet it was observed that clinical activity took place. People saw the doctor, had medication, went to groups and were observed and noted to be better or worse. This project is not an audit either of what psychiatry would call face-to-face clinical contact or its efficacy. Therapeutic norms might underpin much activity, but were not so labelled by either nursing staff or patients to any great extent. Instead, people talked about getting through the day; these were task-orientated activities for nurses and instrumental behaviours by patients, as are evident in other hospital ethnographies, where clinical demands are balanced against institutional demands and where mental health nurses were aware of the gap between desirable role activity and actual behaviour (Buus 2008).

Nurses were aware that there were particular screws and dinosaurs in their midst, though both could confound expectations at times. These terms were common currency and some people were proud of their long-standing personal, familial and social allegiance to Smithtown. Others saw it as a place of work. Not all staff wished to alter the situation of patients. Relations between radical staff and those who liked the status quo could be difficult. There were especially delicate issues if people came from different disciplines. Examples cropped up in the fieldwork of both ridicule and intimidation of individuals who sided with patients against staff. Non-nursing staff saw themselves, as did the researchers, as having to fit in with the dominant nursing culture. Doctors who were not part of the Smithtown network were considered in relation to nurses for whom they are either a supportive or unhelpful presence in times of crisis. Criticism or a reputation for criticism could lead to being ostracized or worse.[3] Where the balance of staff was in favour of liberalization, more conservative staff could behave as dead weights and reduce the energy staff brought to their work. The tensions within the staff group with regard to doing things differently were signalled by the prevalence of the term 'dinosaur', so immediately comprehensible. In contrast to many other Smithtown terms, it was also a new word for the hospital.

From the patients' viewpoint, the formal differentiation of staff role had a certain reality. Doctors were seldom present and nursing assistants were useful. But patients' main understanding of staff was that this was a relationship of inequality, where confrontation would serve you badly

---

[3] Material justifying this assertion is sufficiently delicate and compromising of particular individuals for it to remain unelaborated.

and taking advice and keeping a low profile would serve you well. As one woman put it, 'They like you to be sleepy.' Although she meant it literally, it is metaphorically meaningful as well. As a group, staff provoked mixed feelings among patients.

Patients were able to sort out the good guys from the bad guys, although they might disagree among themselves. Also, for some patients, as we have seen, all staff were 'screws'. There were many aspects of daily life where the way in which a member of staff fulfilled their role, as opposed to the nature of the role, made a real difference to someone's day. This was not about how many staff were on duty but rather who was on duty.

Life below stairs

Downton Abbey has gripped the nation. Every Sunday night, with the exception perhaps of a disdainful intelligentsia, Britain has watched a version of its past. This act of self-absorption must have many roots, including a harking back to the Imperial past, a time when life was ordered and civility the norm. That is, apart from the destitution, criminality, sexism and sexual violence evident in the programme, along with Lady Mary's latest admirers and wonderful clothes. This is not a new phenomenon. *Upstairs, Downstairs*, written not by a Lord like Downton's Julian Fellowes, but by the daughters of women house servants, Eileen Atkins and Jean Gordon, dominated evening viewing forty years ago. There is something peculiarly British about this. In France, the equivalent series are more to do with land, landscape and regional identity, e.g. Les Oliviers and Tramontane, than obsessed with the details of an aristocratic household. But then France had a revolution.

So is Smithtown like Downton? No, precisely because downstairs there is no given social hierarchy. There are no footmen and butlers and valets, cooks and parlour maids and housekeepers. So, in a way, they are created.

The informal patient categories, the attempts at social domination through comment and incident, are efforts to create, sustain and enhance social subdivisions and a social hierarchy amongst patients by patients. The high-status jobs and goods that follow from contact with staff enhance distinctions in the patients. It was a given that being a patient meant you had to knock to enter certain rooms. Staff expressed concern about patients and often expressed a liking for patient contact. They were more likely to highlight the vulnerability of the mentally ill than the psychopathic. The latter group was seen as potentially exploitative and disruptive, linked with a strand of thinking which suggested that patients were essentially undeserving and had too many rights. However, they were also relied upon to take part in the running of the wards. The discretion of staff in awarding jobs was, as in prison, something that restated the key components of the social order. This is despite the reality that a few 'trusted' patients did the things staff did as part of their ward work, or did more complex work than some of the tasks included in nursing assistant roles but still retained patient status.

From the patients' point of view, being a patient was far from ideal. It meant little control over your future and possibly indefinite detention in Smithtown. The exceptions to this were few and far between. Other anxieties which stemmed from confinement included being concerned about your vulnerability both in relation to staff and to patients. You might also be scared of the outside world and your ability to cope, as well as the outside world's ability to characterize you as undeserving and dangerous. Like staff, patients knew their reputation and that of the institution might precede them.

For patients their physical confinement had immediate implications for their social world, which was defined by their ward. Staff always go home; patients are in the world of the institution twenty-four hours a day and have no possibility of escape from each other. Perhaps in response to such inevitable proximity this is an impersonal social world where privacy is maintained by the absence of confiding relationships and a fear of exploitation and violence. Patients live not so much with each other but alongside each other, with an uneasy reliance on staff to prevent such excess.

What is in a ward?

The wards were places of confinement as well as places of daily existence. Without doubt most patients did not want to be there, disliked it and wanted to leave. A very small number wanted to stay, and had few if any complaints. Many would put up with it without complaining too much, as this was seen to be, and obviously was, counterproductive. This was true in all three wards.

Staff and patients on the three wards also overlapped in their ideas about themselves and each other. This overlap did not preclude the emergence of ward differences of a kind that showed the wisdom of those who said this could not be a study of Smithtown but only of certain parts of it. Wards had characters, perhaps even cultures. The extent to which these ward attributes were independent of the discernible clinical and criminological characteristics of the patient population is hard to discern.[4] Whether staff work on particular wards because of the ward characteristics or despite them varies, as clearly each ward contains a wide range of views. The *degree* to which the values of the staff are produced in reaction to the patient group or are brought into the patient group is outside the scope of this study.

There were obvious 'hard' differences between the three study wards. Two were male and one female; they had different numbers of patients and were designed to cope with different patient groups. They varied in terms of the numbers and types of formal meetings and their patient–staff ratios were different. Input from additional staff was also varied. However, in considering the different social relations on the ward these variables can only form an incomplete explanatory backdrop.

Paris had the least happy staff group, some finding no source of job satisfaction, and were viewed most negatively by the patients. The patients were wary of each other and the least able to get off the ward to work or play. The women's ward is less well characterized and conclusions are generally less robust because there was less opportunity to follow up emerging issues. A more mixed picture emerges, with some patient anxiety about other patients and mixed dissatisfaction and gratitude to the staff. The staff themselves seemed unhappy but at least able to laugh and joke on a regular basis. Toulouse seemed the most relaxed. Its staff group was certainly not free from tensions but the patients were active

---

[4] Confidentiality of patient information precludes more detail about the different profiles of the three wards.

and relatively at ease with each other, and more likely to see the staff as helpful.

All three wards run on consent. This is the only sensible conclusion from the staffing ratios. It is true that there is a well-established emergency system to render assistance but there were almost always more patients than staff on the ward at any one time. Just to make this clear, there are carceral institutions where consent has been almost completely replaced by control. People are locked in all day as well as all night. This level of physical coercion, simultaneously creating social isolation, allied to deprivation of possessions and activity, is seen in seclusion rooms in psychiatric hospitals and segregation units in British prisons. Otherwise, it is not what normally happens in the UK. A regime of almost total control, where consent, or even assent, is irrelevant, is best exemplified in American 'supermax' prisons (King et al. 2008; Rhodes 2005).

The system of jobs and perks in Smithtown provides incentives for good behaviour; they are mechanisms that encourage consent. This is an interesting reflection when we consider that the external imposition of social hierarchy, as rehearsed earlier, is not just about the abstractions of the law, the state or the Department of Health, but also about the way in which things might be run. It is interesting to reflect on the extent to which how things run within institutions is paralleled by the way in which wider society is ordered, i.e. whether and to what degree it is authoritarian, democratic or anarchic.

Social determinism and contemporary juggernauts

Race and gender

When anthropologists got bored with society, social class and culture, they turned to race and gender. Both have been considered, with good reason, to be critical to social differentiation and social hierarchy. As we move in a global world towards cultural hypercomplexity and superdiversity (Vertovic 2007), the value of these lumbering vehicles of understanding is in some doubt. However, they are of some relevance to Smithtown. The secure hospitals, even more than British psychiatry in general, have a controversial history of race relations and gender sensitivity.

First, the levels of gender segregation in Smithtown made it quite unlike external society. These practices had their roots both in historical asylum practice and also in a grasp of the patients' histories both of victimization and violence. Segregation was not an accident, nor, therefore, was the limited integration that occurred. For male staff on women's wards, an unpopular placement, there were constraints on their role governed by decency and possibly additional stresses. Non-nursing staff who were women on male wards were much talked about, sometimes in a sexually insulting way, and not always by patients. For patients of either gender who had heterosexual relationships within the hospital (or outside it), ward life and the limits imposed by virtue of patient identity made things tricky. For patients who wished to avoid such heterosexual entanglements, ward life was useful, albeit artificial. For male staff on male wards and for female staff on female wards, there was less daily engagement with a problematic set of issues, but for male staff, the women's wards had a reputation for being very difficult.

These are complex gender issues, behind which lie one of the main purposes of all secure hospitals, that is, the care of men who have been violent to women. Although the distinctions between staff and patients had to be maintained at all costs, dismissive attitudes to women were not confined to the patient group. This overlap in attitude between male employees of the public sector and violent 'others' has been previously noted (Milner 1996; Smith 1989; Thurston 1996). It remained a taboo area, precisely because of its immediate juxtaposition, in the context of Smithtown, with extreme acts of violence. The delicacy of the gender relations of men on the women's ward was evident. Though potentially construed as positive role models, for women patients previously deprived of contact with men, male staff confronted gender-based challenges on a regular basis. As the objects of desire and ridicule, and not in charge of the wards, they embodied, at times, a reverse masculinity. They also ran the risk of reinforcing women patients' existing ideas about masculine hegemony and abuse (Bartlett and Hassell 2001).

Race and its discussion have had a high profile in all secure hospitals (Department of Health 1992, 2005; Kaye and Lingiah 2000; Prins et al. 1993). Perhaps because of this, it was little discussed; when it was, it was done either with an air of caution or defensively. It was hard not to conclude that this was an institution, like other parts of the NHS and the public sector, ill at ease with these sensitive issues. The small number of black staff were relatively isolated, but felt they could offer the relatively larger proportion of black patients cultural reference points not otherwise available. They were hard-pressed to protect themselves or patients from the overt racism detectable on occasion in both staff and patients. But the significance of race or ethnicity was of secondary importance to the major social categories of staff and patient, as it was these that were more likely to determine existence in a day-to-day sense.

Articulating agency

That a power differential existed between staff and patients is not news, and was part of the explicit remit of the institution. It becomes news if this power differential is *not* maintained (Fallon et al. 1999), or if it goes beyond the professionally acceptable into the realm of abuse (Department of Health 1992).

This analysis of ward life resonates with that found in much of the early social science literature on psychiatric hospitals (e.g. Goffman 1961; Scheff 1961) as well as the sporadic later ethnographic material (McCourt Perring 1994). This literature usually emerged from units where many wards contained long-stay patients and where the total hospital population ran into thousands. Though it emphasized the extent to which individuals were cut off from the outside world, it was more concerned with the social relations and concepts of staff and patient roles which made that possible. This was an analysis predominantly of social structure, of a hierarchical system with patients at the bottom of the heap and in a position to exercise little control over their everyday life. This message was expressed without resort to impenetrable social theory and said something of importance to those involved in psychiatric settings. It is understandable that this seminal work is still known outside anthropological circles many years later. Observable social phenomena were presented against a critique of ideas rooted in medicine; these medical ideas had provided intellectual and practical legitimacy for the psychiatric enterprise (Foucault 1989; Jones 1993).

However, that was then, and there are important differences between that literature and the fieldwork material from Smithtown. This material had as a primary aim the purpose of delineating the social rather than the individual, notwithstanding the fact that the distinction would only be partly recognized by the inhabitants of Smithtown. However, real people kept intruding, saying and doing things that necessitated an analysis of the contribution of individual behaviour to the manifest culture of the wards. There was room for the 'I' in life, independent of the attributed or accepted social identities. Then I decided to make tea, go to first breakfast, go to the social function or ring his/her mother. Then I made time to see a particular patient or found the sex offenders' group stressful that morning. There was room in the job of staff or patient for individual expression, and any focus on the social tends to emphasize similarity and to downplay particularity. The importance of the 'I' may be special within an institution with classificatory zeal, especially since some staff and probably many patients did not want the identities thrust upon them by others.

This situation seems to have much in common with the observation of Rapport (2009: 198):

> . . . under a structuralist dispensation, in short, individual agency comes to be overwritten, more or less vulgarly, by social structure and institutionalism, hierarchy and history, habitus and hegemony.

The patients spoke little; the wards were quiet places. They acted as individuals, both dictated to and oblivious to the origins of institutional hegemony. My personal view is that this is to do with madness. They were ill equipped for collective resistance. Some of their solitary modes were a consequence of intense personal preoccupations, some to do with caution about others on the ward. The net effect, interpersonal indifference and incomprehension, made collective thought, belief and action against institutionally imposed rhythms and rules non-viable.

A psychoanalyst might say that there is evidence of 'malignant mirroring' between staff and patients, who on the ward formed each other's most significant other, and perhaps also between patients and patients. Both patients and staff were wary, could be dangerous to the other and were perceived as such. For patients the message of daily life and also of anecdote (framing of troublesome patients, deaths in seclusion) was that staff, even if personally pleasant much of the time, could say and do nasty things to you with sometimes irreversible consequences. The staff rationale might be ill understood or understood and disputed, and the person concerned might not have seen the sanction coming. Less alarmingly, but unfairly, staff could make racist or humiliating remarks.

Staff were armed with the knowledge of what the patients had done. Sometimes, mental health staff would have been victims, adding personal resonance to the account. For them the avoidance of injury was important. It is well known in victimology that if you have been a victim once you are more likely to be one again. Thus, as a member of staff, both for yourself and for your group, order must be maintained. Small-scale disruption to the usual institutional order could only be tolerated if it is the gift of staff to know about it and forgive or sanction it, or as is said in prison studies, to use discretion. Such displays of power served to prevent the arrival of chaos. Perhaps the representation of madness itself, both historically and currently, contributes. An overturning of staff authority, the upset of the usual social order, however brief, fits with the idea of madness as 'disorder' (the term used in the Mental Health Act) and with an unpredictable mind and body.

These social relations that were the daily life of the wards were about saying what you were not, as much as saying how you related. As Massey (1999: 16) put it, these are identities established by 'distinctions from' rather than 'relations to'.

In seeking to find out how you would know who was in charge, which seemed like a straightforward question, what became clear was that there was no single answer. The mechanisms of power involved not only those on the ward, but also those outside it whose system of values, theoretical and practical, determined much that happened. Yet, this was not entirely hegemonic. Individual agency was salient to the actual social relations on the wards.

Chapter 7

Ward life under the microscope: the maintenance of power

The previous chapter made much of social relations between types of people. This has told us about who is in charge of what but not much about how that remains the case. Social distinctions and social hierarchies are not just announced and known thereafter. To do that at all, ward life needs to be scrutinized in greater depth, to be visible under a microscope, to see what might be generic to the maintenance of power in organizations and what might be culturally specific to this particular institution. This is conceptually important, as if there is nothing specific, Goffman's conflation of boarding schools, concentration camps and asylums might be reasonable.

Smithtown wards are very particular environments. The material culture of the ward, the things people had and how they used them, as well as how people lived in that world, literally how they used the space, are highly relevant to the understanding of the social order and thus to the maintenance of the social relations described previously.

Theorizing about space or the use of space in hospital environments is not new. In this instance the focus is on space and power. Geographers are now interested in carceral geography, i.e. migration and imprisonment, and these macro-social movements create theory (Allen 1999; Soja 1989). This is a more anthropological understanding of 'the micro-specificities of day to day routines and practices' (Moore 1996b: ix) and how they happen in local inhabited spaces. This takes us into the territory of the panopticon (see Fig. 7.1) and the cultural messages transmitted by the use of material culture that inform the generation and maintenance of social inequality in hospital settings (Parrott 2010).

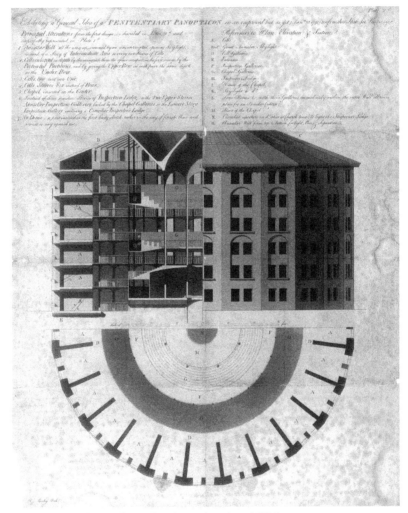

Fig. 7.1 A general idea of a penitentiary panopticon (1791)
Courtesy of UCL Library Services, Special Collections.

It is easy to believe that status distinctions between staff and patients are in some way unique to a setting like Smithtown. The following vignette sounds a note of caution and also brings to life how symbolic aspects of the physical environment can structure human behaviour. The way in which this is perceived depends on the context. So, the same kinds of things can happen but their import may vary according to the particular setting.

We go unbidden to where we think we should be. Our documents are checked. We join a line of people. Ahead of us people start removing their clothing. We are among strangers but we do so too, encouraged by the people in uniform. We show these people our possessions. Some of the people in uniform have guns. Still, we stand now in socks and have no belts. All our outer clothing is removed. In fact, we remove the very things we would need if we had to run away. We are told that this is because of potential problems with these items. We are scanned. Sometimes we have to step into a machine, our bodies encased, and we put up our arms and spread our legs. We are told both that the scanner, a form of X-ray, will do us no harm and that soon we can reclaim our clothing, just not until we are the other side of the scanner. We are social animals, so we follow the behaviour of the person in front.

In fact, this is an airport. We do get our clothes back and we presume that the scanner has done us no harm with its invisible rays. To anyone familiar with the literature or films on the Jewish Holocaust it looks rather familiar. The arrival at a concentration camp involved queues, sorting of possessions, removal of clothing and subjection to procedures which at first sight were not always as worrying as they should have been (Frister 2000). Other people were in uniforms and had guns. In the later days of the war, the time taken from arrival on a train to death could be under an hour, less time than it takes to clear security on bad days.

In passing through the airport, we are controlled, under surveillance and become obedient. We seldom ask, if at all, whether the risk from the scanner is too great and could harm our health. What, I wonder, would happen if it were decided, in the interests of security, that coats, shoes and belts were not enough? For thorough searching maybe we must strip to our underwear. Would public decency, outraged by the proximity and gaze of strangers, triumph over a culture of ever-increasing security and surveillance?

In the event that we are not obedient there is a real risk the people in uniforms will take issue with us. Minor infringements of the rules, like having 150 mls of hair shampoo or some nail scissors, will result in a degree of public humiliation and will irritate everyone else in the queue. In the entire hell that is using budget airlines, you may be publicly chastised if you have two bags, not one. But you will not be summarily shot.

Recently, I and no doubt millions of others celebrated the new freedom to take a carrier bag onto a Ryanair jet. Personally, I tested this new freedom. I put my notebook in my airport bag, not just the newspaper. When does this become an infringement, I wondered? Was it on a par with 'smuggling' cheese in my coat when my bag was too heavy? Standing in line, I saw a woman of 70 plus, with an inner coat of many pockets. She systematically took things out of her case and put them into the many pockets. We have become, we careful law-abiding middle classes, a bunch of rule benders. This is scarcely new. My grandfather, a doctor, evaded cheerfully the currency restrictions of post-war Europe by selling watches. Before leaving England he had sewn them into his coat in anticipation of expensive, continental hotel bills.

The behaviour of Holocaust victims is ours. We are compliant. The behaviour of prisoners, whose rule breaking in prison (drug use, trading pills), major and minor, is well known, is also ours. We, when necessary, look for ways in which to circumnavigate the rules. Restrictions on our personal autonomy make us all subversive. So, it is important not to imagine that it is solely the inhabitants of Smithtown who might hide contraband teabags in their rooms when possible and necessary.

Rooms and keys

Children seldom have keys. It is a rite of passage en route to adult status to be given the keys to your parents' house. In Smithtown the possession of keys meant that staff could go into places when they wanted. Patients were often dependent on staff for access. They were, perhaps, infantilized. The possession of keys by staff, perceived as both normal and legitimate by them, was perceived by patients as normal; but it symbolized a social division. Being able to enter spaces at will is not necessarily the same as 'ownership' of them. The subtleties of the negotiation of space come into play when spaces are open physically, i.e. when a door is either open or unlocked. Shutting doors with or without locking them is both about shutting in and shutting out. The wards, and for that matter the hospital, were divided into these different kinds of spaces, an analysis of which shed light on exactly what was shut in and out and why. Power differentials were made manifest and more importantly, repeatedly reinforced in the small actions of the day, rather than the less frequent but more overt statements to the same effect. The illustrations that follow also suggest that whilst an understanding of these issues hangs on the differences between the two groups, staff and patients, there were exceptions to the rules.[1]

The rules about access were so well learnt that they were seldom remarked upon; it was only through long periods of observation on individual wards that they became apparent. The existence of this shared understanding was also evident in the occasional breaches of, or challenges to, what was usually the case.

Staff space

Two rooms on each ward were, from their names, staff areas—the staff mess and the nursing office. These rooms were locked when no member of staff was in them.

The staff mess did not contain any staff personal items and sometimes contained staff metal cutlery. The exception to the basic access rule was when the mess on Toulouse was being cleaned by the ward worker—he was permitted to be there on his own but only for the duration of his duties. At mealtimes, which were in fact nurses' mealtimes, as all other disciplines ate elsewhere, the door was closed but not locked. For staff this was a way of escaping patient contact and relaxing. In other circumstances they would have gone to a staff cafeteria. This did exist but was so far away as to be impracticable. When the room was used for cups of coffee and tea the door was usually open. Staff were approachable during these times, and patients could legitimately request assistance. Certain patients, in combination with certain staff, would sit in the mess. The vast majority of patients on Toulouse would not step across the threshold of the door even when in conversation with a member of staff inside. On Lille, no patient ever entered the staff mess. On Paris, only one patient, the ward committee man, was regularly given access.

---

[1] For reasons of confidentiality it is not possible to include maps of the wards

On Toulouse, the nursing office was used for administration and was in use most of the time. It contained patients' files in an unlocked cupboard, as well as a variety of potential weapons in the desk drawers. Patients adopted different strategies when conversing with staff—some would never cross the threshold, some would come in and have their query dealt with and others might sit and chat. The rules changed if the doors were shut, e.g. for the nursing handover. Any interruption required knocking and would be unlikely to be dealt with at that time; the transfer of information between professionals took precedence over anything else. Lille, with large numbers of nursing staff, also used their nursing office most of the day. On Paris this was less true, as the supervision of telephone calls and the allocation of work chits and arranging of escorts were done from another room.

Negotiated space

Staff areas that were locked in the absence of staff had an unequivocal quality. Unlocked spaces acquired and transmitted meaning in different ways, principally through occupancy and exclusion. Several rooms on all three wards were not locked at all. There were four such areas on Paris, the ward with the smallest patient population, four on Toulouse—though the quiet room was small—and two on Lille. These rooms were free for staff and patients to use but in practice they could be taken over for meetings of different kinds. This was non-negotiable; for instance, it would not be possible for a patient to hold up the ward round by saying they had to finish a snooker game or complete a letter they were writing on the computer. Equally, a member of staff who was finishing their snooker game would have to do so. Meetings, regardless of the number of patients involved, were instigated by staff. Access to different meetings varied. In a similar vein, the cleaners (paid staff) on Lille locked patients out of the dayroom when cleaning it. In all these cases staff determined access and egress once occupancy had been established.

For illustrative purposes, consider Toulouse. Toulouse case conferences and management rounds took over a 'public room'. During these meetings, members of staff of whatever discipline arrived late, left early and would at times come in and go out. In contrast, patients could only refuse to come in or leave precipitately (the exception to this was the ward worker, who serviced the ward round with cups of tea). Patients would be asked to come in and would be informed when their interview was over. In many ways this is not dissimilar to a job interview—but the rules there only apply to a small area of life, and they are not echoed in the rules affecting the whole of daily life.

Therapy groups on Toulouse were different but also the same. Once occupancy for the purpose of the group was established, the shutting-in of staff and patients to a therapy group invoked the idea that, in contrast to the ward rounds, this was the creation of a confidential space for more than one patient at a time. The ethos of such groups is that the private space created is such that information divulged to the group is not to be shared outside the group. The importance attached to this idea on this ward was indicated by the fact that, in contrast to all other formal happenings on the ward, the researcher was not invited either into the groups or the debriefings by staff. A small number of patients disagreed with this, on the basis that the groups were relevant to an understanding of ward life. The rest of the ward was also shut out of such groups. The confidentiality of the group setting is of course broken by the transmission of information derived from the group between staff. On occasion the researcher was privy to this. Some patients pointed out that in their view patients also told non-group patients some of the things that had been said.

Not all groups on Toulouse had this ethos of confidentiality, nor did it apply to the groups on Paris. On Paris, the community meeting was conducted with a closed door. In practice, people sat through it, be they staff or patients. Its equivalent on Toulouse was more flexible; not only did both staff and patients wander in and out but at times, patients from other wards appeared in it.

Patients' rooms

For patients, the acquisition of a personal room (never called a bedroom), as opposed to sleeping in a dormitory, conferred on them the possibility of excluding both other patients and staff. The facilities on the three wards varied. They had, between them, a mixture of single rooms and dormitories. A few patients had to sleep in a dormitory located on another ward. Some single rooms had what is termed 'integral sanitation', a curious term which really means that in your modestly sized room you sleep next to the lavatory. This has been welcomed as an advance in prisons and hospitals. Much depends on design. Sleeping in close proximity to a lavatory, with no door separating your bed from it, is something really only done by the comatose drunk, so it is debatable that it represents a more normal design solution.

Possession of a single room was in part an illusion of ownership, though one for the most part maintained. There was a boundary between you and other people that could be invoked. The room was not always available to you. Not all the study wards allowed free access by patients to their rooms. Lille and Toulouse did, but Paris operated a system of privilege. Roughly half the rooms on Paris were open during the Smithtown day. The others were locked on weekdays during the hours when patients were supposed to be at work. The nurses' intention was to prevent certain patients from shutting themselves away and to disallow the option of staying in bed rather than going to work. Similarly it was forbidden on Paris to lie on your bed under the bedclothes during the day. The potential sanction was having your room locked, meaning you could not access it. Fellow patients might be legitimately shut out but not in. These rules governed patients' access to their own rooms.

Some patients believed they understood the basis of these rules; some confessed the system was incomprehensible. It is relevant that sexual practices on single-sex wards were frowned upon. Some effort went into reducing the possibility that patients might use their rooms for sexual activity with other patients.

The situation for those without rooms was very different—both in terms of their ability to be physically alone and in terms of personal possessions. Most patients wanted to have a room. Many of the male and female patients in the study did not have them. However, there were patients who did not want rooms. Their reasons varied: they might have found it difficult to maintain an acceptable level of tidiness or hygiene, they might have feared dying alone and without anyone noticing or they might have wanted the company of a dormitory. At the opposite extreme there were instances of the successful refusal of, or disenchantment with, a move to a ward where a newcomer would have to wait for a room, in the meantime having to make do with dormitory accommodation.

Rooms were a major currency for most patients but it was not only having one that mattered. Decisions and the basis for decisions about allocation were not transparent and relevant information resided with staff. Daily use was also subject to regulation by staff.

More than that, staff access to patients' rooms was regularly reinforced. Staff checked for death and did so each morning. They checked by flash-light at night. They could disturb people in their rooms where there was concern that they might harm themselves and they could encourage the use of seclusion rooms for self-protection. A more extreme example of this capacity was the search. Several searches occurred on the study wards during fieldwork, demonstrating the unequivocal power of staff to enter patients' rooms and to go through their possessions with no warning.

The search

One search followed concern by staff that drugs were available on the ward. From Smithtown's point of view not only was this illegal but it was also dangerous for some vulnerable patients. In addition, it potentially formed part of a patient economy which the hospital dis-couraged. The bulk of the search was conducted on another ward but several patients' rooms on the study ward were targeted, primarily because they were thought to have been involved in similar activities in the past. The patients targeted knew this was the case. The search was conducted by staff from the 'Control and Restraint' department; these were nursing staff who to some extent continued to work on the wards but on these occasions wore black romper suits, as one researcher termed them, and big boots; black romper suits were also worn by the SAS. They were accompanied by three policemen with sniffer dogs. They began their search of rooms on the study ward 45 minutes after everyone had gone to bed. The search found no drugs on this occasion.

Another search was prompted by the disappearance of a knife from a staff area. This search had comic elements. Staff searched their own lockers in case the external search team found illicit goods. As it was someone's birthday, liqueur chocolates had been brought in and this caused consternation. The ward manager was trapped on the ward for the search, which had been ordered by a more senior nurse. The staff areas were searched by a three-man security team. As the knife was not located, the patient areas were searched next. The following field note extract explains what happened next:

> The patients were asked to go into the dining room and all their rooms were locked off. No one so far had told them what was going on . . . The feeling among the patients was one of bewilderment, and also anger, as the search was obviously being conducted and they felt it was yet another invasion of their privacy. Marthe was getting quite irate at the prospect of yet another room search. She said there was no respect for their privacy and she banged her fist angrily on the table. Odette said that she was sick of the fact that whatever is missing they assume it has to be the patients. She said that was the feeling when the CD player went missing and it was the feeling now. She said sarcastically that we know the staff would never take anything, don't we? Simone said she had been in the bath . . . and she had been told to get to the dining room immediately. She was really cheesed off because she had taken some cereal and milk into her room and was looking forward to eating it after her bath and now they were going to confiscate it. Therese said that she had just piled her clothes up neatly and God knows what state they would be in now. . . . Unlike on previous occasions, the search team, who were not from the ward, did not call patients to their rooms as they searched them. . . . They did not use metal detectors and they did seem to be whizzing through it, although I expect that they are more experienced at these things than ward staff . . . The staff were annoyed because they felt it was an overreaction and the knife had probably been thrown out in the rubbish . . . Finally, after the search was almost completed, Berthe told the patients that a knife was missing, but they were not told until much later that it was from the staff area and that it was a sharp one . . . There was talk amongst the staff of there being a major search tomorrow, as they had not found it.

In fact, there was no subsequent search and the knife remained missing. The process of searching is interesting because it indicates double standards; the staff got a warning about illicit goods, the patients did not. The search was unpredictable and invasive, and it was perhaps a more potent reminder of just who was in charge because it was both rare and unpredictable. Animal experiments show that events that are intermittent but unpredictable are powerful reinforcers of behaviour.

Being locked in rooms

Staff could and did lock people in rooms; this happened as part of every-day life. There had been a tiny number of incidents, though there have now been none for many years, when patients had obtained keys and locked themselves or other patients or staff in rooms.

At night, the day staff locked patients in their rooms. This meant that you could not get out but nor could anyone else get in, providing a degree of safety from other patients. This was not available for patients in dormi-tories. As a counterpoint, dormitory accommodation in prisons is seen as a risk. Theft and bullying, as well as the protection afforded by wit-nesses, are seen as features intrinsic to this kind of space (HMIP 2013). As patient-on-patient violence was clearly not unknown in the High Secure Hospital system, this was a real issue for some patients.

Seclusion

Seclusion, defined as 'the supervised confinement of a patient in a room, which may be locked, to protect others from significant harm' (MHA Code of Practice 2008), was infrequently used on the study wards. Seclu-sion rooms are differently designed and furnished from ordinary patient rooms, being devoid of fixtures and fittings that can be easily turned into weapons. On one of the study wards, the seclusion room was turned into a bedroom. On a ward elsewhere, where I was subsequently a consult-ant, the seclusion room was turned into a laundry drying room. This was viewed by all of us, staff and patients alike, as both a statement and a bit of a victory. In six months on Toulouse, there was one incident of patient-on-staff violence, which resulted in the seclusion of the patient for a few hours but rates of seclusion varied and on certain other wards were high. Seclusion is an extreme example of the staff's capacity to con-trol patients. In a ward setting, it is also visible to other patients.

Seclusion was, and is, the legitimate sanction for a serious threat of patient violence. Its use was both authorized and constrained by the Code of Practice of the 1983 Mental Health Act (Department of Health and Welsh Office 1993), the hospital's own seclusion policy and by a case taken to the European Court of Human Rights by a Special Hospital patient (*A v The United Kingdom* 1980). It is only one of a range of pro-cedures in use in European hospitals that reduce freedom of movement:

other examples are physical restraint by staff or mechanical restraints applied to the person. England and Wales have low rates of physical restraint (Di Lorenzo et al. 2012). This case of A is illuminating about historic practice. The patient was thought to have started a fire in the Special Hospital in which he was detained and he was secluded for five weeks. No final judgement was made but a consequence of pursuing the case was that changes were made to seclusion policy (Gostin 1986: 69–70).

At the time of fieldwork, the seclusion policy for Smithtown was under review; this was not long after the Ashworth Inquiry (Department of Health 1992: 203) had recommended that seclusion be phased out in the Special Hospitals. The Inquiry reasoned that its use for self-harm was inappropriate and the threshold for use of 'deviant behaviour' was too low, as it encompassed 'anything that interferes with the smooth running of the ward or challenges the authority of staff. Thus, patients may be secluded for failing to obey instructions, or failing to carry out ward tasks, or venting anger or abuse on another. We believe this to be unacceptable'. The abolition of seclusion was the only recommendation of the Inquiry with which the SHSA substantially disagreed. But it did review its policies, and draft documents were circulated to staff as part of the consultation process. The Patients' Council was also part of the consultation process. That it had been very difficult to decide on a seclusion policy was borne out by the fact that Smithtown was on to its fourth draft six months after fieldwork had finished.

In reality, what seclusion is, what it is for and what it feels like depend very much on the person concerned. It is a form of solitary confinement in that the person is locked in a room alone, with a bed that is immovable. It is normal to remove from the patient any item which they might use to harm themselves, such as shoelaces or pens, as well as often their own clothing. Seclusion lasts for variable lengths of time but should be for as short a time as possible. Not all the patients in the study had been in seclusion but for those that had, it could be an important issue.

Reflections on seclusion experience among the male patients interviewed suggested a range of responses. For some with substantial experience of the prison system, it was familiar; for them it was the same

as being 'banged up'. Others disliked it; at best it was thought to be boring and lonely. One or two feared it: 'They can inject you, they done that
to C—and they killed him. It was pretty miserable at times because I had
bad visions and cruel voices'. No one construed it as helpful, and a number of patients viewed it as punishment. They recognized that it was used
to deal with fighting and escapes but saw the periods of seclusion, that
were previously part of routine admission practice and applied wholesale, as unacceptably different, precisely because they were non-specific.

Hostage taking

The opposite experience for staff was hostage taking. This was a real fear
for staff. These fears were exemplified by a horrific, historical incident.
The potency of this incident is unsurprising; the incident involved loss
of control of a unit by staff and extreme sexual violence by patients. The
details of this incident and the relevant type of garrotte were used in the
induction course attended by the first two but not the third researcher. The potential dangerousness of the patient group as a whole was
emphasized to all potential key holders—a motley crew of nurses, porters, catering staff and researchers. One man explained it as follows:
'You dread a riot or being taken hostage. If you are taken hostage you
are dead. Slowly and horribly. In the old days you wouldn't ever go out
of sight of colleagues without telling a colleague; now we have become
complacent.' The hostage-taking incident is the ultimate reversal of the
normal power structure, and requires staff disempowerment and ultimately impotence. I use the word impotence deliberately, as its double
meaning and resonance correctly describe the staff's state of mind in an
institution occupied by sexually violent men.

Men and women and space

It is already clear that there were spaces in Smithtown where women are
absent. The fact that men were present in predominantly women's spaces
is also known. Both of these raised issues of power and risk.

On the women's ward, male nursing staff were present in small numbers. There were delicate issues in the balance of power that were gendered; this was informed both by the past and the present. Common

sense would dictate that there were tasks on the women's wards that should only be undertaken by women. In practice, men felt restricted in what they could do on women's wards and there was a widespread reluctance to undertake overtime. The least anxious of male staff said this was because they felt redundant; the more anxious ones said it was because of the possibility that they would be accused of inappropriate behaviour with women patients. Men regularly working on women's wards had a range of approaches. There were examples of men who stayed in public spaces and seldom saw patients on their own; equally, others were relaxed and joked with the women patients in ways that the women concerned appeared to like. This was despite the fact that accusations of inappropriate behaviour by male staff were made during the lifetime of the study by women patients and required investigation. Gender differences on women's wards compromised staff's overall ability to go anywhere at any time.

> Henri asked me to come with him as a female presence to the dining room . . . He told me that he never went out of sight of another staff member on his own. He said he would walk up and down the corridor in view of someone but he would never go into one of the rooms off the corridor. Neither Jacques nor Phillippe can do this.

However, women patients gave examples of where they thought women's privacy had not been respected and men had been present when women were only partly clothed. Both the breach and observance of these social spatial rules were important in the life of the ward. Male staff were at risk from possibly unjustified accusations of impropriety but were also, by virtue simply of being staff and undertaking staff duties, potentially intrusive into women's private space. This was therefore different from the men's wards where this did not apply. The men could not claim, as the women could, that there were customs and codes of decency that held outside of Smithtown but which also applied inside Smithtown and could not be abandoned by virtue of staff and patient roles. Indeed, for the reasons set out here, perhaps they required greater observance.

Within the life of the women's ward, complex gender issues were being played out. Moore (1996b: 177) has pointed out that the difference between what men and women say men and women are, and what they do, can be considerable. On this ward, there were few men and a lot of women. Women are of course not all the same (Probyn 1995; Strathern 1981) and their experience of this environment would be nuanced by their own histories. Neither the men nor the women on this ward were just men or just women, they were also staff or patients. What is known now about the clinical characteristics of secure hospital women patients is that their early life has been characterized by far more adverse experience than is common (Bartlett and Hassell 2001; Department of Health 2002). This has usually been at the hands of men who should have been looking after them but actually sexually and physically abused them. Increasingly, this is understood to be linked with poor self-worth, self-harming behaviours and a tendency for extreme emotional states, sometimes triggered by experiences, smell, gesture or sound of voice that remind the woman of her abuse. Sexual abuse is an invasion of the body but it often requires an invasion of private space, such as a child's bedroom or playroom. If this is grasped, the complications for male staff in women's space look more obvious. One aspect that is particularly hard to untangle is the difference between intention and reception (Probyn 1995). The signals and behaviours of male staff as they themselves understand them may be a poor guide to how they are perceived. Not all of this is under their control, and some of it hinges on a notion of men being not only men but straight men, since that is the origin of the discretion shown by men in this particular circumstance. The issue of the clothed, and in this case uniformed, male staff and the unclothed women was that of the possibility of abuse. In almost all cases this would be *more* abuse (Bland et al. 1999). Institutionally determined staff proximity to patients and access to patient space, in this regard, as elsewhere in medical practice, challenged the idea that proximity implies membership of the same cultural group (Ilcan 1999).

Some of these issues were also played out off the ward, between patients. Contact between male and female patients almost exclusively happened off the ward, at social functions and work. Relationships across gender and ward were discussed, both informally and formally. Recognized couples had some opportunity to meet, and marriage was discussed and sometimes took place. In practice, the fact that men and women patients had no shared domestic space was an effective way both to safeguard the women patients and to undermine these relationships, since they were never able to develop in the privacy thought both necessary and ordinary in most of the outside world.

All patients in Smithtown were under surveillance but the women were doubly the object of the male gaze, from staff and patients. The impact of such surveillance had additional connotations in view of their pasts. The maintenance of spatial separation was more than usually important.

Public space

Privacy in various forms is highly valued by patients. The inevitable use of public spaces provides additional evidence of strategies that are designed to enhance privacy. These could be to manage concerns about other patients' hostility or simply to avoid meaningful contact. Staff strategies propelled patients into these public arenas more than the patients wished. Public space was used for meals and drinks, for snooker and table tennis and for smoking. However, patients on all three study wards preferentially used their rooms for large parts of the day. This might have been a consequence not only of personal inclination, e.g. reading or writing, but also a response to aspects of ward life. Patients on one ward complained of feeling physically threatened when using public space; on another ward, the researcher saw evidence of intimidation between patients. When dormitories or rooms were locked off, the use of public space was inevitable. Some patients adopted methods that lessened the likelihood of interaction with others in public space, e.g. not washing or not initiating conversation. Being silent could be a way of being private, even in the midst of people; it is like reading on a packed tube train. Privacy inside one's head might be more problematic. Silence might be accompanied by a cacophony of voices that other people could not hear. Voices could make it hard to be alone, and for that to be witnessed in a public arena provoked unwanted attention.

Meals and the minutiae of power

We all eat and drink; it is fundamental to life. This and the regularity with which people ate and drank on the wards lent itself to description and analysis. Just by being there and watching and listening you learn a lot. Rooms and keys are about the regular and the untoward. Both help maintain status differentials but meals, with their mundane but complex quality, showed how little untoward needs to happen for social order to be reinforced. It need never be consciously known because it is done that way.

A number of authors have commented on the organization of patient meals (Alasewski 1986; Goffman 1961) in psychiatric settings but to date there has been no attempt to think about staff in this context. This is remedied here. The three wards organized themselves both differently and the same, with varying contributions from patients and staff. Most of what follows is from one ward but the differences we picked up on elsewhere are referenced. What comes through strongly is concrete evidence of the minutiae of control; the experience of precisely these minutiae work to reinforce the status differentials between staff and patients identified by people in Smithtown and documented earlier. This builds on the broader brush analysis of space and its meaning in the last section by bringing together fine-grain activities in small areas of the ward.

The other contribution to, and consequence of, the status differential was an abuse of staff role, in this case taking food allocated to patients. This was only possible with the cooperation of key members of the patient group who were in privileged positions; it required as well the tacit acceptance of this practice by all patients. Taking food in this context had little practical import but it indicated the way in which staff rule-breaking in institutions can go undetected and as such is an important message, in this case, to the patient group. It indicated that staff were confident that patients would not complain.

Patients' food

There were three formal meals a day for patients on all three wards, and these were provided for them. This food was eaten publicly in contrast to self-catering, which was less communal. Standard Smithtown food was also supplemented by meals organized for special occasions, for instance those which were integral to social events. Both the public nature of most meals and the possible variation in food preparation practices were different from an English prison, where, as Earle and Phillips (2012) note, most meals are collected by individual prisoners, transported and eaten in the relatively private but cramped space of a cell. Startlingly different again is the situation in Canadian medium or minimum secure prisons, where prisoners were unable to choose where to eat or what clothes they wore when eating (Godderis 2006).

Big meals

Toulouse ward meals were announced by the call for carriers—patients doing this as regular ward work. Everyone on the ward knew the meal-times, and when the delivery of food to the ward was late, patients grumbled about the state of the hospital or went to check out the dining room in case they had missed the Tannoy. The meal could not begin without the arrival of four large yellow food boxes. These came from central kitchens, brought by porters to the bottom of Loire. The Tannoy was based on the ground floor. No one on the ward had any control over the arrival of the yellow boxes, or the use of the Tannoy. Even when the food arrived particularly late and patients were complaining, no attempt was made to hurry the central kitchen staff, who kept to their own rhythms.

The carriers took the food through to the patients' kitchen, and it was unloaded onto the servery by kitchen worker patients. Kitchen workers were never seen to be prompted into activity, moving automatically into gear.

The dining area adjacent to the servery contained square Formica-topped tables. The ward manager had introduced tablecloths in an attempt to render the environment more domestic and less institutional but the consequence of this had been to create more work for the laundry man—twenty-seven tablecloths a day; this did not go down well. Water-jugs on the table seemed less problematic. Alain commented that he had seen the re-emergence of the communal teapot, with milk being added to the pot for convenience. There was room for four men at every table, though the numbers varied; no one regularly sat alone. Cutlery was laid by a kitchen worker before the meal. The level of activity in the dining area contrasted with the smooth efficiency of the kitchen workers. These were men who knew their jobs. A queue formed at the servery for most meals but at breakfast, cereals were laid out just outside the kitchen door where access to them was controlled in practice by the senior kitchen worker. Most of the food was dished out through the servery. Tradition and current practice has it that this onerous task could only be carried out by members of staff. Many staff found this absurd and, in front of the researcher, there were jokes about the kitchen workers taking this over. Further status subtleties were revealed by the fact that items such as orange juice were taken out of the fridge by kitchen workers and passed through the servery to patients. The serving of large trays of food was truly restricted to staff. What ended up on anyone's plate was read out by one of the kitchen workers who was responsible both for menus being filled in by patients and telling staff who had ordered what. Meals were both rapid and quiet. The noise level on the ward rose dramatically as patients left the table. On other wards in the past, staff had been responsible for the removal of cutlery, which encouraged patients to eat quickly. The contrast that springs to mind is that of other public food consumption, for example restaurant meals are leisurely. But a more appropriate comparison might be with the hurried domestic meal, where the pressure is on to complete the washing-up to reach the end of domestic work. It would be hard to connect the atmosphere in this setting to that described but not witnessed by Godderis (2006), who notes the tendency for prison dining areas to be the site of riots.

Meals on Toulouse were substantial. This was in marked contrast to past asylum practice. Scull (1979: 292) comments that the consequence, intended or otherwise, of nutritional deficiency in nineteenth-century asylums was that it was easier for staff to maintain order. Crammer (1990) notes that in Buckinghamshire Asylum, in the first half of the twentieth century, the mortality rate was directly correlated with the generosity of the food allowance. The meaning of the excess food supply in this instance is unclear. Breakfast could include fruit juice, cereals and fried food (though the eggs appeared to have lived a bit before arriving on the ward), and there were plentiful supplies of bread. Midday and evening meals consisted of two courses, though this was not necessarily taken up. Attempts were made to cater for minority food tastes, though these were not always considered successful. At the start of fieldwork food was chosen in advance from a choice of three menus. If a patient did not fill in the menu, he risked not getting any food. Subsequently, the choice was broadened to six. One patient who had spent a few days in a local district hospital expressed his surprise at finding there both relatively little food and relatively little choice. On Toulouse there was always more food. At times, this resulted in an unseemly dash for seconds, with those served first and those nearest the servery standing a better chance of getting seconds. In an effort to combat this, teams for seconds were created and took turns. This was in part recognition of the fact that despite officially being able to sit wherever they wished, the patients, in fact, sat in the same combinations. Place changes were brought about more by patients leaving than anything else.

Goffman (1961: 188) documents various social practices evident in his study of the Central Hospital. His 'male chronic service', 900 patients, ate in shifts in a cafeteria. Second helpings were obtained by a number of different means including eating the desired part of the serving, binning the rest and getting more with an empty plate, wrapping up portable food and leaving it by the plate in order to get seconds and have a snack for later. In another dining room he notes the theft of these night-time snacks by other patients before the 'inmate' returned from the counter. The level of observation on Toulouse ward would have made such practices difficult if not impossible; nursing staff could see all nine tables from the servery and patients were not allowed to move freely between tables during courses. There was no bin in the dining area, so food could not be jettisoned in this way. There was no requirement for patients to eat food they did not want, as they chose it and could refuse it if it looked unpalatable.

At the start of the fieldwork period on Toulouse, cutlery was collected by one of the patients—not a kitchen worker—then washed up and dried and counted by staff, and put away by them in a locked cupboard. Patients were then able to leave the dining area following a signal from staff. The more important signal was of course that patients could not, in their own time, rise from the table.

The later system, where cutlery was washed not by hand but by machine, entailed a change in routine. Patients returned their own cutlery, and until the counting was correct, patients were not able to leave the room. Washing-up took longer and nursing staff had to wait until this was complete in order to lock it away. For some staff, who commented spontaneously on the subtle signals this gave off, how this was achieved was an indication of a member of staff's relationship with patients. There were those, it was remarked, who did not feel confident to remain in the patients' kitchen on their own. The paradox of this concern when four sets of metal cutlery were routinely available to the kitchen workers was also noted.

Inside the kitchen other tasks were carried out by the kitchen team during meals. The staff tended to vacate the kitchen—a small space, and one in which they were redundant after serving food. Rather than enter the dining room itself, they would hang around in the corridor space. Plates were returned to the area by patients and excess food from the food trays and plates jettisoned. The washing-up machines were loaded and some hand-washing-up done, tables wiped down and the yellow boxes taken back downstairs. The kitchen workers, who kept food back on the hotplate for themselves, settled down to eat last in the dining room after everyone else had gone.

Alasewski (1986: 157) argued that in his study of institutional care in a mental handicap hospital 'the main "message" encoded in the meals was about the nature of the relationship between the patients and their nurses'. The relationship identified in his account of mealtimes on three wards is of different degrees of patient dependence on staff. Some of his patient group needed to be brought to tables and required assistance with feeding. Only on his 'high grade' ward was there any involvement by patients in food distribution. Staff determined where patients sat according to a perception of their 'problems'. In Smithtown it is not so easy to link social practice to staff perception of the patients' problems. No patient was unable to feed him/herself—even in the presence of significant side effects from medication. Staff practice seemed to be deeply embedded. This, in the case of Toulouse, was at odds with the expression of ward ethos—Toulouse prided itself on innovation. The emphasis was on making patients responsible for aspects of daily life, within the constraints of the hospital's security procedures. Cutlery items were always potential weapons. In truth, meals could not have happened without the involvement of the kitchen workers as there were not enough staff. So, while staff controlled materials, counting cutlery and serving the actual meals, they were dependent on the active participation of patients whose behaviour was that of a well-oiled and in turn well-fed machine. In Maidstone Prison (Earle and Phillips 2012), a Category B prison, where men were in the unusual position of frequently self-catering, the management of the kitchen by prisoners was considered by them to be an achievement, particularly given the range of available weapons and limited space. Smithtown and Maidstone practices represent different points on a spectrum from self-management to total staff control.

Not eating

Not everyone wants to eat all the time. On Toulouse, patients could absent themselves from any of the meals providing they indicated as such, since staff needed to know who was absent because the other agenda at mealtimes is patient numbers, another security issue. Patients were counted at breakfast time. Reasons for missing meals varied—at weekends patients wanted a lie-in, at other times they might not be hungry or might be dieting (weight problems being very common), or they might have planned to cook or to eat at a function. Alternatively, as the ward operational policy remarks, their psychiatric illness and their abstinence could be linked. Personal preferences for independent eating were constrained by budget, or access to functions or external food supplies— from the canteen or the catering manager.

Personal catering

Private food existed. On Toulouse, individual cups of coffee were common. They were made either in the servery or from personal flasks of hot water that patients were permitted to use when the servery was closed. Coffee and other drinks could be consumed in any of the public rooms on Toulouse and in private space. By contrast, the consumption of food was restricted to the patients' dining area, apart from sweets and snack bars. Some patients, as in Goffman, smuggled food to eat elsewhere. Private food of this kind was eaten separately from the institutional meals and might be solitary or communal. Caudill et al. (1952) observed that this kind of social eating represented conscious resistance to routine, a plausible explanation in Smithtown.

Non-perishable food was kept in lockers and there were rules about its storage. Glass jars were forbidden items on the ward. Lockers on Toulouse were both in the games room and along the ward corridor. Access to those in the games room was constrained by the use of this room for meetings.

There were additional rules about access to certain types of kitchen implements for cooking. Patients did not have access to sharp knives or tin openers, and when preparing their own food they would eat with plastic cutlery. The use of such items highlighted differing attitudes to security. There had previously been a tin opener attached to part of the furniture on Toulouse, available for use without necessitating staff–patient contact. This broke and the new tin opener gave rise to conflicting attitudes amongst staff, some of whom favoured less access than previously. Some of the items in the staff mess could be used by patients, e.g. the microwave.

Communal food was usually prepared by patients without the assistance of staff at the cooking stage, one example being the farewell meal cooked for the researcher. Alcohol was banned throughout the hospital but alcohol-free beers and wine were permitted. Food not normally available from the hospital shop, e.g. raw meat, could with some effort be ordered from Smithtown catering staff, who would obtain it for a particular day. Basic foodstuffs could be purchased from the hospital shop. Relatives also brought food, which for many ethnic minority patients could be something of a cultural lifeline. Take-away food could also be organized, and was on an occasional basis. So, food practices were more varied than those described by other authors but the routine of three meals a day was just that for most of the patients on Toulouse.

Comparison of all three wards

The two other study wards showed the same basic pattern of food supply but there were subtle differences. These are worthwhile remarking, as they indicate small but important differences in the degree to which patients' behaviour was circumscribed within the institutional regime.

Food was brought to both Paris and Lille by the portering service. Patients on both wards were involved in the preparation of the dining area. On Paris, this was the one public room in which smoking was permitted. Ashtrays needed emptying, which discouraged anyone from sitting and smoking there at that time. The fact that on this ward the only smoking room was the dining room highlighted differences in opinion between patients about the appropriateness of smoking in a food area. Crockery and cutlery were laid out by the kitchen workers. In theory, no patient, other than the kitchen workers, was allowed in the dining room with the cutlery out until the meal was announced. This rule was breached. The meal was announced by one of the patients shouting out when the delivery van was seen. Patients queued for food; their name and choice of food were usually broadcast by the kitchen worker. The staff served the food and seconds were handed out on a first-come-first-served basis. Plates and cutlery were rapidly collected and the cutlery immediately washed by a kitchen worker. Once the cutlery had been accounted for by staff, they gave a shout, allowing patients to get up from the table. It was noticed that the odd patient breached this security rule by moving to the dispensary early. Attendance at meals was not compulsory; however, in contrast to Toulouse, patients were not allowed to remain in their rooms over mealtimes and were required to be in the dayrooms.

On Lille, the dining room was light, with dried flowers on each table. At the start of fieldwork, food arrived from outside the ward and the nursing staff took it to a corner of the dining room. The meal was announced over the Tannoy system and patients went to the dining room and sat down. When their name was announced by staff, they got up, one by one, went over to the food trolley and were served. As on the other two wards, eating happened in relative silence. Seconds were called out and a patient collected the cutlery in a bucket. The cutlery was washed and counted while the patients sat and waited. When the cutlery was accounted for and the signal to move given, the patients rushed to the door. Patients were entitled to miss breakfast and tea but not lunch. There was little incentive to miss breakfast for many patients, as the only room in which they could smoke, the dayroom, was cleaned during breakfast by the domestic staff. In order to clean the room, they locked themselves in and locked the patients out. At lunchtime, even if you were not eating it was necessary to sit there and wait for the meal to finish. Towards the end of the fieldwork period the system had changed. Tablecloths had reappeared. Also, patients served themselves, although they still had to approach the serving trolley one at a time. This had always been the intention but became a reality only much later. Staff had raised objections when it was discussed in staff meetings (one had said there were insufficient spoons), and one nurse explained that the change caused problems, as patients are slow and staff found it difficult not to serve them to speed up the process. The same nurse commented on patients taking large portions so that there was little left for others.

This detailed examination of wards' routines shows different degrees of involvement by patients in the process of mealtimes and different degrees of control exerted by staff on patients' whereabouts at this time. To summarize, on Lille and Paris, patients did not collect food; on Toulouse, they did. On Paris and Toulouse, you could miss any meal but on Paris, you had to remain in public areas. On Lille, you were locked out of the dayroom and had to sit in the dining room even when not eating a meal. On Paris and Toulouse, men queued and patient ward workers indicated previous food choices; on Lille, women came up one at a time, and making sure patients got what they ordered was down to the staff. There were thus several features of the female ward system which suggested both a higher degree of control of women patients and greater passivity on their part. Even the giant leap forward of a degree of self-service could scarcely be said to have wholehearted staff support.

The meaning of missing cutlery

All three wards require the complements of metal cutlery to be complete before patients move from the table, and this was always done. That staff took this area of security seriously is further evidenced by the consequences of an item going missing. On Toulouse ward, one of the patients put a spoon in his breast pocket, possibly mischievously; no patients moved from the dining area until it was found. On Lille, a fork went missing, and the cutlery was triple counted and all the patients searched with a metal detector; they were confined to the dining room area during this time. When released, their rooms had been locked, and were then searched one by one with the patients present and staff using a metal detector. This search did not detect any forks but it found various items of contraband food. The responses of the patients included anxieties that something might be planted on them, how someone might be hiding it in their vagina, how it was a staff tactic to avoid escorting the patients that night, and tales of how cutlery had previously been used as a weapon. The staff expressed a variety of views including distaste at the state of some patients' possessions, suspicion of certain patients and joking suspicion that the researcher had taken it to have something about which to write. Ward routine on the night of the search dissolved and the fork remained missing. In some contrast, Lille count teaspoons at the end of meals even though all patients had metal teaspoons—to say nothing of metal knitting needles, which were in use throughout the ward. The rationale for these procedures was that these implements could be used as weapons and the less potential weapons there were the better. It is hard not to think that if anyone so wished they could have sharpened their teaspoons or impaled someone on a knitting needle.

Whatever the institutional rationalization for such practices, which were at times mocked by staff, they were the constantly repeated reminders of the staff's ability to control the physical movement of the patient group, as well as to keep them in view and to count them. This control, like other aspects of routine life, was contingent on the cooperation of the patients in view of the total number of staff manning the ward or the hospital at any one time. However, when discussion takes place in the mainstream media about the need for nursing staff to feed patients, it is hard to see that this is the system they had in mind. The balance here is tilted towards supervision and surveillance, not least because the timing of meals made it simple to add the counting rituals of security roll calls. In a building ill suited for surveillance, the dining rooms were open spaces with good sight lines; no cosy corners and dimmed lighting in Smithtown.[2]

Staff food

Smithtown has a cafeteria outside the main gate. To get to the cafeteria it is necessary to walk off the ward, across the site, give in your keys and walk for a further five minutes. The alternative is to go home—for those who live on the Smithtown estate this is convenient; for those who live any distance away it can make a lunch break a waste of time. In the past, staff meals were provided on the hospital site. The shift pattern for the periods of fieldwork was the same. The only meal for which staff were allowed off the ward was lunch. During this time the absence of staff from the ward was covered either by the next shift or by staff coming onto the ward briefly from other areas of the hospital. For staff undertaking long days, i.e. a morning and evening shift, lunch was the only point in a fourteen-and-a-half-hour day when they could guarantee to be off the ward. Even then this might not happen.

Breaks were built into the day at breakfast time and teatime. These were taken formally by almost all staff and happened behind the closed door of the nurses' mess. The main points about staff meals can be made using the case of Toulouse ward; where relevant, reference will be made to the other two wards.

On Toulouse, staff meals were a way of not supervising patients' meals. Those going to 'first mess' at breakfast and tea would not supervise the food but might find themselves available for something else, e.g. manning a social function. Breakfast also included the arrival of milk and the newspapers. Though these papers were subsequently handed on to

[2] Special meals were subtly different from the everyday. On Christmas Day, breakfast was cooked by staff and patients on Paris. It was eaten in near silence by the patients. Staff breakfast was eaten uniquely en masse and with the staff mess door open. Christmas lunch was accompanied by presents from hospital and ward staff. There are no visits to patients on 25 December. The researcher found it a sad day. Birthdays were celebrated on Lille. Patients' tea became something you might really want to eat. The researcher was told that unlike other occasions, staff were allowed to eat the food.

the patients, they were first available to the staff. In the mess, the staff had their own set of cutlery but like the patients lacked decent kitchen knives. This canteen of cutlery was locked after meals. There was a supply of hospital crockery also kept in the mess, as well as personalized mugs. Inside the staff fridge there were hospital issue milk and assorted sauces, which originated in the patient supply kept elsewhere. Bread was plentiful and left in the cupboards. Staff often stored their own food in the fridge. Tea was always hospital issue. Coffee was organized by the staff following the arrival of a filter machine—eyed with some envy by certain patients. When this system collapsed, the occasional private staff supply could be raided.

The commonest meal was conducted with the door shut and additional food being brought by one of the kitchen workers from the dining area to the kitchen. Patients' food had been put aside during the meal. It was then eaten as well as food brought in by staff for their own meals. The practice of reassigning patients' food involved the active cooperation of all kitchen workers and the silence of the entire patient group who were aware of the practice. A number of patients objected to the practice but did not complain about it; another found the attempts at secrecy comical. The researcher was initially told that evening meals were brought in by staff; this was commonly the case. However, after an initial period of concern, staff relaxed and it was not unusual for whole meals to arrive from the patients' kitchen. This relaxation was accompanied by the "corruption" of the researcher who was offered and accepted breakfast. It was intended that it would be impossible for me to write about an illegitimate behaviour having colluded with it. On all three wards subtle tactics were used to seduce the researchers into consumption of patients' food. One researcher was told that within the Smithtown nurses' job description is a clause saying they should be prepared to participate in eating food with patients. This particular informant exerted caution eating in front of senior nursing staff.

The fact that the illegitimacy of this practice was unnecessary and that its continuation serves another purpose, is illustrated by reference to other secure hospital units. At the Longridge Clinic, food for the staff at mealtimes is included in the food order and patients and staff sit in the same area of the ward at 'mixed' tables to eat. At the Raeside Clinic, both patients and staff eat in a cafeteria inside the purpose-built medium secure unit. Along the same lines at Springfield Hospital, a mental hospital, patients access what was previously only the staff cafeteria. In Smithtown, the separate areas of food consumption meant staff were distinct from patients and avoided relating to them for the duration of the meal. This echoes Bray's (1999) view that mental health nurses use 'distancing techniques' with regard to patients and their emotional demands.

The repeated transgressions of the staff eating patients' food served several purposes. In involving powerful, well-paid patients who brought or gave the food it emphasized how the ward's smooth functioning relied upon collusion. Implicitly, it suggested that if you wanted a job like the kitchen workers, you too had to be prepared to make compromises and not complain. That it was so flagrant meant it bound staff together in illicit activity. Lastly, in being so overt it indicated three times a day how things really were, i.e. that the staff could break the rules and were unafraid to do so publicly, so sure were they of their position. It is pertinent to all of this, since this was so definitely not a concentration camp, a nineteenth-century asylum or an early twentieth-century prison in Devon (Brown 2007), that there was neither a food shortage nor was the food inedible. It could all have been addressed by management had they so wished. That it was not addressed supports the controversial idea that regardless of the type of institution, '[e]ach institution has its rate of illegalism which is necessary and sufficient for it to exist' (Foucault 2009: 20).

This particular practice is a good example of what Foucault saw as a more general issue in society, that is:

[t]he differences people in power make between different illegalities, the different ways of dealing with their own illegalities as opposed to those of other people (Foucault 2009: 24).

Space exploration and the demonstration of social status

The Americans were the first to put a man on the moon. In so doing they demonstrated their technological and, from their point of view, a more general supremacy over the Soviet Union. By implication, it was thought capitalism had triumphed over communism. Technology was not politically neutral, as Bertold Brecht had observed about Galileo who invoked the Pope's displeasure by messing around with telescopes.

This insight into space and power is deliberately far from this ethnography. It illustrates the range of interdisciplinary interest in space and power (Cieraad 1999). Key issues in recent years appear to have been the relationship of language about space, social relations, the built environment and the symbolism of space. Different academic disciplines have had particular interests, for instance the geographers claim their territory as 'space, place and nature' (Massey et al. 1999: 4); gender and sexuality theorists analyse hegemony and ownership (Graham 1998; Moore 1996a; Probyn 1995) of space; and linguistics and psychology explore perception and language (Bryant and Campbell 1997). These contributions have been followed by an academic and public discourse on virtual space, the 'ownership' of the Internet (exemplified by disputes in China about Internet providers and restricted access to the World Wide Web) and by the escape from the hands of their owners of sensitive electronic material of international interest, as seen in the recent cases of Julian Assange and Edward Glover.

Anthropologists' concerns are diverse and overlapping with other disciplines and include the cultural specificity of spatial action (Duranti 1992) and language (Levinson 1996), the relation of domestic and public space (Reed-Danahay 2001) and symbolic elaboration of spaces and places (Aase 1994; Fog Olwig and Halstrup 1997). Discipline-specific contributions often acknowledge their debt to key figures such as Bourdieu and Giddens. My interest here is in the spatial arrangement of social practices on the study wards and how reasonable it is to connect the ethnographic material on rooms and meals to the maintenance of power.

How is the physical environment of the ward used?

The social relations described previously are manifest not only through social interaction but also through static and dynamic features of the built environment. A church is a church but it is also a place that looks like a church because people go and pray there. It remains a church but it is violated if a massacre takes place there (Keane 1996). This is more shocking precisely because it is known to be a sacred place. In the case of Smithtown, the physical environment provides a substrate for the primary mechanisms of control, those applied to patients by staff. The use of the word substrate, with its specific biological sense, is deliberate. It conveys the idea that knowing the physical environment and how it is deployed is necessary but not sufficient for an understanding of the social world in which the researchers found themselves. These mechanisms of control are critical to the management of dangerous, or potentially dangerous, madness. This rationale provides the basis for practice and informs the detail of everyday practice at the same time.

Everyday practice can be considered at two different levels of spatial action. One dimension is the macro-architecture of individual wards and their symbolic associations, rooms, keys and ward rounds. These are maintained by speech acts but also by repetitive action, and openly acknowledged when challenged. The other dimension is the choreography of the individual social actor in a given ward space; the 'where does the staff nurse stand to serve food?' dimension. Here the individual body in space is the focus of analysis, though it is not so much as an individual but as a person in role.

McCourt-Perring (1994) has drawn attention to the distinction between the institution as a built environment as opposed to the idea of institution in Douglas' wider sense (Douglas 1987), invoking 'models of thought and action'. In the analysis that follows, the institution is seen both as bricks and mortar, laid down architecturally in particular ways, and, as such, also related to 'models of thought and action', in line with Foucault's understanding of prison design (Foucault 1979: 250–1).

Who goes where: macro-view

In Smithtown it mattered where patients and staff were physically located. Reflected in the design and use of Victorian asylums were prevailing ideas about appropriate contact between men and women. Patients were grouped into wards; the sexes were segregated for all activities, except the occasional 'lunatics ball' (Showalter 1987: 38–40). This sexual segregation was still true for Smithtown. Although many hospitals, both psychiatric and otherwise, had had mixed wards for the last twenty years, the Department of Health returned to the view that sexual segregation was desirable, and in medium and low secure hospital units this has been substantially achieved (Department of Health 1997; Harty et al. 2012). This has developed from concerns about the safety and vulnerability of women in mixed wards (Mezey et al. 2005; Thomas et al. 1995). Smithtown, in having failed to achieve integration of men and women, was one step ahead.

It also mattered how ward space was occupied or emptied. Control was exercised over large movements (leaving the ward, going to bed) and small ones (serving food and doing the washing-up, picking up metal cutlery). The distinction between large and small was really about moving within a room or moving outside it. There was a highly specific association of activity and physical space, i.e. patients could decide to have dinner in their bedrooms or see friends of the opposite sex on the ward. They could have possessions in their bedrooms and they could sleep there. In some parts of Smithtown, patients could be in their rooms during the day. They could only see friends of the opposite sex in public places like the sports field or the visitors' hall. Places retained meaning even when unoccupied but their regular and highly restricted associations invited the newcomer to learn the social rules of a ward quickly. These associations reinforced the social relations that everyone understood but might otherwise forget. They were perhaps necessary to, and certainly assisted, the maintenance of social status differentials.

Within the ward there was a working knowledge of the territory— what you could enter at will, what you might be able to go into sometimes and in what circumstances, and what was essentially forbidden to the patient group. The ward was literally, with walls and doors but also symbolically compartmentalized. Some spaces were always staff spaces, some negotiable, and some usually but not invariably patient spaces. Patient ownership or occupancy was never absolute. Staff power resided in this capacity to deprive. Such fluidity of ownership has been recognized in other, less restrictive psychiatric settings (Van Dongen

1997) and in non-institutional environments (Moore 1996b: x) where 'space . . . is never neutral, but neither is it ever fixed or static'.

This is most easily demonstrated by the example of individual rooms. Having your own room was highly prized by most patients but it could be taken away and be searched at will by staff. You were locked in your room regularly and you could be placed in a seclusion room by staff. The nearness of 'own room' and 'the seclusion room' was illustrated on one of the study wards, which was alternately a rather bleak bedroom or the seclusion room, depending on demand.

Who goes where: micro-view

At a level of detail beyond the room is the spatial symbolism of conduct at mealtimes. Valentine (1999: 48–59) notes Bourdieu's interest in the cultural capital of food and adds her own contribution on the relation-ship of food practices, e.g. shopping for food and what is eaten, to iden-tity, in her case to gender identity. In Smithtown, what is important is what is eaten, by whom and where. In fact, put another way, it is the not eating together of staff and patients that stands out and informs iden-tity. Equally, the highly institutional patient meals, eaten in haste and without conversation, tell you this is not a domestic shared experience. This is perhaps different from the prison situation described by Ugelvik (2011) and Godderis (2006), where refusal of institutional meals is a refusal to succumb to institutional power. Few patients in Smithtown did refuse the meals. The private preparation and consumption of addi-tional food by patients is a statement of agency and individuality but not obviously of regime resistance; the institutional regime of Smithtown not only allowed it but at times also encouraged it. An ethos of psychi-atric rehabilitation supports the development of practical, independent skills of which cooking is one.

Douglas (1975: 249) knew this a long time ago, arguing that '[i]f food is treated as a code, the messages it encodes will be found in the pattern of social relations being expressed. The message is about different degrees of hierarchy, inclusion and exclusion, boundaries and transactions across the boundaries. Like sex, the taking of food has a social component'. Like Valentine (1999), Douglas is more interested in the symbolism of the actual food, not in terms of its consumerist status allusion but rather in terms of what kind of a meal is indicated by the content. What you offer people to eat tells of your relationship to them. This is perhaps different from observant Hindu, Islamic or Jewish cultures, where what you eat can tell you what you are to yourself (Douglas 1975).

In Smithtown, we have already established that the degrees of overlap in terms of which people eat what are culturally important. But the spatial aspects of consumption give the best clues to the social relations embodied in food practices. Down to the last square foot you can read a Smithtown person's identity from *where* they are at mealtimes. Reed-Danahay (2001: 49–50) suggests that in her analysis of a nursing home for the elderly demented, Auge's idea of 'non place', i.e. of transience, conventionally linked to places such as hospitals and airports, and Bourdieu's idea of 'lieu', where social position and place are linked, apply to her material. The residents of the nursing home are going somewhere else as their capacity for independent living declines; where they are going no one wants to go. The issue for Smithtown is slightly different. Patients do not want to be there and few patients, if any, believe they are going anywhere fast. Status and place are meaningfully linked at an institutional, ward and personal level.

Subtle issues of individual relationship are visible or audible in specific interactions such that social roles can be modified by the individual personifying them. Pointing out that staff must serve the food in Smithtown can reinforce the idea but also undermine it, depending on how such observations are made.

Much of this is about the meaning of the space and, as Duranti (1992: 657) summarized, is in keeping with the idea that 'other studies of the cultural organization of space (Bourdieu 1977; Giddens 1984; Moore 1986; Pader 1988) have already argued that a space is given meaning by the particular actions performed by an individual inside of it'. But space, as is easily seen, has meaning without people being in it. Gardens are often empty but they are seen and known in the mind's eye; other senses are invoked by the memory of the fragrance of wisteria, the sound of birds, the touch of raindrops dripping from roses in the rain. Such meaning is determined by the memory of the garden's physicality, not by its visitors. Other spaces derive meaning from what is known about how people have been in them, and how they will be in them in the future. The spaces themselves then convey identity to the people in them—religious people go to church, children play in playgrounds, Smithtown patients were locked up at night.

The interaction of people in a space, and with it, can both reinforce and change meaning. Isolated challenges to the received order such as stray patients in the staff mess are about both contested space and negotiated meaning but also pave the way potentially for a new order with an altered hierarchy. Describing and analysing Smithtown at that moment is not to render it completely static; indeed, the tensions in the staff group about ways of working have already been rehearsed. Rather, it is to describe the way things were at that point. Change becomes more likely if the meaning is transported not only by more, and repeated, observed and lived, unusual social action but also by the telling of what has happened differently. This creates possibility out of the *in situ* understanding of the new in relation to the established social order. To make this idea more concrete, if patients repeatedly occupy the staff mess, the symbolism of the space alters. If, as happened recently in North London, an Anglican Parish Hall begins to be used for bar mitzvahs, the nature of what happens there on Saturdays says something important about local Jewish, Christian relations. This is different from Duranti's (1992) observation that individuals can change their position within a given social order without the order itself changing. Such individual negotiation of, to use a spatial metaphor, social distance is recognized within the asylum literature (Pearlin and Rosenberg 1962; Scheff 1961; Segal 1962).

The end of the ward and the ends of the world

The social life of the ward is informed by outside forces at an ideological level and, to some extent, at a practical level. This is a given, in the sense that the Mental Health Act applies to Smithtown but is also uncertain. The uncertainty stems from the extent to which external forces determine what happens, as opposed to what happens being determined by people on the ward operating collectively or individually. The wards' physical structures and routines have social consequences. We have considered how the repeated positioning of patients as individuals and as a group, deprived of goods and freedom of movement in the ward, can reinforce a discernible social hierarchy.

Life outside the ward has received scant attention. There was less of it, and access to it was determined by physical, virtual and social boundaries.

Definite physical boundaries controlled access and egress. This would be true of any physical ward, in a general or psychiatric hospital. What was radically different in Smithtown was the degree of permeability. Some boundaries, like the end of the ward on Toulouse, were ordinary doorways; others, like the wall around Smithtown, were physically and psychologically intimidating.

Patient physical access to other parts of Smithtown, beyond the ward, was contingent on the staff. You could just have walked out of Toulouse onto a stairwell but that was not done. Decisions to grant degrees of freedom were almost exclusively the preserve of nursing staff in a day-to-day sense but were periodically reviewed in more multidisciplinary case conferences and ward rounds. In such settings, it was considered whether or not you could go to a particular work area or go 'on a visit' to chat to your girlfriend. Much of the information provided at these meetings came from nursing staff, as medical and other staff seldom had time to talk to patients about such day-to-day activity. The exception to this access rule was 'social functions'. One of the ward's patients organized these, and in so doing occupied a hierarchical position somewhere between staff and patients.

The wards sat within substantial external space, as was common in asylum design during the last two centuries; this was mainly either courtyard or garden space. Much was visible from within the ward, creating a tantalizing sense of the possible into which the privileged might venture. The consequence was also a lack of visual complexity, created by the tedium of gazing at the same things every day, reinforcing the sameness of social action.

Patients' virtual access to the outside world was very different to that found in the historical asylum, the two obvious reasons being the telephone and the television. Televisions were seldom switched off except to signal 'time for bed'. Television gives quick access to major events and entertainment. My impression was that many patients viewed television as separate from their lives; even the news took on a fantasy quality, as it was so far away from their immediate existence.

Some years later, I was standing in a medium secure unit watching in real time the events of 9/11. I experienced what must have been a common response, which was that the planes could not really be crashing into the World Trade Centre. I enquired of the patients watching whether it was a film. They said no, it was really happening. I took that perception away and went, anxiously, to check on my sister's fate. I do not know if anyone in that ward did the same but if they did, it would have been differently negotiated because of the constraints on their access to the outside world. That would have been very worrying.

The telephone in Smithtown was valued by patients with outside contacts but for others it was an irrelevance. Visitors to Smithtown were similar, important for some but non-existent for others. Thus, the control of time spent on the telephone or allowed in the visitors' hall was only effective in a proportion of cases.

The fieldwork was conducted before access to the Internet or social media and smart phones became components of everyday life. All have privacy, safety and security implications for individuals and for institutions; all of us negotiate what personal privacy and safety mean in the twenty-first century, and the goalposts are moving. These technologies are relevant to detained populations but the way in which they work as valued commodities may not differ so much from use of the ward telephone. As tools for life, they join the list of toys with which some secure hospital patients, by virtue of long-term detention, are unfamiliar, like electric cars and supermarket self-checkouts. A new generation of patients is also being created who already have familiarity with the global possibilities of the Internet and digital technologies before they are hospitalised.

There were rules about real access to the outside social world. In many large psychiatric hospitals in the twentieth century, the fact that a patient was detained against his/her will did not mean incarceration in a building, although it sometimes did. Everyone in Smithtown was locked in, and trips outside were few in number and needed official approval, not only from Smithtown but also from the then Home Office. Their significance to patients was in inverse relation to the number undertaken. Being allowed out on such trips signalled progress. Necessary trips out, such as for urgent medical attention, were correspondingly problematic for staff if they involved high-profile patients or those thought likely to escape. All of this marked Smithtown as different from most psychiatric hospitals, where patients considered less dangerous can access the outside world (Van Dongen 1997) and indeed visitors can turn up and see people without appointments. In such other settings, commodities are less controlled; visitors can bring gifts and/or contraband. Quirk et al. (2006, cited in Buus 2008) observe the relative openness of contemporary psychiatric wards and the corresponding need for nursing staff to monitor the availability of street drugs and the risk of abscondion.

In sum, the experience of patients was that they are not of the ordinary world. Not only was their ward life regimented and prescribed but the fact of detention was also brought home by the invasion of the external in the form of telephones and TVs, while they were unable to walk more than 30 metres without permission. Their world ended for the most part at the end of the ward, even as the real world intruded, highlighting their situation. In a world where catching planes is regular, call cards for cheap phone calls to every country in the world are sold in a corner shop, where Facebook shows what your friends and family are doing instantaneously and everyone can Skype, the detention of a patient in Smithtown appeared more different than in the past. Their virtual and actual isolation seemed stranger because everyone else is connected.

Why does such power need to be maintained?

Foucault (1979: 135–69) argued that institutions have favoured organizing bodies in 'complex spaces that are at once architectural, functional and hierarchical'. This is to begin to see institutions as more similar than different, though not to deny the validity of the insight. Smithtown wards were exactly as he says. Foucault included in his list of examples institutions that have ambiguous connotations, i.e. hospitals for infectious disease, factories and schools. He takes the people out of the organizing, seeing the institutions with their ways of going about things as responsible for the patients' frame of mind and the practices. As Gillespie (2010: 40) observes, this 'affords almost no possibility for interpretation by inhabitants, creating an ideologically saturated space with little room for deviance or defiance'. Taking Foucault's argument into the specific place of Smithtown, his characterization of space has an immediate plausibility. The fieldwork material suggests that the social relations manifest in physical separateness are tribute to the fragility of a sense of difference. To be different from the patients, he would say, is important to staff. The language they used often placed the patient in another, lower, realm. Such physical proximity on the part of nursing staff (less so for others) invites the shared stigma that Perucci (1974) highlights and is inevitable in closed institutions where, as Rowe (2012: 113) remarks, life is 'inescapably and pervasively social'. Hence the drive to be separate, to have staff rooms, to maintain separateness in the sub-divisions of action in space are to remain a different category of person, one with power over the other category.

In line with this, the institution demands of its staff that they know where all the patients are all of the time and indeed that they count them on a regular basis. This is Foucault's (1979: 143) partitioning. The physical aspects of the wards in Smithtown were particular, though not unique; it was far from normal. Doors were locked, windows did not open very much, there was a lack of privacy for patients and also a requirement for the staff to be both vigilant and intrusive. This may have worked in exaggerated ways for patients whose experience of the outside world created a sense of intrusion and powerlessness. For women previously 'objectified' within a 'male gaze' that included sexual and physical violence, and for ethnic minority individuals whose difference has previously made them the object of harassment by authority, this could be particularly difficult. In this way, the resonances of the physical practices of necessary surveillance might have had unintended clinical consequences. These, in turn, might be reinforced by routine clinical process that documented and analysed individual behaviour, to test it against pre-existing clinical categories and expectations. These clinical activities are a more specifically personalized, internally directed surveillance. Anything a patient did might be of clinical interest. Relatedly, Crewe (2011) notes the extension of what he calls 'the "psy" disciplines' in prisons. The behaviour of individual prisoners is now considered in line with an increasingly individualized framework of understanding of their criminality. Crime is no longer 'social'; it is 'psy', an individual problem. This appears to be built on the idea that how someone is inside a closed institution can predict their behaviour outside it. This assertion provides legitimacy for Mental Health Review Tribunals and for Parole Boards amongst others but can neglect the effect of the institution on the individual. It favours seeing endogenous continuities in the person's unwanted ideas and behaviour (see Camp and Gaes 2005).

Components of secure environments can reinforce patients' understanding of power differentials that have contributed to their problems (Potier 1993). For staff, the institutionally legitimate practices were routines but were also seen as a way of staying safe; this was not a school. Both the individual and social panopticon approaches are supported by the risk agenda.

Social theory is just that. It can bring out the pedant in the empiricist. It is all very well to gloss over difference but it does not do justice to the lived experience of either staff or patients. This works in three ways. First, it certainly matters to them what kind of place they lived and worked in, and embedded in the regular features of life was a profound awareness that this was neither a death camp nor an army barracks. It was frankly quite enough that they were in a High Secure Hospital. Second, as is evident from the descriptions of what people say and do, they brought not only compliance and implementation with institutional ordering to their daily life but also themselves. They, the individuals, are the people that social science struggles to consider. To return to Delvecchio Good et al. (2008), there is a problem in anthropology, as there is in criminology (Bosworth 1999, cited in Godderis 2006) in understanding individual agency. Third, an analysis that says, fundamentally, that institutions have agency, are all the same and not only inform but also determine your life, does not necessarily mean very much to a patient group that was clear that Smithtown was better, and therefore different from prison.

Part of why the similarities between institutions are easy to emphasize is because they are largely visible. This is interesting in an institution where therapy was happening. To use a clinician's perspective, therapy did not only happen in the therapy group. It was invisible and happened inside patients' heads as they digested and pondered on their situation, aided at times by new insights they reached either alone or in a group. The iterative process of therapeutic work for patients on the three wards was no doubt slow and painful, as befits the seriousness of their disability and the gravity of their actions. The imperative for privacy prevented much of this being known, though it was glimpsed. So it may be in part true that as Douglas (1987: 92) puts it, [i]nstitutions systematically direct individual memory and channel our perceptions into forms compatible with the relations they authorize'. But that is not the whole story. Douglas's institutions are not bricks and mortar, they are people and ideas, and yet it is the people she too leaves out, the ones who dare, in the face of institutional pressure to conform, to be themselves. Sometimes, they do hide the teabags successfully, sometimes they write a story. To see individual preference only in reaction to institutional rules and regulations is to give those rules and regulations too much power. This leads us to consider whether the balance between such individual and social action allows space for a sense of what can reasonably be termed ward culture to emerge.

Part 4

Culture and change

Chapter 8

Did wards have cultures?

Reasons for caring about hospital culture

Wards in Smithtown went about life in particular ways. This may or may not lead us to conclude they had particular cultures. To address the question, 'Did wards have cultures?', two things are necessary. First, there should be some rules to convert raw fieldwork findings into an account, to see how they might fit or not any understanding of culture. This is known to be anthropology's weak spot. Second, there need to be some versions of culture available for a comparison—given the research method is participant observation, this should be an anthropological one, not T S Eliot's high culture for instance. This exercise might be academically sterile. So we might reasonably ask what is added if that is done?

This is where the managers come back into the frame. They had largely disappeared from view as we drilled down into ward life, an interesting observation in its own right. In Smithtown, managers were easy to spot precisely because of the commotion caused if they did arrive on a ward. They were a separate species, not easily confused with frontline practitioners as they might be in other organizations. We know they were not well liked. Their particular understanding of culture is important because they had power, in terms of the formal hierarchy and because they thought they had a cultural problem, i.e. for them, culture was a word with real meaning and was important in the real world, outside academe. They had concerns about the depth of that power and their capacity to reach into wards, as the start of this project illustrated, but their version of culture offers us an important understanding.

So the reason for undertaking this analysis is twofold, both philosophical and practical. Philosophical, because what words mean, and now we are in the territory of words, are very important. 'Let him have it' sounds very simple as a phrase. Its inherent ambiguity and the resolution of that ambiguity in a criminal trial was the difference between a death sentence or not. There is a real difference between handing a loaded gun over to the police and firing it at them. Derek Bentley (*R v Bentley* 1998: 97/7533/S1) was hung after being found guilty of murder, because one interpretation of the phrase 'Let him have it' was favoured over another. Practical, because the word culture is not confined to the modest, academic discipline of social anthropology. 'Culture' has gone on a long and meandering journey, changed its appearance as it has pottered about and been adopted by any number of other academic disciplines who have seen good in it; it is barely recognizable to its anthropological parents.

Institutional and individual accountability

We have seen that in Smithtown, what happened in daily life on a ward appeared to emerge from a combination of institutional practice and individual agency. These are blurred when we discuss such topical and fundamental ideas as 'culture of care', 'hospital culture' and a 'culture of blame', to cite a few common examples. These are coat-hangers for the consideration of the adequacy of health care. This is as true now as it was for Smithtown at the time of the fieldwork. Recent examples of this usage are both the Winterbourne Inquiry (Department of Health 2012) and the Mid Staffordshire Inquiry (Francis 2013). Once again, we are in an era of hospital inquiries, just as we saw for two decades leading up to the 1980s (Martin 1984). These inquiries into institutions can be contrasted with those into the care of single patients, the approach of almost all of the so-called psychiatric homicide inquiries in the 1990s. All these issues are part of a public debate about standards of care and, specifically, the balance of responsibility between organizations and individuals. The balance between these is poorly theorized in social science and yet crucial in adjudications of poor professional practice. This was also true in early reports into secure hospital care (Boynton Report), where the institution rather than the individuals was held accountable. Emerging from the Mid Staffordshire inquiry are not only wholesale recommendations to take effect within the entire NHS, but also individuals being held to account by their professional regulatory bodies. The reality of any inquiry is that the gaze is interrogatory and perhaps persecutory. It is helpful and perhaps radical to consider, in these three wards, outside of investigation, review or inquiry, two more neutral questions: first, what, if anything, is cultural, and what is the result of individual agency; and second, can social science address this or should it be left to the lawyers? What follows is an attempt to engage the reader not in whether Robert Francis is right, but how we can theorize organizational life using the case of Smithtown's three hospital wards.

There are of course many other ways of studying the social phenomenon of the ward. From different methods of study emerge a number of overarching concepts such as 'social climate', 'psycho-social atmosphere' and 'ward climate' (see Day et al. 2012), often determined with admirable mathematical exactitude. Such concepts pay less attention to the continuing power of organizational memory and meaning and more to the easily measureable present. They are of importance because of the potential link between the measureable components of wards or prison wings and their capacity both to engage with patients and inmates and to affect long-term recidivism and well-being (Day 2011).

In Smithtown, the gist of ward life is that the devil is in the telling details. Long-term participant observation is revealing about informal rules, as well as formal rules of behaviour and codes of conduct. Researchers remain familiar with the micro-environmental details of the ward. They can chat and see in their minds, even after some years, the corridors, the smoke staining, the pool table and the way men passed each other in the corridors, avoiding each other's gaze, engrossed in private ritual, the bars on the windows and the penchant for shell suits among the patients. To say such imagery is powerful is an understatement. It is one of the reasons why anthropology, in its reliance on participant observation, is right to claim that it is distinctive and allows the anthropologist to think about the world in an interesting and important way. Researchers who pop in or who use ethnographic method to produce thin accounts of life have missed the point; it needs to get into your bones. As a tool to get at the hard-to-know parts of life, wherever on earth participant observation is *sans pareil*. But, its resultant in-depth experiential knowledge is always partial. It is possible to hear the world they inhabited described by staff and patients, and to see first hand the distinctive characters of wards. That is not the same as answering important questions about methods of translation from data to conclusions.

From ethnographic material to cultural account

Things we could not know

This ethnographic material arose in this fashion as the process of fieldwork was adapted to the specific field (Josephides 1997). As such, it can claim to be a valid reflection of at least some aspects of Smithtown's existence; other aspects were hidden from the researchers, not witnessed, deliberately obscured or unnoticed as such. Thornton (1992: 18) comments on the encyclopaedic quality of early anthropology but also notes the impossibility of one person getting to grips with 'social wholes'. The content of the ward life material is not encyclopaedic in content, nor is it disguised as such by rhetorical strategies designed to make it more credible.

What follows is a discussion of what counts and why it should. This is about the status and transformation of data as well as the relationship of interpretation to data and to disciplinary concerns. The separation of data and interpretation is of course not as easy as it is to write the words. The artificiality of such separation, the glossing over of mental processes and technology constitute part of this analysis, and are reflected in the construction of what follows. In turn, we consider:

- the relationship of ethnography and anthropology; and
- whether the ethnographic material from the wards speaks to an anthropological idea of culture.

Anthropology and ethnography

The first hurdle is whether ethnography is always anthropology, i.e. whether it is a technique that can just be applied or whether there is something special about the anthropological apprenticeship.

There are differing views on the definitions of, and relationship between, anthropology and ethnography. Hammersley and Atkinson (1995: 1) are reluctant to get drawn into a sterile debate about such key words and suggest a 'liberal' approach, where ethnography is 'referring primarily to a particular method or set of methods'. They suggest any social researcher can be an ethnographer providing the data is used to address issues. They explicitly separate data and issues. Strathern (1995: 155) notes the borrowing of ethnography, previously one of the 'distinctive anthropological concepts'. Marcus and Fischer (1986: 18) emphasize the ethnographer's immersion in culture, and the need for 'descriptive detail' in the account of the culture. They suggest (1986: 22) that the position of the ethnographer is between 'traveller's discovery and science', noting that the people who are most aware of the importance of fitting things into genres are those writing about 'ethnography for the doctoral dissertation' (1986: 37).[1]

Wright (1994: 4), an anthropologist, is acutely aware of such interdisciplinary tensions in the analysis of organizations. She suggests that for a piece of work to become anthropology it has to involve not only fieldwork with participant observation, but also 'problematizing' in an anthropological way, whereby fieldwork is tested against theory.

So far then, the ward life material which has been ordered, coded, selected, thought about and written down falls at this last hurdle. Analysis of a kind has been done, but not such as to transform the material into something distinctively anthropological. To do so requires not just description of the social world of the ward but also an analysis of it against something anthropologists will recognize as an anthropological concern, i.e. something on which we could reasonably expect anthropology to be expert and which would create something meaningful within the discipline, even if the analysis never spilled out into other domains.[2]

Culture indubitably has that status in anthropology, but it has been both differently defined and used (Kuper 1999), and its usefulness and

---

[1] Though it occurred to me that it might as easily be true of people who read doctoral dissertations.

[2] Anthropology unconsciously manifests an evolutionary perspective. It believes in the progress of the discipline through markedly self-referential writing. This is curious given that important shifts in anthropological style have been prompted by outsiders like Foucault, or external theory in the arts.

use have a taken-for-granted quality within anthropology (Strathern 1995; Wright 1994). This is a problem.

Culture is far too big a topic; arguably it is *the* topic of anthropology. But this was not always the case; it is not now just the preserve of anthropologists (Kuper 1994, 1999) and this worries them (Weiner 1995).

From fieldwork to culture: seeing culture, thinking culture

The second hurdle is whether the ward-based ethnographic material allows for the development of an understanding of culture within Smithtown in *any* anthropological sense, given that anthropology, as ever, does not agree with itself. For clarity in the developing argument, I will use the two main strands of culture within anthropology: first, culture as intrinsic ideational norms manifesting themselves in the 'out there' social world, whose appearance they inform; and second, culture as primary observable phenomena. The context is a broader debate about the status and value of theoretical elaborations of culture, which owe much to the preoccupations of an academic discipline whose original wish, paradoxically, was to grasp the 'native's point of view' (Geertz 1983).

To explain this distinction a little more, we should consider Geertz (1993), who sees culture as ideational. The primacy of ideas in the definition of culture has a long history (Kroeber and Kluckhohm 1952) but Geertz's twist on it is that the same question must be asked of all 'the things of this world', i.e. what do they mean? Observable social phenomena have no stand-alone quality, and in being observed and articulated they are already interpreted. The art of anthropology is to isolate the indigenous filters that make things what they seem, that is, to elucidate the shared symbolic meanings which constitute cultural knowledge.

This is in part a difference of emphasis. At one level, primary observable phenomena do have a stand-alone quality; otherwise there would be nothing around which to weave ideas. Early positivists were clear about that but perhaps too emphatic about the rock-solid, unchallengeable nature of their own views. It is of note that law, medicine and political strategists and pollsters seem immune to post-modernism and remain wedded to social empiricism; of necessity they continue to grapple with social attitudes and behaviours as if they were real things. The AIDS epidemic, breast cancer screening and anti-smoking campaigns have relied on public information systems which, in turn, are based on understanding the attitudes and behaviours of the target groups, be they gay men, middle-aged women or teenagers. With this British empiricism in mind, Sahlins (1999: 399–400) observes that British social anthropologists were not anthropologists at all, but sociologists. He finds that '[i]t is possible to conclude from several decades of disciplinary self-reflection that anthropology doesn't exist since if it isn't sociology it's humanities'.

The third hurdle is whether the analysis of power, which relies on and is mediated by the social relations of individuals and groups within a symbolically loaded physical environment, lends itself to an anthropological perspective on culture.

The first problem is using terms such as 'social relations' and 'space'. These ideas invoked in the account so far acquire validity, not through precise definition in an abstract sense, but through the absorption of the complex meaning and bulk of the writing, what Cohen (1994: 4) has called 'extended demonstration'. What appears in those sections derives from first-hand experience of Smithtown, a place where things have happened and other things were expressed by the people living and working there. They talked about each other and they did things to, beside and independent of each other, in terms of *kinds* of people, to some extent.

The preliminary analysis of social relations suggests that social categories were important in the life of Smithtown, but only partially account for what was noted in the research. Individual consciousness, interpretation and the particularity of interaction and attribution were also part of the picture. The rich symbolism of the use of space contributes a connected but alternative explanatory framework. It uses, preferentially, the routine rather than the exotic, except where the exotic is illustrative of prevailing ideas. The framework of space, notably action in space, has received important attention in anthropology and elsewhere in recent years, some in the anthropology of health care settings (Page and Brooke-Thomas 1994; Reed-Danahay 2001). Moore (1996b: 200) argued that 'the choice of space as an object of study is partly the result of its materiality and everyday relevance, and partly because it is the context in which all other cultural representations are produced and reproduced'. One might argue on this basis that no account of a social setting is complete without it. However, the particular bricks and mortar physicality of Smithtown, plus its overt and known rules and regulations about who goes where, made space an essential analytic vehicle. Space is necessary to give a proper account of Smithtown. Equally, the analysis makes sense because the meanings generated in space indicate indigenously important values within particular social relations, most obviously how power differentials are maintained.

To conclude, it was legitimate in the context of Smithtown to describe life in the institution within the two overlapping frameworks of social relations and the meaning of space, but other frameworks might also tell us much that was both interesting and valuable, e.g. evaluations of clinical practice.

Both analyses of social relations and of space give information that fits commonly under the umbrella of culture in both the observable and ideational sense. Both are necessary for an ideal of completeness in that they add to understanding. Self-evidently, neither in isolation results in a total description of culture. Similarly, in combination they are still subject to the reservation that any cultural analysis is incomplete (Geertz 1993: 29): 'Cultural analysis is intrinsically incomplete. And worse than that, the more deeply it goes the less complete it is.' These are conceptual dilemmas. There are also situationally specific dilemmas arising from the fieldwork process, including the amount of data, implicit knowledge and the problem of ownership of cultural accounts.

From fieldwork to culture: the technology of anthropology

The amount of data

One area of incompleteness relates to the volume and balance of data. The participant observer is not there all the time, so she/he cannot record even what she/he witnesses, and remain ignorant of what she/he does not witness which has still occurred. Even with a dataset as large as the one underpinning this book, there are more absences than presences. As Woolf (1975: 189) wrote of fiction:

> . . . examine . . . an ordinary mind on an ordinary day. The mind receives a myriad impressions—trivial, fantastic, evanescent or engraved with the sharpness of steel.

> From all sides they come, an incessant shower of innumerable atoms; and as they
> fall, as they shape themselves into the life of Monday or Tuesday.

Even if we did what all ethnography manuals and Geertz recommend, and immerse ourselves in the world of the other, to sort out saying from doing, and what they say and do from what the researcher says and does (to paraphrase Kuper (1999: 105)), we would fail. Woolf's modernist particular will always be so much greater than what is possible.

Specifically, in Smithtown, the women fared badly. In contrast to the staff and patients on the two male wards, there were no interviews. Therefore, although the voices of the strident and socially confident come through, quieter women were muted, limiting the understanding of gender and making conclusions about Lille more tentative. Given my recent interest in the care of women, it is a source of frustration that this opportunity was lost and only partly alleviated by the fact that there are now no more than 50 women left in High Secure Hospital care, far fewer than was the case then.

The problem of the implicit

The problem of the implicit is evidential. This has three components: one is the capacity and availability of fieldwork data to address ideas such as how 'human existence is symbolically constituted, which is to say culturally ordered' (Sahlins 1999: 400) and how that can be identified unequivocally; the second is the relevance of culturally congruent ideas to cultural practice; and the third is the relationship of implicit cultural ideas to individual consciousness. These will be considered in turn. Put another way, this section discusses the difference between knowing, being able to say, saying, being signed up to and living in accordance with particular cultural norms.

For the grand old man of psychiatric institutions, this was not a problem. It seems no anxiety was associated with moving from social relations to the underlying ideology (Goffman 1961: 186):

> In the main, state psychiatric hospitals do not function on the basis of psychiatric doctrine, but in terms of a 'ward system'. Drastically reduced living conditions are allocated through punishment and rewards, expressed more or less in the language of penal institutions.

Geertz (1957: 33–4) has suggested that '[c]ulture and social structure are . . . different abstractions from the same phenomena'. The social relations on the ward at Smithtown hinge on the demonstrable mutual recognition of social identity and status lived out on the ward. If you like, the observable bits of culture are easier to identify, whatever the reservations about adequacy. Geertz (1993) accepted that the relationship between fieldwork material and the theory of anthropology was a problem, and suggested it can be resolved by focusing on the particular, i.e. the individual events, behaviours and material culture from which meaning is read, but it is less clear what principles govern this activity. How then to wade through a methodological morass to discuss a Geertzian ideational concept of culture invoking shared symbolic meanings in the way that Goffman, and many anthropologists do so effortlessly?

This empirical dilemma really does apply to Smithtown. If the identities of staff and patients are separable, important and interdependent, then the shared symbolic meanings we are looking for may be hard to find. If the social groups are so distinct, it must be foolish to imagine they share symbolic systems when their descriptions of the other indicate the absence of a shared outlook. Smithtown is a two-tier society: one tier, the patients, is only living there because coerced; the other tier, the staff, is only there for part of the day. In both cases, the key identity, being a member of staff or a patient, is only part of the self, albeit an important one. To suggest joint investment in the culture of the ward or indeed of Smithtown seems to fly in the face of what the fieldwork material already reveals. Both staff and patients would be significantly appalled if they were invited to change places with each other and extremely surprised to hear it would not make any difference to how they view the world or how they behave. It might be wiser to look for shared symbolic meanings, at least in the sense of being signed up to them, *within* rather than *across* social groups.

Pursuing this subdivision for a moment, we can return to the evidence from other studies of psychiatric and penal institutions. Earlier hospital studies had difficulty with patient culture (e.g. Alasewski 1986; Perucci 1974; Stanton and Schwartz 1954). This study has identified certain values of which patients were aware, even if they did not always observe them. But it is hard to say that the shared ideas, and shared enforced patterns of behaviour, which follow from the imposition of an unwanted identity, constitute a shared symbolic world in the same way that they might for less coerced social groups. You are part of a group with a heterogeneous history. Your relationship to your value system and the felt balance between it and other aspects of your social or individual identity might be highly ambiguous. This is less of a problem if shared symbolic meanings simply indicate an awareness of them, rather than agreement on their definition or importance.

For the staff, being such is also only part of the self, but they have, as individuals, opted into the social group. Doctors choose to become doctors, nurses to become nurses and so on. And they can all leave. So the existence of tensions within the ward staff group, dinosaurs and nurses, suggests a degree of cultural crisis. This is a crisis seen in the variable expression of views and behaviours in relation to the patients. Staff are not agreed about the nature of the patient. In contrast, the patients differ not about whether the staff are 'screws' or 'nurses' but rather how many and which ones are. The attributes of the other in Smithtown, which has a symbolic dimension, do inform daily life. These 'others' exist both in and outside social action, but they are easier to grapple with as they become explicit. They rely less on the intuition and imagination of the anthropologist in that they feature within fieldwork material as objects, linguistic ones, picked up in the field. They have a very different quality from the analytic categories applied to prisoners recently by Crewe (2012), whose 'retreatists', 'pragmatists' and 'stoics' come from the criminologist, not the criminals. Anthropology demands that indigenous meaning is privileged in understanding the symbolic world of other people.

The critical social identities of staff and patients exist, to some extent, both in immediate social action and in the abstract. This points to a potential difference between cultural understandings and actual practice (Sahlins 1999: 404). The mechanical determinism of social structure (Radcliffe-Brown 1940) studiously ignores the relationship between the abstraction and the action. Bourdieu (1990: 85) disliked the 'ostentatious rigour of so many diagrams of social organization offered by anthropologists', but it would be entirely possible to generate such a map of social relations, perhaps with accompanying arrows about power and influence. Bourdieu's argument is one that is meaningful here, and one that has been emphasized throughout the material both on reflexivity and life on the wards. The 'uncertainties and ambiguities' of social action need acknowledgement; diagrams will not do. In the artificial, theoretical and metaphorical potential space between cultural ideas and cultural practice, a space owing more to Geertz than to the structural functionalists, there is room for manoeuvre. To consider this in more depth, it is helpful to think about the anthropological self and its composition, because this sheds light on this theoretical space.

Much that is ideational, that might or might not relate to shared symbolism, or cultural knowledge more generally, and which is inside people's head, is unknown. Cohen (1994: 142) suggests that:

> it has become a commonplace of symbolic anthropology that the meanings of symbols are not exhausted by their shared or public elements, but are a matter of private interpretation and, as such, may well be inaccessible to others (including alas, to ethnographers).

Within Smithtown the sense of wariness that characterized the researcher's day-to-day access and the way in which many questions could be posed and answered meant many things were known to be unknown. There is uncertainty about the understanding, potentially available, of the individual social actor's consciousness about discernible cultural ideas and observed social acts. In Smithtown, the physical environment is known in both approved daily use and in transgression, in the history of the building and in the repetition of group existence. The use of space is both casual and unacknowledged, seen but not necessarily stated and largely implicit. The symbolic dimensions of these concrete actions are harder to evaluate. Everyone knows who is in charge, but they may not say so very often, even to themselves. Unknown to the researcher is what is potentially conscious. This can be what might, in certain situations, be brought to bear on social action, where in the moment of action, it is relevant. Equally, it may be deliberately held back from the researcher within deliberate inquiry.

The reason why these comments are important is that the researcher can articulate this dilemma, as I have done, and through a reflexive approach access and articulate his/her own consciousness—and even point towards what might be missing. The difficulty for the material on the 'other' is that you cannot do that with the same rigour. The private remains an abstract notion that is not filled out. Even where it is apparent in fieldwork, it may well be ironed out of the final account which is, for disciplinary and storytelling reasons, more interested in similarity than difference. Cohen (1994: 5) views this as unacceptable on the grounds that anthropologists deny to others the 'self-consciousness' that reflexivity has permitted researchers. Clifford (1988: 94) is aware not only that this reflexive self is itself culturally constituted but also that the others are identified by this reflexive self.[4] Thus a notion of self-consciousness may be highly culturally specific, in concept and detail. Nonetheless, it may have value in Smithtown, which is not Papua New Guinea.

The problem of ownership

In turn, this absence of 'self-consciousness' may contribute to our last local difficulty, the ownership of cultural accounts. There are several ownership issues in the specific case of Smithtown: first, there is the difficulty of recognizing your own society in the account of the anthropologist; second, there is the problem of agreeing with the interpretation; and third, there is the availability of information given the jargon of anthropology. Even though data, interpretation and writing can be only partially separated because data is always interpreted and interpretation is always ultimately written, a self-conscious attitude to the understanding of the creation of written culture from written fieldwork material seems important in this project.

The anthropologist's enthusiasm for symbolism and understanding deeper issues creates a potential danger, that is, of providing a non-indigenous cultural analysis. Kuper (1999: 111–14) suggests that in his

---

[4] The self of the subjects of anthropology may or may not have much in common with a Western notion of self. For contributions to this debate see Hollan (1992), Spiro (1993), Moore (1994a) and Morris (1994), and for its historical perspective see Baumeister (1987).

work on the Balinese Cock Fight, a particularly vivid and well-known exposition of a cultural phenomenon, Geertz imposed an essentially external analysis, using the ideas of a Western system of thought, psychoanalysis. Moore (1996a) suggests that the origin of many, if not all, of the analytic categories in contemporary anthropology is in the West. This means anthropology, or at least that undertaken by Western anthropologists elsewhere, is still shooting itself in the foot. Moore's comments are part of the broader discussion of speaking with authority about the 'other' without simply designing the 'other' in terms of one's own, predominantly Western, preoccupations (Appadurai 1992). The more distanced the interpretation is from the language and detail of the field notes and the more interested the anthropologist is in extending his/her pet metaphor, the more likely this is.

In the context of Smithtown, when Goffmanesque or Foucaultesque ideas can be thought to drive the machinery of daily existence, the danger is that, however worthy the analysis, its artificiality, most obviously its theoretical status in an atheoretical world, undercuts its value. As such, it is non-indigenous. Giving such ideas an importance they do not warrant on the ground is to be untrue to the setting. Whether or not the 'natives' of Smithtown would or will recognize this picture of themselves seems highly debatable.

Recognition and agreement are different beasts. Marcus (1998) points to the dangers of institutions disliking the analysis. Although he would seem to be discussing financially powerful entities, this concern must equally apply to Smithtown. Smithtown's high public profile makes it potentially sensitive to anything it would construe as an unhelpful analysis, whatever the author's intentions. To suggest that this would be mediated solely by social phenomena and independent of individual interests seems to ignore what the fieldwork tells us, i.e. that individuals can see themselves threatened, not just because they are part of a group.

Whatever the value of anthropological observations, the way it is written can render it inaccessible. Marcus (1998: 210) argues that anthropologists have pondered whether 'the discourse that the anthropologist has produced would be meaningful to the natives, and whether the latter would even be able to comment at all on what the anthropologist says (writes?) about them'. I have often thought that length is off-putting. Executive summaries with bullet points are all some people, often including me, can manage. To make matters worse, discussion of social relations, symbolism, cultural knowledge (even though I have avoided 'habitus') and culture, all in the same place, is a peculiarly anthropological act that limits the audience.

Maybe in the end, culture is just too big. Certainly, there are sound reasons to be wary of what purports to be a comprehensive cultural analysis, even of a rather modest ethnographic field, like this one. But some key elements of a cultural analysis have emerged with an ethnographic approach. This has conveyed what is shared, but also pointed towards what is hard to fit in a conventional ethnography, which is the way in which people can and do subvert, seduce, reinforce or simply ignore supposedly structuring principles of social organization and in so doing undercut the idea either of a single ward culture or indeed of staff culture or patient culture. This is therefore at odds with the managers' view.

Culture as thing: anthropology and the managers

In Smithtown, the managers came in with two concepts that relate to Wright's (1994: 2) ideas. They described the 'concepts, attitudes and values' of the workforce and found them lacking. This was the 'staff culture' problem they confronted (SHSA 1991b: 6); 'staff development' and 'cultural change' were explicitly linked in their five-point agenda for change (SHSA 1991b: 2). At the same time but in a different sense, they brought their own ideas about appropriate, managerially led management values and practices with which they hoped to influence the workers' culture. In many ways the formal system went into battle against an assumed, and not very well-characterized, informal system. However, the perception of the culture problem within the workforce is an interesting sleight of hand. The obvious historical origins of these practices and their historical legitimacy were conveniently forgotten. Thus, the institution was encouraged both to rewrite and to disown its history.

As Strathern (1996: 60) said of society, for anthropological theory, culture might become 'a salient cultural artefact'. It has taken on an independent existence; it has become a thing, but not necessarily a very useful thing.

The SHSA perhaps did the same thing as the anthropologists; they talked about culture, whereas no one in Smithtown actually did so. Unlike queer culture or black culture, people did not talk about Smithtown culture inside Smithtown. They talked, often about themselves and each other and sometimes about Smithtown, and the substance of that debate and discussion might be called, by others, culture. To clarify this distinction, my son—when very young—knew and talked about and related to 'mummies' and 'daddies', but did not talk of families or family structure, though that would be one analysis of what he voiced. At that point, the implicit analytic word meant nothing to him.

Interestingly for a management perspective which has traditionally mainly been concerned with formal culture, i.e. intentional culture, the criticism of the SHSA was intended for informal culture. But, as indicated, it was a truncated version of both the cultural ideas that informed practice in Smithtown and an oversimplification of that practice. They took for granted the primacy of staff culture, and the irrelevance of the patients to the culture of a unit. Like Alasewski (1986), who conflated the culture of the institution with the culture of staff, they neglected the impact of patients and patienthood on social existence. The patients were both there, because otherwise there would be no Smithtown, but also not there, because they were not actors in their own lives, just passive recipients of staff culture, denied group or individual agency.

The managerial view failed to recognize the importance, ambiguity and interdependence of the social categories of staff and patients. This complex social scene on the ward contrasts with a non-empirical but powerful notion of culture identified with staff alone, emanating from a managerial discourse most often associated with formal structures and explicit organizational goals. The managers of the SHSA, in this instance, reified culture to a 'thing', as anthropology can do, and put this conceptualization to use in their five-year plan. This lends itself to a discussion of the nature of cultural change and of resistance to such management imperatives.

Chapter 9

Culture on the move: resistance and reality

Models of change: structures, organizations, institutions and cultures

Smithtown was, at the time of the study, an NHS organization. The three wards provided a unique opportunity to examine structural, organizational, institutional and cultural change. These terms are not straightforward and the subtleties of meaning and use will be discussed further in this section. Some of what happened at Smithtown was specific to its position as a High Secure Hospital but it sat within the broader change management processes that have characterized the NHS since its inception.

Welfare to business: the NHS and its journey

To characterize the journey of the NHS as from welfare to business is overly simplistic. However, the balance in the ethos of the organization has changed. It began with a simple idea of free health care at the point of delivery as part of a welfare state. It is now a complex, modern health care delivery system contemplating unaffordability. Solutions to this certainly include paying for treatment. The history of the NHS has been of constant change, and the variation has been in the pace of change, not the fact of it. Change has frequently been opposed, notably by doctors but also by other trade unions. Doctors did not want the NHS in the first place and, having had it for enough years for it to become a cherished object, have vehemently opposed its recent notional re-privatization via the Health and Social Care Act 2012. The BMA, the doctors union, in particular has been a thorn in successive governments' sides.

Repeated structural change

The NHS has gradually been affected by an enthusiasm for market forces, i.e. purchasers and providers of health care and the associated business practices. Thirty years ago the implementation of the Griffith's (1983) Report on health service management was considered to be bringing Sainsbury's to the NHS and emphasized the need for strong, business-style leadership by managers; this was not welcomed by those working in the public sector. This Report was followed by the introduction of the first attempt at an internal market (Mynor's Wallis 2011) for health care, which collapsed. The internal market was intended to provide business-style incentives to excellence and better financial accountability for services.

Commissioning structures gradually took hold, in line with World Class Commissioning (Department of Health 2009) but there was never the appetite for it that had originally been envisaged amongst GPs. Primary Care Trusts were managerial entities, not clinical ones. They controlled the allocation of funds with varying adequacy of performance management, and were supplemented by specialist commissioning groups in areas of high-cost, low-volume services such as secure hospital care. Few services were actually transferred between service providers, i.e. hospitals and Trusts, as few were actually put out for commercial tender. The established distinction between providers and commissioners heralded the arrival of the Health and Social Care Act 2012, which was intended to put purchasing power into the hands of local GPs. Andrew Lansley, Secretary of State for Health at the time, had wanted much more radical change but the final product of much lobbying and parliamentary time is a more complex set of structures, checks and balances than he had intended (<http://www.youtube.com/watch?v=8CSp6HsQVtw>). The legislation did away with most of the existing commissioning structures while retaining the idea of a commercial market for health. It also levelled the playing field, significantly encouraging the commercial tender process and effectively inviting both commercial companies and the voluntary sector to take a larger market share. The full effect of these structural changes is still being played out but it has led to concern about the perceived privatization of health care delivery.

It is both relevant and irrelevant to the world of secure hospital care, as the independent sector, largely comprised of for-profit organizations, already had a very substantial foothold (Laing 2013). The independent sector accounts for just over half of all secure hospital beds.

During the lifetime of the wider NHS evolution, there is evidence to suggest that overall management costs have risen from 5% of health spend to nearly a quarter (Mynors Wallis 2011), inevitably linking the overt business practices of buying and selling health care to a creeping managerialism.

Empirical understanding of organizational change

This study of Smithtown is useful in this wider health service context because it provided a rare opportunity to look at change management as it happened. But, there is a further twist which applies uniquely to the High Secure Hospital system and follows from its own history. External commentators had seen the High Secure Hospitals as immovable objects, impervious to efforts to bring them into line with the rest of the psychiatric world. In sum, they were considered *resistant* to change. This contrasted with an *insistence* on change typical of those with management responsibility for the NHS in general, and commentators on the High Secure Hospitals in particular (Bynoe 1992; Department of Health 1992).

Anthropology and institutional change

The related theoretical issue for anthropology and the wider world is how change occurs and in particular, how cultural change, as opposed to structural, organizational, institutional or indeed personal change, occurs. Key questions are what are the elements that allow, evidence and constitute such transformations?

These questions are of continuing relevance to psychiatric institutions, large and small, publicly and privately run. The era of community care never led to the abolition of psychiatric hospitals in this country (Thornicroft and Bebbington 1989). Disillusionment with the capacity of mental health services to protect the public has also led to the funding of an increasing number of locked hospital units (Hassell and Bartlett 2001;

Laing 2013). Current estimates suggest the number of high, medium and low secure beds provided nationally within the NHS has gone from 2,383 in 2001 to 4,022 in 2012, and that in 2013 around four thousand additional low and medium secure beds were available in the independent sector. In contrast to preceding decades there has been no change in the number of psychiatric inpatient beds nationally, with the number stuck at around thirty-five thousand. The recent change has been the increasing proportion provided outside the NHS.

To ensure humane care, it is accepted that we must study and learn from where institutions went wrong; it is also useful to think about what they got right. Recent events reinforce the view that malpractice is never far away. Understanding how institutions change for good or for ill is a contribution to the long-term protection of what remains a large cohort of patients in the present generation of hospitals.

We consider first, how, if at all, life on the wards had changed and second, how this was construed by staff and patients. In so doing we compare and contrast attitudes to historical and recent changes and those with private or general impact.[1] It became apparent that the staff and patients had very different views of change. This empirical evidence provides a context in which to place the managerial mandate for change and clarifies and explains critical areas of apparent resistance to managerial authority.

Staff perspectives on change: the past is a number of places

The management of change was very relevant to staff on the ward. Change was a hot topic. Staff 'dinosaurs', who disliked and feared change, were new arrivals to the Smithtown lexicon. Left to their own devices, members of staff discussed either imminent changes or those being implemented—and their 'knock-on' effects, or how past changes still mattered. Much time was spent in reflecting on the state of the

---

[1] The analysis is based on field notes, particularly incident material, from all three study wards and interview material from the two male wards.

institution. The impression gained from the staff on the ward in the course of the research was of an organization in transition.

Long discussions with several key informants brought to light a variety of perspectives on the past and on recent institutional change. Some staff had been affected by the introduction of ward managers; they had either kept their pay but lost their status, or moved to work elsewhere in the hospital. Others had only worked in Smithtown for a few years. The following account came from someone who had been there for over twenty years. This view was far from unusual:

> He said that morale at present amongst the staff was terrible. He says 'they' are destroying the place. By 'they' I assume he means management. He said there used to be a terrific rapport between the staff and the patients but that is going and he compared current attitudes of 'them' and 'us' such as that found in prisons which is creeping into 'Smithtown' now . . . He said I was not to get him wrong, he can be fierce if he has to. You know, just like with children . . . he thought that they had got it finely tuned on how to do things and how the hospital should be functioning and then they turn round and say it is all wrong and that the things they have been doing for all these years have been done incorrectly. He was very annoyed at that and got quite animated . . . He said Smithtown never used to be in the paper so much, it never used to have the bells going all the time . . . which just demonstrates the effect of the current upheaval on the atmosphere of the hospital.

New staff could be sympathetic to the position of the 'dinosaurs' who had been overtaken by events. Others, who saw themselves as reformers, had little patience with such attitudes, which were thought to be self-serving on the part of long-established staff. New staff could comment negatively on the continuing influence of 'dinosaurs' who could damage the ward.

Other features of the past that were genuinely mourned included the role of the old charge nurse (who was seen as a repository of knowledge). Charge nurses reigned supreme, owned their chairs in the staff mess and no one else was required to make decisions—including medical staff who were substantially irrelevant, apart from the Physician Superintendent. Ward staff were promoted on the basis of 'dead men's shoes' rather than talent, and that was fine. This ordered progression through the nursing ranks was replicated in the general running of the institution, where everyone knew where they were. Ward staff were said to form a supportive staff group. There was said to be a more relaxed attitude to smoking and drinking, doctors played croquet with patients, visitors were not searched and there were picnics on the grass. Patients were said to appreciate the staff's sense of humour.

'Order' and 'discipline' were key words. Some staff referred to the use of threat and physical assault as occasional methods of informal sanction of patients. In this way, psychopaths would be manageable and the mentally ill cared for with a judicious combination of recreational activities (which were helpfully compulsory) and seclusion for bad behaviour.

But long-established staff, from both male and female wards, gave accounts of their own entry to Smithtown where they were virtually ignored, asked to stand and watch patients without talking to them, and were likely only to be accepted into the staff group once they had acquitted themselves well in a violent incident.[2] Staff who questioned the charge nurses would be 'sent to Coventry'. Such a time was seen as oppressive by some.

The past was undated. In consequence, it was hard to understand its relevance to the period of the fieldwork, not least because it contained obvious contradictions and paradoxes around safety. It seemed that one person's order and discipline was another person's repression and arbitrary punishment of patients who were unable or unwilling to be subject to unnecessary and demeaning institutional practice.

Among staff who regretted the move away from the past was a genuine and understandable sense of bewilderment. They had been shocked and surprised by criticism. They thought they had been doing their jobs well and that they had been a credit to the hospital. They had liked coming to work. In finding themselves suddenly out of step with contemporary psychiatric nursing, they consoled themselves by saying that the old-style routines of the day, whereby everyone got up on time and went to work, had been better rehabilitation for patients than the laxness of the present day.

---

[2] More recent initiation rites involved testing people's sense of humour rather than being tests of physical courage.

Political power and historical forces

Explanations offered by staff to account for what was a transformation, whether or not they agreed with it, were several fold and not mutually exclusive.

First, that the POA, which had been a powerful union, had lost power during the 1980s. Like other unions it had been affected by changes brought in by the Conservative governments. Mawson (1998: 183), a doctor almost uniquely well positioned to comment, as he worked in senior positions in the Special Hospitals in the 1980s, refers to the POA as the 'principle and long standing blemish of the Special Hospitals'. In the course of fieldwork we obtained the following insider's account:

> He said Smithtown would not strike and the management tended to know that. The legislation of the 1980s made industrial action more difficult for the unions. Balloting meant there was no industrial action for at least three weeks after the ballot and that management tended to know the secret result, which led to negotiations. Overtime bans run the risk of UKCC problems and interestingly a strike does not. He thinks that the change in the climate about the unions means that Jean's position (as current chair of the POA) is not as strong . . . He thought that perhaps 500 or 650 nursing staff belonged to the POA. Many have joint membership with the RCN. He thinks in general people are less supportive of the POA currently. He thinks the changes have led to an increasingly professional attitude to their work.

We were told that in the past the POA could veto changes with which it disagreed by threatening management with industrial action. This linkage of a specific Smithtown issue to a wider government agenda is echoed in the following field note on staff attitude:

> Ludovic thinks it is quite likely that MI5 are bugging some staff telephones. I smiled and he explained it was because the Government wants to beat the POA. He said the POA is the last bastion of powerful Trade Unionism. He said there is a very short chain of command from {the Chief Executive} to {the Secretary of State for Health} who will use whatever means necessary to beat the POA. . . .[A]pparently . . . HMT were seen jumping up and down with glee when the Union backed down and returned to normal working.

Second, the new managers—both general and ward—had swept through changes since 1989 at the instigation of the SHSA. Wards previously had several charge nurses. The introduction of ward manager positions had altered the nature of the hierarchy among nurses on the ward. Two team leaders worked to the ward manager following the restructuring. Some charge nurses had not bothered to apply either for team leader or ward manager posts. Some had moved to nights and some to non-ward based posts. Some had become staff nurses but maintained their pay on the old rates. Discontented staff suggested that Smithtown had got rid of the wrong people. In contrast to many charge nurses all three ward managers had experience outside Smithtown. They were alleged to bring with them an unhealthy preoccupation with budgets and management structures, including a new system of performance appraisal for nurses.

Senior managers were depicted as insensitive to staff stress, injury or reward. Particular individuals were discussed at times by staff with a startling degree of personal animosity and their transgressions of institutional rules were pointed out with glee, for example:

> Michel then explained, saying Noel (senior manager) had said to the press what he thinks of us. He said Noel said we are all racists. Too military and too custodial. Too much like prison officers. Olaf said, 'And then he goes and recruits them.' Olaf proceeded to name three ex-prison officers who have just started . . . Pierre said that all the ex-prison officers that he has worked with have been good people. Michel said he is fed up with 'the management giving everything to the criminals and kicking the staff in the teeth all the time' . . . Pierre said Noel is a liar.

Contemporary, continuing change

Two institution-wide changes added a very contemporary dimension to what would otherwise have been reminiscence or reconstruction. Changes to the nursing shift system and to the complaints processes directly affected staff. Following the progress of these changes shed light on the dynamics of power between the different social groups, most particularly staff and management and staff and patients. They also highlighted the difficult role of the ward manager, whose allegiances were debatable.

The shift system and twenty-four hour care

As already described, the nursing staff on the study wards and in Smithtown generally were divided into day and night staff. During fieldwork the proposal was developed that this distinction be abolished. All nursing staff would do some nights and night staff would work on some days. This proposal was linked to another initiative to have patients unlocked at night, known curiously as twenty-four-hour care. The following field note illustrates both the tone and the basis of staff views:

> The change in the shift system had been suggested and Nadine (ward manager) was looking to see what the staff opinion was to pass it on to the powers that be. . . . Alain and Paulette quite strongly felt that taking the day staff off the days and taking primary nurses away from their patients for three months or whatever was suggested, as the time period when staff do nights would be detrimental to continuity of care. Nadine's argument for this was that there was going to be twenty-four-hour care and the doors were going to be opened so primary nurses would have access to their patients and vice versa, all through the night as well. Paulette said that the patients were not going to want to talk to their primary nurse at 3 a.m. There was a further point made by Alain that some of the night staff had been on nights for thirty years and would be totally out of touch with how to deal with patients during the day and it would take an awful lot of training to get them up to the same standard of care that the patients are used to from the ordinary day staff. Nadine said again that the fact that night staff were possibly out of touch was not a good reason, as it was a question of training people and this would be a gradual process. Odette raised the practical point that both she and her husband worked at Smithtown, so what would they do if they were both on night shifts together? Who would look after their children? Nadine was very sympathetic to this . . . and she felt sure some arrangement could be made. Both Sandrine and Therese gave physical reasons for their objections. They both said they had tried to do nights before but had great difficulty adjusting . . . their body clocks. Nadine said that in cases like that . . . there was a case for not doing nights.

At this point in the project there was little information available about the details of the system. However, it was viewed by staff as a way of saving money and became a vehicle for dissent often expressed as concern for patient welfare. Later, the details of the proposals became clearer but still encountered opposition from staff.

> He said Marcel has appointed compliant ward managers. He said we are better off than most but Karine will not stand up to management. He said ward managers just accept what management say. He said, however, that the management think that twenty-four-hour care is good for patients on the grounds that being locked in your room is bad for you. . . . He said the management would be better off spending the £2 million on staffing during the day to have more therapy. . . . He said the staff will not accept the new shift system. The management are just trying to keep up the pressure on staff. Marcel was appointed to bulldozer through change.

The awkward position of the ward managers as neither fish nor fowl is clear in the next extract.

> Veronique {ward manager} asked Yvette about the new shifts. . . . Veronique said that Angelique had refused to talk to her about that but she was concerned that people would not get the days off they wanted if they did not tell her what days they wanted. . . . She says she cannot please 100% of the people 100% of the time. But she said, 'I'll try my damnedest.' . . . Quentin said he would rather wait until after the union meeting. Yvette said that was fair enough. Sylvan said that what will happen about the new shift system is that the union will have an overtime ban for a day or two, then the new system will go ahead as planned. . . . He said the new system will bring some improvements . . . He said that some staff who do loads of overtime are against the new shift system, yet they spend so much of their time here it will make no difference to them.

The POA and other unions took a view on the proposals. At one point the POA's decision was not to work the new rotas. Although staff went to the meetings, there was concern as to whether the position of the POA would safeguard its members and was legally sound. Talks with management were known to be fraught. Other unions were involved and balloting their members about the issue of shifts. Rumours circulated among nursing staff that the SHSA had intervened with hospital management and instructed them to leave the shift system alone. It seemed to the researchers that the POA had not kept their members fully abreast of the situation. Eventually, the issue was resolved, but it was said that the POA had been isolated by the other unions and that they had no legal loophole left to oppose the new system. They and the other unions had all agreed.

The shift changes were implemented but later than intended. They also had teething problems, which some staff felt required the hospital to rely on the rapidly eroding goodwill of the nursing staff.

Great discontent was voiced about the POA. Individual staff contemplated resignation from the union, feeling let down by a union whose function was to protect them. This was contrasted with the perceived role of the RCN as a professional body, or as one person put it, not so much a union but more a college, like the medical colleges.

This long saga is interesting partly because the major industrial relations issue signalled a defeat of the POA: it did not have the industrial muscle of earlier times (Brindle 1991; Carvel 1990a,b,c). Ward managers were 'piggy in the middle' of the staff they were meant to be leading and the managers they were meant to obey. The analysis of the POA insider cited earlier proved to be correct. Things had changed.

There is an irony in the fact that, within the High Secure Hospital system, locking in at night has subsequently been reintroduced. This was apparently on the grounds of safety but without doubt it would have saved money on night staff as well.

The consequences of complaints

Complaints were a sensitive area. Historically, the resolution of complaints in High Secure Hospitals had been problematic (Department of Health 1992). Complaints procedures varied over time but new guidelines were introduced in all three High Secure Hospitals in April 1992.

Following the Boynton Report (DHSS 1980) into Rampton Hospital, the Rampton review board reported for several years and found that 'of over 40 complaints made by patients not one was upheld' (Gostin 1986: 73). Gostin went on to remark that both MIND (National Association for Mental Health) and NCCL (National Council for Civil Liberties) received complaints from patients. MIND, by the mid-1980s, had attempted to provoke the Department of Health into producing independent arbitration of complaints. One issue was the difficulties posed by complaints of ill treatment where criminal offences might have occurred. In these instances, nurses who were members of the POA were instructed not to cooperate with an internal hospital investigation. In 1992 the investigating team at Ashworth found that referral to the police for allegations that could constitute criminal offences meant that the internal hospital examination of the complaint stopped. This meant the issues of professional discipline were never adequately considered. As the team comment (Department of Health 1992: 85), 'And if the police concluded that there was insufficient evidence, that invariably was the end of the matter'.

Other difficulties with the existing Ashworth policies they identified were that patient witnesses were often disbelieved, whereas it was almost inconceivable for staff to be disbelieved. Those investigating complaints for the hospital confused this with making pre-emptive conclusions.

Where patient complaints were withdrawn, they were assumed to have been malicious.

In the light of these concerns, a single new policy was introduced in all three hospitals, which emphasized the right of a patient to complain about any aspect of care. It also stated that regardless of referral to the police, staff had to cooperate with any internal consideration of a complaint. At the time of its introduction, the POA believed this conflicted with the legal right of their members to remain silent. Complaints are variable, and there are important differences between complaints of unfair loss of parole and complaints of physical assault. This was reflected in the adoption of four distinct categories of complaint, the allocation to be done by a senior member of hospital staff. Certain complaints would be independently adjudicated.

The consequences of an internal complaint in the NHS nowadays vary. Many are resolved quickly, some trigger a detailed internal inquiry and may result in organizational changes, others are mediated by patients' representatives, e.g. solicitors or voluntary sector organizations, and a small number result in civil litigation, e.g. negligence cases, European Court of Human Rights action or criminal prosecution. Feedback to teams and individuals including family and carers is now commonplace. We should remember, however, that patients' complaints triggered the Mid-Staffordshire inquiry, too late for many patients. This is an area of struggle not only for High Secure Hospitals but also everywhere else in the NHS.

This account, drawn from field notes, highlights the realities of serious complaints using an anonymized version of a real incident.[3]

> A patient complained that they had been seriously assaulted at night by a member of staff. There was immediate involvement of senior hospital staff. A particular member of staff was rung at home and told that they were accused. The person concerned was upset by the phone call, the accusation, and the way the telephone call was conducted, subsequently saying it was the 'third degree' but was unfazed

---

[3] The account is a heavily edited account based on field notes. Details have been altered to protect those involved, to the detriment of the account. The account is written primarily to emphasize the essence of the story and is completely, and necessarily, lacking in local detail.

by the accusation itself. Proof of the accusation would have led to dismissal. All the staff thought the accusation was false. Various suggestions were made about the patient's motivation—they were known to lie, perhaps they had a dream. The staff viewpoint was supported by early forensic evidence, which suggested an assault was unlikely. At this point the senior staff involved in the emergency phone call said that the person who had been rung was not accused directly. No other member of staff was rung in this way. The patient insisted that things can happen at night without the night staff being aware, that the incident had happened but the assailant was unidentifiable. The patient cited evidence of ward staff behaving inappropriately at other times in support of their allegation. Since the allegation the patient alleged the staff had been behaving oddly and had offered no support. Staff insisted they had offered the patient support but in their view the allegation had little substance and it was reconstructed as a clinical problem for a patient known to have fabricated stories in the past. Other staff were less than sympathetic and when the question of support was again raised, in the privacy of staff handover, one wag suggested 'scaffolding'. The patient's allegations then broadened to include a general view of staff as racist. Coincidentally, other inquiries were happening at the same time. The same member of staff, along with others, was investigated in relation to an apparently similar issue.[4] The main allegation of assault was to be the subject of a full-scale internal inquiry. Staff continued wholeheartedly to back their colleague and were disgruntled with the choice of hospital staff conducting the inquiry. Colleagues suggested that with this level of stress the member of staff should go off sick. Throughout this the member of staff continued to work on the ward. The patient stuck to their story but wrote a letter of apology about the accusation of racism and denied ever having directly accused the member of staff rung at home. The patient said it could not have been this member of staff, who was not in the hospital at the time. The patient also disclosed to the researcher that further forensic reports were inconclusive but expressed no surprise. Meanwhile, the apparently accused member of staff continued to have meetings, with their union representative present, with senior hospital staff, much to the irritation of their ward manager. It transpired that there should have been no phone call to the staff member's home and it should not have been conducted in the way it apparently was. The story, which had gone on for weeks, and appeared in the end inconclusive, found its way into the media. This breach of confidentiality was distressing to the patient.

There were no winners in this narrative, only losers. Other inquiries conducted at the time of fieldwork seemed to confirm the staff view that anxious senior staff, operating in the potential glare of publicity, might

---

[4] This investigation was undertaken by a member of staff reputed to have been eager to fight with patients when on the ward.

leap to conclusions prejudicial to staff. Equally, this incident confirms what some patients knew, which was that sparking off a major investigation was unlikely ultimately to be to your advantage as a patient, despite the obvious changes made to the system. For the ward manager it once again suggested that they could not be relied on either by ward staff or by senior management. Equally illuminating was another major incident which occurred during fieldwork, where the ward manager stuck by the nursing staff and left themselves open to difficulty with senior management as a result. Their position illuminates an unhappy dynamic, characterized by distrust between staff and management, starkly illuminated at times of crisis.

These two examples of events unfolding during fieldwork illustrated something about the changing nature of social relations within Smithtown. It appeared that some things were being done differently and that vociferous staff had strong and often negative views about this. Direct questions provided a more representative view about organizational change on the male wards.

Major changes: staff views

Staff of all disciplines on Paris and Toulouse were asked about important, positive and negative changes, their understanding of the process and what they themselves would change if in charge. There were no limits placed on the timescale of identified change, nor was the level of description, i.e. ward, hospital or external to Smithtown, specified.

From this more systematic approach to staff views, several major areas of recognizable change stand out: patients' rights, aspects of ward life and issues to do with management. Two particular political 'hot potatoes', which constituted crucial components of staff management relations, were sufficiently frequently mentioned to stand out in their own right; these were the possible loss of uniforms and, as already rehearsed, the abolition of the shift system.

Patients' rights

'Patients' rights' can be understood in a number of ways. Patients have legal rights enshrined in statute law by virtue of being citizens, by virtue of being patients and by virtue of being detained mental health patients. In accordance with this last identity, rights are also taken away, e.g. liberty, freedom of association and voting rights. All these rights are considered to some degree by the statutory agency charged with maintaining standards in the High Secure Hospitals, at that time the Mental Health Act Commission. Equally, a High Secure Hospital has a responsibility to safeguard the welfare of its patient population, which includes, as in the case of other hospitals, vigilance with regard to the behaviour of its own staff. Patients' internal complaints procedures are the first port of call. Recourse to the law is in a formal sense possible, usually by way of lawyers who deal with appeals against detention under the Mental Health Act.

Daily existence requires regular negotiation about rights and entitlements writ small, e.g. going to social functions, being able to use the telephone or getting a room. The permissions and refusals of these activities are often what staff meant when talking about rights, as these were the things over which they had control. Their importance is already clear; the quality of life of patients could hinge substantially on these seemingly small issues.

Nursing staff are not lawyers, although because they use the law more in practice, doctors and social workers will be aware of the statutes and to some extent the principles that lie behind them. They are charged with interpreting this in a clinical way—the medico-legal interface. There have been de facto changes in obvious and easily identifiable rights in recent years. The statutory rights of mental health patients with regard to hospital treatment and detention increased in the 1983 Mental Health Act. Patients have automatic Mental Health Review Tribunals after a period of detention. For many patients there is significant and highly valued contact with a trained advocate to whom they can turn for advice about other matters. These rights apply both to patients entering the Special Hospitals from prisons and courts and from the health care system.

The Mental Health Act Commission had a responsibility both to see patients' legal rights observed, and to respond to patient complaints in relation to care and placement. Its remit varied from ensuring that allegations of brutality are investigated to seeing if ward shower fittings work. The Commission devoted considerable energy to the Special Hospitals (Mental Health Act Commission 1999). Commissioners visited regularly. Whether or not its enthusiasm was matched by influence is less clear.[5] Many patients viewed the Commissioners' visits as either irrelevant or actually dangerous to them. Fieldwork observations suggested that disparities of background between Commissioners and patients and the fact that many Commissioners had mental health training did not engender confidence in them. Patients knew that their concerns could be fed back to the clinical team on the same day, and for some, to be identified as a complainant in this way appeared risky; nonetheless, they did sometimes use the system. Commissioners appeared, at times, worried at the low take-up on visits. They may or may not have grasped the reasoning behind it. Staff were aware that the patients' reluctance could be attributed to staff intimidation. The other task of Commissioners was to check the clinical notes. This bureaucratic task was performed diligently. It was perhaps less demanding than obtaining meaningful views from patients about the quality of service offered.

The Commissioners' visits were relatively few. Day-to-day implementation of patients' legal rights was delegated, as in all psychiatric hospitals, to the Patients' Affairs department, which would tell patients when their Tribunals are occurring. Where patients believe their rights, of whatever kind, have been infringed they have the option of complaining. Interview evidence supported the fieldwork in suggesting that staff were conscious of a new, real capacity to complain. But more than that, there was a perception of patients' rights generally increasing. In most cases, they felt that was inappropriate. A constellation of related attitudes and ideas can be detected behind this general observation in both nursing assistants and qualified staff. The following nursing assistants' remarks are illustrative:

> In those days you could have a laugh and a joke with patients. Now this is frowned upon. Now you are afraid to open your mouth. Now the patients are treated better

---

[5] The impotence of the Mental Health Act Commission in dealing with the practice of one of the special hospital consultants was illustrated in a television documentary.

than the staff. Now the management write . . . 'staff allege', 'patients say'. Any complaint a patient makes, however bizarre, is checked out by management. Some of them are total liars, e.g. Xavier.

Morale is at an all-time low. Comradeship was much better then but now staff are frightened—not of the dangerous patients but of management. . . . Of course the internal inquiries only find the nurses at fault.

Patients have been given more say and more rights. They have far too many rights. When you consider what they have done they have far too many rights, e.g. they have whatever they want. No one is prepared to say no, e.g. Yves destroys his clothes so he gets new ones.

Another nursing assistant who considered patients 'the scum of the earth' was in favour of turning 'the clock back'. By this he meant 'no telephone calls', 'no outside party' (meaning no patients working outside of the hospital) and a 'harsher regime on the ward . . . if you're told you will do it'. This, he felt, would lead to a 'better relationship between staff and patients'. Staff were, in his view, frightened of a 'laugh and joke'. If something happens, the patients were believed and the staff suspended.

This view is contradictory to that described in the case analyses from the Ashworth Inquiry (Department of Health 1992), which had shown how hard it was for patients to be believed. The case study in the project cited earlier tells us much about the experience of complaint but it was not found to be a justified complaint.

An easy assumption would be that untrained nursing staff were isolated in their views. Their lack of exposure to the illness/treatment model might be thought to account for their preference for military-type order and hierarchy. However, there was no consistent nursing assistant opinion. Antoine, another nursing assistant who occupied a position of respect amongst his colleagues, and was cherished by the patients, expressed himself differently and held complex views. He recognized the power of old charge nurses to lock people up, pointing out that there were 'some good ones but there were some bad ones . . . it was a system that was wrong'. He expressed frank views on the previous victimization of individual patients often by clearly identified staff with a reputation to match. Now, many such staff had either gone or reverted to staff nurse status while maintaining their income. Patients had increased power and staff 'backed right off' for fear of possible complaint. Previously, 'if a patient hit a staff man he'd be in trouble', but for him, 'discipline had gone too far the other way', so that patients could not be told to get out of bed.

The nursing assistants' view was inconsistent but so was the view of qualified staff. Although the detail of their responses differs from what is already cited, there was the same fear in their minds of complaints. The consequences of complaints against trained staff, as one informant said, are potentially different, since complaints against them can be made to the UKCC. Built into the issue of complaint was the sense that certain staff behaviours were now likely to be seen as at best inappropriate, whereas in the past they would have passed unremarked, for example:

> Lots of the fun has gone. You could have a laugh and a joke and with some even a wrestle with them. Now it would be seen as very unprofessional. A lot of the patients think that a lot of the humour has gone out of the place.

> Now so many petty allegations are made, e.g. in the past a patient would pour some water on your head . . . you would end up having a water fight. It didn't hurt anyone, you were interacting with the patients. Everyone enjoyed it. People let off steam. A bit of horseplay. On Calais ward staff were suspended recently for playing about with water. The old management used to listen to the staff. If things did get out of hand the charge nurse would call you in and tell you not to do it again. If you did it again you would be up in front of the nursing officer. If you did it a second time you went in front of the chief nursing officer. You only appeared before him once. The next time you were out. Now it just goes straight to the top and you are suspended 'pending an enquiry'.

The reality may not be as extreme but even for confident staff, asked to work closely with patients who might nurture great hostility to the system of care, specific complaints left them less than sanguine about the institutional response. The following account comes from an experienced qualified nurse:

> Patients can make allegations which can affect your professional status. I personally feel this and patients have made allegations against me, e.g. Guillaume was very abusive and aggressive. I got him to sit down. I explained to him that if he didn't calm down I'd have to seclude him. He alleged that I was always threatening to seclude him . . . Eventually, it was found to have been nonsense. At this time Guillaume was making lots of complaints. The investigations made everyone feel quite shitty and did no good for Guillaume's treatment plan. Everyone thought that management wanted to find staff guilty. . . . Once the complaint is over you have to pick up the pieces. Every time you interact with him there is this stress factor there.

Concern about how they could be construed was particularly evident in relation to the female wards. Few male staff would risk allegations and work with female patients.

Most nurses saw changes in this area as negative but a few welcomed the enhanced patients' rights. One man, coming from outside of Smithtown, commented that he could cope with patients' rights, whereas some of his colleagues could not. He was in favour of the Mental Health Act Commission and thought that the public attention given to patients' complaints had flagged the fact that something was wrong. If it had not, he argued, 'It would still be going like that.' Another man, with over thirty years of experience in Smithtown, thought a patients' charter was a good idea and commented that the law could usefully be changed such that untreatable psychopaths could return to prison rather than simply occupying a hospital bed. This last observation is in line with the government's current approach to high-risk personality-disordered men who are likely to be managed by the Ministry of Justice, not hospital services. This change of emphasis came on the back of an expensive treatment experiment with high-risk men in high secure care; units commissioned to do this have now had their funding redirected elsewhere. For men in Smithtown who could not or would not engage with staff, this option would have avoided pointless hospital detention.

Senior nurses and staff from other disciplines were less preoccupied with patients' rights per se but it was acknowledged that the ward staff had a specific fear of litigation and that this had altered their practice with regard to calling in doctors. There was support for the concerns of staff; it was felt that nursing staff were blamed when things went wrong and that suspension was the response to incidents. Senior staff felt less at risk from complaint and did not have the same issues with personal authority in relation to patients. This is interesting in the light of the consequences for senior staff both at Ashworth and in the SHSA of the Fallon Inquiry (1999). The tone of this inquiry is severely judgmental. Individuals in senior medical, social work and management positions were named. Resignation and disciplinary action were recommended for some.

The maintenance of ward-based power relies in part, but not exclusively, on these areas of rights and privileges. In daily life, this was a crucial dynamic for ward-based staff who responded to requests and made decisions whose basis could seem opaque. Many nursing staff perceived an increase in patient power as in some way being at their expense. They saw themselves as losing their grip and unable to be as strict with patients as would be ideal. Staff had lost room for manoeuvre, as what had previously been privileges had become rights. The balance of power between staff and patients was like a see-saw, as one goes up, the other goes down. Few staff welcomed this idea, and many found it observably stressful.[6]

Ward life

Although paradoxical, the majority of nursing staff welcomed practical changes in ward routine. Individuals with long memories recalled the levels of overcrowding, notably in dormitory accommodation. No one opposed the reduction in numbers and no one regretted the major effort that had gone into creating individual rooms for patients. This process was not complete. Individual rooms and access to rooms was seen almost without exception as a good thing.

Arguably these improvements were elements of what many saw as more relaxed wards. Levels of tension can be decreased on wards if patients are able to use their rooms to stay out of conflict. Very overcrowded facilities are known to provoke physical violence (Paulus et al. 1985). At the time of the fieldwork, 'sleeping in' beyond 7 a.m. was pioneered. Compulsory bathing, where patients had no choice about bathing routines and might be forced to stand naked in corridors waiting for access to a bathroom, was a thing of the distant past. Concern was expressed about limited access to the outside world for patients.

For other staff the details of ward life were generally less apparent, presumably because fewer doctors or psychologists spent long periods of time on the ward. When mentioned, they welcomed the change towards a less restrictive and rigid ward routine.

---

6 One other aspect of patients' rights was mentioned, which was that patients' marriages were universally condemned as doomed to failure.

Management issues

Management, as far as ward staff were concerned, started with the clinical area manager for nurses and members of the hospital management team for most others. The overwhelming view of the nursing staff was that managers were a bad thing. There were several strands to this frank dislike. First, it was thought there were simply too many managers. The management structure was viewed as top heavy, generating too much paperwork. Second, because professional managers, as opposed to clinicians, were now running the hospital, managers were thought to be ignorant of clinical issues. Third, in line with previous material, and mirroring the staff view of them, managers were also thought to have a negative view of staff. Specifically, they were viewed as a different species from clinical staff and predisposed to ignore the views and wishes of ward staff. The following accounts convey the spirit of these concerns:

> It is top heavy. A director for everything. Many faceless people in offices. All chiefs and not enough Indians. . . . Bertrand knew the score. He came up through the ranks. He knew the kind of people we were dealing with. If you had a problem you would bring problems to his attention. Not now. The managers knew your name. Lots of the staff were family jobs but I got the job on my own merits and I had a rapport with him. This management have no idea. They don't care about the staff. They are not approachable. In the past, management were human and there. This management you only see if you are in trouble. They sit in their ivory towers.

> They keep relaxing the way Smithtown is run. Our patients are not here for scrumping apples. The management need to start realising the sort of patients we have and the sort of treatment this needs. Nursing staff are scapegoated every time things go wrong. No one else gets blamed. Only nurses. No one knows who the management are, let alone the management know the staff. . . . The goodwill of the nurses is gradually going, e.g. Claude often stays on for half an hour . . . Eventually, they will lose the goodwill.

> HMT are trying to bring in so many new ideas. They are trying to treat it like a general hospital. Christian is trying to focus on the money but care is important. . . . he knows nothing about the sort of patients we have. Every week they are finding new office space for admin staff, more office workers, less nurses.

> Too much empire building, too much bureaucracy, it's just gone crazy as far as I can see . . . escalation of staff on non-nursing side.

There were a number of reasons put forward to explain the way management approached staff. These included the idea that there were financial pressures on management and that the clinical staff, or more particularly the nursing staff, were to bear the brunt of this. This was seen as a major motivation behind the attempt to change the shift system and to introduce '24-hour care'.[7] Worry was expressed at the idea that staffing levels would drop and jeopardize the safety of both patients and staff.

The second explanation for what was understood as the management style was that they intended to break the power of the POA. A potent symbol of the union's historical domination of the hospital was the earlier uniform worn by staff, with peaked hats and gold braid. The military overtones of this uniform were obvious, with all its implications in terms of hierarchy. Thus, the battle over uniforms on which the managers embarked was revealing; it illuminated the extent to which staff saw their authority located in the lounge suit (into which the gold braid had metamorphosed) as well as the extent to which the POA was prepared to confront the managers. Some staff still mourned the white socks and peaked hats of earlier days, some still sported the white socks. Others were unconcerned about the potential move to 'civvies'. As it turned out, the transition was postponed as a result of its unpopularity with staff, and perhaps because of a need to get through the shift changes.

The third explanation for managerial behaviour was that they were ruled from above. A third of the nursing staff thought that the important changes brought about had originated outside the hospital and that the hospital management team were simply carrying out orders.

The non-nursing staff echoed this political analysis and also expressed concern about managerial style. As one senior member of staff said, 'You as a member of staff are treated in exactly the way you're not supposed to treat the patients'; another said that there was a widespread mistrust of the hospital management team and their insensitive handling of change made it hard to achieve sensible goals. Another commented that '[i]t was a very closed institution. Some of the staff were little Hitler's. But the medical director interviewed all the staff himself and knew them. But it was very incestuous, fathers, sons, husbands and wives working here. The regime now is much more liberal', adding that the HMT 'are out

---

7 All nursing staff would work days and nights. The rigid distinction between day and night staff would be lost. The existing shift system was ill suited to this change.

of touch with what is going on in the hospital. They are not picking up on the staff's dreadfully low morale'. Witnessed exchanges with senior managers were few and far between but they indicated that when senior managers came to the ward, they only talked to staff and that the staff were unimpressed.

Both individual managers and managers as a non-clinical class were criticized, either as pawns of their political masters or as deficient in their own right. The vehemence of this critical analysis was unmistakable. There was a profound reluctance to do anything differently at the instigation of people who were considered non-clinicians.

Though this was a parochial dispute, many of the views cited here could be found almost anywhere in the NHS from the 1990s onwards and are not unique to High Secure Hospitals. Spending on management in the NHS (Klein 1995: 209) was either money diverted from patient care, or a sensible investment which would result in increased efficiency. He suggested that those holding different views shouted loudly in a 'dialogue of the deaf', a term that might equally be applied to general relations between clinical and non-clinical staff in Smithtown. It was not a dialogue audible to many patients.

Personal perspectives and private preoccupations: patient views

The past is a private place?

Patients were not exercised about changes. The contrast with intensity of the debate in staff conversation was striking. Even when asked directly, they might evade the question or say nothing had altered.

Didier, a patient, explained that during most of his years in Smithtown he had not left the ward; his work during this time was as a ward cleaner. The consequence of this was that for the first twenty years of his stay he had not seen a woman. Like many observations early in a period of fieldwork, this remark proved to be something of a red herring. Although other patients in the first few days talked spontaneously about the past and the present, such remarks were peripheral to the main business of life on the ward.

Other patients told me how they themselves had changed since arriving in Smithtown. More general comments occurred only sporadically in ordinary conversation. How Smithtown ran in the past, or what it was now, seemed to be more a matter of occasional comment than a topic of regular and open debate.

Some people had noticed the impact of the new management and commented on differences in the patterns of ward routine, not always favourably. One man said his visitors were not searched in the past and he used to have picnics on the grass. Another said the choice of food was better now but meals are late. He added that the routines for the escorting of patients were less efficient than in the past and made getting to work difficult. Seclusion practices had also changed. In the past, 'dumb insolence or arguing' would get you put into seclusion, in line with the attitude 'you are the criminal, we are the screws'. A few patients recalled periods of overcrowding and having to sleep elsewhere.

On the women's ward the personalization of memory was if anything more true. Time to many patients had gone quickly, defying their expectations. This was time in years, whereas, as has already been mentioned, each day, especially at weekends, was boring for many patients. Their sense of things past was enshrined in personal memories rather than in institutional ones; such expressed memories were of life before Smithtown.

The ages of the women patients ranged from 22 to 76. At least ten patients had been there for ten years or longer. There were also at least seven women who had been there less than eighteen months. This meant that about a third had a long continuous timeframe on which to base their views; a further two had been readmitted and in Smithtown for some years previously. One older woman described the changes, and lack of, to her life in the following field note:

> I asked her about the blue and white scarf which I had seen her knitting in the sewing room and she told me it was for a man. Apparently, it was for a different man from her current boyfriend! She told me that her boyfriend does not know about that and was quite mischievous about it. On her two other days of work she goes to the sewing room. She told me that she liked doing that and could not say which she preferred, the day centre or the sewing room. She told me she had been going to the sewing room for . . . years. She used to do the mending and alterations years

ago and said that that was really hard work and that she did not enjoy that, as it was far too much to do. She described various alterations to shirts and trousers that she had to do. For six years she, Isobelle and another patient had to finish socks. Apparently, they came knitted up like tubes and they had to tie the toes together. She said that Isobelle was very lazy and did not do very many, so Sandrine had to do loads to compensate. She said that she found it affected her eyes and she always looked as though she was crying with watery red eyes. In the end, a social worker coming in to the sewing room picked up that this work was affecting her and she was taken off doing it . . . She said she has a large room here now which has a TV in it. She likes to watch it, though she does not much in the dayroom . . . She said she used to have a radio but it went wrong and she did not miss it. Sandrine was very happy to chat to me about sewing and knitting and so on but was not very forthcoming when I asked her about the changes that she had seen over the many years she had been there. I do not think she was being deliberately evasive, I just do not think she thought about it very much. In the end she went back to her knitting because I was distracting her and she had 'to get on'.

The past has public dimensions

Women's reflections on the institution were random remarks, which formed no coherent theme but did relate to issues raised more common-ly by the men. The seven women who did identify differences had either been in Smithtown for some years or had been readmitted. They com-mented on changes in the powers of staff with regard to ward routine, use of seclusion and medication. Ward routine had become more easy-going. Seclusion was no longer used as a punishment, more care was taken by male staff to respect the modesty of women and patients came out of seclusion and back into regular ward life more quickly. Patients were not 'drugged up' as they were in the past. In keeping with what seemed to be pointers towards liberalization was the view that there was more freedom of expression nowadays. There was a lone dissenter who felt that staff were more prison oriented than in the past.

Only two issues during fieldwork attracted interest from significant numbers of patients: changes in the rates of remuneration for work and the smoking policy. The smoking policy, which also affected staff, was part of the plan to bring the hospital in line with the rest of the NHS, where smoking has been gradually eradicated. Smithtown was starting from the opposite extreme, and several things happened. Staff were not allowed to smoke in front of patients, which meant that if they did, they might be in trouble. Patients were no longer able to get cigarettes easily from the canteen and visitors were banned from bringing them. Needless to say, this led to considerable consternation among the large group of patient smokers, made worse by wild rumour mongering.

Payment for work also attracted some interest. This complex issue of payment, like the smoking issue, provoked comments from staff. The complexity of the previous system and the likely complexity of the subsequent system precluded the researchers from ever fully grasping what was proposed. At least partly led by disgruntled staff, patients were antagonistic to the proposed alterations which became associated with wage cuts.

These hospital-wide issues were also discussed by staff and, like the use of seclusion and the relative freedom of expression mentioned by some patients, represented crude agreement between staff and patients. Patients welcomed altered changes in seclusion practice and greater freedom of speech. As we already know, not all staff did.

But it was far from clear that the issues known to matter to staff and to some patients were of widespread importance. Interpreting an absence of information seemed risky. A more systematic approach to the issue of institutional change was possible in longer interviews with male patients on Paris and Toulouse.

Daily life dominated patients' perceptions of change

Male patients were invited to say what they thought had changed during the time they had been resident in Smithtown, what they thought about that, what they would change if they were in charge and what was being discussed that might lead to further changes and what they thought about this. These questions reflected the fieldwork material in two ways.[8] First, while not all the patients had volunteered notions of change, none had said that nothing had altered. Second, from the researchers' point of view it was an inescapable fact that both ward- and hospital-level changes had occurred within the immediate past.

---

[8] Questions to staff and patients that covered the same issues were in places differently phrased in response to the differences emerging from field note material.

The decision to move beyond key informants was helpful, as it revealed that most men thought there had been changes but also that a quarter thought nothing was different. Most men's hospital detention spanned years, on average eight years. Men detained under the Mental Health Act term "psychopathic disorder" as opposed to "mental illness" were more likely to identify changes than the mentally ill.

What is different?

Several men who identified changes had frames of reference spanning decades, as they had been resident in Smithtown for many years. From these oldest residents came some of the most thoughtful and articulate ideas about Smithtown. The group included men with long-term mental illness as well as most of the men detained for 'psychopathic disorder'. Their responses indicate that most had what might be termed a parochial outlook. They focused on what had changed for them as individuals but had less of a perspective on life 'beyond the end of the ward'. Some men talked at length about this issue, while others confined themselves to a couple of sentences.

By far the commonest topic was the social relations of staff and patients, followed by discussion of rooms and dormitories and personal access to the world beyond the ward (see also Appendix A). Patients made three times as many positive comments, welcoming change, as negative ones, objecting to changes; this is very different from the pattern of staff responses.

Staff attitudes to patients

In essence, the patients suggested that there had been a move towards less harsh attitudes to them. Some accounts came from patients who recognized that their attitude to the system in which they found themselves was, in the words of one of them, 'very anti'. One commented that in the past there was a hard core of staff who saw patients as 'no better than scum'. Previously, he said, but no longer, these members of staff were in the majority. Another made the following complex assessment of how he and the staff had changed. On arrival, he found himself amongst people for the first time whose behaviour was startlingly unpredictable. As he learnt about the symptoms and signs of mental health problems amongst his fellow patients he felt some were picked on for 'bugging the staff'. He thought these observations were made by other patients too and that this situation no longer pertained. His own attitude to staff became negative and was only retrieved by individual staff who, he added, took the trouble to understand him. He also pointed out objective changes, such as being able to sit where you wanted at meals instead of in your allocated place. This is part of what he sees as moves by staff to give patients choices, to the extent that he remarked that the staff had, in the everyday sense, 'allowed patients to run the ward'. He saw his life as less at the mercy of rules and regulations. Another patient, again cautious about the changes in his own outlook, said that 'patients have more clout' and as a consequence he sees 'a subtle air of caution in staff'. One older patient had lived through the days of 'the monkey house', a block ward with the reputation of housing large numbers of patients with mental illness. His recollection was of 'psychotics having the piss taken out of them'. His understanding was of less formality between staff and patients than in the past, and the patient group were 'allowed opinions'. He saw these changes as accompanied by more emphasis on aspects of therapy. This was echoed by a patient on another ward, who said, 'It's much better for patients . . . the staff are kinder and more health orientated. Before they were more prison orientated. They are very good.' Objections to the liberalization in staff–patient relations came from two patients. Discipline could be considered in some ways desirable, one advantage being fairness. It was thought reasonable for patients who had committed dreadful crimes. Where discipline had relaxed, it could be seen as giving rise to more 'fiddles' and resulting in 'the ever-increasing potential for violence'.

Use of seclusion

An illuminating area of staff–patient relations was patients' understanding of the use of seclusion. Patients had commented anecdotally on changes in its use in Smithtown. The interview material suggested that it was used both for more serious behavioural disturbance as well as less punitively than in the past. One man explained that he had once been placed in seclusion:

I complained about my medication. I said it made me feel I couldn't concentrate and Henri locked me up to teach me a lesson. He gave me no tea. They came to see me later and Henri tried to wind me up to hit him. There were two staff hiding round the corner. I didn't hit him. Patients are no longer beaten up here.

Did you ever see it happen?

When I was on Boulogne ward a patient hit a staff man over the back of the head with a snooker cue and badly injured him. Jean-Paul, a nurse, told the staff to give him 'the usual treatment'. I didn't see it but I heard the beating they gave him. I later heard that he was beaten up twice more. It was clearly understood that if you hurt a staff man you got a beating. That doesn't happen now.

The importance of this account lies both in the accuracy or otherwise of his recollection of what did or did not happen to his fellow patient, and in his understanding of the rules of hospital life. It is not feasible to evaluate his testimony on issues of fact. However, his account suggested that he believed staff could behave in a way that, in terms of their professional role, was quite illegitimate. It also suggested that this potential sanction for attacks by patients on staff was recognized by the patients. It can only have operated as a considerable incentive for good behaviour.

Patients who commented on changes in the use of seclusion were clearly not quoting statistics about changing frequencies of use but were speaking from their own experience of what you had to do to be secluded.

[I]f you had told a member of staff to fuck off previously you would have been in seclusion . . . refusing medication was a seclusion offence.

In the past if you were caught with a cigarette lighter, a bit of dope or if you had a fight or if you had an argument and wouldn't shut up, you were sent to the punishment block; they called it the intensive care [laughs]. Now they are far more tolerant. There are more groups and talking now. Also they look at the patients' point of view more now, for example, they think you are joking when you are. You couldn't joke with them before. There is more tolerance now, they tolerate people a lot more, for example, . . . a patient said he would kill all the staff and they let him shout and after a while asked if he would like to lie down. When I was first here they would have dragged him to the seclusion room. Now they also use different procedures to take people to seclusion. Restraint. This is a vast improvement. I experienced the wristlocks and it did not injure me. When I first came they used to get you in a headlock and you could easily get hurt. I saw people being dragged off in a headlock. The memory sticks in my mind. It is quite terrifying.

I was secluded x years ago. I can't remember what it was for. I was in the room for three or four days. You had to eat your food with a spoon. You used to be let out for a smoke once or twice a day . . . Nowadays you don't get secluded for very long, only about a day. Other times I was secluded when I first got sent to the punishment block for the first few days. When you were secluded no one spoke to you and you were only let up once or twice a day. It was not very nice.

Francois commented that the reasons for seclusion had changed as well as the way it was monitored. He and a member of staff independently said that when a particular charge nurse had authorized the seclusion it might not be lifted until that man returned to duty two weeks later. Francois thought you might be secluded in the past for swearing at staff, whereas now, even for getting into a fight you would not automatically be secluded. Another patient who hit someone during the project was surprised to find himself not secluded; he viewed the staff response as 'very lenient'.

Another man, who had never been in seclusion despite a long Smithtown career, said he had once hit a 'staff man' whom he thought on this occasion was 'asking for it'. Instead of seclusion being imposed, the 'staff man' held him up against the wall in a sluice room (where the bed pans are emptied and whose interior is not visible from the main corridor) and threatened him. No further action ensued and the patient never complained, pointing out that in the past 'they would find a way of getting back' if patients did complain. This echoed the remarks of at least two of the long-serving staff.

Patients' general view was that as staff–patient relations had relaxed, the use of seclusion was better regulated. There was a degree of consensus between staff and patients about what had changed but they framed it differently—patients' rights rather than staff attitudes—and evaluated it differently. Correspondingly, patients disliked the enhanced security procedures. Objections were voiced to the more thorough inspections of dormitories at night and to the introduction of visible surveillance cameras.

This discussion covers similar terrain to the material from staff framed around patients' rights but it is different. The conceptual difference is illuminating because only rarely did patients consider or articulate their formal rights; they seldom used the term. Patients had to consider staff attitudes because that was the concrete, rather than abstract, reality of their existence.

Rooms and dormitories

Wholly positive remarks about personal rooms were unsurprising. Patients reinforced what staff had said about the bad old days of over-crowded dormitories thankfully being replaced with individual rooms. Even the continued dormitory accommodation was better run. As one man said, you no longer had to get into your dressing gown to go to bed at half past eight in the evening. Both increased access to rooms and the possibility of having your own things in them, e.g. televisions and videos, were welcomed, especially as you were locked in your room early in the evening.

Rehabilitation trips and parole

Rehabilitation trips had increased in number since the advent of the SHSA. Directors of rehabilitation had been created as part of the hospital management team. Rehabilitation trips took various forms, and could include visits to family, shopping trips or outings to places of general interest. Patients might go out with two 'escorts', or as part of a ward outing. They were universally popular with the patient group, although the first one for many years could be anxiety inducing; although the world is transmitted through the television, radio and newspapers, it could seem very foreign to patients who had been confined for many years.

Rehabilitation trips of this kind were entirely cancelled for a period of some months when a number of trips ran into problems with absconding patients. This paradoxical action was the response of the senior management in the hospital. Given that this relatively normal contact, often with important people in their lives, was highly valued, this was a considerable hardship for the affected patients. It was a blanket ban and entirely non-negotiable from the patients' perspective.

Some patients had never been allowed rehabilitation trips. Sometimes, this was a consequence of how their psychiatric condition was viewed; however, it could equally be a comment on their escape potential, and if they were construed as potentially too competent, then trips might be refused and/or permission from the Home Office not requested.

For some people who had not have left Smithtown for years, rehabilitation trips were a non-issue. For others, the increase in trips was seen to be a good thing and the cancellation of all trips was terrible. Similarly, cancellation of social events and outside working parties were thought retrograde steps.

By comparison, the issue of 'parole', a term with continuing meaning in the criminal justice system, was, within Smithtown, of little concern. Historically, it had granted access to large parts of the hospital site and in other secure hospital settings was referred to as 'leave'. It was whittled away so that it was 'just a bloody fag lighter' rather than a genuine marker of increased freedom and trust.

Management style and structure

This was of little interest to the patients by comparison with staff. Only a quarter of patients observing changes made any remarks about any aspect of management, at ward or hospital level. In this, they showed little awareness of staff anxieties. The only aspect of management mentioned by more than one patient was the welcome introduction of ward managers.

Nothing had changed

A quarter of the men had proved immune to the changes in their accommodation, to the staff losing their peaked hats, to the introduction of ward managers, to an apparent enhancement in their rights and to the use of a telephone. For the two who had been there less than two years it is possible their answers reflect their short stay, while for the others it was a view based on many years in Smithtown.

The fact that those classified as mental illness are disproportionately represented among this group suggests that chronic psychosis may have limited some individuals' ability to notice changes. It is possible that their relative preoccupation with their psychotic internal worlds may effectively have precluded any interest in the outside world. By virtue of their mental disorder, their perception of events and time was sufficiently abnormal that nothing *appeared* to have changed.

Alternatively, the lack of stimulation consequent on long-term hospitalization may have rendered them indifferent to the world around them. The numbing effect of long-term institutional care was such that their environment had ceased to have any meaning and they no longer *noticed* changes. The social role of 'patient' precluded them from acting on the social world to bring about their wishes. Their position in the stratified hospital system was so low that they could not walk out of the ward, let alone change it as they would have wanted. They had acquired indifference.

Lastly, they may have observed changes but considered them irrelevant in the overall scheme of things. This might say something important about the attempts at transformation so enthusiastically instigated by the SHSA. That nothing had changed in terms of *their* lives even though certain things were to them observably different, meant they remained *insignificant* in terms of their personal experience. Given the importance patients attach to the fact of incarceration this should be unsurprising. There were parts of Smithtown the SHSA could not reach. There is evidence in partial support of all three propositions.

The relevance of incarceration and mental disorder to the process of 'institutionalization' has been considered by social scientists and psychiatrists. Much of the focus has been on why the individual appears to alter within an institution. The essence of the historical debate is not what institutionalization is, about which there is substantial agreement but rather the contribution of madness to its manifestation (Abrahamson 1993). Wing (1962: 38) comments that whatever the nature of the institution, being there a long time tends to give rise to the same sort of problems, i.e. 'apathy, resignation, dependence, depersonalisation and reliance on fantasy'. In his investigation of what he terms, slightly confusingly, institutionalism, he highlights three variables relevant to the generation of this pattern: the social pressures of an institution, susceptibility to institutional pressures and length of exposure to institutional pressures. His early work suggests that the longer you stay in hospital, the less likely you are to want to leave, and the less interested you are in the outside world.

Goffman (1961) lays the blame for this at the feet of the institution. He argued that when hospitalized, the patient adjusts their sense of self and ultimately agrees with the hospital's view of him/herself as sick. When this has happened they become indifferent to the prospect of leaving hospital. In this model the social pressures of the institution create the problem. Townsend (1976) suggested that this theory, while appealing, is not borne out by empirical research on patient groups; they do not generally consider themselves mentally ill. Goffman's work also stresses the similarities between different institutions which generate similar patterns of behaviour independent of the type of inhabitant.

Conversely, Johnstone et al. (1981) emphasized the intrinsic process of schizophrenia, that of gradual deterioration, and the relative irrelevance of someone's environment in determining such behaviours.

Wing's later work goes on to attempt to establish the extent to which aspects of institutionalism can be affected by altering the environment. Wing and Brown (1970: 178–80) emphasized the importance of 'poverty of the social environment' (by which they meant access to the outside world, personal possessions, constructive occupation and a lack of optimism in members of the clinical team about their future) in determining 'social withdrawal, flatness of affect and poverty of speech' in women patients with schizophrenia. Their 'Three Hospitals Study' suggested that manipulation of the environment could provoke changes in these phenomena; improving the material world of the patient made them less institutionalized. The features they regarded as institutionalization were correlated with length of stay in hospital.

This ethnographic material was not measuring 'apathy', nor for that matter 'poverty of the environment'. Nor was the environment manipulated, as in the classical Wing and Brown study. But it had changed. The fact that of the quarter of male patients who were indifferent to change, almost all were classified under mental illness, suggests that the medical model may have some validity (Johnstone et al. 1981). How the illness operates to achieve this state of indifference is less clear. But the fact that some of those categorized under mental illness did observe change suggests that either illness is a complex variable per se, which it is, or that additional factors are relevant to the individual case. This holds true if we accept that there is sensibly a parallel between the individual's interest in the outside world and their interest in their immediate world in Smithtown.

The issue of insignificance and irrelevance is addressed by McCourt-Perrin (1994: 170), whose study of psychiatric patients who went on to be rehoused in the community revealed that 'change had to be understood in a very limited and relative sense. Residents felt that important aspects of their experience and identity were still framed in the way they had been as hospital patients'. We know that what patients really minded about was still being in Smithtown, and no amount of tinkering with the shower timetable was going to affect this more fundamental point.

The danger is that those who see no change in the circumstances of their life can be explained away by the argument of 'institutionalization'. Privileging this construct undermines the views of the unimpressed patients. If we take the patients' views as valid in their own terms, they are an intriguing commentary on the relevance of what the staff uniformly saw as important changes.

Resistance to change

This commentary on change and its identification and practical impact has skirted around the significance of change and the extent to which it should be seen as cultural change. Managerial imperatives, ultimately coming from the SHSA, altered what was done on the surface of daily life and these had followed a more gradual process of change that was articulated by most staff and many patients. Getting under the surface of visible changes in practice and exploring not only social but also cultural, change is next. The possible disjunction between ideas and practice invites consideration of staff resistance to change and the role of the POA in particular.

Remembering and forgetting

The process of institutional change invites both forgetting and remembering (Douglas 1987: 69), so what becomes important in its analysis is precisely what is remembered and what is forgotten. This tells us much about the present, perhaps mainly what it is acceptable to say but also what means of communication are currently culturally congruent and what needs to be forgotten. That which is forgotten may be irretrievable. It may be truly forgotten, or it may be important to 'forget'. In fieldwork you may never know what people choose not to tell you, as they build a picture of their history to suit present time, and their immediate audience.

In the case of Smithtown, there is extensive documentation of certain aspects of life—there are for instance annual reports, old case notes and government inquiries. This does little or nothing to affect the personal editing and manipulation of past everyday experiences, processes which illuminate current value systems. This issue is of particular importance, as some aspects of the Special Hospital past are considered at best regrettable, and at worst frankly unsavoury (Brindle 1991a, 1992, 1992a,b,c; Department of Health 1992; Department of Health and Social Security 1980; Gostin 1986). Such things militate against honesty, straightforwardness and free expression of views.

The process of fieldwork and its longevity were useful. The impression of the researchers was, a little unexpectedly, of an organization in flux, not one that was stuck. But there may be good reasons for following Douglas (1987: 69) in her assertion that there may be 'shadowed places' in Smithtown's past, whose nature or extent is unguessable.

Not in the shadows: changing life on the ward

A degree of consensus had emerged about staff and patient reports of practical changes in daily life. They agreed about what had changed and substantially approved such changes. No one mourned the loss of either widespread dormitory accommodation for patients or the levels of overcrowding that had characterized the past. An increase in permitted personal possessions and patients' access to rooms was also welcomed. A more relaxed set of ward routines was seen as a good thing. None of these was introduced during the timeframe of the study and placing them chronologically was hard, not least because they were gradual.

But these undisputed changes had not been apparent to a fair number of male patients. Also, some of the changes, e.g. the ability to lie in bed until 9 a.m. at weekends, seemed still very institutional and divorced from real life.

Social relations

Staff and patients saw themselves and each other very differently. They assessed change from different starting positions but agreed that staff–patient social relations were different. Patients saw this as a more relaxed and lenient attitude. Staff were less likely to respond coercively to any kind of dissent from patients and more likely to want to hear their views. They saw this as liberalization. Nursing staff framed the change in social relations differently and were not agreed amongst themselves. Patients were seen as more powerful, principally in their capacity to complain. Nursing and other staff felt that the balance of power had shifted but not all saw this as undermining of authority. Some saw it as a way of controlling staff excess. But many staff believed they were vulnerable in a way that previously had not been the case.

There was something of a paradox in the staff attitude of welcoming practical and material changes but fearing the impact on their capacity to remain in charge of the wards. In reality, their day-to-day authority remained largely unassailable.

But the staff–patient dynamic is only part of the understanding of change. Management matter. There had been obvious changes in the social structures of the staff group, principally in the introduction of ward managers, who occupied an uncomfortable position between senior management and ward staff. Some charge nurses had gone effectively underground, as they left senior positions but were still employed. Among the staff group on the wards there were therefore individuals who had lost power and influence as a result of the new line management system for nursing staff. Everyone knew of others who had had to retire or to move off the wards. It appeared some staff were attracted to Smithtown because of its reputation and others despite it.

Beyond the ward there had been other changes in line management, notably the introduction of a hospital management team and a chief executive. During fieldwork the attempt to bring about further changes in practice, i.e. shift changes, twenty-four-hour care and the abolition of uniforms, provoked discussion that revealed the nature of social relations. The fact that shift changes were effected but the uniform issue was resolved by making it optional, said something about the locus of power within Smithtown. Management could make major changes but could not always force them upon a reluctant staff group.

The effect of change had in fact been to engender resistance. The sense of shifting power on the wards and the increasing vulnerability of staff to management oversight, allied to distrust of management, created considerable hostility, reduced the capacity of all staff to operate together and encouraged front-line staff of all grades and disciplines to coalesce around the issue and see themselves as the only people who understood the patients.

The role of the unions in mediating or fostering these tensions is uncertain. The POA continued to be central to an understanding of change, not least because the POA was and is only its members. Members of the POA discussed issues not only at union meetings but also on the ward. The union was a key player in terms of ward practice in so far as it affected the way in which shift and uniform changes were received and implemented. But not all staff were in the POA and the POA was not the only union, though you could be forgiven as a researcher for leaping to that conclusion. The POA had long been a target for those who characterize themselves as reformers of the Special Hospitals (Bluglass 1992; Bynoe 1992; Murphy 1997) and had allowed itself to be seen as the defender of unprofessional values and reluctant to embrace change. More than one author suggested it had no place in the High Secure Hospitals (Kaye and Franey 1998: 276; Murphy 1997). However, belonging to the POA did not automatically map onto resistance to change.

The real views of individual staff were to some extent opaque; we know what they said and what they did but we do not know what they said to themselves in the privacy of their heads.

Organizational and cultural change: what's the difference?

Wearing institutional blinkers

An important caveat to the perception of institutional change and one that applies equally to staff and patients, and to researchers, comes from Douglas (1987), who sees an intrinsic problem in the process of classifying and in noticing how institutions change. First, she argues (1987: 100), 'How can we possibly think of ourselves in society except by using the classifications established in our institutions? If we turn to the various social scientists, we find their minds are still more deeply in thrall', adding (1987: 102), 'institutions survive by harnessing all information processes to the task of establishing themselves. The instituted community blocks personal curiosity, organises public memory and heroically imposes certainty on uncertainty'. Put more simply, we see things the way institutions want us to, without realizing that. She also suggests that when things change, institutions can hide the process. These comments act as an effective critique on what has been so far established. Whatever staff and patients noticed as different, the way in which they framed it might be constrained by their pre-established identities within the institution. It is true that the analysis of change offered so far uses the available and institutionally generated categories of patient and staff. It is also true that my comments on why things appear as they do owe something to both psychiatry and social science, reflecting personal institutional blinkers. However, the work of anthropological empiricism, if not anthropological theory, is to document the other in its own terms. So although the framing of change is constrained by pre-existing institutional perspectives, this at least allows an analysis to emerge that informants could recognize.

The evidence to date would not easily support the idea that the institution, as a whole, or the wards, in particular, were static. Most staff, most patients and all three researchers understood that the past, however dated, was different and so too would be the future. Dissent did exist. In staff it was clearly characterized as resistance to the forces of modernity.

Anthropological theory was not well equipped to think about social change. Geertz (1983: 143) explained why. As he put it, 'the emphasis on systems in balance, on social homeostasis, and on timeless structural pictures, leads to a bias in favour of "well integrated" societies in a stable equilibrium and a tendency to emphasise the functional aspects of social usages and customs rather than their dysfunctional implications'. Not much of what has been written so far suggests ideational equilibrium, rather the opposite, although the changes on the ward, while significant, scarcely create a sense of anarchy but evidence a level of unease in the staff group and cautious optimism from the patients.

So, did the managers prevail?

The emergence of a confident managerial class in the NHS made it unsurprising that it was a managerial entity, the SHSA, rather than a professional one that was charged with changing the High Secure Hospitals. Smithtown had followed Griffiths (1983) in having strong leadership within the institution. However, there was little evidence that the 'natural managers' were doctors.[9] Smithtown had a history of powerful physician superintendents but otherwise lacked powerful doctors. This is unlike the rest of the NHS (Haywood and Alasewski 1980; Hunter 1979; Walby and Greenwell 1994: 58–60).

The direction of the SHSA appeared strongly influenced by the inquiries and governmental responses. Policy shifts and initiatives often follow adverse publicity about clinical standards, so this is no different from the rest of the NHS (Department of Health 1998, 1999) or for that matter the prison service. Genders and Players (1995: 9) note that in the context of Grendon Underwood, the therapeutic prison, the policy emphasis on rehabilitation and treatment, or their absence, had a real impact on the ground. The SHSA (1991b: 6) had wished to 'bring about changes in the overall culture and to foster positive attitudes in staff; to promote partnership with staff and patients in tackling change; to develop professionalism and pride in performance; and to develop our managers at all levels with particular emphasis on middle grades'. The tone of this was echoed in Smithtown.

The view from Fantasy Island

For ward-based staff, Fantasy Island was the universally acknowledged nickname for the administration block in Smithtown. The island exported large numbers of policy documents and memoranda. During the induction course all three researchers came across a further paper product, an upbeat glossy document specific to Smithtown. It came from the Change Facilitation Group, in its own words 'set up to establish a framework for developing new initiatives'. The introduction to 'Partnerships in Care: the

---

[9] Subsequent to this study, one of the special hospitals, Broadmoor, appointed a doctor as chief executive.

Smithtown Initiative for Excellence' reads as follows: 'Smithtown Hospital has always been a place of progressive change—after all that's our business. But now we are entering perhaps the most demanding period of change so far. The changes will challenge many of the standards and methods we are used to.' A very explicit statement of management philosophy was evident from reading on: 'Management do not wish to make the decisions about change in isolation and then ask the rest of us to do all the hard work. A dialogue between all staff levels is essential—it's about time we all started listening to each other—so let's get cracking!'

This document did not emanate directly from the highest tier of the hospitals bureaucracy. It was glossy in appearance and in tone and language similar to that of the SHSA brochures. It referred to 'corporate culture' and made clear that a hospital mission statement was to follow. In the cartoon pictures there was a threat. It is suggested that '[i]f you don't see yourself as part of the solution, you must be part of the problem'. A disconsolate or disgruntled cartoon bird disappears off the page. In a document where birds represent the staff, the message is clear. In its final paragraph, it said, 'Changes are not always popular or desired. But they are inevitable.' As a statement of the new management, this was revealing.

According to Walby and Greenwell's (1994: 57) distinction between 'Taylorist' and 'new wave' approaches, Smithtown were adopting a Taylorist approach. This means success relied on detailed scrutiny and incentives, as opposed to productivity arising from feeling good about the organization and the work. An apparently previously proud workforce had, for the best of reasons, had its morale sapped. But, as Giri (2000: 183) pointed out, self-examination was not a feature of organizations prior to the recent emphasis on audited activity. The assumption of satisfactory work with which many of us operated in health, education and other areas of the public sector may have been complacent.

The Special Hospitals faced criticism from 1980 onwards and could not easily defend themselves, at least in part because they had not been self-questioning and lacked a capacity, now routine, to demonstrate satisfactory quality and performance. Regular service user feedback, use of peer support workers, clinical activity figures, Care Programme

Approach audits, patient-based outcome measures and transfer times, all made easier by electronic records, are new. No unit twenty years ago had a comprehensive self-scrutiny at its fingertips. With the Care Quality Commission dropping in unexpectedly, these measures have to be ready to fly and are updated through standard governance structures. This does not prevent disaster but it helps organizations defend themselves. Massaging of the figures or failing to feed elderly patients or neglecting death rates from MRSA remains possible. But it is true to say that when high secure care is subject to routine or unusual inquiry now, its response includes a different order of evidence about the adequacy and modernity of its clinical approach.

The question to ask at this point is whether the staff and patient material suggests the SHSA and Smithtown management had, to coin a phrase, met their own objectives. The disingenuous document of the Change Facilitation Group contains an implicit message about the location of power within the hospital; strikingly, management are not staff. And staff clearly agreed. The SHSA did develop middle management. Ward managers at the time of the study had an uncomfortable but significant role for the staff but many staff felt demoralized, unsupported and vulnerable, so it was little wonder that they continued to see the POA as a necessary protection from managerial scrutiny. What earlier pride they had had in their work had been reframed as ignorance and brutality. Some staff welcomed particular changes which affected patients but most were wary. Patients had barely featured in the SHSA's discussion of cultural change (and in terms of ward life did not feature elsewhere in SHSA strategy). Many patients had noticed a relaxation in what had been construed by many staff, patients and outsiders as an overly coercive environment, but a quarter had noticed nothing at all.

Judged by the people they most wanted to affect, the SHSA had only partially succeeded. At the level of Smithtown there had been organizational change, coincident with the introduction of management language and values. There had been visible changes in institutional practices and recognizable differences in the staff's and patients' understanding of each other. But it was less clear that this represented cultural change in the way that the SHSA intended when they referred to staff culture. Equally it was not clear that cultural change had been achieved in any wider anthropological sense.

One of the difficulties in determining whether the SHSA had succeeded in their own terms is that they were imprecise in determining what would constitute cultural change; it was easier to operationalize organizational structures. This imprecision has been a repeated feature of those writing on the perceived culture of the Special Hospitals but was not remarked upon (Bluglass 1992; Department of Health 1992; Fallon et al. 1999). It is in some contrast to the use of the term culture in other areas of mental health review, where the discussion of race and ethnicity has led to ideas of cultural competence and precise measures to be adopted by organizations (Mental Health Act Commission 1999).

Staff were not signed up to the managers' agenda. If a requirement of cultural change was taking your workforce with you, then the management of Smithtown had not succeeded. But workers in other areas of work do not necessarily believe managers are working to their advantage (Shore and Wright 2000). There is no reason to assume this would be different in the health service. If cultural change were simply imposing organizational structural change, then the SHSA could say it had succeeded to a significant degree.

This relates to the anthropological issue of ideas and practice. Here, Geertz (1993: 144–5) is helpful. He suggests that '[o]ne of the more useful ways . . . of distinguishing between culture and social system is to see the former as an ordered system of meaning and of symbols, in terms of which social interaction takes place: and to see the latter as the pattern of social interaction itself'. Later in the same passage, he adds: 'Culture is the fabric of meaning in terms of which human beings interpret their experience and guide their action: Social structure is the form that action takes, the actually existing network of social relations.' Rather than returning to the earlier discussion of what culture is *in* anthropology, I want to use Geertz to help us, with his use of social structure and culture, to consider what the empirical material on change means. In the day-to-day life of the ward, staff and patients are the critical others for each other, and we have information on both what they believed and what they did. But we know much less about managers, who were the drivers for a particular version of 'cultural change', as they are only seen through written communication. Managerial life impinged largely indirectly on the ward and was both known and opaque, evidenced in the amount of rumours around key decisions and multiple interpretations of managerial acts.

Some though not all changes in social structure and social practice were attributed to managers. Language changed, and they brought initiatives, performance indicators and quality standards. These, if you like, were also their sacred symbols. Social relations altered. Staff and patients looked different and a new social grouping acquired power. There is good evidence, then, of ideational and practice changes.[10]

Hearts and minds

But the problem the managers had is rather the same as that of the French invaders in 1066 (Weir 2000). Only the elite spoke French. William the Conqueror measured his kingdom but was not universally popular. He, like the Smithtown management, did not have the hearts and minds of his people but for different reasons. The staff, rather like the old English aristocracy, were anxious about a loss of power; in a day-to-day sense this loss was more perceived than real. The feudal system remained in place under William, rather like the hierarchical system of staff and patients. But, unlike the English peasants, at least some patients noted a softening in the social interactions with those more powerful than them.

The symbolic and ideational systems of staff and patient had not been replaced with managerial values and beliefs, and they remained discernibly separate and distinct. There was a level of either indifference or antagonism to those of the managers as well as some enthusiasm.

It is tempting to suggest that where there were two cultures there were then three but then cultures would be things, like bags of flour that you

---

10 An alternative analysis is that mentioned by Wright (1994: 17) as characterizing many organizational studies. Organizations were characterized as having formal systems (organizational structure, job descriptions, decision-making hierarchy, policies, rules and goals). Informal systems were the way in which people in the system related. She comments that the weakness is that the formal system is not seen as a cultural manifestation, whereas the informal system is. For this reason the distinction is not explored further in this thesis.

can weigh. But there were three cultural forces which all impinged on ward life, and even if what people did changed, it was clear that at best what they thought had only shifted slightly.

In the final reckoning the issue is not the *reality* but the *depth* of change. Clarke et al. (1994: 3) suggested that the ideological change of 'managerialization' required the change in the balance of power observed by the staff and felt by many of the patients. Whether it has achieved its objectives where practices have altered but many staff dissented and many patients continued to focus not on day-to-day life but rather on ultimate liberty, is less clear.

The anthropological perspective helps clarify these organizational issues. In terms of profound change, the reality is more complex than is permitted by managerial discourse. It is both less reassuring to those who would have approached the high hospitals with a new broom, and thought-provoking for those who would have written them off as stagnant. This discussion is also of more general relevance to both ongoing and wider change in the NHS, where the difference between organizational and cultural change can be glossed over, with corresponding indifference to staff morale.

Part 5

Thinking ahead

Chapter 10

Looking back

This is a rather sober, unsensational book. It has attempted to make explicit the mindset and behaviour of those living and working in part of a High Secure Hospital, to go beyond the quick scout around of the TV documentary and to avoid the prejudicial gaze of hospital inquiries. It has not taken at face value what people have said, be they staff or patients. Nor has it accepted uncritically the professional or public discourse on what should be or is happening in a High Secure Hospital. Informants in Smithtown appeared remarkably frank, given the context of the study. Sometimes they entrusted the research team with information, which if attributed, might have had negative consequences for them. Patients and staff presented complex views on their situations, and their institution. These have been contrasted with the goals of the then SHSA and the managers of Smithtown, whose voices were only audible through their actions.

Both the gathering and exploration of data were informed by the original aims of the study and by the anthropological imperative to ask additional questions as these emerged in the course of fieldwork. In getting to know people over time, there are insights into the informal social world of staff and patients that go beyond caricature but do not rely on friendship.

The focus throughout has been on several different understandings of culture and cultural change in the context of a single complex institution, one that is a physical structure and also symbolic, comprising too literal spaces of social practice with their made meanings and iteration. This analysis of power and ways of understanding what happened in a particular health organization is of course of ongoing relevance to the evolving public sector, including both the world of secure care and the wider NHS. The culture of care has been and is a vital issue (Delamothe 2013; Department of Health 2012; Francis 2013).

The analysis of power, how that is manifest, maintained and is understood in a complex institutional environment, involved an institution that was made of bricks and mortar, and had pool tables, communal cigarette lighters and a chapel. Managerial, staff and patient groups contested ideas and space in a place laden with symbolic meaning, consciously and unconsciously wielded in a way that many clinical staff might not normally register or even imagine informs what they do or how they are perceived. Secure hospitals lock people up. Staff in secure care everywhere should be attentive to this and think actively about how it would feel if it was them. Dutch forensic psychiatry, post war, was run by men some of whom had been incarcerated during the Second World War, including in Japanese prisoner of war camps. As a result, the post-war Dutch forensic system became a beacon of humane practice throughout Europe, as that experience was used imaginatively.

Studying hospitals from perspectives other than management and organizational studies is currently rather unfashionable. Studying secure hospitals and their informal social systems has always been and remains unusual. This is in contrast to a concern about who is confined (e.g. Carlen 1998; Kesteven 2002; Mauer 1999). Instead, their lives have been considered routinely by the Mental Health Act Commission and now by the Care Quality Commission, or, when something goes wrong, by an inquiry. Public policy, most particularly the introduction of such wholesale audit arrangements, has been driven not so much by a political concern that everyone should be operating within a band of acceptable practice, but by the need to respond to rare catastrophes.

Revisiting this kind of old social science territory brings to the fore contemporary anthropological and social policy questions. It requires engagement with the real world even as it addresses academic issues. Being 'between the lines' of anthropology and psychiatry necessitated reading between the lines to make any sense of Smithtown at all. Time has passed. The continuing relevance of the empirical findings and accompanying analysis is obvious: history teaches us we must look backwards to go forwards. There are immediate challenges, in anthropology and in secure hospital care. The next two chapters discuss aspects of their shared uncertainty in a rapidly changing world.

The context is a society in which surveillance has breached the perimeter walls of the asylum as well as the prison, and invaded all our lives. In wider culture, the erosion of privacy provokes a broader set of questions about the rights and agency of individuals. Specifically, technological and social changes have shifted the terms of the debate about privacy and security. There is an appetite to open oneself up for semi-public and sometimes public amusement and scrutiny. This is the new context in which we provide confidential health care, itself monitored and scrutinized as never before, even as the government contemplates the use of all such records for research. Institutional care and the culture of care are no longer permissibly secret or known only to a few. It is reported on the Care Quality Commission website. This cultural change might be halted by the demise of the silicon chip but it and its paradoxes seem likely to be sustained, and it is the discussion of this issue that concludes the book.

Chapter 11

Anthropology and the individual: knowing me, knowing you

As the embodiment of the tension between anthropology and psychiatry, I have been concerned throughout the book to be explicit about the issues this raises. Anthropology and psychiatry are now, but were not always, two very different bodies of knowledge with more in common than they might like to admit (Skultans 2000).

The nature of the anthropological subject and of the inquiring self have both been discussed at length. Their status and relationship to agency, what individuals do and what responsibility they bear for their actions within a social world where they are seen to have role congruent or incongruent views, roles, attitudes and behaviours is not a theoretical question. It is a question for our times. Our answer to this question leads to our understanding of where, when things go wrong (in easily unequivocal ways, e.g. patients die, people are assaulted), blame is to be laid. Do we understand our caring institutions to be full of real people with names and individual autonomy and responsibility, or comprised of creatures whose actions are determined by their social world, or some combination thereof? If a combination, how can we establish degree in the way that the law or investigation or inquiry often, with its binary precision, demands?

So, this seemingly abstract issue of personhood and agency has profound implications for both the maintenance of standards of care and the analysis of cultures of care. The framework we believe in and/or adopt channels and constrains the attribution of blame.

Anthropological subjects and whole people

Anthropology is concerned with the partial and contextual identity of the anthropological subject. Post-modernist lip service is paid regularly nowadays to the impossibility of the completeness or accuracy of description. Anthropology is concerned with an idea of identity that is social rather than individual, psychological or biologically based. Although this helps it carve out areas of intellectual inquiry that are, at least to some extent, distinctive, it leaves anthropology with a major difficulty. The anthropological subject is individually embodied. Theorizing social action's relationship to individual personhood and the social practice of that individual, rather than to types of individual, is not a new task, either for anthropology or psychiatry (Sahlins 1999). Nor is the question resolved (Moore 2007).

Within Smithtown, individuals kept intruding, adding complexity and difficulty to the analysis. What to do with disagreement when the idea was to capture similarity on which the idea of cultural wholes relies? This issue of individual agency is not so much about partial identity but is rather a problem of aggregate individuals and outliers. More than that it is about private thoughts, desires and imagination set in a cultural landscape, with some capacity to limit and direct the possible but not to determine it.

Psychiatry is approaching these issues from a very different starting point. Perhaps it is less explicit about the conceptual dilemmas therein. It shares with anthropology a problem of completeness. Clinical psychiatrists would not frame it like this, but one way of describing what psychiatry does, using a multidisciplinary team, is that it deals in a reduced, but whole, patient self. This is a partial identity too. The gathering of the life history information in professional examinations will take no more than 45 minutes. This is very different from the life history work of the social sciences (Crapanzano 1978; Faraday and Plummer 1979). The wholeness pretended to in the case notes is a consequence of the working theory or conceit that all the important elements of the person have been identified. These elements will account for the pattern of behaviours a person exhibits. In practice, the incompleteness of the process is acknowledged by the practical addition of information throughout clinical care. This is different from the upfront notion of incompleteness in ethnographic accounts (Clifford 1986: 7; Geertz 1993: 29).

A separate but linked issue relates to the anthropological notion of incompleteness discussed earlier. Western-based ethnographies such as this one rely on particular lexicons of emotion, in this case in English, a language which lends itself to discussion of relationship. The question for the ethnographer and the medical ethnographer is why not use this? To discuss relationship is in the reflexive tradition, as well as being a style of expression we use all the time and it is conspicuously missing. It would facilitate discussion of the individual embodiment of social practice. Applied to the subject other (or the inquiring self), it would have a naturalness not noticeable in discussions of the 'habitus', with its determining structures and the apparent absence of human agency (see Moore 1994d: 77). It would address what Douglas (1994: 213) called 'muffled, conflicting and inconclusive' discussions of the Western industrial self, which contrast with anthropological authority in relation to other parts of the globe. This would lead to a more sophisticated discussion of attributed and owned identity, particularly where the identity is unwanted and egodystonic, as is the case for many patients.

The other related issue is the relationship of the elements of the self. It is easy to imagine metaphors (e.g. jigsaws, layers, packs of cards) which might provide models of the self, and anthropology is not alone in such model building and explication (Baumeister 1987; Douglas 1994: 211–34; Hollan 1992), with dubious claims to ethnographic validity. Moore (2007: 41), for instance, uses the latest term, subjectivity, to propose that the self achieves a balancing act between the determining forces of power and difference and what is self-created. Such models of 'selves' and 'subjectivity' have a metaphorical concreteness necessary to the telling of a story of what it is to be human. But they have to be balanced against the amorphous nature of real social encounters and the difficulty of determining real people's perceptions of their own reality.

That individuals are different from one another is often a given. However, intrinsic to diagnostic practice is the sense that there are also groups with similar abnormal rather than normal attitudes, beliefs and behaviour. Psychiatry is in that sense the mirror image of anthropology.

The self of the anthropologist

However, if there are differences in the formulation of the *object* of inquiry between anthropology and psychiatry, this is more pronounced in terms of the inquirer. The self of the psychiatrist is seldom thought about by the psychiatrist, whereas anthropologists increasingly think and write about themselves.[1]

The extended earlier discussion of how the researcher's identity matters pinpoints the contemporary challenge for ethnography to represent the complexity of the anthropological self and other succinctly, while bearing a relationship of truth to the ethnographic encounter. Discussion of the ways in which identity is controlled appears and affects the subsequent personae of the anthropologist, and emphasizes that postmodern truism about the fluid and multifaceted nature of identity. As Okely memorably put it, 'Details of my past, important to me, were irrelevant to the gypsies, other details to which I felt indifferent were to them most meaningful. All this can be both shattering and exhilarating' (1996: 42). It may yet be possible not to get lost in the post-modern fog.

These questions have been taken up through a contextualized discussion of reflexivity, in which the relationship aspects of this fieldwork were explored. My own identity as a psychiatrist was important to the negotiation and reality of fieldwork and has implications for other health-care-based ethnography. That many medical anthropologists are psychiatrists seems not to have been addressed within the seam of reflexive writing. Historical studies of institutions were often done by those who had a personally relevant identity (Alasewski 1986; Coggeshall 1988; Goffman 1961; Kauffman 1988; Stanton and Schwartz 1954) in terms of occupation before or during fieldwork. For ethnographic illness narratives to be constructed by doctors (Kleinman 1980; Littlewood 1988), or other health care professionals (Krause 1989), needs problematizing. This work is often made possible through the auspices of medical institutions and relies at times on the privileged access of the doctor to the patient. This requires incorporation into the published analysis of the ethnographic encounter.

---

[1] This is true even with the advent of cultural and gender awareness in the NHS, with programmes designed to connect individual selves and understandings of ethnicity and gender.

Chapter 12

Secure care

Cultures in secure care

The analysis uses the word 'culture', not necessarily reflecting the day-to-day use of the word within Smithtown. However, one achievement of examining the nature of culture in this formal sense instead of using it casually, and in a 'taken for granted' manner (Strathern 1995: 154), is to compel a recognition of the politicized, rather than technical nature of health service management. This should not be confused either with agreement or disagreement with its various and changing objectives (Ham 1994, 1995; Klein 1995). Management culture in Smithtown was not politically neutral but rather instrumental and believed itself to have a connection with the overall performance, in a managerial sense, of Smithtown. This belief is nuanced by the understandings of health service staff of managerial initiatives.

In addition, the empirical material not only highlights the active contribution of patients but also of staff, to the construction of ward life. They clearly inhabit different places while also sharing one place, the ward. Their actions and expressed views resonate with the commentary of Keesing (1981: 371) on the Trobriand Islanders' use of 'obeisance', which is both given and received according to social position. Both givers and receivers understand the meaning. Smithtown staff and patients can similarly decipher the same cultural codes, from different social positions. Unlike Keesing's example, they do not share identity. Within the one place, a culturally specific place, they start in different places.

The state, society and secure hospital care

Power without glory

The religious overtones of this phrase, in fact the title of a Dirk Bogarde film, seem appropriate to Smithtown. Smithtown is an institution where moral judgements about good and bad are intended to be, if not suspended, then subsumed into, and perhaps disguised by, professional practice. Staff have day-to-day and minute-to-minute power over patients. This is, to use that classical distinction, legitimate power, i.e. authority, and authority based on a view of the merits of the staff not as individuals but as a group and, more importantly, on the negative attributes of the patient group. Patients, whom society has judged, have had power over the victims of their offences, even if only briefly. They can frighten the staff. This was, and is, illegitimate power, though their prevailing sense of the world may be of their own powerlessness.

In Smithtown the physical environment and its constraints reminded patients of their second-class status and provided a physical medium for the repeated demonstration of this social status. Patients had rights but fewer than the average citizen. For the most part, these social relations were maintained within the formal rules of professional practice. Illegitimate staff activity, such as the regular use of patients' food, and the rarer examples of overt rudeness, pointed to the undisputed nature of this power differential. Managers, technically in charge, could live in ignorance of such infringements. Patients seldom complained. Staff complaints about each other had been held in check in the past. This might be attributed to a genuinely uncritical view of certain activities or to the threat of social exclusion from the staff group.

The limits of consensus: power and control

It has been argued that secure settings rely on consensus between those detained and those detaining for the unit to operate (Genders and Player 1995; Kauffman 1988; Liebling and Price 2001). Staff as a group, and as individuals, cannot rule solely by coercion. In American 'supermax' prisons, a culture of extreme control has arisen: the absence of alternatives to punishment, a modern technology of control and surveillance as well as old fashioned physical restraints cause punishment to escalate and risk the dehumanization of the prisoner and the guard (Haney 2008). Where regimes are harsh, it is known that opposition can develop (Irwin and Cressey 1962; Thomas and Zingraff 1976) and inmates can be harmed by combinations of material deprivation, lack of meaningful activity, social isolation as well as physical brutality (Haney 2008). Coercion judged by the recipients to be disproportionate or otherwise unreasonable can create further discord and an escalation of tension (Gillespie 2010). In hospital practice, there are limits to any escalation in sanctions. Where staff are outnumbered in settings by patients with a track record of violence, and daily routines are maintained by talking, this is because there is, for almost all of the time, tacit acceptance of the social order. Individuals are neither isolated nor deprived in the way that the US, the land of the free, appears to have made routine in some custodial settings (Rhodes 2010). In Smithtown, the visible social order was backed up by the possibility of specific actions that were uncommon but which would make a patient's life more uncomfortable, e.g. seclusion or sedation.

Within secure environments these issues are never absolute, rather they are matters of degree. The SHSA came to the Special Hospitals with the clear intention to address a staff culture they saw as unacceptable, because it was both too custodial and insufficiently therapeutic. The explicit message of dissatisfaction with the past invited the patient group to reconsider the staff. A managerial culture that explicitly emphasized solidarity with the patient could be seen as sapping the morale of a suddenly beleaguered staff group.

Liberalization in other secure environments has at times had violent consequences (see Bowker 1977; Kauffman 1988), which have demanded a reassertion of control. The fears of staff about hostage taking, which had a special significance in Smithtown, seemed to point towards the presence of this anxiety in the staff group.

However, given the nature of the specific patient population, their predisposition to violent emotion, to hatred and to acting on these intense and at times uncontrollable feelings, as well as their difficulties in understanding other people's perspectives, it is entirely unsurprising that some staff felt vulnerable. This may be a simple descriptive point but there is every reason to emphasize it. Staff thought that the managers did not appreciate, in any real sense, what their jobs on the ward were like.

The practices of Smithtown might be said to have evolved, as in other similar institutions, precisely to avoid experiencing emotionally demanding contact with the patients. One purpose of excessive custodial practice is to distance staff from the unacceptable, intolerable experience of getting near the patients and their pain. Changing social practices at the level of the ward without equipping the staff with the psychodynamic skills and clinical supervision necessary for them to feel safe in a more liberal institution was tried. Fallon et al. (1999) in a critical inquiry suggest that staff lost control of at least one area of Ashworth Hospital in the wake of an initial inquiry into custodial practice. Deacon (2004), who was intimately involved in these events, argues that staff are asked to do something unusual by wider society, i.e. to contain 'monstrous, murderous and perverse impulses in phantasy and reality' and that to do that well requires actively thinking about the anxiety that task engenders, not just reacting to it. From his account, the staff group in Ashworth at the time of the Fallon report were as much in the institution as the patients and struggled in a regime in which care and control were seen as paradoxical. Bennett and Shuker (2010) highlights the critical importance of both staff empowerment and personal flexibility in running successful therapeutic regimes in contained conditions, frankly acknowledging the fragility of the enterprise. Frontline staff in the wards studied did not necessarily feel empowered.

What do we want of our secure hospitals now?

Equally paradoxically, as Smithtown was told to focus on therapy, not just custody, the rest of psychiatry was being compelled to do exactly the opposite. If Foucault had a pendulum, Smithtown and the rest of psychiatry were at different points of its swing.

Since the fieldwork was completed there has been a sea change in the practice of psychiatry, not just forensic psychiatry. This was led by successive governments' anxiety about acts of serious violence committed by the mentally ill (Department of Health 1998). At all levels of care, practitioners are expected to focus not so much on treatment and therapy but on the analysis and management of risk. This threatens to transform the nature of the practitioner–patient relationship in routine mental health work. Psychiatry has moved towards greater surveillance of community patients and increasing detention of hospital patients (Department of

Health 2000) in order to accommodate increasing numbers of individuals who are deemed both ill and dangerous.

In the secure hospital programme, money has gone into the creation and purchasing of more locked beds (Harty et al. 2012; Hassell and Bartlett 2001; Laing 2013). There has been a significant reduction in the number of high secure beds (Butwell et al. 2000, see High Secure Hospitals websites) but their external security was increased at great cost and despite the absence of any recent escapes (Department of Health 2007; Tilt et al. 2000). There are more medium secure beds with intended length of stay up to, and in some cases beyond, two years (Bartlett et al. 2007; Hassell and Bartlett 2001; SHSA 1995). The advantage of this dispersal of patients into lesser tiers of security is first, that morally, this might constitute more proportionate secure detention, and second, that the stigma associated with being in the highest form of hospital security applies to fewer people.

Beyond the institution

Simultaneously, the government involved the psychiatric profession, against its will, in the wholesale detention of individuals with personality disorders who were thought to pose a high risk to other people (Department of Health and Home Office 2000). This involved the creation of a new category of person, the 'Dangerous and Severe Personality Disordered' (DSPD) person, who has been researched (Haddock et al. 2001) and treated. We are looking at the creation of a larger group of doubly stigmatized individuals, dangerous and mad, whose conceptualization owed more to legal principle than to previous understanding of illness categories (Eastman 1999). This process is an up-to-date version of Foucault's earlier analysis:

> ... he appears as a villain, a monster, a madman, perhaps a sick and before long, abnormal individual. It is as such that, one day, he will belong to a scientific objectification and to the 'treatment' that is correlative to it (Foucault 1979: 101).

The risk of the DSPD programme was always that they were looking at long periods of hospital detention, during which time many of those detained might have failed to engage in treatment, proved hard to change and might have lost all hope of release. This may have happened. Money is in the process of being redeployed from expensive and in part newly built hospital facilities into community and prison-based programmes. Incorporated into the revised funding is a recognition that many anti-social men do not want treatment and cannot even begin a process that might result in a fundamental change that reduced their perceived risk to others. A more pragmatic and less clinical model of intervention based on actuarial risk and clinical psychological formulations has been adopted. However, this kind of service of case formulation and management by the NOMS is spreading the 'psy' into the community, so that the whole person, not just the offending, is under scrutiny. Such services are being funded in prison but most conspicuously in the community too.

Blurring the boundaries of health and justice

The DSPD programme, now the Offender Personality Disorder (PD) programme, has constructed a new reality, in which money is dangled in front of health providers to join with criminal justice agencies to undertake partnership work to reduce risk. Even as I am personally involved in parts of this interesting endeavour, I am struck by the mission creep of both health and criminal justice organizations.

The criminal justice system is being told to have integrated health practitioners and the health service is told to focus on risk, not treatment. The specificity of these agencies has been eroded on both sides and they begin to look very similar. The way this is done, i.e. partnership working, is to privilege pragmatism over historical models of ethical practice. Information sharing is becoming more and more common, so that not to share information is seen as difficult but also improper. This change followed the CJS Act 2003, which mandated cooperation between state agencies in the name of public protection and led directly to the setting up of Multi-Agency Public Protection (MAPP) panels.

The criminal justice system is bursting at the seams and our prisons have never been so full. Crewe's fieldwork (2011) and this ethnography both suggest that immediate staff/secure hospital patient or prisoner interactions may have become less authoritarian. However, the apparatus of surveillance and control through massive paper trails (CPA,

CTO, SO with conditions of Rx, the OMS) and holistic understanding (and thus documentation) has grown like Topsy. We are desperately attempting to find ways of managing offender populations safely in the community. The Offender PD programme and the implementation of Transforming Rehabilitation are the latest wholesale attempts to do this, while playing explicitly to a welfare and quasi health agenda. Paper spills out of the asylum and the prison, and tumbles down the road into the community-based probation office or local Community Mental Health Teams (CMHT). We tag prisoners and now some patients: the electronic tagging of patients is seen more as a technical than a moral or an ethical issue (Tully et al. 2014). In the past, leaving the institution meant leaving behind an unwanted identity. Now, prisoner and inpatient identities are transformed, as they live outside a bricks and mortar institution but remain subject to the call of the state. In the community, a combination of the multiplicity of workers' roles and responsibilities can only enhance the individual's sense of bewilderment about process, progress and the impossibility of real independence.

It would be nice to say this was driven by a wish to enhance quality of life or reduce restrictions on liberty but a more compelling argument might be the relative costs of community and institutional care.

Do we need High Secure Hospitals?

The odd consequence of this newly created community monitoring and decant to lower tiers of security is that it becomes possible to imagine a world in which high secure care might be redundant. This would be closure not for the reasons originally articulated by Lois Blom Cooper, i.e. that the institutions were unacceptable but rather that they are unnecessary. This would perhaps represent a real triumph. In the US, the proliferation of "supermax" prisons, to manage supposedly terrifying individuals, is a demonstration of how societies can genuinely differ in their response to what is perceived to be a very dangerous group of people. Britain has steadfastly avoided, both in hospital and in prison organizations, creating conditions of deprivation which may, in some ways, exceed even those imposed within Nazi concentration camps.

One hundred and fifty years after the opening of Broadmoor, a calm debate about its future and that of its two sister hospitals, Rampton and Ashworth, might be timely. England has older hospitals but no older secure hospitals. The weight of history must be a burden but the loss of unusual clinical knowledge and understanding would be significant. To some extent, the hospitals' incorporation into larger NHS organizational entities has hidden them from view but they continue to do something not done by other units, notably to care for a small number of both high-profile and probably highly dangerous individuals.

Changing the cultural landscape

Maybe Foucault had a point, or why we should worry

The wholesale change in secure care and community practice in the last twenty years has been paralleled by a change in our understanding of what constitutes surveillance and monitoring and control, as well as by changes in the technology that creates new possibilities of knowing and positioning. The new culture of continuous surveillance applies to the deviant and non-deviant, and is available to the state and the market as well as being chosen freely and imposed. It is an extended application to individual life and whole communities, to children and adults, and relates to people and spaces. It involves access to the movement of the child molester and the mind of a child. It can create an illusion of near-total knowledge where, just as in the old-fashioned institution, there are universal processes that locate, classify, document and observe.

Expanding surveillance in ordinary society

There is a desire, often located in local government and perhaps in the communities too, to use the paraphernalia of dogs, cameras and security guards to monitor their own streets. Boyne (2000: 302) has called this 'a general condition of Panoptical surveillance'. In short, surveillance, which was previously noticeable, has become routine. Instead of simply being imposed, it is now additionally welcomed. It has been suggested that 'the disciplinary societies are being replaced with societies of control' (Jones 2000: 9). It seems much more convincing to suggest that the desire for control remains present within institutions, and is sometimes taken to extreme lengths (Bauman 2000; Krutschitt et al. 2000), though remains subject to the vagaries of institutional fashion. In addition, external society is now itself being increasingly observed.

The boundaries of the person have changed. This has been provoked by a digital revolution that has spread cameras, microphones and telephones around the world. Tiannamen Square versus Tahrir Square. This new capacity for comprehensive documentation is protective but also intrusive. The person on the tube next to you is playing their music too loud but the woman being manhandled in Tehran is instantly on NBC, the pictures sent in from a single phone camera. Such hyperconnectivity, both instant and relying on a myriad of individual global links, has become ordinary rather than extraordinary and includes countries where telephone landlines were never commonly installed. Life on Facebook at 14—your conversation, diary, homework crises and judgement at stake—what is private and what is not. No time to decide as you talk to four people on 'chat' at one go. We can see around the world on Google Earth, we can see our street and sometimes our car. Celebrities are not safe anywhere. We are almost transparent. Our every move is documented, whether it is a click on a website or a walk down the High Street.

Surveillance which was unwanted is now welcomed, no longer an invasion of privacy, it is now a protector and friend.

Applying new technology to social deviance

In line with this level of documentation of ordinary life, the life of the social deviant is subject to control beyond the wall of the institution. Foucault (2009), writing in 1976, noted the trend within penal systems to find alternatives to custody. Asked to speak on the failure of prisons, he remarked instead on their success. He argued that the practices of surveillance they had honed, built on physical separation, enforced labour and the encouragement of penitence, had spread beyond the walls. Community supervision, 'approved premises' or partial imprisonment mean that for the offender, 'it is a surveillance over his whole environment' (p. 17). Tagging had not been invented then. Many would see alternatives to custody as more liberal, more benign. Being locked in a cell with no access to a phone has an immediate reality, whatever the symbolism. The Corston Report (Home Office 2007) argued strongly for alternatives to custody on these grounds and because they might, in a positivist rehabilitation framework, also be more successful at reintegrating offenders into mainstream society. Foucault profoundly disagrees, seeing such moves as the 'transmission of the old carceral functions' (p. 18) into the community, effectively retaining precisely the same principles of control over the person and his or her body but spreading them further.

The lessons learnt from the analysis of space within the prison and the asylum, of the linkage of architecture, social practice and social position, have informed the proliferation of supervisory arrangements of offenders and led to similar contemporary mental health practices in the name of clinical risk management. As Chow and Priebe (2013) argue, the use of Community Treatment Orders and the practices of assertive outreach mental health services move 'institutionalization' into the community. Not only are patients subject to continued monitoring but it may also erode their capacity to operate effectively and independently while not preventing re-institutionalization (Burns et al. 2013).

Mental institutions have not failed. Many of the buildings may have been closed but they have colonized our thinking and their practices live on outside the asylum: 5,218 people were made newly subject to a Community Treatment Order (CTO) (a 10% increase) in 2012/13. The total number of people detained under the Mental Health Act in the same year in hospital, despite reduced numbers of available NHS beds, was over fifty thousand, also an increase on the previous year (<http://www.hscic.gov.uk/catalogue/PUB12503> accessed 09.05.14).

Surveillance and audit of health culture

The limits of surveillance are as yet unknown. Here we consider its promise of ever-expanding knowledge and its application not to the individual subject of health care, the actual patient but the performance of health care delivery, often confused with health gain itself. Such audit of health care comes from the managerial world with an assumption of moral neutrality.

In line with the society-wide preference for such surveillance, we now monitor the insides of our institutions. The dimensions of the psychiatric encounter are, and were, broader than doctors and patients. Although this was true of the older literature, so it is true of contemporary psychiatric practice, inside and outside the hospital's institutional setting. Managers, staff and patients are all active players in the manifestation of institutional life.

It is important that secure hospital care practitioners and managers, and politicians have an understanding of how secure institutions really work, rather than how they are supposed to work. It is also important that the 'technology' of secure hospital care, i.e. the 'needs assessments' and the building programme, is not perceived as divorced from its wider political context and the trends apparent within it. There is a maxim in forensic psychiatry that in risk assessment, the past predicts the future. For secure hospitals it would be better if that were recognized.

A desire to avoid repetition of the past, both in mental health services and throughout the NHS, as well as a preoccupation with value for money (Klein 1995: 131–75) have led to audit systems requiring what has been termed 'Herculean micro-management' in a system of 'hypercomplexity' (O'Neill 2002). It is less clear that such labour-intensive strategies ensure that the wider objectives, such as those of the now defunct SHSA, will be met. Given the National Service Framework (Department of Health 1999) and its successors, with its directives on minimum standards for health care and the need for health care trusts to audit their compliance, this is a question of considerable importance. Audit surveillance of the workforce is a necessary component of these initiatives, which are accompanied, in the NHS as a whole, by expensive quangos.

The burden of proof

If it is accepted that there is little or no existing proof that instruments of audit capture the important components of service delivery within the public sector, be it education or health, this is a remarkable investment of time, energy and money. Audit processes themselves surely warrant systematic cost-benefit research. We should know what such processes both prevent (i.e. homicide, manslaughter and other major incidents) and facilitate (i.e. cost effectiveness, targeting need, ensuring best practice). But what audit techniques can and do capture may be unhelpful. Bean counting counts beans, and does not look at how they grow, why they have not done so or what would be the best conditions for growth.

Surveillance and audit, inside and outside our hospital buildings and other institutions, approach each other. Strathern's (2000) phrase 'Audit Cultures' captures the spirit of the times. Surveillance is not audit and audit is not surveillance but in the current climate of suspicion and blame they tell us that not only do we not trust the dangerously mad but nor do we trust the professional classes. In Smithtown, at the time of the study, this convergence of meaning was apparent, and perhaps appropriate.

Fundamental truth eludes us if the tools of surveillance capture only the surface and perhaps the transient. The illusion if not of total knowledge then of more knowledge is that safety and good governance are ensured. But what this book demonstrates is that it is what lies beneath the surface that determines an ethos of care. In the absence of recent hospital or community ethnography, this is a call to arms for methods of inquiry whose power lies in a capacity to address informal social systems, without being judgemental in the way characteristic of inquiries. It is crucial that this approach is taken in advance of difficulties. Prison ethnography has undergone a renaissance; health ethnography should do too. We need to understand what is normal in complex health organizations, rather than simply relying on inquiry information obtained too late, from the bereaved or defensive. As the UK has gone twenty years essentially without hospital ethnography and the NHS is facing the most serious financial challenge ever (Iacobucci 2014), this might be the right moment. The task of maintaining staff morale and good services for patients against a backdrop of flat-line funding to the NHS will be, if it is not already, actually impossible. Documentation of that challenge using multiple methods is critical.

Two issues stand out as particularly worthy of attention: the understanding of agency in health care work and the formulation of change. In Smithtown, these emerged as fundamental to a grasp of the organization at that time but they are of more general and enduring significance as well as being tough to tackle. They warrant theoretical and empirical development. In this way, the established methods of social anthropology would make a valuable contribution to the understanding of how good health care can be delivered and go some way to avoid the kind of shadowed places that have failed patients in the recent past. Ethnography should not be exotic; it should be routine and a bit mundane.

Appendix A

Additional notes on method and data analysis

The research objectives (approved by Smithtown's Ethics Committee) that generated fieldwork included in this book were as follows:

1 What are the components of institutionalization as experienced by the patients and staff?

2 How are staff networks established and what is the relationship of staff networking to resistance to change in work practice?

3 What are the informal, as opposed to the formal, power structures? What is the currency of power and how does it relate to interactions between staff and staff, patients and patients, and staff and patients?

4 What are the factors perceived by patients and staff to affect the progress of patients through the hospital system towards release?

The intention was for the main researcher (the author) and two assistants to address these aims through a participant observation and interview study of daily life, for staff and patients. This was to be based on three wards in Smithtown. Three wards were used in order to compare and contrast life on each of them. This was what was done.

The original timetable of the study was affected by access to the various wards. The following periods of time were spent on the wards:

Researcher 1 (the author): six months, followed by an interval of six months, then a further three months on the ward

Researcher 2: five months

Researcher 3: six months[1]

---

[1] Three additional days were spent on the ward.

Researchers did not go onto the ward every day. In total, the researchers were present on the wards for 214 nursing shifts. Researcher 1 spent seventy-three days doing participant observation; Researcher 2 spent sixty-three days on this; and Researcher 3 spent seventy-eight days. Systematic interviewing was conducted by Researcher 1 during the later period of fieldwork and by Researcher 3 at the end of fieldwork.

As the main researcher, I had the unusual luxury of having two research assistants, one woman (Researcher 2) and one man (Researcher 3) of similar age to each other and some five years younger than me. The woman researcher had an undergraduate degree in law and a postgraduate degree in research methods, as well as previous research experience, and the man researcher had a range of work experience, including being a police officer, and an undergraduate degree in anthropology. Each of us undertook participant observation on one ward. This was originally intended to be contemporaneous; with the benefit of hindsight, it was neither practical nor appropriate.

The role of the two research assistants was specific and subordinate to that of the main researcher. Prior to embarking on fieldwork, they undertook a period of selective reading on anthropological method and the Special Hospitals, and were fully briefed about the issues of conducting fieldwork in such a setting and the aims of the fieldwork. They approached the day-to-day conduct of fieldwork in line with advice from me, and wrote, and subsequently dictated, notes for transcription. Regular meetings took place between the individual fieldworkers and me, and later in the coding process between all three of us. These meetings were to review the conduct and progress of fieldwork, to generate lines of inquiry and for mutual support in a testing fieldwork setting.

Most of the fieldwork was based on the ward. Researchers were attached to a given ward; Researcher 1 was attached to a men's ward (Toulouse) in the old part of Smithtown, Researcher 2 to a women's ward (Lille) and Researcher 3 to a men's ward (Paris) in the new part of Smithtown.

Choosing three wards gave us the opportunity to compare and contrast two male wards whose institutionally determined functions were distinct, as well as to compare and contrast male and female wards. No wards are representative of Smithtown. The study was concerned to encompass as far as possible the experiences of men and women who lived and worked in Smithtown (see Table 1).

These were clearly differentiated in the field notes. Different parts of the wards were the scenes of different activities and social interactions, and systematic and geographically located information was obtained. Key areas were nursing offices, the nurses' mess, day areas and rooms used for formal meetings, e.g. ward rounds, case conferences (both characterized by relatively in-depth clinical discussion of individual patients) and community meetings. Relatively less time was spent in areas considered to be private by researchers and potentially unsafe and private by staff, i.e. bedrooms, dormitories and washrooms. The analysis devotes attention to the negotiation of space and its relation to the built environment; aspects of the built environment and other elements of

Table 1 Timetabled ward-based meetings (weekly, unless otherwise stated)

	TOULOUSE	PARIS	LILLE
MONDAY AM	group x 1 (1)		
MONDAY PM	group x 1 (4)		
TUESDAY AM	groups x 2 (1)	community meeting (3) canteen	clinical team meeting (2)
TUESDAY PM	case conference (2)	clinical team meeting (2)	
WEDNESDAY AM	canteen		clinical team meeting (2)
WEDNESDAY PM			
THURSDAY AM	management round (2) group x 1 (1)		
THURSDAY PM		group x 1 (4)	
FRIDAY AM	yoga		
FRIDAY PM	group x 1(1)		
SATURDAY AM	patients' meeting (3) (monthly)		
SATURDAY PM			
SUNDAY AM			
SUNDAY PM			

the material world were also documented. It became clear as the field-work progressed that particular spaces were associated with the different social groups, and care was taken to include adequate data on staff and patient joint or single occupancy.

Material was gathered by all researchers over twenty-four-hour time-frames; relatively little time was spent on the night shift in view of the fact that all patients were locked either in rooms or dormitories from 9 p.m. until 7 a.m. A smaller number of staff were allocated to wards at night with a limited range of explicit functions in comparison with day staff.

Other parts of Smithtown were also accessed; these were systematically but relatively infrequently visited. Areas covered included the workshops and other work areas, the Central Hall, the canteen and the education centre where social activities took place, the area of Smith-town designated for Control and Restraint courses, the Staff Club and the medical centre.

To add detail to what was emerging as an appropriate focus of the study and to increase the likelihood of hearing from as many potential inform-ants as possible, longer interviews were conducted with both staff and patients. But, for both staff and patients perhaps rendered silent in the ward, it was an opportunity for them to describe their experiences in a way that did not invite public comment, not that privacy guarantees honesty.

Researcher 1 (the author) interviewed on Toulouse and Researcher 3 interviewed on Paris. It was not possible to conduct interviews in the same way on the female ward, both because of the stage of data analysis and the researcher's personal timetable.[2] Individual informed consent was obtained prior to all interviews. Researcher 1 interviewed after a period of preliminary data analysis (see timetable) and Researcher 3 interviewed at the end of the fieldwork period.

Forty-five members of staff and forty-four male patients agreed to dis-cuss the various topics. Informants could and did talk for as long as they wanted and interviews lasted between 20 minutes and 4 hours. A con-versational style was possible because the informants were very well

---

[2] The Ward Manager of the female ward was interviewed individually, but before the sched-ule had been developed.

known to the researcher and the schedule allowed topics to be addressed in different orders. Most interviews took place on the ward, but not all. Although others on the ward could see what was happening, i.e. that the interviews were taking place, they were not overheard. They offered people more privacy than was routinely available on the ward. Even though individuals often did talk alone to researchers, the overcrowded nature of ward life meant these conversations were usually interrupted and often overheard.

Thirty-five nurses were interviewed, thirteen on Toulouse, twenty-two on Paris. Four men were Team Leaders, twelve Staff Nurses, six Enrolled Nurses and thirteen Nursing Assistants.[3] Paris employs proportionately more nursing assistants. No member of staff refused to be interviewed, but four had moved on from the wards. Participation should not be read as unbridled enthusiasm for the project, but it can be seen as a consequence of months of participant observation and relationships on the ward. The researchers did feel that one or two interviews were almost useless as a guide to what interviewees really felt, since the opinions uttered were at odds with other information about how people were perceived, or so guarded as to be self-evidently limited. Equally, previously reticent members of staff took advantage of the relative privacy of the interview space to speak their minds, and at times to bare their souls. The emotional pitch of the staff interviews was unexpected, and indicated that we had tapped into issues which were inherently important.

As many of the ward-related staff as possible were interviewed where they had a significant involvement with the ward; they were three doctors, three senior nurses and four others. These individuals were considered as informants with particular knowledge bases, e.g. knowledge of management initiatives. Their contact with the ward was variable.

All male patients present on the ward in the later stages of fieldwork were asked to undertake the topic-based interview. It is reassuring that on both Toulouse and Paris men refused to take part, eight in total. Their reasons included concern that the project would not change anything

---

3 All Toulouse staff interviewed were day staff. Three of the Paris staff interviewed were night staff. The numbers of night staff at the time of the study were small in comparison with the day staff. Staff did not rotate to nights at that time.

and a view that not talking represented an area of autonomy they valued; these reasons were not always forthcoming, but in some cases came from men who had previously avoided contact with researchers. Nine men had also either left hospital or moved wards; their replacements were not approached, as their relative lack of involvement in the study made this seem inappropriate. As with the staff, at times the researchers felt privileged to be told information.

Field notes were taken as contemporaneously as possible by all three researchers. My notes were less detailed than those provided by the other two fieldworkers, though in the course of the later analysis, notes trigger visual and auditory memory. They, like I, paid attention to time, place and person in our recording and put in as much detail as was possible. These handwritten notes were then dictated by the researchers and transcribed by a secretary. The purpose of the dictation was to encode the identities of all staff and patients, such that material removed from Smithtown protected all informants from subsequent identification. Dictation also offered a valuable opportunity for reflection. Analytic notes and memos were dictated at the same time. The fieldworkers met regularly to discuss the practicalities of the fieldwork, to ensure sampling was adequate and to discuss emerging analytic issues and preliminary coding. The process of the fieldwork was assisted by both emerging foci and the opportunity to test out ideas as they developed. Topic-based interviews were recorded in the same notebooks as the field notes. Tape-recording had not been approved, and would have been intrusive and at odds with the informality achieved by the fieldwork. The emphasis in the data recording was on verbatim accounts; this was most easily achieved in this context by sitting down to talk to someone individually.

Early in the fieldwork, as already described, the recording of field notes was accompanied by the writing of memos. As the other two researchers entered the field there was regular discussion of analytic ideas, and in the case of Researcher 2 on the women's side, testing out of analytic ideas, as it was clear that interviewing was not a possibility.[4] Preliminary

---

[4] This was a consequence of the researcher's personal timetable, not the study design.

codings were developed as field notes were transcribed, and these were discussed by all three researchers and amended and enlarged in the light of these discussions. The volume of data was considerable and the initial purpose was to create descriptive codes in an effort to get an overview of the material. Similarly, at the end of the field-work the entire database, i.e. all field notes and interviews, was read twice through, with analytic notes and revisions to preliminary codes being made contemporaneously. The purpose of this was to generate ideas. An early version of Nudist was used to facilitate storage, coding and retrieval, and field notes were coded in detail using this computer package. Coding was inclusive in order to decrease the likelihood of missing relevant material and the same text units could be multiply coded. Codes continued to expand and hierarchies of code developed. Some initially obvious descriptive codes proved useless for analytic purposes and some infrequent codes, i.e. those that represented small amounts of text, were useful in that they addressed important but rare phenomena, e.g. explicit racism. However, subsequent detailed analysis of field notes and interviews was done by hand and checked by frequent returns to the raw text. This resulted in analytic ideas cutting across basic descriptive codes and there was significant recoding. Throughout this process of analysis, analytic memos were written, which proved a valuable source of ideas. Analytic concepts were both observer identified, as in the overarching idea of institutional change, and indigenous, as in the extensive Smithtown lexicon. As the analysis developed and the volume of text grew, so did anxieties about the extent to which the analysis was evidence-based. This was exacerbated by the length of time involved in writing up and by differential knowledge of my and the other researchers' notes. This meant exhaustive and exhausting returns to data to compare and contrast material between databases and between researchers, to note negative case material and the absence of information. A limitation of the study may be that the analysis is stronger for my own material than for that of the other two researchers.

Content analysis of the interview material with nursing staff indicates that very few changes came without a positive or negative

Table 2 Frequency and kind of nursing staff comments on institutional change

Category of comment	Toulouse Positive	Paris Positive	Positive Subtotal	Toulouse Negative	Paris Negative	Negative Subtotal
Ward life	7	11	18	2	5	7
Patients' rights	3	0	3	9	16	25
Management issues	2	1	3	8	13	21
Staff employment	3	3	6	5	10	15
Treatment	3	5	8	0	4	4
Vulnerability	0	0	0	6	4	10
Hospital atmosphere	3	0	3	4	2	6
Physical environment	2	6	8	0	0	0
Uniforms	0	1	1	2	5	7
Shift system	0	1	1	2	4	6
Training of nurses	0	2	2	1	2	3
Money	0	0	0	1	3	4
TOTALS	23	30	53	40	68	108

value attached. No staff said nothing had changed. Seven of thirty-five said nothing positive had happened and five said nothing negative had. The seven staff unable to identify positive changes had on average worked at Smithtown for eight years (range two to twenty-one years). The five staff only identifying positive changes had been there on average six years (range one to eight years). The three staff nurses who said nothing negative stood out were all externally trained, as was one of those who said nothing positive had happened. Table 2 indicates there were twice as many negative remarks as positive ones.

There were fifteen members of the nursing staff who expressed negative views in the area of patients' rights (Table 3). Seven of these were N/As and eight were qualified staff, whereas thirteen interviews were with N/As and twenty-two with trained staff. Though the numbers are small, it suggests that trained staff were less likely to see an increase in patients' rights as a problem (Table 4).

Table 3 Nursing staff interviews: frequency and attribution of comments on institutional change

Category of Comment	Total Number of Mentions	Total Number of Individuals Mentioning Categories	Number of Individuals on Toulouse	Number of Individuals on Paris
Patients' rights	28	18	8	10
Physical environment	8	7	2	5
Ward life	25	17	5	12
Uniforms	8	8	2	6
Shift system	7	7	2	5
Training of nurses	4	4	1	3
Staff employment	21	15	7	8
Management issues	24	15	6	9
Treatments	12	9	3	6
Money	4	4	1	3
Hospital atmosphere	9	7	5	2
Vulnerability	10	8	4	4

Table 4 Male patients' perception of institutional change by ward and Mental Health Act classification

	Changes perceived	No changes noted	Total
Toulouse	18	3	21**
Paris	14	8	22
Psychopathic Disorder	11	1	12***
Mental Illness	21	11	32***

** One Toulouse patient who was interviewed was unable to comment on this issue.

*** Two patients are dually classified as having Psychopathic Disorder and Mental Illness and data is missing for one patient.

The length of stay for all patients was an average of 8.4 years. The length of stay of 'no change' group varied from eighteen months to eighteen years, averaging 6.7 years. This is slightly less than the length of stay for the 'change' group, which ranged from one year to thirty-two years, averaging 8.9 years.[5] (Table 5)

[5] This includes the length of stay for one man whose classification is unknown.

Table 5 Length of stay of male patients who did and did not perceive institutional change by Mental Health Act classification

	Toulouse		Paris		Toulouse and Paris	
	no change	change	no change	change	no change	change
Mental illness	10.5	7.95	5.3	9.2	6.8	8.5
Psychopathic disorder	N/A	9.18	1	8	1	8.9

Table 6 Patients' perceptions of institutional change: frequency and type

Category of Comment	Total Number of Comments	Positive Comments	Negative Comments	Number of Patients Mentioning Topic
Staff attitudes to patients	25	23	2	14
Rooms and dormitories	10	10	0	8
Rehabilitation trips and parole	9	7	2	8
Management style and structure	9	6	3	8
Ward routines	8	6	2	5
Patients' work	7	5	2	6
Physical environment	7	7	0	6
Food	6	6	0	6
Recreation	6	2	4	6
Security practices	4	0	4	4
Smoking policy	4	1	3	4
Formal rights	2	2	0	2
Personal finance	2	1	1	2
TOTALS	99	76	23	N/A

N.B. The small number of comments about access to treatment or perceived changes to an individual's mental health have not been included in this table.

Table 6 indicates the frequency with which patients focused on particular issues.

Sixteen patients out of thirty-two evaluated at least one change negatively. Five of the patients only identified negative changes. Twenty-seven patients identified at least one positive change. Sixteen patients only mentioned positive changes. There were three times as many positive comments as negative ones. Patients who identified changes were, by comparison with nursing staff, more likely to see change as positive.

References

A v the United Kingdom, application no. 6840/74. Report of the European Commission of Human Rights, adopted on 16 July 1980.

Aarvold Committee. 1973 Report on the Review of Procedures for the Discharge and Supervision of Psychiatric Patients Subject to Restrictions. London: HMSO.

Aase, T. H. 1994 Symbolic Space: Representations of Space in Geography and Anthropology. *Geografiska Annaler*, **76**, 1, 51–8.

Abrahamson, D. 1993 Institutionalisation and the Long-term Course of Schizophrenia. *British Journal of Psychiatry*, **162**, 533–8.

Agar, M. H. 1980 *Professional Stranger*. Orlando, Florida: Academic Press Inc.

Alaszewski, A. 1986 *Institutional Care and the Mentally Handicapped: The Mental Handicap Hospital*. Beckenham: Croom Helm.

Allderidge, P. 1979 Hospitals, Madhouses and Asylums: Cycles in the Care of the Insane. *British Journal of Psychiatry*, **134**, 321–34.

Allen, J. 1999 Spatial Assemblages of Power: From Domination to Empowerment, in Massey, D., Allen, J., and Sarre, P. (eds), *Human Geography Today*. Cambridge: Polity Press, pp. 194–218.

American Psychiatric Association (APA). 1994 *Diagnostic and Statistical Manual*, 4th edn. Washington, DC: American Psychiatric Association.

American Psychiatric Association (APA). 2013 *Diagnostic and Statistical Manual of Mental Disorders*, 5th edn. Arlington, VA: American Psychiatric Publishing.

Anderson, F. 1988 Special Hospitals Set to Get General Management. *The Health Service Journal* (May), 521.

Appadurai, A. 1992 Putting Hierarchy in its Place, in Marcus, G. E. (ed.), *Rereading Cultural Anthropology*. Durham: Duke University Press, pp. 34–47.

Ardener, E. 1975 Belief and the Problem of Women 1–17, in Ardener, S. (ed.), *Perceiving Women*. London: Dent.

Barratt, R. J. 1988a Interpretations of Schizophrenia. *Culture, Medicine and Psychiatry*, **12**, 357–88.

Barratt, R. J. 1988b Clinical Writing and the Documentary Construction of Schizophrenia. *Culture, Medicine and Psychiatry*, **12**, 265–99.

Barratt, R. J. 1998c The 'Schizophrenic' and the Liminal Persona in Modern Society. *Culture, Medicine and Psychiatry*, **22**, 465–94.

Bartlett, A. 1993 Rhetoric and Reality: What Do We Know about the English Special Hospitals? *International Journal of Law and Psychiatry*, **16**, 27–51.

Bartlett, A. 2000 Racism and the Expression of Identity in Special Hospitals, in Kaye, C. and Lingiah, T. (eds), *Working with Difference*. London: Jessica Kingsley, pp. 74–85.

Bartlett, A. 2002 *Social Difference and Division: Women*. Liverpool: National R & D Programme on Forensic Mental Health.

Bartlett, A. 2010 Medical Models of Mental Disorder, in Bartlett, A. and McGauley, G. (eds), *Forensic Mental Health: Concepts, Systems and Practice*. Oxford: Oxford University Press, pp. 5–20.

Bartlett, A. and Hassell, Y. 2001 Do We Need Women-Only Secure Hospital Services? *Advances in Psychiatric Treatment*, **7**, 302–9.

Bartlett, A., Johns, A., Jhawar, H., and Fiander, M. 2007 Report of the London Forensic Units Benchmarking Project.

Bartlett, A. and Kesteven, S. 2010 Organisational and Conceptual Frameworks and the Mentally Disordered Offender, in Bartlett, A. and McGauley, G. (eds), *Forensic Mental Health: Concepts, Systems and Practice*. Oxford: Oxford University Press, pp. 327–38.

Bartlett, A. and McGauley, G. (eds) 2010 *Forensic Mental Health: Systems, Concepts and Practice*. Oxford: Oxford University Press.

Bartlett, A., Phillips, P., and King, M. 2001 Straight Talking? An Investigation of the Attitudes and Practice of Psychoanalysts and Psychotherapists in Relation to Gays and Lesbians. *British Journal of Psychiatry*, **179**, 545–9.

Bartlett, A., Somers, N., Reeves, C., and White, S. 2012 Women Prisoners: An Analysis of the Process of Hospital Transfers. *Journal of Forensic Psychiatry and Psychology*, **23**, 4, 538–53.

Bartlett, A., Somers, N., Fiander, M., and Harty, M. (2014) Pathways of Care for Women in Secure Hospital: Which Women Go Where and Why? *British Journal of Psychiatry*, **205**, 4, 298–306; doi: 10.1192/bjp.bp.113.137547

Bartlett, A. E. A. 1994 Spatial Order and Psychiatric Disorder, Parker-Pearson, M. and Richards, C. (eds), *Architecture and Order: Approaches to Social Space*. London: Routledge, pp. 178–95.

Bartlett, A. E. A., Cohen, A., Backhouse, A., Highnet, N., and Eastman, N. L. G. 1996 Security Needs of South-West Thames Hospital Patients: 1992 and 1993: No Way Out? *Journal of Forensic Psychiatry*, **7**, 256–70.

Bauman, Z. 2000 Social Issues of Law and Order. *British Journal of Criminology*, **40**, 205–21.

Baumeister, R. F. 1987 How the Self Became a Problem: A Psychological Review of Historical Research. *Journal of Personality and Social Psychology*, **52**, 1, 163–76.

BBC NEWS 1982 ON THIS DAY 'God's Banker' Found Dead <http://news.bbc.co.uk/onthisday/hi/dates/stories/june/19/newsid_3092000/3092625.stm> (accessed 21.05.14).

BBC News 1998 Scissors Death Report Criticise Health Workers <http://www.bbc.co.uk/search?q=1998%20scissors%20death> (accessed 08.06.15).

BBC NEWS 2013 Pope Francis Sets Up Vatican Child Sex Abuse Committee <http://www.bbc.co.uk/news/world-europe-25235724> (accessed 21.05.14).

Belknap, I. 1956 *Human Problems of a State Mental Hospital*. New York: McGraw Hill.

Bell, D. 1993 Yes, Virginia, there is a Feminist Ethnography: Reflections from Three Australian Fields, in Bell, D., Caplan, P., and Karim, W. J. (eds), *Gendered Fields: Women, Men and Ethnography*. London: Routledge, pp. 29–43.

Bennett, J., Crewe, B., and Wahidin, A. (eds) 2012 *Understanding Prison Staff*. London: Routledge.

Berrios, H. and Porter, R. 1995 *A History of Clinical Psychiatry: The Origin and History of Psychiatric Disorders*. London: Athlone.

Bland, J., Mezey, G., and Dolan, B. 1999 Special Women, Special Needs: A Descriptive Study of Female Special Hospital Patients. *Journal of Forensic Psychiatry*, **10**, 1, 34–45.

Blom-Cooper, L., Hally, H., and Murphy, E. 1995 *The Falling Shadow: One Patient's Mental Health Care 1978–1993*. London: Duckworth.

Bluglass, R. 1992 The Special Hospitals Should be Closed. *British Medical Journal*, **305**, 323–4.

BMJ. 1978 The Normansfield Inquiry. Extracts from the Report of the Committee of Inquiry into Normansfield Hospital, Including the Main Conclusions and Recommendations. *British Medical Journal*, **2**, 1560–3.

Bodenhorn, B. 2006 Learning to be an Anthropologist in the Field, in De Neve, G. and Unnuthan-Kumar, M. (eds), *Critical Journeys: the Making of Anthropologists*. Aldershot: Ashgate, pp. 17–30.

Bourdieu, P. 1990 *The Logic of Practice* (trans. Nice, R.). Cambridge: Polity Press.

Bowers, L., Ross, J., Cutting, P. and Stewart, D. 2014 Sexual behaviours on acute inpatient psychiatric units. *Journal of Psychiatric and Mental Health Nursing* (April), **21**(3), 271–9; doi: http://dx.doi.org/10.1111/jpm.12080.

Bowker, L. H. 1977 *Prisoner Subcultures*. Lexington: D. C. Heath and Co.

Boyne, R. 2000 Post-Panopticism. *Economy and Society*, **29**, 2, 285–307.

Bradley, Lord K. 2009 The Bradley Report. Lord Bradley's Review of People with Mental Health Problems or Learning Disabilities in the Criminal Justice System. Department of Health.

Brindle, D. 1991 Secure Hospital Nurses Face 'Strike' Charges. *The Guardian*, 21 February.

Brindle, D. 1992 Women Patients 'Stripped Naked in Solitary'. *The Guardian*, 3 March.

Brindle, D. 1992a Women Patients 'Were Left Naked'. *The Guardian*, 3 March.

Brindle, D. 1992b Staff Who Tell of Cruel Patient Treatment Risk Death Threats. *The Guardian*, 10 March.

Brindle, D. 1992c Mental Patients Terrified by Pig's Head at 'Repressive' Hospital. *The Guardian*, 10 March.

Bronson, E. F. 2006 Medium Security Prisons and Inmate Subcultures: The 'Normal Prison'. *Southwest Journal of Criminal Justice*, **3**(2), 61–85.

Brooks, A. and Johnson, R. 2010 Exposed Yet Unrevealed: Reflections on the Poetry of Women Prisoners. *Gender Issues* (December), **27**(3–4), 146–64.

Brown, A. 2007 The Amazing Mutiny at the Dartmoor Convict Prison. *British Journal of Criminology* (March), **47**(2), 276–92.

Bryant, D. J. and Campbell, J. 1997 Representing Space in Language and Perception. *Mind and Language*, **12**, 3–4, 239–77.

Bucher, R. and Schatzman, L. 1962 The Logic of the State Mental Hospital. *Social Problems*, **9**, 337–49.

Bureau of Justice. 1997 *Correctional Populations in the U.S. 1995*. Washington, DC: Department of Justice.

Burke, T. 2010 Psychiatric Disorder: Understanding Violence, in Bartlett, A. and McGauley, G. (eds), *Forensic Mental Health: Concepts, Systems and Practice*. Oxford: Oxford University Press, pp. 35–52.

Burns, T., Rugkåsa, J., Molodynski, A., Dawson, J., Yeeles, K., Vazquez-Montes, M., Voysey, M., Sinclair, J., and Priebe, S. 2013 Community Treatment Orders for Patients with Psychosis (OCTET): A Randomised Controlled Trial. *The Lancet*, **381**, 1627–33.

Burrow, S. 1991a Therapy versus Custody. The Special Hospital Nurse and the Dilemma of Therapeutic Custody. *Journal of Advances in Health and Nursing Care*, **1**, 3, 21–38.

Burrow, S. 1991b Therapy versus Custody. *Nursing Times*, 87, **39** (September), 25, 64–6.

Butler, M. and Drake, D. H. 2007 Reconsidering Respect: its Role in Her Majesty's Prison Service. *Howard Journal of Criminal Justice* (May), **46**(2), 115–27.

Butwell, M., Jamieson, E., Leese, M., and Taylor, P. 2000 Trends in Special (High-Security) Hospitals 2: Residency and Discharge Episodes, 1986–1995. *British Journal of Psychiatry*, **176**, 260–5.

Buus, N. 2008 Negotiating Clinical Knowledge: A Field Study of Psychiatric Nurses' Everyday Communication. *Nursing Inquiry* (September), **15**(3), 189–98.

Bynoe, I. 1992 *Treatment, Care and Security: Waiting for Change*. London: MIND.

Calloway, H. 1992 Ethnography and Experience: Gender Implications in Fieldwork and Texts, in Okely, J. and Callaway, H. (eds), *Anthropology and Autobiography ASA Monographs 29*. London: Routledge, pp. 29–49.

Camp, S. D. and Gaes, G. G. 2005 Criminogenic Effects of the Prison Environment on Inmate Behavior: Some Experimental Evidence. *Crime Delinquency* (July), **51**(3), 425–42.

Cardozo-Freeman, I. 1984 *The Joint Language and Culture in a Maximum Security Prison*. Springfield, USA: Charles C Thomas.

Care Quality Commission. 2013 Monitoring the Mental Health Act in 2012/13 <http://www.cqc.org.uk/public/publications/reports/mental-health-act-2012/13> (accessed 21.05.14).

Carlen, P. 1998 *Sledgehammer: Women's Imprisonment at the Millennium*. London: Macmillan Press.

Carrabine E. 2005 Prison Riots, Social Order and the Problem of Legitimacy. *British Journal of Criminology*, **11**, 45(6), 896–913.

Carstairs, G. M. and Kapur, R. L. 1976 *The Great Universe of Kota: Stress, Change and Mental Disorder in an Indian Village*. Berkeley: University of California Press.

Carvel, J. 1990a Special Hospitals' Staff to Take Action. *The Guardian*, 3 October.

Carvel, J. 1990b POA Offers Deal to End Special Hospital Strike. *The Guardian*, 10 December.

Carvel, J. 1990c Nurses Allege POA Strike Intimidation. *The Guardian*, 11 December.

Casale, S. 1989 *Women Inside: The Experience of Women Renamed Prisoners in Holloway*. London: Civil Liberties Trust.

Caudill, W. 1958 *The Psychiatric Hospital as a Small Society*. Cambridge: Harvard University Press.

Caudill, W., Redlich, F. C., Gilmore, H. R., and Brody, E. B. 1952 Social Structure and Interaction Processes on a Psychiatric Ward. *American Journal of Orthopsychiatry*, **22**, 314–34.

Chagnon, N. 1983 *Yanomamo: The Fierce People*, 3rd edn. New York: CBG College Publishing.

Chow, W. S. and Priebe, S. 2013 Understanding Psychiatric Institutionalization: A Conceptual Review. *BMC Psychiatry* (June), **13**, 169.

Cieraad, I. (ed.) 1999 *At Home: An Anthology of Domestic Space*. Syracuse: Syracuse University Press.

Clare, A. 1980 *Psychiatry in Dissent*. London: Tavistock.

Clarke, J., Cochrane, A., and McLaughlin, E. 1994 Introduction: Why Management Matters, in Clarke, J., Cochrane, A., and McLaughlin, E. (eds), *Managing Social Policy*. London: Sage, pp. 1–12.

Clemmer, D. 1940 *The Prison Community*. Boston: The Christopher Publishing House.

Clifford, J. 1986 Introduction: Partial Truths, in Clifford, J. and Marcus, G. E. (eds), *Writing Culture: The Poetics and Politics of Ethnography*. Berkeley: University of California Press, pp. 1–26.

Clifford, J. 1988 On Ethnographic Self-Fashioning: Conrad and Malinowski, in Clifford, J., *The Predicament of Culture: Twentieth-Century Ethnography, Literature, and Art*. London: Harvard University Press, pp. 92–113.

Codere, H. 1986 Fieldwork in Rwanda, 1959–1960, in Golde, P. (ed.), *Women in the Field: Anthropological Experiences*, 2nd edn. Berkeley, California: University of California Press, pp. 143–66.

Coggeshall, J. M. 1988 Ladies Behind Bars. *Anthropology Today*, **4**, 4, 6–8.

Cohen, A. P. 1992 Self-conscious Anthropology, in Okely, J. and Callaway, H. (eds), *Anthropology and Autobiography ASA Monographs 29*. London: Routledge, pp. 221–41.

Cohen, A. P. 1994. *Self Consciousness: An Alternative Anthropology of Identity*. London and New York: Routledge.

Cohen, S. and Taylor, L. 1972 (and 1981) *Psychological Survival*. Harmondsworth: Penguin.

Coid, J. W. 1984 How Many Psychiatric Patients in Prison? *British Journal of Psychiatry*, **145**, 78–86.

Coid, J. W. 1988a Mentally Abnormal Prisoners on Remand I—Rejected or Accepted by the NHS. *British Medical Journal*, **296**, 1779–82.

Coid, J. W. 1988b Mentally Abnormal Prisoners on Remand II—Comparison of Services Provided by Oxford and Wessex Regions. *British Medical Journal*, **296**, 1783–4.

Coid, J., Kahtan, N., Gault, S., and Jarman, B. 2000 Women Admitted to Secure Forensic Psychiatric Services: I. Comparison of Men and Women. *Journal of Forensic Psychiatry*, **11**, 2, 275–95.

Coid, J. Yang, M., Tyrer, P., Roberts, A., and Ullrich, S. 2006 Prevalence and Correlates of Personality Disorder in Great Britain. *British Journal of Psychiatry*, **188**, 423–31.

Commons, M. L., Bohn, J. T., Gordon, L. T., Hauser, M. J., and Gutheil, T. G. 1992 Professionals' Attitudes towards Sex between Institutionalized Patients. *American Journal of Psychotherapy*, XLVI, 4, 571–80.

Cooper, J., Murphy, E., Webb, R., Hawton, K., Bergen, H., Waters, K., and Kapur, N. 2010 Ethnic Differences in Self-harm, Rates, Characteristics and Service Provision: Three-City Cohort Study. *British Journal of Psychiatry*, **197**, 212–18; doi: 10.1192/bjp.bp.109.072637.

Copes, H., Brookman, F., and Brown, A. 2013 Accounting for Violations of the Convict Code. *Deviant Behaviour*, 10/15, **34**(10), 841–58.

Cosgrove, L., Bursztajn, H. J., and Krimsky, S. 2009 Developing Unbiased Diagnostic and Treatment Guidelines in Psychiatry. *New England Journal of Medicine*, May, **360**, 2035–6; doi: 10.1056/NEJMc0810237.

Covington, S. S. 1998 Women in Prison: Approaches in the Treatment of Our Most Invisible Population. *Women and Therapy*, **21**(1), 141–55.

Crammer, J. 1990 *Asylum History: Buckinghamshire County Pauper Lunatic Asylum—St Johns*. London: Gaskell.

Crapanzano, V. 1977 The Life History in Anthropological Fieldwork. *Anthropology and Humanism Quarterly*, 2, 2–3, 3–7.

Crewe, B. 2007 Power, Adaptation and Resistance in a Late-Modern Men's Prison. *British Journal of Criminology* (March), **47**(2), 256–75.

Crewe, B. 2011 Soft Power in Prison: Implications for Staff–Prisoner Relationships, Liberty and Legitimacy. *European Journal of Criminology*, **8**(6), 455–68.

Crewe, B. 2012 *The Prisoner Society: Power, Adaptation and Social Life in an English Prison*. Oxford: Oxford University Press.

Crewe, B. and Bennett, J. (eds) 2012 *The Prisoner*. London: Routledge.

Crewe, B., Bennett, J., and Wahidin, A. 2012 Introduction, in Bennett, J. Crewe, B., and Wahidin, A. (eds), *Understanding Prison Staff*. London: Routledge, pp. 1–13.

Davidson, R. T. 1974 *Chicano Prisoners: The Key to San Quentin*. Prospect Heights, Illinois: Waveland Press.

Day, A., Casey, S., Vess, J., and Huisy, G. 2011 Assessing the Social Climate of Australian Prisons. *Trends & Issues in Crime & Criminal Justice*, **9**(427), 1–6.

Day, A., Casey, S., Vess, J., and Huisy, G. 2012 Assessing the Therapeutic Climate of Prisons. *Criminal Justice Behaviour*, **39**(2), 156–68.

Deacon, J. 2004 Testing Boundaries: The Social Context of Physical and Relational Containment in a Maximum Secure Psychiatric Hospital. *Journal of Social Work Practice* (March), **18**(1).

Delamothe, T. 2013 Culture Change: Robert Francis's Prescription for the NHS. *British Medical Journal*, **346**, f979.

Dell, S. 1980 Transfer of Special Hospital Patients to the NHS. *British Journal of Psychiatry*, **136**, 222–34.

Dell, S., Robertson, G., and Parker, E. 1987 Detention in Broadmoor. Factors in Length of Stay. *British Journal of Psychiatry*, **150**, 824–7.

Delvecchio Good, M.-J., Hyde, S. T., Pinto, S., and Good, B. J. 2008 *Post-colonial Disorders*. Berkeley, California: University of California Press.

De Neve, G. 2006 Hidden Reflexivity, Assistants, Informants and the Creation of Anthropological Knowledge, in De Neve, G. and Unnuthan-Kumar, M. (eds), *Critical Journeys: The Making of Anthropologists*. Aldershot: Ashgate, pp. 67–89.

Department of Health. 1989 Prejudice and Pride: A Report about Rampton Hospital Ten Years after the Boynton Report.

Department of Health. 1992 Report of the Committee of Inquiry into Complaints about Ashworth Hospital Vols I and II. London: HMSO.

Department of Health. 1994 Report of the Working Group on High Security and Related Psychiatric Provision. London: Department of Health.

Department of Health. 1997 The Patient's Charter: Privacy and Dignity and the Provision of Single Sex Accommodation. NHS Circular EL 97(3). London: Department of Health.

Department of Health. 1998 Modernizing Mental Health Services: Safe, Sound, and Supportive. London: Department of Health.

Department of Health. 1999 National Service Framework for Mental Health: Modern Standards and Service Models. London: Department of Health.

Department of Health. 2000 In-patients Formally Detained in Hospitals under the Mental Health Act 1983 and Other Legislation, England: 1989–1990 to 1999–2000. London: Department of Health.

Department of Health. 2002 Women's Mental Health: Into the Mainstream. Strategic Development of Mental Health Care for Women. <http://webarchive. nationalarchives.gov.uk/20050315021049/http://www.dh.gov.uk/Consultations/ ClosedConsultations/ClosedConsultationsArticle/fs/en?CONTENT_ ID=4075478&chk=yY6aB3> (accessed 24.12.13).

Department of Health. 2005 Delivering Race Equality in Mental Health Care: An Action Plan for Reform Inside and Outside Services and the Government's Response to the Independent Inquiry into the Death of David Bennett. London: Department of Health.

Department of Health. 2007 Best Practice Guidance Specification for Adult Medium-Secure Services, Health Offender Partnerships DH 2009 World Class Commissioning: An Introduction <http://www.lcr.nhs.uk/Library/ worldclasscommissioninganintroduction.pdf> (accessed 21.08.14).

Department of Health. 2008 Code of Practice Mental Health Act 1983 [online]. Norwich: The Stationery Office <http://www.lbhf.gov.uk/Images/Code%20of%20practice%201983%20rev%202008%20dh_087073[1]_tcm21-145032.pdf> (accessed 01.01.14).

Department of Health. 2011 Consultation on the Joint Department of Health / NOMS Offender Personality Disorder Pathway Implementation Plan <webarchive.nationalarchives.gov.uk/ + /www.dh.gov.uk/en/Consultations/Liveconsultations/ DH_124435> (accessed 21.05.14).

Department of Health. 2012 Transforming Care: A National Response to Winterbourne View Hospital: Department of Health Review Final Report <www.gov.uk/ government/publications/winterbourne-view-hospital-department-of-health-review-and-response> (accessed 19.05.14).

Department of Health. 2013 Draft Guidance on Mental Health Currencies and Payment—Monitor <www.monitor.gov.uk/> (accessed 21.05.14).

Department of Health and HM Prison Service. 2001 Changing the Outlook: A Strategy for Developing and Modernising Mental Health Services in Prisons <http://www. dh.gov.uk/prod_consum_dh/groups/dh_digitalassets/@dh/@en/documents/digitalasset/dh_4034228.pdf> (accessed 12. 12. 11).

Department of Health and Home Office. 1992 Review of Health and Social Services for Mentally Disordered Offenders and Others Requiring Similar Services. Final Summary Report. London: HMSO.

Department of Health and Home Office. 2000 *Reforming The Mental Health Act. Part II High Risk Patients*. London: HMSO.

Department of Health and Social Security. 1980 *Report of the Review of Rampton Hospital (Boynton Report)*. London: HMSO.

Department of Health and Welsh Office. 1993 *Code of Practice: Mental Health Act 1983*. London: HMSO.

De Rosia, V. R. 1998 *Living Inside Prison Walls*. Westport, CT: Praeger.

de Viggiani, N. 2012 Trying to Be Something You Are Not: Masculine Performances within a Prison Setting. *Men and Masculinities* (August), **15**(3), 271–91.

Dhami, M. K., Ayton, P., and Loewenstein, G. 2007 Adaptation to Imprisonment: Indigenous or Imported? *Criminal Justice Behaviour* (August), **34**(8), 1085–100.

Di Lorenzo, R., Baraldi, S., Ferrara, M., Mimmi, S., and Rigatelli, M. 2012 Physical Restraints in an Italian Psychiatric Qard: Clinical Reasons and Staff Organization Problems. *Perspectives in Psychiatric Care* (April), **48**(2), 95–107.

Dolan, B. and Coid, J. 1993 *Psychopathic and Antisocial Personality Disorders: Treatment and Research Issues*. London: Gaskell.

Dooley, E. 1990 Prison Suicide in England and Wales 1972–1987. *British Journal of Psychiatry*, **156**, 40–5.

Douglas, M. 1975. Deciphering a Meal, in Douglas, M., *Implicit Meanings: Essays in Anthropology*. London and New York: Routledge and Kegan Paul plc, pp. 249–75.

Douglas, M. 1987 *How Institutions Think*. London: Routledge and Kegan Paul plc.

Douglas, M. 1994 Thought Style Exemplified: The Idea of the Self, in Douglas, M., *Risk and Blame: Essays in Cultural Theory*. London: Routledge, pp. 211–34.

Duncker, P. 1996 *Hallucinating Foucault*. London: Serpent's Tail.

Duranti, A. 1992 Language and Bodies in Social Space: Samoan Ceremonial Greetings. *American Anthropologist*, **94**, 3, 657–91.

Earle, R. and Phillips, C. 2012 Digesting Men? Ethnicity, Gender and Food: Perspectives from a 'Prison Ethnography'. *Theoretical Criminology* (May), **16**(2), 141–56.

Eastman, N. L. G. 1999 Public Health Psychiatry or Crime Prevention? *British Medical Journal*, **318**, 549–51.

Eastman, N. 2006 Can There be True Partnership between Clinicians and the Home Office? *Invited Commentary on . . . The Home Office Mental Health Unit Advances in Psychiatric Treatment*, **12**, 459–61.

Einat, T. and Chen, G. 2012 Gossip in a Maximum Security Female Prison: An Exploratory Study. *Women and Criminal Justice* (April), **22**(2), 108–34.

Ellen, R. F. (ed.) 1984 *Ethnographic Research: A Guide to General Conduct*. London: Academic Press.

Etzioni, A. 1960 Interpersonal and Structural Factors in the Study of Mental Hospitals. *Psychiatry*, **23**, 13–22.

Evans, P. 1988 Management Board is Suspended in Broadmoor Review. *The Times*, 29 August.

Fabrega, H. 1982 Culture and Psychiatric Illness: Biomedical and Ethnomedical Aspects, in Marsella, A. J. and White, G. M. (eds), *Cultural Conceptions of Mental Health and Therapy*. Dordrecht: D. Reidel, pp. 39–68.

Fallon, P., Bluglass, R., Edwards, B., and Daniels, G. 1999 *Report of the Committee of Inquiry into the Personality Disorder Unit, Ashworth Special Hospital. Volume I*. London: The Stationery Office.

Faraday, A. and Plummer, K. 1979 Doing Life Histories. *Sociological Review*, 27, 4, 773–98.

Fazel, S. and Benning, R. 2009 Suicides in Female Prisoners in England and Wales, 1978–2004. *British Journal of Psychiatry*, **194**, 183–4.

Fazel, S. and Seewald, K. 2012 Severe Mental Illness in 33,588 Prisoners Worldwide: Systematic Review and Meta-regression Analysis. *British Journal of Psychiatry*, **200**, 364–73.

Flanagan, T. J. 1980 The Pains of Long-Term Imprisonment: A Comparison of British and American Perspectives. *British Journal of Criminology*, **20**, 2, 148–56.

Fog Olwig, K. and Halstrup, K. 1997 *Siting Culture: The Shifting Anthropological Object*. London: Routledge.

Forrester, A., Henderson, C., Wilson, S., Cumming, I., Spyrou, M., and Parrott, J. 2009 A Suitable Waiting Room? Hospital Transfer Outcomes and Delays from Two London Prisons. *Psychiatric Bulletin*, **33**, 409–12.

Foucault, M. 1967 *Madness and Civilisation: A History of Insanity in the Age of Reason* (trans. Howard, R.). London: Tavistock.

Foucault, M. 1979 *Discipline and Punish: The Birth of a Prison* (trans. Sheridan, A. M.). Harmondsworth: Penguin.

Foucault, M. 1989 *The Birth of the Clinic: An Archaeology of Medical Perception* (trans. Sheridan, A. M.). London: Routledge.

Foucault, M. 2009 Alternatives to the Prison: Dissemination or Decline of Social Control? *Theory, Culture and Society* (November), **26**(6), 12–24.

Frances, A. 2009 A Warning Sign on the Road to DSM-V: Beware of Its Unintended Consequences. *Psychiatric Times*, 25 June.

Frances, A. 2013 The New Crisis of Confidence in Psychiatric Diagnosis. *Annals of Internal Medicine*, 159 (2), 221–22.

Francis, R. 2013 Report of the Mid Staffordshire NHS Foundation Trust Public Inquiry <http://www.midstaffspublicinquiry.com/report> (accessed 19.05.14).

Gaines, A. G. 1982 Cultural Definition, Behaviour and the Person in American Psychiatry, in Marsella, A. J. and White, G. M. (eds), *Cultural Conceptions of Mental Health and Therapy*. Dordrecht: D. Reidel, pp. 167–92.

Galanek, J. D. 2013 The Cultural Construction of Mental Illness in Prison: A Perfect Storm of Pathology. *Culture, Medicine, and Psychiatry* (March), **37**(1), 195–225.

Gamwell, L. and Tomes N. 1995 *Madness in America: Cultural and Medical Perceptions of Mental Illness before 1914*. New York: Cornell University Press.

Garber, M. 1993 *Vested Interests: Cross Dressing and Cultural Anxiety*. London: Penguin.

Geertz, C. 1957 Ritual and Social Change: A Javanese Example. *American Anthropologist*, **59**, 32–54.

Geertz, C. 1983 'From the Native's Point of View': On the Nature of Anthropological Understanding, in Geertz, C., *Local Knowledge: Further Essays in Interpretative Anthropology*. New York: Basic Books, pp. 55–70.

Geertz, C. 1988 *Works and Lives: The Anthropologist as Author*. Cambridge: Polity Press and Oxford: Blackwell Publishers Ltd.

Geertz, C. 1993 *The Interpretation of Cultures*. London: Fontana Press (originally published 1973, New York: Basic Books).

Geertz, C. 2000 *Available Light: Anthropological Reflections on Philosophical Topics*. Princeton: Princeton University Press.

Genders, E. and Player, E. 1986 Women's Imprisonment: The Effects of Youth Custody. *British Journal of Criminology*, **26**, 4, 357–71.

Genders, E. and Player, E. 1995 *Grendon: A Study of a Therapeutic Prison*. Oxford: Clarendon.

Giallombardo, R. 1966 *Society of Women: A Study of a Women's Prison*. New York: John Wiley.

Giallombardo, R. 1974 *The Social World of Imprisoned Girls*. London: John Wiley.

Gillespie, K. 2010 The Social Life of Space: Post-Apartheid Prisons, and the Problem with Architectural Reform. *Prison Service Journal*, **187**, 40–7.

Gilligan, J. 2000 *Violence: Reflections on Our Deadliest Epidemic*. London: Jessica Kingsley.

Ginn, S. 2012 Elderly Prisoners, *British Medical Journal*, 345; doi: http://dx.doi.org/10.1136/bmj.e6263 (published 15 October 2012).

Giri, A. 2000 Audited Accountability and the Imperative of Responsibility: Beyond the Primacy of the Political, in Strathern, M. (ed.), *Audit Cultures: Anthropological Studies in Accountability, Ethics and the Academy*. London. Routledge, pp. 173–95.

Godderis, R. 2006 Dining In: The Symbolic Power of Food in Prison. *Howard Journal of Criminal Justice* (July), **45**(3), 255–67.

Goffman, E. 1961 *Asylums: Essays on the Social Situation of Mental Patients and Other Inmates*. New York: Anchor Books (reprinted Harmondsworth: Pelican, 1968).

Goldingay, S. 2007 Jail Mums: The Status of Adult Female Prisoners among Young Female Prisoners in Christchurch Women's Prison. *Social Policy Journal of New Zealand/Te Puna Whakaaro*, **31**, 56–73.

Gooberman-Hill, R. 2006 Among the Crowds: Learning Anthropology and Learning Multi-disciplinarity, in De Neve, G. and Unnuthan-Kumar, M. (eds), *Critical Journeys: The Making of Anthropologists*. Aldershot:Ashgate, pp. 117–28.

Good, A. 2006 Writing as a Kind of Anthropology: Alternative Professional Genres, in De Neve, G. and Unnuthan-Kumar, M. (eds), *Critical Journeys: The Making of Anthropologists*. Aldershot: Ashgate, pp. 91–113.

Good, B. J. 1994 *Medicine, Rationality and Experience: An Anthropological Perspective*. Cambridge: Cambridge University Press.

Good, B. J., Herrerah, H., Good, M. D., and Cooper, J. 1985 Reflexivity, Counter Transference and Clinical Ethnography: A Case from a Psychiatric Cultural Consultation Clinic, in Hahn, R. A. and Gaines A. D. (eds), *Physicians of Western Medicine, Anthropological Approaches to Theory and Practice*. Dordrecht, Holland: D. Reidel, pp. 193–221.

Gostin, L. 1986 *Special Hospitals 56–92 in Institutions Observed: Towards a New Concept of Secure Provision in Mental Health*. London: King Edward's Hospital Fund.

Graham, M. 1998. Follow the Yellow Brick Road: An Anthropological Outing in Queer Space. *Ethos*, **63**, 1, 102–32.

Greenblatt, M., York, R. H., and Brown, E. L. 1955 *From Custodial to Therapeutic Care in Mental Hospitals: Explorations in Social Treatment*. New York: Russell Sage Foundation.

Griffin, M. L. 1999 The Influence of Organizational Climate on Detention Officers' Readiness to Use Force in a County Jail. *Criminal Justice Review*, **24**, 1, 1–26.

Griffiths, R. 1983 *NHS Management Inquiry: Report to the Secretary of State for Social Services*. London: DHSS.

Grounds, A. T. 1987 Detention of 'Psychopathic Disorder' Patients in Special Hospitals: Critical Issues. *British Journal of Psychiatry*, **151**, 474–8.

Haddock, A. W., Snowden, P. R., Dolan, M., Parker, R., and Rees, H. 2001 Managing Dangerous People with Severe Personality Disorder. *Psychiatric Bulletin*, **25**, 293–6.

Hales, H., Somers, N., Reeves, C., and Bartlett, A. 2015 Criminal Behaviour and Mental Health. Article first published online 24.03.15; doi: 10.1002/cbm.1953 (accessed 10.04.15).

Halleck, S. L. and Herstko, M. 1962 Homosexual Behavior in a Correctional Institution for Adolescent Girls. *American Journal of Orthopsychiatry*, **32**, 911–17.

Halstead, N. 2008 Others In and Out of the Field: Anthropology and Knowledgeable Persons, in De Neve, G. and Unnuthan-Kumar, M. (eds), *Critical Journeys: The Making of Anthropologists*, Aldershot: Ashgate, pp. 48–66.

Ham, C. 1994 Where Now the NHS Reforms? Making Them Up As They Go Along. *British Medical Journal*, **309**, 351–2.

Ham, C. 1995 Private Finance, Public Risk. *British Medical Journal*, **311**, 1450.

Hamilton, J. 1985 Special Hospitals, in Gostin L. (ed.), *Secure Provision: A Review of Special Services for the Mentally Ill and Mentally Handicapped in England and Wales*. London: Tavistock, pp. 84–125.

Hammersley, M. 1992 *What's Wrong with Ethnography?* London: Routledge.

Hammersley, M. and Atkinson, P. 1995 *Ethnography: Principles in Practice*, 2nd edn. London: Routledge.

Haney, C. A. 2008 Culture of Harm: Taming the Dynamics of Cruelty in Supermax Prisons. *Criminal Justice Behaviour*, **35**(8), 956–84.

Hansard. 1972 Col 1673–1685, 29 June.

Hansard. 1999 Col 601–603, 5 February.

Hare, E. 1983 'Was Insanity on the Increase?' *British Journal of Psychiatry*, **142**, 451.

Harty, M., Somers, N., and Bartlett, A. 2012 Women's Secure Hospital Services: National Bed Numbers and Distribution. *Journal of Forensic Psychiatry and Psychology*, **23**, 5–6, 590 –600.

Hassell, Y. and Bartlett, A. 2001 The Changing Climate for Women Patients in Medium Secure Psychiatric Units. *Psychiatric Bulletin*, **25**, 340–2.

Hastrup, K. 1987 Fieldwork among Friends: Ethnographic Exchange within the Northern Civilisation, in Jackson, A. (ed.), *Anthropology at Home. ASA Monograph 25*. London: Tavistock Press, pp. 94–108.

Haywood, S. and Alasewski, A. 1980 *Crisis in the Health Service: the Politics of Management*. London: Croom Helm.

Heads, T. C., Taylor, P. J., and Leese, M. 1997 Childhood Experiences of Patients with Schizophrenia and a History of Violence: A Special Hospital Sample. *Criminal Behaviour and Mental Health* (June), 7, 2, 117–30. Article first published online 10.03.06; doi: 10.1002/cbm.157.

Health Advisory Service. 1988 DHSS Social Services Inspectorate Report on Services Provided by Broadmoor. HAS-SSI-88. SHI. July.

Heidensohn, F. 1985 *Women and Crime*. Basingstoke: Macmillan.

Hensley, C., Wright, J., Tewksbury, R., and Castle, T. 2003 The Evolving Nature of Prison Argot and Sexual Hierarchies. *Prison Journal*, **9**, 83, 3, 289.

HM Chief Inspector of Prisons for England and Wales. 1990 *HM Prison Brixton*. London: Home Office.

HM Chief Inspector of Prisons for England and Wales. 1992 *HM Prison Holloway*. London: Home Office.

HM Chief Inspector of Prisons for England and Wales. 1997 *Thematic Review: Women in Prison*. London: Home Office.

HMIP 2013 Report on an Unaannounced Inspection of HMP Holloway by HM Chief Inspector of Prisons, <http://www.justice.gov.uk/about/hmi-prisons> (accessed 08.05.15).

Hoffman, E. 2010 *Shtetl: The Life and Death of a Small Town and the World of the Pol-ish Jews*. New York: Public Affairs.

Hollan, D. 1992 Cross-Cultural Difference in the Self. *Journal of Anthropological Research*, **48**, 283–300.

Hollan, D. 1997 The Relevance of Person-Centred Ethnography to Cross-Cultural Psy-chiatry. *Transcultural Psychiatry*, **34**, 219–34.

Home Office. 1984 *Managing the Long-Term Prison System: Report of the Control Review Committee*. London: HMSO.

Home Office 1990 Circular no. EL (90) 168. Provision for Mentally Disordered Offenders.

Home Office. 1991 *The Prison Disturbances: Report of an Enquiry by Rt. Hon. Lord Jus-tice Woolf (Parts 1 and 2) and His Hon. Judge Tumin (Part 2)*. London: HMSO.

Home Office. 1999 *Statistics on Women and the Criminal Justice System*. London: Home Office.

Home Office. 2007 *The Corston Report: A Report by Baroness Jean Corston of a Review of Women with Particular Vulnerabilities in the Criminal Justice System*. London: Home Office.

Hospital Advisory Service. 1975 Unpublished Report on Broadmoor Hospital.

Howard League for Penal Reform. 2014 Weekly Prison Watch <http://www.how-ardleague.org/weekly-prison-watch/> (accessed 21. 03. 14 from The Howard League for Penal Reform website).

Hulley, S., Liebling, A., and Crewe, B. 2012 Respect in Prisons: Prisoners' Experiences of Respect in Public and Private Sector Prisons. *Criminology and Criminal Justice*, **12**, 1, 3–23.

Hunter, D. J. 1979 *Coping with Uncertainty: Policy and Politics in the National Health Service*. Chichester: John Wiley and Sons.

Iacobucci, G. 2014 NHS Finances: The Tanker En Route for the Iceberg: Will it Hit before Next Year's General Election? *British Medical Journal*, **348**, g3129.

Ilcan, S. 1999 Social Spaces and the Micropolitics of Differentiation: An Example from North-West Turkey. *Ethnology*, **38**, 3, 243–56.

Ingleby, D. 1981 Understanding Mental Illness, in Ingleby, D. (ed.), *Critical Psychiatry: The Politics of Mental Health*. Harmondsworth: Penguin, pp. 23–71.

Ingold, T. 1996 Concept of Society is Theoretically Obsolete: Introduction, in Ingold, T. (ed.), *Key Debates in Anthropology*. London: Routledge, pp. 57–9.

Ireland, J. L. 1999 Provictim Attitudes and Empathy in Relation to Bullying Behaviour Among Prisoners. *Legal and Criminal Psychology*, **4**, 51–66.

Ireland, J. L. 2000 'Bullying' among Prisoners: A Review of Research. *Aggression and Violent Behavior*, **5**, 2, 201–15.

Irwin, J. and Cressey, D. R. 1962 Thieves, Convicts and Inmate Culture. *Social Problems*, **10**, 142–55.

Jackson, A. (ed.) 1987 *Anthropology at Home. ASA Monograph 25*. London: Tavistock Press.

Jamieson, E., Butwell, M., Taylor, P., and Leese, M. 2000 Trends in Special (High Secure) Hospitals I: Referrals and Admissions. *British Journal of Psychiatry*, **176**, 253–9.

Jensen, G. F. and Jones, D. 1976 Perspectives of Inmate Culture: A Study of Women in Prison. *Social Forces*, **54**, 3, 590–603.

Johnsen, B., Granheim, P. K., and Helgesen, J. 2011 Exceptional Prison Conditions and the Quality of Prison Life: Prison Size and Prison Culture in Norwegian Closed Prisons. *European Journal of Criminology*, **8**, 6, 515–29.

Johnstone, E. C., Cunningham Owens, D. G., Gold, A., Crow, T. J., and MacMillan, J. F. 1981 Institutionalization and the Defects of Schizophrenia. *British Journal of Psychiatry*, **139**, 195–203.

Joliffe, D. 2010 Violence in a Criminological Context, in Bartlett, A. and McGauley, G. (eds), *Forensic Mental Health: Concepts, Systems and Practice*. Oxford: Oxford University Press, pp. 21–34.

Jones, J. G. 1987 Stress in Psychiatric Nursing, in Payne, R. and Firth-Cozens, J. (eds), *Stress in Health Professionals*. London: John Wiley, pp. 189–210.

Jones, K. 1993 *Asylums and After: A Revised History of the Mental Health Services: From the Early Eighteenth Century to the 1990s*. London: Athlone.

Jones, R. M. 1996 *Mental Health Act Manual*, 5th edn. London: Sweet and Maxwell.

Jones, R. 2000 Digital Rule: Punishment, Control and Technology. *Punishment and Society*, **2**,1, 5–22.

Jones, H. and Cornes, P. 1977 *Open Prisons*. London: Routledge and Kegan Paul.

Josephides, L. 1997 Representing the Anthropologist's Predicament, in James, A., Hockey, J., and Dawson, A. (eds), *After Writing Culture: Epistomology and Praxis in Contemporary Anthropology*. London: Routledge, pp. 16–33.

Kane, S. 2002 *Phaedra's Love*. London: Methuen.

Kapoor, R., Dike, C., Burns, C., Carvalho, V., and Griffith, E. E. H. 2013 Cultural Competence in Correctional Mental Health. *International Journal of Law and Psychiatry*, **36**, 3–4, 273–80.

Kauffman, K. 1988 *Prison Officers and Their World*. Cambridge, Massachusetts: Harvard University Press.

Kaye, C. and Franey, A. 1998 Achievements and the Future, in Kaye, C. and Franey, A. (eds), *Managing High Security Psychiatric Care*. London and Philadelphia: Jessica Kingsley, pp. 271–80.

Kaye, C. and Franey, A. 1998a The Inheritance, in Kaye, C. and Franey, A. (eds), *Managing High Security Psychiatric Care*. London and Philadelphia: Jessica Kingsley, pp. 39–50.

Kaye, C. and Lingiah, T. (eds) 2000 *Race, Culture and Ethnicity in Secure Psychiatric Practice: Working with Difference*. London: Jessica Kingsley.

Keane, F. 1996 *Letters to Daniel: Despatches from the Heart*. London: Penguin/BBC.

Keesing, R. M. 1981 *Cultural Anthropology: A Contemporary Perspective*. New York: Holt, Rinehart and Winston.

Kesteven, S. 2002 *Women Who Challenge: Women Offenders and Mental Health Issues*. London: NACRO.

Kidd, B. and Stark, C. 1995 Role of the Organisation, in Kidd, B. and Stark, C. (eds), *Management of Violence and Aggression in Health Care*. London: Gaskell, pp. 123–39.

King, M. and Bartlett, A. E. A. 1999 British Psychiatry and Homosexuality. *British Journal of Psychiatry*, **175**, 106–13.

King, R. and Elliott, K. W. 1977 *Albany: Birth of a Prison—End of an Era*. London: Routledge and Kegan Paul.

King, R. D. and McDermott, K. 1989 British Prisons 1970–1987: The Ever-deepening Crisis. *British Journal of Criminology*, **29**, 2, 107–28.

King, R. D., Raynes, N. V., and Tizard, J. 1971 *Patterns of Residential Care: Sociological Studies in Institutions for Handicapped Children*. London: Routledge and Kegan Paul.

King, K., Steiner, B., and Ritchie Breach, S. 2008 Violence in the Supermax: A Self-Fulfilling Prophecy. *The Prison Journal* (March), **88**, 1, 144–68.

Kirby, S. 1997 Ward Atmosphere on a Medium Secure Long-stay Ward. *Journal of Forensic Psychiatry*, **8**, 2, 336–47.

Klein, R. 1995 *The New Politics of the National Health Service*, 3rd edn. London: Longman.

Kleinman, A. 1977 Culture, Depression and the 'New' Cross-Cultural Psychiatry. *Social Science and Medicine*, **11**, 3–11.

Kleinman, A. 1980 Core Clinical Functions and Explanatory Models, in Kleinman, A., *Patients and Healers in the Context of Culture*. Berkeley: University of California Press, pp. 71–118.

Kleinman, A. 1987 Anthropology and Psychiatry: The Role of Culture in Cross-Cultural Research on Illness. *British Journal of Psychiatry*, **151**, 447–54.

Krause, B. 1989 The Sinking Heart: A Punjabi Communication of Distress. *Social Science and Medicine*, **29**, 4, 563–75.

Kroeber, A. and Kluckhohn, C. 1952 Culture: A Critical Review of Concepts and Definitions. Cambridge, Massachusetts: Papers of the Peabody Museum, Harvard University, 47, 1, 153 (cited in Kuper, A. 1999 *Culture: The Anthropologist's Account*).

Kruttschnitt, C., Gratner, R., and Miller A. 2000 Women's Responses to Prison in the Context of the Old and the New Penology. *Criminology*, **28**, 3, 681–717.

Kulick, D. and Wilson, M. (eds) 1995 *Taboo: Sex, Identity and Erotic Subjectivity in Anthropological Fieldwork*. London: Routledge.

Kuper, A. 1994 Culture, Identity and the Project of a Cosmopolitan Anthropology. *MAN*, **29**, 537–54.

Kuper, A. 1999 *Culture: The Anthropologist's Account*. Cambridge, Massachusetts: Harvard University Press.

La Fontaine, J. S. 1998 *Speak of the Devil: Tales of Satanic Abuse in Contemporary England*. Cambridge: Cambridge University Press.

Laing, W. 2013 *Mental Health Hospitals and Community Health Services UK Market Report 2013*. London: Laing and Buisson.

Leamy, M., Bird, V., Le Boutillier, C., Williams, J., and Slade, M. 2011 Conceptual Framework for Personal Recovery in Mental Health: Systematic Review and Narrative Synthesis. *British Journal of Psychiatry*, **199**, 445 –52. doi: 10.1192/bjp. bp.110.083733.

Leff, J. 1988 *Psychiatry Around the Globe: A Transcultural View*. London: Gaskell.

Lester, H. and Gask, L. 2006 Delivering Medical Care for Patients with Serious Mental Illness or Promoting a Collaborative Model of Recovery? *British Journal of Psychiatry*, **188**, 401–2; doi: 10.1192/bjp.bp.105.015933.

Levinson, S. C. 1996 Language and Space. *Annual Review of Anthropology*, **25**, 353–82.

Lewis, A. 1974 Psychopathic Personality: A Most Elusive Category. *Psychological Medicine*, **4**, 133–40.

Lewis, G., Croft-Jeffreys, C., and David, A. 1990 Are British Psychiatrists Racist? *British Journal of Psychiatry*, **157**, 410–15.

Liebling, A. and Arnold, H. 2012 Social Relationships between Prisoners in a Maximum Security Prison: Violence, Faith, and the Declining Nature of Trust. *Journal of Criminal Justice*, **40**, 5, 413–24.

Liebling, A. and Price, D. 2001 *The Prison Officer*. Leyhill: Prison Service and Waterside Press.

Liebling, A. 2007 Why Prison Staff Culture Matters, in Byrne, J., Taxman, F., and Hummer, D. (eds), The Culture of Prison Violence. Boston, MA: Allyn and Bacon, pp. 105–122.

Lindberg, O. 2005 Prison Cultures and Social Representations. The Case of Hinseberg, a Women's Prison in Sweden. *International Journal of Prisoner Health*, **6**, 1, 2–4, 143–61.

Littlewood, R. 1988 From Vice to Madness: The Semantics of Naturalistic and Personalistic Understandings in Trinidadian Local Medicine. *Social Science and Medicine*, **27**, 129–48.

Littlewood, R. 1990 From Categories to Contexts: A Decade of the New Cross-Cultural Psychiatry. *British Journal of Psychiatry*, **156**, 308–27.

Littlewood, R. 1991 Against Pathology: The New Psychiatry and Its Critics. *British Journal of Psychiatry*, **159**, 696–702.

Littlewood, R. and Lipsedge, M. 1985 Culture Bound Syndromes, in Granville-Grossman, K. (ed.), *Recent Advances in Clinical Psychiatry*. **5** Edinburgh: Churchill Livingstone, pp. 105–42.

Littlewood, R. and Lipsedge, M. 1988 Psychiatric Illness among British Afro-Caribbeans. *British Medical Journal*, **296**, 950–1.

Lockwood, D. 1980 *Prison Sexual Violence*. New York: Elsevier.

Lutz, C. A. 1988 *Unnatural Emotions: Everyday Sentiments on a Micronesian Atoll and the Challenge to Western Theory*. Chicago: University of Chicago Press.

MacCormack, C. and Strathern, M. (eds) 1980 *Nature, Culture and Gender*. Cambridge: Cambridge University Press.

Mackay, G W. 1948 Leucotomy in the Treatment of Psychopathic Feeble-minded Patients in a State-Run Mental Deficiency Institution. *Journal of Mental Science*, **94**, 834–43.

Maden, T., Swinton, M., and Gunn, J. 1994 Psychiatric Disorder in Women Serving a Prison Sentence. *British Journal of Psychiatry*, **164**, 44–54.

Maden, A., Taylor, C. J. A., Brooke, D., and Gunn, J. 1995 *Mental Disorder in Remand Prisoners*. London: Institute of Psychiatry.

Malinowski, B. 1967 *A Diary in the Strict Sense of the Term*. London: Routledge and Kegan Paul.

Mandaraka-Shepherd, A. 1986 *The Dynamics of Aggression in Women's Prisons in England*. London: Gower.

Mantel, H. 2009 *Wolf Hall*. London: Fourth Estate.

Mantel, H. 2012 *Buy Up the Bodies*. London: Fourth Estate.

Marcus, G. E. 1998 *Ethnography Through Thick and Thin*. New Jersey: Princeton University Press.

Marcus, G. E. and Fischer, M. M. 1986 *Anthropology as Cultural Critique: An Experimental Moment in the Human Sciences*. Chicago: University of Chicago.

Marsella, A. J. and White, G. M. 1982 Introduction: Cultural Conceptualisation in Mental Health Research and Practice, in Marsella, A. J. and White, G. M. (eds), *Cultural Conceptions of Mental Health and Therapy*. Dordrecht: D. Reidel, pp. 1–38.

Marsh, A., Dobbs, J., Monk, J., and White, A. 1985 *Staff Attitudes in the Prison Service. Office of Population Censuses and Surveys, Social Survey Division*. London: HMSO.

Martin, L. 1984 *Hospitals in Trouble*. Oxford: Blackwell.

Massey, D. and the Collective. 1999 Issues and Debates, in Massey, D., Allen, J., and Sarre, P. (eds), *Human Geography Today*. Cambridge: Polity Press, pp. 3–21.

Mauer, M. 1999 *Race to Incarcerate*. New York: The New Press.

Mawby, R. I. 1982 Women in Prison: A British Study. *Crime and Delinquency*, **28**, 24–39.

Mawson, D. 1998 A Doctor's View, in Kaye, C. and Franey, A. (eds), *Managing High Security Psychiatric Care*. London and Philadelphia: Jessica Kingsley, pp. 181–92.

Mazower, M. 2009 *Hitler's Empire: Nazi Rule in Occupied Europe*. London: Penguin.

McClellan, D. S., Farabee, D., and Crouch, B. M. 1997 Early Victimisation, Drug Use and Criminality: A Comparison of Male and Female Prisoners. *Criminal Justice and Behaviour*, **24**, 4, 455–76.

McCourt Perring, C. 1994 Community Care as De-institutionalization, in Wright, S. (ed.), *Anthropology of Organizations*. London and New York: Routledge, pp. 168–80.

McGovern, D. and Cope, R. 1987 The Compulsory Detention of Males of Different Ethnic Groups with Special Reference to Offender Patients. *British Journal of Psychiatry*, **150**, 505–12.

McKenzie, K. and Crowcroft, N. S. 1996 Describing Race, Ethnicity and Culture in Medical Research. *British Medical Journal*, **312**, 1054–6.

McKnight, D. 1986 Fighting in an Australian Aboriginal Supercamp, in Riches, D. (ed.), *The Anthropology of Violence*. Oxford: Blackwell.

Mental Health Act 1983 (revised 2007).

Mental Health Act Commission. 1999 *Eighth Biennial Report 1997–1999*. London: The Stationery Office.

Mental Health Strategies. 2009/10 National Survey of Investment in Adult Mental Health Services Report Prepared for DH 2010 Mental Health Strategies.

Menzies, I. E. P. 1960 A Case Study in the Functioning of Social Systems as a Defence against Anxiety. *Human Relationships*, **13**, 95–121.

Mezey, G., Hassell, J., and Bartlett, A. 2005 Safety of Women in Mixed Sex and Single Units. *British Journal of Psychiatry*, **187**, 579–82.

Miles, M. B. and Huberman, A. M. 1984 *Qualitative Data Analysis: A Sourcebook of New Methods*. London: Sage.

Millar, B. 1991 When is a Nurse Not a Nurse? *The Health Service Journal* (January), 13.

Miller, P. 1986 Critiques of Psychiatry and Critical Sociologies of Madness, in Miller, P. and Rose, N. (eds), *The Power of Psychiatry*. Cambridge: Polity Press, pp. 12–42.

Miller, P. and Rose, N. (eds) 1986 *The Power of Psychiatry*. Cambridge: Polity Press.

Milner, J. 1996 Men's Resistance to Social Workers, in Fawcett, B., Featherstone, B., Hearn, J., and Toft, C. (eds), *Violence and Gender Relations: Theories and Interventions*. London: Sage, pp. 115–29.

Ministry of Justice. 2012 *Prisoners' Childhood and Family Backgrounds*. Ministry of Justice Research Series 4/12 March 2012. London: Ministry of Justice.

Ministry of Justice. 2013 Story of the Prison Population 1993–2012 https://www.gov.uk/government/statistics/story-of-the-prison-population-1993-2012 (accessed 21.05.14)

Ministry of Justice. 2013 Transforming Rehabilitation—A Revolution in the Way We Manage Offenders <https://consult.justice.gov.uk/digital-communications/transforming-rehabilitation> (accessed 25. 03. 14, from Ministry of Justice website).

Minnis, H., McMillan, A., Gillies, M., and Smith, S. 2001 Racial Stereotyping: Survey of Psychiatrists in the United Kingdom. *British Medical Journal*, **323**, 905–6.

Moore, H. L. 1988 *Feminism and Anthropology*. Oxford: Polity Press and Blackwell.

Moore, H. L. 1994a Embodied Selves: Dialogues between Anthropology and Psychoanalysis, in Moore, H. L., *A Passion for Difference: Essays in Anthropology and Gender*. Bloomington and Indianapolis: Indiana University Press, pp. 28–48.

Moore, H. L. 1994b Master Narratives: Anthropology and Writing, in Moore, H. L., *A Passion for Difference: Essays in Anthropology and Gender*. Bloomington and Indianapolis: Indiana University Press, pp. 107–28.

Moore, H. L. 1994c The Feminist Anthropologist and the Passion of the New Eve, in Moore, H. L., *A Passion for Difference: Essays in Anthropology and Gender*. Bloomington and Indianapolis: Indiana University Press, pp. 129–50.

Moore, H. L. 1994d Bodies on the Move: Gender Power and Material Culture, in Moore, H. L., *A Passion for Difference: Essays in Anthropology and Gender*. Bloomington and Indianapolis: Indiana University Press, pp. 71–85.

Moore, H. L. 1996a The Changing Nature of Anthropological Knowledge: An Introduction, in Moore, H. L. (ed.), *The Future of Anthropological Knowledge*. London: Routledge, pp. 1–15.

Moore, H. L. 1996b *Space, Text and Gender*. New York: The Guilford Press (originally published 1986 Cambridge: Cambridge University Press).

Moore, H. L. 2007 *The Subject of Anthropology: Gender, Symbolism and Psycho-analysis*. Cambridge: Polity Press.

Moore, H. L. 2013 Female Genital Mutilation/Cutting. *British Medical Journal*, 347; doi: http://dx.doi.org/10.1136/bmj.f5603.

Morris, P. 1969 *Put Away: A Sociological Study of Institutions for the Mentally Retarded*. London: Routledge and Kegan Paul.

Morris, B. 1994 *Anthropology of the Self: The Individual in Cultural Perspective*. London: Pluto Press.

Morris, N. and Rothman, D. (eds) 1998 *The Oxford History of the Prison: The Practice of Punishment in Western Society*. Oxford: Oxford University Press.

Mott, J. 1985 *Adult Prisons and Prisoners in England and Wales. Home Office Research Study No. 84*. London: HMSO.

Murphy, E. 1997 The Future of Britain's High Security Hospitals. *British Medical Journal*, **314**, 1292–3.

Murray, K. 1996 The Use of Beds in NHS Medium Secure Units in England and Wales from 1999 to 2007. *Journal of Forensic Psychiatry*, **7**, 3, 504–24.

Mynors-Wallis, L. 2011 Co-operation or Competition? *Proposed Changes in Healthcare Provision in England*, **35**, 441–3.

Naish, J. 1991 Nursing's Last Frontier. *Nursing Standard* (May), **5**, 33, 21.

NCI. 2011 National Study of Self-Inflicted Deaths in Prison Custody <http://www.bbmh.manchester.ac.uk/about-us/search> (accessed 21.05.14).

Newman, J. and Clarke, J. 1994 Going about Our Business? The Managerialisation of the Public Sector, in Clarke, J., Cochrane, A., and McLaughlin, E. (eds), *Managing Social Policy*. London: Sage, pp. 13–32.

NHS Commissioning Board. 2013 2013/14 NHS Standard Contract for High Secure Mental Health Services (Adults) Particulars, Schedule 2—the Services, A—Service Specifications, <dh.gov.uk c02-high-sec-mh pdf> (accessed 04.05.14).

NICE. 2009 Borderline Personality Disorder: Treatment and Management <http://www.nice.org.uk/CG78> (accessed 01.04.14).

NICE 2009a Anti-Social Personality Disorder: Treatment and Management <http://www.nice.org.uk/CG77> (accessed 01.04.14).

NOMS. 2012 41/2012—Sentence Planning, https://www.google.co.uk/search?q=noms+2012+41/2012+sentence+planning&ie=utf-8&oe=utf-8&gws_rd=cr&ei=RhMZVpfhFMH5UonWscgF this works accessed 10.10.15

Offender Management Statistics. 2013 Table 2.1a Total Receptions into Prison Establishments by Type of Custody, Sentence Length and Age Group, April–June 2011 to April–June 2012, England and Wales <http://www.gov.uk/government/uploads/system/uploads/attachment_data/file/218124/omsq-q2-2011-prison-reception-tables.xls> (accessed 22. 03. 14 from gov.uk website).

Okely, J. 1992 Anthropology and Autobiography: Participatory Experience and Embodied Knowledge, in Okely, J. and Callaway, H. (eds), *Anthropology and Autobiography*. London: Routledge, pp. 1–28.

Okely, J. 1996 *Own or Other Culture*. London: Routledge.

O'Neill, O. 2002 Reith Lectures 2002: A Question of Trust. Lecture 3: Called to Account <http://bbc.co.uk/radio4/reith2002> (accessed 23. 06. 15).

Ortner, S. B. 1974 Is Female to Male as Nature is to Culture? in Rosaldo, M. Z. and Lamphere, L. (eds), *Woman, Culture and Society*. Stanford: Stanford University Press, pp. 67–88.

Page, H. and Brooke-Thomas, R. B. 1994 White Public Space and the Construction of White Privilege in U.S. Health Care: Fresh Concepts and a New Model of Analysis. *Medical Anthropology*, **8**, 1, 109–15.

Parker, E. 1985 The Development of Secure Provision, in Gostin, L. (ed.), *Secure Provision: A Review of Special Services for the Mentally Ill and Mentally Handicapped in England and Wales*. London: Tavistock Publications, pp. 15–65.

Parker-Pearson, M. and Richards, C. 1994 Ordering the World: Perceptions of Architecture, Space and Time, in Parker-Pearson, M. and Richards, C. (eds), *Architecture and Order: Approaches to Social Space*. London: Routledge, pp. 1–37.

Parrott, F. R. 2010 'Real Relationships': Sociable Interaction, Material Culture and Imprisonment in a Secure Psychiatric Unit. *Culture, Medicine, and Psychiatry*, **34**, 4, 555–70.

Paulus, P. B., McGain, G., and Cox, V. C. 1985 The Effects of Crowding in Prison and Jails, in Farringdon, D. P. and Gunn, J. (eds), *Reaction to Crime: the Public, the Police Courts and Prisons*. London: John Wiley and Sons Ltd, pp. 113–34.

Pearlin, L. I. and Rosenberg, M. 1962 Nurse–Patient Social Distance and the Structural Context of a Mental Hospital. *American Sociology Review*, **27**, 56–65.

Peel, J. D. Y. 1996 The Concept of Society is Theoretically Obsolete: Against the Motion, in Ingold, T. (ed.), *Key Debates in Anthropology*. London: Routledge, pp. 67–71.

Perucci, R. 1974 *Circle of Madness: On Being Insane and Institutionalised in America*. Englewood Cliffs, New Jersey: Prentice Hall Inc.

Peugh, J. and Belenko, S. 1999 Substance-Involved Women Inmates: Challenges to Providing Effective Treatment. *Prison Journal*, **79**(1), 23–44.

Phillips, C. and Earle, R. 2010 Reading Difference Differently? Identity, Epistemology and Prison Ethnography. *British Journal of Criminology*, **50**(2), 360–78.

Porter, R. 1987 *Mind-Forg'd Manacles: A History of Madness in England from the Restoration to the Regency*. Harmondsworth: Penguin.

Potier, M. A. 1993 Giving Evidence: Women's Lives in Ashworth Maximum Security Psychiatric Hospital. *Feminism and Psychology*, **3**, 3, 335–47.

Prins, H., Backer-Holst, T., Francis, E., and Keitch, I. 1993 Report of Inquiry into the Death in Broadmoor Hospital of Orville Blackwood and a Review of the Deaths of Two Other Afro-Caribbean Patients: 'Big, Black and Dangerous'. London: SHSA.

Probyn, E. 1995 Lesbians in Space. Gender, Sex and the Structure of the Missing. *Gender, Place and Culture*, **2**, 1, 77–84.

Putkonen, H. and Taylor, P. J. 2014 Women as Offenders, in Taylor, P. and Gunn, J. (eds), Forensic Psychiatry—Clinical, Legal and Ethical Issues, 2nd edn. Boca Raton: CRC Press, pp. 498–522.

R v Bentley 1998:97/7533/S1) [1999] Crim LR 330, [1998] EWCA Crim 2516, [2001] 1 Cr App R 21 <http://www.bailii.org/ew/cases/EWCA/Crim/1998/2516.html> (accessed 23. 06. 15).

Radcliffe-Brown, A. R. 1940 On Social Structure. *Journal of the Royal Anthropological Institute*, **70**, 1–12.

Rader, N. E. 2005 Surrendering Solidarity: Considering the Relationships among Female Correctional Officers. *Women and Criminal Justice*, **16**, 3, 27–42.

Raftery, J. 1992. Mental Health Services in Transition: The United States and the United Kingdom. *British Journal of Psychiatry*, **161**, 589–93.

Ramon, S. 1996 *Mental Health in Europe: Ends, Beginnings and Rediscoveries*. Basingstoke: Macmillan.

Rapaport, R. N. 1960 *Community as Doctor: New Perspectives on a Therapeutic Community*. London: Tavistock.

Rapport, N. 2009 Power and Identity, in Clegg, S. R. and Hanguaard, M. (eds), *Sage Handbook of Power*. London: Sage, pp. 194–209.

Rawlings, B. 2005 Researching Therapeutic Communities in Secure Settings. *Therapeutic Communities*, **26**, 4, 465–74.

Reed-Danahay, D. 2001 'This is Your Home Now!': Conceptualizing Location and Dislocation in a Dementia Unit. *Qualitative Research*, **1**, 1, 47–63.

Rhodes, L. A. 2005 Changing the Subject: Conversation in Supermax. *Cultural Anthropology*, **8**, 20, 3, 388–411.

Rhodes, L. A. 2010 Risking Therapy. *Howard Journal of Criminal Justice*, **49**, 5, 451–62.

Ripa, Y. 1990 *Women and Madness: Incarceration of Women in 19th Century France* (trans. du Peloux Menage, C.). Minneapolis: University of Minnesota Press.

Rosaldo, M. W. and Lamphere, L. (eds) 1974 *Woman, Culture and Society*. Stanford, California: Stanford University Press.

Rosenhan, D. 1973 On Being Sane in Insane Places. *Science*, **179**, 250–8.

Rosenhan, D. L. 1981 The Contextual Nature of Psychiatric Diagnosis, in Grusky, O. and Pollner, M. (eds), *The Sociology of Mental Illness: Basic Studies*. New York: Holt Rinehart and Winston, pp. 319–29.

Rowe, A. 2012 Women Prisoners, in Crewe, B. and Bennett, J. (eds) *The Prisoner*. London: Routledge, pp. 103–16.

Rycroft, C. 1972 *A Critical Dictionary of Psychoanalysis*. Harmondsworth: Penguin.

Sahlins, M. 1999 Two or Three Things that I Know about Culture. *Journal of the Royal Anthropological Institute*, **5**, 399–421.

Said, E. W. 1989 Representing the Colonized: Anthropology's Interlocutors. *Critical Inquiry*, **15**, 205–25.

Sartorius, N., Jablensky, A., Korten, G., Ernberg, G., Anker, M., Cooper, J. E., and Day, R. 1986 Early Manifestations and First-Contact Incidence of Schizophrenia in Different Cultures. *Psychological Medicine*, **16**, 909–28.

Scheff, T. J. 1961 Control Over Policy by Attendants in a Mental Hospital. *Journal of Health and Human Behavior*, **2**, 93–105.

Scheff, T. J. 1966 *Being Mentally Ill: A Sociological Theory*. Chicago: Aldine.

Scheff, T. J. 1981 The Role of the Mentally Ill and the Dynamics of Mental Disorder: A Research Framework, in Grusky, O. and Pollner, M. (eds), *The Sociology of Mental Illness*. New York: Holt Rinehart and Winston, pp. 54–62.

Schmid, T. J. and Jones, R. S. 1993 Ambivalent Actions: Prisons' Adaptation Strategies of First-Time, Short-Term Inmates. *Journal of Contemporary Ethnography*, **21**, 4, 439–63.

Scull, A. T. 1979 *Museums of Madness: The Social Organisation of Insanity in Nineteenth-Century England*. London: Allen Lane.

Scull, A. 1989 *Social Disorder and Psychiatric Disorder: Anglo-American Psychiatry in Perspective*. London: Routledge.

Segal, B. E. 1962 Nurses and Patients: Time, Place and Distance. *Social Problems*, **9**, 257–64.

Shah, P. and Mountain, D 2007 The Medical Model is Dead: Long Live the Medical Model. *British Journal of Psychiatry*, **191**, 375–7.

Shore, C. and Wright, S. 2000 Coercive Accountability: The Rise of Audit Culture in Higher Education, in Strathern, M. (ed.), *Audit Cultures*. London: Routledge, pp. 57–89.

Showalter, E. 1987 *The Female Malady: Women Madness and English Culture 1839–1980*. London: Virago.

Shweder, R. A. 1997 The Surprise of Ethnography. *Ethos*, **25**, 2, 152–63.

Singh, S. P. 1997 Ethnicity in Psychiatric Epidemiology: Need for Precision. *British Journal of Psychiatry*, **171**, 305–8.

Singh, S. P., Greenwood, N., White, S., and Churchill, R. 2007 Ethnicity and the Mental Health Act 1983. *British Journal of Psychiatry*, **191**, 99–105.

Singleton, N., Meltzer, H., Gatward, R., Coid, J., and Deasy, D. 1998 *Psychiatric Morbidity among Prisoners in England and Wales: The Report of a Survey Carried Out in 1997 by Social Survey Division of the Office of National Statistics on Behalf of the Department of Health*. London: The Stationery Office.

Skultans, V. 2000 Remembering and Forgetting: Anthropology and Psychiatry: The Changing Relationship, in Skultans, V. and Cox, J. (eds), *Anthropological Approaches to Psychological Medicine*. London: Jessica Kingsley, pp. 94–104.

Smith, R. 1988 Broadmoor Slammed: Reforms Proposed. *British Medical Journal*, **297**, 1357.

Smith, J. 1989 There's Only One Yorkshire Ripper, in Smith, J., *Misogynies*. London: Faber and Faber, pp. 117–51.

Smith, G., King, M., and Bartlett, A. 2004 An Oral History of Treatments for Homosexuality in Britain Since the 1950s I: The Views of Patients. *British Medical Journal*, **328**, 427–9.

Soja, E. W. 1989 Spatializations: A Critique of the Giddensian Version, in Soja, E. W., *Post-Modern Geographies: The Reassertion of Space in Critical Social Theory*. London: Verso, pp. 138–56.

Special Hospitals Service Authority (SHSA) 1991a *SHSA Review 1991*. London: SHSA.

Special Hospitals Service Authority (SHSA) 1991b *SHSA Development Plan 1991–1996*. London: SHSA.

Special Hospital Service Authority (SHSA) 1995 *Service Strategies for Secure Care*. London: SHSA.

Spillius, E. B. 1990 Asylum and Society, in Trist, E. and Murray H. (eds), *The Social Engagement of Social Science: A Tavistock Anthology: Volume 1: The Socio-Psychological Perspective*. Philadelphia: University of Pennsylvania Press, pp. 586–612.

Spiro, M. 1993. Is the Western Conception of Self Peculiar within the Context of World Cultures. *Ethos*, **21**, 107–53.

Stanton, A. H. and Schwartz, M. S. 1954 *The Mental Hospital: A Study of Institutional Participation in Psychiatric Illness*. New York: Basic Books.

Strasser, S. and Kronsteiner, R. 1993 Impure or Infertile? Two Essays on the Crossing of Frontiers through Anthropology and Feminism, in Del Valle, T. (ed.), *Gendered Anthropology*. London: Routledge, pp. 162–77.

Strathern, M. 1981 Culture in the Netbag: The Manufacture of a Subdiscipline in Anthropology. *MAN*, **16**, 4, 665–88.

Strathern, M. 1987 The Limits of Autoanthropology, in Jackson, A. (ed.), *Anthropology at Home*. London: Tavistock, pp. 16–37.

Strathern, M. 1995 The Nice Thing about Culture is that Everyone Has It, in Strathern, M. (ed.), *Shifting Contexts*. London: Routledge, pp. 153–76.

Strathern, M. 1996 The Concept of Society is Theoretically Obsolete: For the Motion, in Ingold, T. (ed.), *Key Debates in Anthropology*. London: Routledge, pp. 60–6.

Strathern, M. 2000 Introduction: New Accountabilities, in Strathern, M. (ed.), *Audit Cultures: Anthropological Studies in Accountability, Ethics and the Academy*. London: Routledge, pp. 1–18.

Strauss, A. L. 1987 *Qualitative Analysis for Social Scientists*. Cambridge: Cambridge University Press.

Struckman-Johnson, C., Struckman-Johnson, D., Rucker, L., Bumby, K., and Donaldson, S. 1996. Sexual Coercion Reported by Men and Women in Prison. *Journal of Sex Research*, **33**, 1, 67–76.

Swinton, M., Oliver, J., and Carlisle, J. 1999 Measuring Quality of Life in Secure Care: Comparison of Mentally Ill and Personality Disordered Patients. *International Journal of Social Psychiatry*, **45**, 4, 284–91.

Sykes, G. M. 1958 *The Society of Captives: A Study of a Maximum Security Prison*. Princeton: Princeton University Press.

Szasz, T. S. 1961 *The Myth of Mental Illness: Foundations of a Theory of Personal Conduct*. New York: Dell.

Tait, S. 2012 Prison Officers and Gender, in Bennett, J. Crewe, B., and Wahidin, A. (eds) *Understanding Prison Staff*. London: Routledge, pp. 65–91.

Taylor, P. J. and Gunn, J. 1999 Homicides by People with Mental Illness: Myth and Reality. *British Journal of Psychiatry*, **174**, 9–14.

The Economist. 2013 November 16th Briefing Ubiquitous Cameras The People's Panopticon, pp. 25–7.

Thomas, C. W. 1973 Prisonisation or Resocialisation: A Study of External Factors Associated with the Impact of Imprisonment. *Journal of Research in Crime and Delinquency*, **10**, 13–21.

Thomas, C., Bartlett, A. E. A., and Mezey, G. C. 1995 The Extent and Effects of Violence amongst Psychiatric In-patients. *Psychiatric Bulletin*, **19**, 600–4.

Thomas, C. W. and Foster, S. C. 1972 Prisonisation in the Inmate Contraculture. *Social Problems*, **20**, 229–39.

Thomas, C. W. and Zingraff, M. T. 1976 Organisational Structure as a Determinant of Prisonisation: An Analysis of the Consequences of Alienation. *Pacific Sociological Review*, **19**, 98–116.

Thomas, J. E. and Pooley, R. 1981 *The Exploding Prison: Prison Riots and the Case of Hull*. London: Junction Books.

Thornicroft, G. and Bebbington, P. 1989 Deinstitutionalisation—from Hospital Closure to Service Development. *British Journal of Psychiatry*, **155**, 739–54.

Thornton, R. 1992 The Rhetoric of Ethnographic Holism, in Marcus, G. E. (ed.), *Rereading Cultural Anthropology*. Durham: Duke University Press, pp. 15–33.

Thurston, R. 1996 Are You Sitting Comfortably? Men's Storytelling, Masculinity, Prison Culture and Violence, in Mac an Ghaill, M. (ed.), *Understanding Masculinities*. Buckingham: Open University Press, pp. 139–52.

Tilt, R., Perry, B., and Martin, C. 2000 *Report of the Review of Security at the High Secure Hospitals*. London: Department of Health.

Toch, H. 1977 *Living in Prison. The Ecology of Survival*. New York: The Free Press.

Townsend, P. 1962 *The Last Refuge—A Survey of Residential Institutions and Homes for the Aged in England and Wales*. London: Routledge and Kegan Paul.

Townsend, J. M. 1976 Self-Concept and the Institutionalization of Mental Patients: An Overview and Critique. *Journal of Health and Social Behavior*, **17**, 263–71.

Treacher, A. and Baruch, G. 1981 Towards a Critical History of the Psychiatric Profession, in Ingleby, D. (ed.), *Critical Psychiatry: The Politics of Mental Health*. Harmondsworth: Penguin, pp. 120–49.

Tully, J., Hearn, D., and Fahy, T. 2014 Can Electronic Monitoring (GPS 'Tracking') Enhance Risk Management in Psychiatry? *British Journal of Psychiatry*, **205**, 83–5.

Ugelvik, T. 2011 The Hidden Food: Mealtime Resistance and Identity Work in a Norwegian Prison. *Punishment and Society*, **13**, 1, s 47–63; doi: 10.1177/1462474510385630.

Valentine, G. 1999 Imagined Geographies: Geographical Knowledges of the Self and Other in Everyday Life, in Massey, D., Allen, J., and Sarre, P. (eds), *Human Geography Today*. Cambridge: Polity Press, pp. 47–61.

Van Dongen, E. 1997 Space and Time in the Lives of People with Long-standing Mental Illness: an Ethnographic Account. *Anthropology and Medicine*, **4** 1, 89–103.

Vertovec, S. 2007 Super-diversity and its Implications. *Ethnic and Racial Studies*, **29**, 6, 1024–54.

Vincent, J. 2014 'Obsessive Selfie-Taking Classified as a Mental Disorder': What We Can Learn from a Hoax (7 April) <http://www.independent.co.uk> (accessed 20.08.14).

Walby, S. and Greenwell, J. 1994 Managing the National Health Service, in Clarke, J., Cochrane, A., and McLaughlin, E. (eds), *Managing Social Policy*. London: Sage, pp. 57–72.

Walmsley, P. 2012 World Female Imprisonment List (2nd edn): Women and Girls in Penal Institutions, Including Pre-trial Detainees/Remand Prisoners <http://www.prisonstudies.org/sites/prisonstudies.org/files/resources/downloads/wfil_2nd_edition.pdf> (accessed 26. 03. 14 from International Centre for Prison Studies website).

Waquant, L. 2002 The Curious Eclipse of Prison Ethnography in the Age of Mass Incarceration. *Ethnography*, **3**, 371–97.

Ward, J. 1982 Telling Tales in Prison, in Frantzenberg, R. (ed.), *Custom and Conflict in British Society*. Manchester: Manchester University Press, pp. 235–57.

Ward, D. A. and Kassebaum, G. G. 1966 *Women's Prison. Sex and Social Structure*. London: Weidenfeld and Nicolson.

Weiner, A. B. 1995. Culture and Discontents. *American Anthropologist*, **97**, 14–21.

Weir, A. 2000 *Eleanour of Aquitaine: By the Wrath of God Queen of England*. London: Pimlico.

Wheeler, S. 1961 Socialization in Correctional Communities. *American Sociological Review*, **26**, 697–712.

Williamson, M. 2006 Improving the Health and Social Outcomes of People Recently Released from Prisons in the UK: A Perspective from Primary Care. London: Sainsbury Centre for Mental Health. (Web paper) <http://www.scmh.org.uk> (accessed 25.06.15).

Wilson, S., James, D., and Forrester, A. 2011 The Medium-Secure Project and Criminal Justice Mental Health. *The Lancet*, **378**, 9786, 110–11.

Wing, J. K. 1962 Institutionalism in Mental Hospitals. *British Journal of Social and Clinical Psychology*, **1**, 38–51.

Wing, J. K. and Brown, G. W. 1970 *Institutionalism and Schizophrenia*. Cambridge: Cambridge University Press.

Woolf, V. 1975 *The Common Reader*. London: Hogarth Press (originally published 1925).

World Health Organization (WHO). 1992 *International Classification of Diseases, 10th edn. Classification of Behavioural and Mental Disorders: Clinical Descriptions and Diagnostic Guidelines*. Geneva: WHO.

Wright, S. 1994 'Culture' in Anthropology and Organizational Studies, in Wright, S. (ed.), *Anthropology of Organizations*. London and New York: Routledge, pp. 1–31.

Yap, P. M. 1965 Koro—A Culture Bound Depersonalisation Syndrome. *British Journal of Psychiatry*, **111**, 43–50.

Index

Notes

vs. indicates a comparison or differential diagnosis

televisions 220–221
therapy 140–141
therapy groups 191
transgression 107
twenty-four hour care 252–255

U
unskilled activities 136–137
Upstairs, Downstairs 177
use of space, maintenance of power
    185–187

V
verbal abuse 138
virtual *vs.* reality 7–8

W
wages 270
ward(s) 125–129, 178–180
    access permission in study design 63–65
    articulating agency 182–184
    changes in *see* ward changes
    characteristics of 128b
    confinement 178
    consent 180
    culture *see* ward culture
    day areas 141
    differences between 128–129b, 179–180

maintenance of power *see* maintenance
    of power
managers *see* ward managers
meal distinction 208–209
mechanisms of power *see* mechanisms
    of power
patient absence 126
researcher allocation 66
social relations 238
study design 316–317
study of 231
ward changes 280
    patients' perspective 268–269
    staff attitudes 264
ward culture 229–244
    managers 229–230
ward managers 132
    introduction of 249
    ward culture 229–230
Winterbourne Inquiry 230
work 132
    payment 270
World Class Commissioning
    (Department of Health 2009) 246
writing of anthropology 75

Y
Young, Graham 160